INTRODUCTION TO EDUCATIONAL LEADERSHIP

HAROLD W. BOLES & JAMES A. DAVENPORT

WESTERN MICHIGAN UNIVERSITY

HARPER & ROW, PUBLISHERS
NEW YORK, EVANSTON, SAN FRANCISCO, LONDON

Sponsoring Editor: Michael E. Brown
Project Editor: David Nickol
Designer: Michel Craig
— Production Supervisor: Will C. Jomarrón

INTRODUCTION TO EDUCATIONAL LEADERSHIP

Library of Congress Cataloging in Publication Data

Boles, Harold W
    Introduction to educational leadership.

    Bibliography: p.
    Includes index.
    1. School administrators. 2. Leadership.
I. Davenport, James, Date— joint author.
II. Title.
LB2831.6.B65   371.2   75-16481
ISBN   0-06-040856-1

CONTENTS

PREFACE

In 1965, John W. Gardner—later to become Secretary of Health, Education, and Welfare and the originator of Common Cause—charged in his final report as president of the Carnegie Corporation that "the academic world appears to be approaching a point at which everyone will want to educate the technical expert who advises the leader, or the intellectual who stands off and criticizes the leader, but no one will want to educate the leader himself."

This was a serious charge, and examinations of academic programs offered around the country for those who aspired to positions in which they could be expected to lead provided considerable credence to the allegation. Nationwide, the situation today remains essentially the same, yet as early as 1964 we and our colleagues at Western Michigan University had already started an extensive review and an updating of our graduate programs of study in educational leadership. However, we found ourselves handicapped in three respects related to materials for courses in those programs, namely: (1) all of the textbooks and books of readings that we could locate were aimed at persons who, the editors and authors seemed to assume, were aspiring to become superintendents or principals of public schools; (2) all available resources, seemingly, equated school administration with educational leadership; and (3) none of the books gave the matter of *how one leads* more than passing attention.

There were further difficulties. None of the editors of readings books nor authors of textbooks had used a leadership—as differentiated from an administration—approach, despite the fact that for years organizations such as the NCPEA had called for leadership emphasis in the preparation of school administrators. During that same period, professors of school administration almost everywhere had been seeking ways to incorporate an interdisciplinary approach that could utilize the wealth of materials already available in the social sciences. In response to such an appeal, apparently only five books—two in the United States, one in Canada, one in Australia, and one in England—had been written with attempts to show how the behavioral and social sciences are related

and can contribute to school administration. Furthermore, in
the literature of school administration, only a few authors and
ideas from psychology, sociology, and management had been
paraphrased or quoted. Even in those works and other literature, there was a tendency to ignore the fact that management
was years ahead of school administration in the use of
behavioral science theory and research.

This textbook and the book of readings[1] that was developed
to parallel and to complement it are intended to overcome
some of the above-mentioned difficulties. The materials they
contain have, to a great extent, been field-tested with students
over an eight-year period. Both books are based on six major
premises that must be understood and accepted by readers
who are to find the books useful. The first is that *public
schools constitute only a portion of the schooling system that
now exists.* There are also hundreds of parochial and private
schools that have leaders who need pre- and in-service
leadership training.

Second, *the positions of superintendent and principal are
only two of many positions in which incumbents are expected
to lead in school matters.* As attendance areas and districts
have increased in size, the numbers of principals and superintendents have decreased, while the numbers of assistants,
aides, directors, and coordinators have increased dramatically.
Leadership positions in intermediate districts, state departments, and professional associations have also proliferated.
Furthermore, research in the behavioral sciences has
indicated that if human resources are to be fully utilized, then
any individual, regardless of position title, must be encouraged
to be an emergent leader in those situations in which he or
she can demonstrate appropriate and necessary knowledgeability or skill in the resolution of organizational problems.

The third premise is that *schools are but one of the formal
agencies of education that now exist.* There are numerous
other formal agencies, including academies, armed-forces
schools, community and junior colleges, four-year colleges,
graduate colleges and universities, as well as vocational and
technical institutes. There are also literally hundreds of
nonformal agencies, along with uncounted informal agencies,
all of which aid individuals in learning for specific purposes,
thus qualifying as educational agencies. All of these agencies,
whether formal, informal, or nonformal, employ certain persons
who are expected to lead others and each designated leader
needs to learn how to lead more effectively and efficiently.

[1] H. W. Boles (Ed.), *Interdisciplinary Readings in Educational Leadership.*
New York: MSS Information Corp., 1975.

A fourth premise is that *leadership is a process.* A process, as used here, is defined as "a series of actions conducing to a common end." Much theory and research evidence exist regarding the actions that are necessary to bring about the achievement of goals, the sequence in which those actions should occur, and how each necessary action may be attained through instruction and practice. Therefore, it should be possible for some to teach and for others to learn the performance competencies needed for each of those actions.

Our fifth premise is that *no one discipline has as its exclusive province all that is known about the effective performance of the various actions that comprise the leadership process.* There is evidence that it is not necessary for all leadership actions to be accomplished by a single individual in order for the process to occur. It is necessary, though, to look to many disciplines in order to coordinate what is known about how and by whom the actions involved in the leadership process can be performed. We have our personal beliefs that the process is always comprised of essentially the same actions, regardless of the enterprise in which the process occurs.

The sixth and final premise is that *educational leaders must be concerned with all of education,* not just with those agencies in which they work. There is no "educational philosophy" extant that can accommodate this premise. Close examination will reveal that any so-called "philosophy of education" is, in reality, only a philosophy of schooling. Any consideration of nonschooling education threatens those who have been accustomed to equating education with schooling— particularly threatened are those who work in schools.

The present lack of synthesis leads to the conclusion that there is almost no rapprochement between schools and other agencies of education. Nevertheless, the need for conservation of resources demands that educational leaders at all levels acquire a panoramic view of the forest rather than maintain the simplistic and telescopic focus on a single tree. This book is intended to help leaders and would-be leaders in all of the agencies of education with that almost-Sisyphean endeavor.

H.W.B.
J.A.D.

INTRODUCTION TO EDUCATIONAL LEADERSHIP

SECTION ONE

THE SOCIAL SETTING OF EDUCATIONAL LEADERSHIP

> *True education . . . emerges from an understanding of the*
> *social order and of the nature of man, and from no other source.*
> —Sizer

This first section is intended to develop an understanding of the social order and of the nature of human beings—to provide educational leaders with true education. They must see the social milieu in which they are expected to function in terms of the institutions formed by human beings and of the agencies which represent those institutions. They must understand the educational organization in which they function as an institutional agency, must conceptualize the place of that agency in the overall institution of education, and must see the place of the institution in society.

To understand their own nature and that of their fellow human beings, educational leaders must understand how organizations allocate responsibilities among positions, how each position eventuates in a role, how roles are delimited by expectations, and how expectations affect behavior.

This section of this book develops understandings of social institutions, social change, organizations, positions, roles, and expectations.

CHAPTER 1

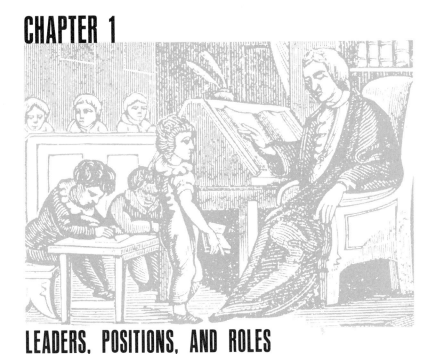

LEADERS, POSITIONS, AND ROLES

While . . . we do not conceive of leadership so narrowly as to restrict its exercise only to specific positions within formal groups, we . . . are concerned primarily with persons who are designated as administrators in a formal . . . setting.
—Sergiovanni and Carver

The present writers conceive of leadership as a process rather than as a personal attribute or a collective noun. We need to consider where the leadership process can and does occur in various educational agencies, in terms of positions in those agencies in which role incumbents are *expected to lead* on a continuing basis. Some writers have designated such positions as *headship* positions, although many of them are found below the apex of the hierarchy. Each is of such a nature that the position-holder *is* at least the nominal "head" of a work group. This chapter also will attempt to relate such positions to organizational positions in general, will discuss roles as they relate to positions, and will differentiate between the role of leader and the role of follower.

POSITIONS IN EDUCATION AGENCIES

The leadership process can occur in all agencies of education. In many of them, a leader is not chosen by the group, but an administrator is appointed and given control by a board of trustees or similar body, whose members are not subject to the appointee's control. In some agencies, including many proprietary schools, leaders appoint themselves because they require a group to achieve purposes that *they* desire. One thing that the two kinds of heads have in common is high visibility.

Appointed administrators are expected to be leaders—that is one of the things for which they are paid. They may be exhorted and implored to lead; they may take courses and degrees in leading, and still they may be unsuccessful. Or they may utilize the ideas of others, along with the abilities of various emergent leaders, to achieve success. Or they personally may be able to both administer and lead. In any event, responsibility for the leadership process resides with them, and many persons can see what they do about it.

Let us consider some specific educational positions (other than teacher, instructor, or coach) in which role incumbents are *expected* to lead, as found in three types of agencies.

Informal Agencies

In informal agencies of education, there usually are no designated leaders, and in some, no designated positions. In the home, for example, one parent or the other usually emerges as a leader. In most social groups, the leader changes frequently, depending on the activities undertaken. Individuals who lead in neighborhood haunts often do so on a fleeting come-and-go basis. In informal occupational groups, leaders are likely to be those with high competence levels, those with causes in which others are interested, or even those who are accomplished tale tellers!

Nonformal Agencies

In the mass media, the *leaders,* those who influence, are the writers and editors who shape the media messages. Church schools usually have designated superintendents. Youth-serving groups have scoutmasters, managers, coaches, and program directors; some, such as 4H clubs, may even call the designated person "leader." In agriculture and home extension services, the head person is called agent. The armed forces schools utilize noncommissioned and commissioned officers of various ratings and ranks, depending on responsibility. Some also employ civilian instructors and administrators. Special governmental programs usually are run by directors of training or by other administrators with a wide variety of esoteric titles. Government schools often are operated under directors or superintendents, as are civic and cultural centers. Social organizations may be presided over by presidents, chairpersons, wardens, officers (as in the Salvation Army), grand wizards, masters, or any of dozens of other individualized—and also esoteric—titles. Company schools usually are supervised by directors—often directors of training and management development.

Special-needs schools may have presidents or directors, and the heads of some may be called managers. Locally situated proprietary schools may have directors or presidents, and the same is true of special proprietary schools that provide instruction largely or totally by correspondence. Unions have presidents and shop stewards; professional associations have presidents and executive secretaries—and the latter more often lead, because their tenure is continuing while that of presidents is limited.

Formal Agencies

In schools, whether public, parochial, or private, one is accustomed to thinking of principals, superintendents, and headmasters as those who are expected to lead, but there are many other positions, some of them staff, whose holders also may be expected to lead. Such positions include assistant principals, assistant or associate superintendents, administrative assistants, and supervisors, along with a sometimes bewildering array of directors and/or coordinators.

In some school districts, there are directors of instruction, personnel, pupil personnel services, community education, adult education, business affairs, purchasing, federal programs (now largely phased out), athletics, intramurals, special education, and many more.

There are coordinators of distributive education, vocational education, career education, curriculum, music, art, special services, learning resources, and so on ad infinitum. Department heads or chairpersons frequently are designated for subject areas. Often overlooked is the fact that counselors also are expected to lead both small groups and individuals.

Alternative and free schools seem to be led either by principals, directors, or headmasters in most instances although some schools use other titles in further attempts to break the establishment mold.

Community, junior, four-year, and graduate colleges tend to follow the same patterns as universities. Usually these institutions have presidents, vice presidents, deans, registrars, and department head or chairpersons. Some have chancellors, provosts, bursars, directors, and coordinators. Leading in certain situations and with certain groups is an expectation for each of the position-holders in most agencies.

These positions may be seen in better perspective through considering the general characteristics of positions and how positions affect roles, expectations, and behavior.

CHARACTERISTICS OF POSITIONS

Ralph Linton (1947) said that:

The average individual's participation in the culture of his group is a function of the series of positions within the social system which he has occupied or expects to occupy. Similarly, at any

*given point in time the demands which the society makes upon
him and the rights which it accords him are functions of his current position in the social system pp. [433–434].*

Most agencies of social institutions are so organized that positions, or relative standings, within them are clearly distinguishable.

As numerous writers have pointed out, one logically starts with
the objectives of the enterprise when designing an organizational
structure. Considerations must include the benefits of specialization,
groupings that will make the best uses of personnel, limitations of
authority, means of communication, and needs for stimulation. A
proper organizational plan sets the bounds of action for individuals,
outlines the ways in which to work, and provides members with a
framework in which to work. Ergo, it delineates positions.

For any educational agency, then, people attempt to:

1. establish an organizational pattern that *assures some permanency*—which more or less guarantees that the agency will
   be maintained;
2. divide the labor to be performed along hierarchical lines;
3. establish *positions* which indicate the particular division of the
   labor—the *tasks*—to be performed in each, *regardless of who
   holds the position;*
4. set expectations regarding the behaviors of individuals or *as-
   sign a role* to the incumbents of such positions as they
   —attempt to carry out their assigned tasks
   —help to maintain the organizational structure
   —try to help achieve agency goals
   —assist in maintaining employee morale
   —may try to bring about changes in the organizational structure or the institution.

Among the widely quoted and used bases for organization are
Urwick's (1963) "Notes on the Theory of Organization" and Rorty's
(1963) "Ten Commandments of Good Organization." However, recent
developments in the theory of organization are at considerable variance with earlier formulations.

Goslin (1965) said:

*As groups become institutionalized (i.e., as they take on func-
tions, specified goals, and a normative structure that give them
an existence and continuity independent of the goals and efforts
of their members), they acquire a new complex of internal (and
external) forces that interact with the groups' goals, its informal
social structural characteristics, and the personalities of its members to determine the ultimate nature of the organization. Formal*

organizational pressures arise at the intersection of function and system, at that point where the instrumental goals of the group (not necessarily of its members) must be translated into action by a particular group of individuals who may or may not already stand in some kind of orderly relationship to one another. As instrumental groups grow in size and complexity, formalized procedures for decision-making, the allocation of responsibility, communication within the group, and the recruitment of personnel becomes increasingly important if the group is to perform its functions in the most efficient way. Formal organizational characteristics of a group constitute those aspects of its normative structure that are both specified (usually in writing) and which pertain primarily to the way the group is to carry out its functions [pp. 131–132].

Today's educational leaders faced with the task of organizing or reorganizing the agencies in which they work would do well to study thoroughly the literature relating to organizations and positions before deciding how to proceed. Exciting new developments are being reported each year.

Among the features which traditionally have distinguished one position from another are the degree of permanence, the responsibility, the status, the authority, and the perquisites which attach to each, along with the skills and knowledge required for each.

Degree of Permanence

A position may be classified as temporary, enduring, or fixed. A temporary position is one which persists for a relatively short period of time when considered in relation to the ongoing function of the agency. The position of chairperson of a study committee is an example. An enduring position is one which is likely to continue unless or until there is a reorganization of responsibilities; the position of training director in an industrial concern is an enduring one. A fixed position is one which is likely to continue as long as the agency of which it is a part, regardless of reorganization of responsibilites. The positions of superintendent of schools or president of a proprietary school are examples. A further characteristic of any position is the amount and kind of responsibility assigned to the incumbent.

Responsibility

A position is characterized by that portion of necessary tasks which is assigned as the responsibility of the position-holder. While it is a manifest impossibility to catalog all of the tasks to be performed by all educational agencies, there are dozens of major tasks which must be accomplished and which relate to learners, to staff personnel, to curriculum and instruction, to activities and services, to facilities, to finance, to administration, to organization, and to public or community relations.

Obviously, responsibility for the multitudinous educational tasks must be apportioned among various individuals. It should be apparent that: (1) some of the tasks are more related to leadership than are others, (2) positions are characterized, in part, by the responsibilities assigned to incumbents, and (3) many kinds of positions are essential to accomplish tasks. A fact of life is that each position is characterized by a certain status.

Status

Sociologists have emphasized that status seems almost nonexistent in cooperative societies. Those readers who saw the videotapes and films, or who read about the discovery, of the aboriginal Tasaday tribe of the Philippines in the early 1970s perhaps observed this phenomenon. There seemed to be almost no distinctions among members in terms of tribal responsibilities. However, in competitive societies such as ours, there are psychological elements in the division of labor that seem to be at least as significant as the structural elements.

Among the elements of status are: (1) consideration of how society regards and rewards the holders of various positions and (2) the motivations that cause people to assume the positions. The amount of power and authority involved, the degree of specialization of work, and the skills required enter into the regard that society accords to positions. Rewards include the legitimization of power and/or authority, plus salary or wages and other tangibles. The latter will be discussed later in this chapter.

The work ethic causes members of the middle class, and aspiring members, to regard their jobs as involving fulfillment and purpose. Working-class persons tend to see their jobs as a way to provide for survival needs. Sometimes a feeling of interdependence and mutual striving pervade an organization, but status does not automatically disappear. Undoubtedly, the psychological benefits that a position-holder experiences are related to his or her individual level of motivation, and Maslow's (1954) suggested levels have been expanded and paraphrased somewhat in Table 1-1. It seems apparent that a person motivated at one of the "lower" levels will neither get as great emotional rewards nor have as much concern for the expectations held for her or him as will someone at a "higher" level. Whether concern for others' expectations diminishes as one comes nearer the "self-actualization" level is indeed a moot point.

It is self-evident that educational positions in which individuals do essentially similar work have different statuses attached to them because of the nature of the agencies in which they exist. For example, compare the relative regard shown instructors in a university, a liberal arts college, a community college, a high school, and an

TABLE 1-1
A POSSIBLE HIERARCHY OF HUMAN NEEDS AND SATISFACTIONS

LEVEL OF NEED			NATURE OF SATISFACTION
Psychological	Ego	Aesthetic	Beauty
		Self-Actualization	Self-esteem Autonomy Privacy Knowing Understanding
		Accomplishment	Order Successful task completion Pride of workmanship Involvement—service to others Realization of potential

	Social	Security	Freedom from threat, or loss of:
			  income and other perquisites
			  protection
			  privacy and other rights
			  affiliation
			  status
			Admiration
			Respect
			Indulgence of idiosyncrasies

		Status	Recognition of influence Praise Credit for work done Feeling needed
		Affiliation	Feeling loved or wanted Feeling accepted Identity Loyalty Conformity to expectations

Physiological		Protection	(from uncertainty) Habituation
			(from territorial invasion)
			  Numerical reinforcement
			(from enemies) shelter, fire,
			  light, group strength
			(from the elements) Shelter, clothing

		Survival	Sensory stimulation Activity Sexual expression Sleep, warmth Air, water, food, bodily elimination

Source. (With credit and apologies to the late Abraham Maslow)

elementary school. Then, compare the regard shown any one of those with that accorded a trainer in industry or an instructor in a proprietary or other special-purpose school! Proficiency on the job seems almost negligible consideration in the award of status.

Zaleznik (1966) said that an unusual amount of justified ego must characterize any leader, and Livingston (1971) had a working hypothesis that every leader, regardless of style, likes to exercise authority. Jay (197) proposed that physical strength, strength of will, determination, courage, and character are characteristics that add to the status of individuals. That individuals often enhance the status of the positions they hold is quite clear.

The authority that attaches to a position certainly is an element of status, but not a complete explanation of it.

Authority
Authority may be either the authority ascribed to the position because of its relative status compared to other positions, regardless of who holds the position, or it may be the *achieved authority* of the particular holder of the position at a given moment. *Ascribed authority* nearly always carries with it a capability for imposing sanctions, which we call power. Achieved authority, on the other hand, nearly always is the authority of ideas or of competence, and should not be confused with the ascribed or positional authority to which a person may fall heir upon achieving a particular position. In the achieved type, a particular individual is considered an authority because she or he knows more about a subject or is more expert in a skill than are those about him. Where achieved authority is recognized in connection with a particular position, it is likely to foresake the position when the holder of the position changes.

Authority ascribed to positions within an organization performs the following functions, according to Simon (1957):

1. It enforces the responsibility of the individual to the next higher or next lower authority figure.
2. It secures expertise in the making of decisions.
3. It permits the coordination of organizational activities.

Ascribed authority, achieved authority, and *influence* all exist outside an organization, and should not be confused with the authority which characterizes positions in it. Influence may seem to attach to positions within an organization, but probably is an attribute of a position-holder rather than a characteristic of his or her particular position. Individuals often are influenced by nonauthority figures because of feelings of admiration, affection, friendship, or respect.

In addition to responsibility, status, and authority, certain perquisites are usually among the rewards for particular positions, regardless of who holds the positions.

Perquisites

Direct compensation is an ever-present reward of position-holders in formal organizations, but it may vary in form from a flat wage or salary to bonus or profit-sharing plans, or to preferential treatment in buying company stock. Fringe benefits range from insurance, savings, and retirement coverages to provision of secretarial or other help, moving expenses, use of an automobile, an expense account, a place to live, or assistance in buying or selling real estate. Privileges may include the right to set one's own work schedule and hours, a larger office, a larger desk, club membership, wall to wall carpeting, or a key to the executive washroom.

Many of the above-mentioned perquisites seldom, if ever, attach to most positions in schools. They may, however, be among the rewards of certain status positions in some of the other agencies of education.

Skills and/or knowledge perhaps should have been among the first-mentioned characteristics of positions. That they were not is in no way indicative of their relative importance.

Skills and Knowledge

The rationale usually given for division of labor within an organization is to get enough specialization to assure proficiency in the performance of assigned tasks. That some specialization is essential, especially in a technological society, cannot be doubted. Even in aiding learners, it is impossible for any one person to know enough or be skilled enough to handle all of the responsibilities suggested earlier in this chapter. Certainly skills and knowledge are characteristics of positions, along with responsibility. They affect status, but status is not dependent on them alone, and they do not account for observable behavior.

ROLES

Most educators probably are familiar with the Getzels-Guba (1957) model of the school as a social system. It is a visual representation of the Parsons-Shils (1951) "general theory of action" applied to the school setting. That theory had its origins in the work of Linton (1945), which asserted that a role, with attendant expectations for behaviors, attaches to status, and status to position. The logic of this view is overwhelming.

For years psychologists believed than an understanding of personality would help to explain why individuals behave as they are observed to behave. When the investigations of personality failed to provide adequate explanations of behavior, social psychologists insisted that the personal development of the individual must be considered in conjunction with expectations held for her or him as the occupant of a certain position, or in terms of role. The Getzels-Guba (1957) model has been extended in Figure 1-1 to portray this essential consideration, and the following discussion relates to that figure.

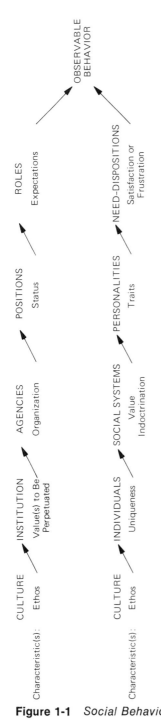

Figure 1-1 *Social Behavior of an Individual*

A culture is characterized by a particular ethos, which leads to the establishment of certain institutions. Each institution is intended to perpetuate certain values, and it does so through one or more agencies. Each agency is comprised of a structured social system that results in an organization in which positions are established. Depending on the status accorded it, and other characteristics, each position results in a role, and certain expectations are held for the role incumbent.

A culture, with its collective ethos, also produces individuals, each characterized by uniqueness. In order to avoid anarchy, individuals are exposed to and made parts of social systems, each intended to indoctrinate all members with certain common values. Personalities result, each characterized by certain traits. Traits result in people expressing themselves in various ways, and when actions become conditioned by anticipation of fixed responses from the environment, they are called *need-dispositions.* Need-dispositions are characterized by satisfaction or frustration, either of which can take various forms.

Thus, observable behavior may be explained by understanding the individual's satisfaction or frustration in relation to the expectations held for him or her. Expectations define roles.

Expectations as Definers of Roles

Once a position is established in an organization, the behavior of any individual who is to occupy the position is prescribed to a great extent. *Because* she or he has certain responsibility and authority, because of the permanence or impermanence of the position, because of a certain status and the rewards which it brings, people both inside and outside hold certain expectations for the position incumbent, regardless of who that person is. While one may have a bit of leeway within group-approved limits due to what Hollander (1958) called "idiosyncrasy credit," the position-holder's behavior is largely prescribed and proscribed by the expectations of individuals other than himself, and of groups. Those individuals and groups exist outside as well as inside the organization.

Each individual's behavior is conditioned by his or her own and others' expectations regarding individuality and conformity, so that each plays a role.

Role-Playing

Most individuals tend, by nature, to express their individuality. Early conditioning determines in great measure how strong this tendency is. However, individuals become part of a group or organization because it can do for them something that they could not do for themselves, or the alliance can help them to do better or more easily something with which they alone would have difficulty. In the group or organization, one is expected to exhibit the behavior that others anticipate, in other words, to play a role.

Thus, the individual is the object of a continual tug-of-war in which one's own nature and desires pull in certain directions while group sanctions of various kinds may pull in other directions. The strength of one's individuality and the significance of group sanctions determine the direction in which the individual ultimately goes. One's degree of ego-involvement in a particular situation is likely to determine which of the forces will dominate. The feeling that he has regarding whether he must assert his independence or can do what others anticipate he will do will greatly influence his behavior. That feeling depends to some extent on the amount of conflict that exists between the person's values and those values imposed by the group.

Effects of Value Conflicts on Roles

Value conflicts may be intrapersonal in nature, related to the individuality-conformity pulls on the individual. Value conflicts, though, often are interpersonal. Whose values are more important? Whose welfare is to be promoted? Each person adopts a referent and unconsciously assumes that others have the same referent. Yet, if four persons attempt to solve an educational problem when one is primarily concerned with what is best for learners, another with teacher influence, the third with what makes for ease of administration, and the fourth with likely voter reaction, agreement is unlikely.

Value conflicts such as illustrated above reach the instrumental-institutional level when a group maintains that dollar costs are more important than benefits to learners. Conflicts are human vs. non-human when jobs are seen as demeaning by the individuals holding them. Value conflicts also may be intergroup in nature, as when a community college faculty wants to make program decisions but is prevented from doing so by bureaucratic administrators.

Value conflicts usually are chronic, and may endlessly stimulate hostility. Such conflicts, along with role conflicts, certainly affect observable individual behaviors. Value conflicts often are inherent in role conflicts.

Role Conflicts

Most individuals simultaneously hold several positions in concurrent and overlapping social systems. One may be a family member, an economic producer, an educator, a voter, and a church member without necessarily encountering role conflict. However, when one's role as economic producer demands unusual amounts of time at the expense of family life, role conflict or conflicts of expectations is experienced.

Linton (1945) minimized the danger of role conflict by stating that at any given time one role is always ascendant over all the others. As an example, he used the classic Scottish tale of the man who found himself host to his brother's murderer; as host, he fed and housed the man, then conducted him safely beyond clan territory. There, as offended brother, he engaged the traveler in combat to the death.

Role conflict resolution becomes impossible if expectations in one role preclude the meeting of expectations in another. It is in this context that the role of leader should be examined.

EXPECTATIONS FOR THE ROLE OF LEADER

Whether verbalized or not, there are certain behaviors expected of leaders. The leader and each of his or her followers hold expectations which may or may not be identical.

A leader is expected to take initiative, to have a "preferred outcome,"[1] in terms of group goals. At the same time, he or she is expected to maintain the organization in good enough shape that it can continue to function. A leader is expected to assume more than a pro rata share of group risk, to endure stress, and to behave in some consistent fashion, or style.

A Preferred Outcome

Leaders have a distant vision of what their organizations could and should be—of what might result from their intervention in a situation that likely would not result without such intervention. They have a *preferred outcome* for that situation, and they need to estimate what would occur if they do not intervene.

"Some men see things as they are and say, 'Why?' I dream things that never were and say, 'Why not?'" A person who says "Why not?" has a preferred outcome. It may have originated from a problem found in one's daily practice, from considering a better way of handling routine, from investigating a hypothesis (*research*), from utilizing an idea of someone else, or from an intellectual consideration of possible order and relationships (*theorizing*).

The preferred outcome may relate to goals themselves or to the means of achieving goals. The leader's motivation for putting forth the preferred outcome, its nature, and its origin are all unimportant to our considerations here. The important point is that the leader has and is expected to have a preferred outcome that will impel him or her to take the initiative to move the group.

Taking Initiative

A leader, by our definition, takes the initiative to move a group (two or more persons) toward a goal or goals that its members find ac-

---

[1] The term "preferred outcome" was used by Mark Crum in unpublished materials at Western University in 1967.

ceptable. Few, if any, leaders spend all or even a major portion of their time in initiatory actions. Much time must be devoted to duties and activities which achieve the outputs for which the social system was formed. However, if leading and the leadership process are to occur, innovation also must occur. Innovation occurs when either a status or emergent leader takes initiative.

Innovation is a process by which new outputs, or techniques that affect those outputs, are introduced into a social system (Nelson, 1968). Innovation, in this sense, results in establishment of new capability of the system, and it includes more than invention. It can include utilization of new tools, such as electronic data-retrieval devices; a managerial concept, such as "management by objectives" or accountability; or an organizational concept, such as differentiated staffing. Tessin (1972) found some interesting results related to flexibility of leaders in his investigation of emergent leaders in small groups in a university setting, and flexibilty certainly is essential to innovation.

A leader, though, is expected to take initiative while at the same time keeping the enterprise operating and producing. To do this, the leader or someone must do some administering.

Administering

Traditionally, an educational administrator has been expected to achieve production (the provision of learning opportunities) while preserving organizational structure, meeting group members' needs, and maintaining morale. Lipham (1964) and others have maintained stoutly that this is the antithesis of what a leader is expected to do, and that wearing both hats is an impossibility.

It may be that the "best" organizational structure would resemble a proprietary school in which there is a vice-president for administration teamed with a vice-president for innovation, both presided over by a president who can keep them in line. No such organization is known to exist in any educational agency. Suffice it to say here that the leader is expected to innovate and *someone* within a group is expected to carry out the administrative function also. Often, that someone is the leader himself.

There are numerous educational leaders who both administer and lead. They "put into effect the policies and rules of an organized group," but they keep the structure flexible enough for easy change when some change of goals makes it desirable. However, they soon learn that change threatens people and is thus an element of the unavoidable risk to which every leader is exposed.

Risk

Any aspiring leader should be advised that risk "comes with the territory." If a group can go only one way or if members have no ego involvement, no leader is needed. With choices possible or egos involved, risk is inevitable and the leader is expected to assume much of it.

Lack of necessary skills may be a source of risk, as may the inability to make decisions or the making of improper decisions. A leader is expected to be skilled and to show sound judgment in decision-making. Imagination may provide many alternatives from which the leader chooses and may be a source of risk if it causes one to go beyond group-sanctioned limits. Lack of imagination, on the other hand, also can generate risk if school principals or other leaders fail to conceptualize how their agencies fit into the total pattern, or if their followers find their chosen course too dull for their tastes.

Pressure groups both within and outside an organization present risks, and the leader is expected to be able to cope with them.

Timing of an innovation or of a critical decision is a very real source of risk. Prematurity or tardiness of action can be as devastating as inappropriate action or inaction. The leader is expected to have a built-in and infallible "sense of timing."

Risk inevitably produces stress.

Stress

The fact that an individual is a leader gives one added visibility which, in addition to making one more vulnerable, adds to the strains of living. The leader is expected to be able to sustain examination of his or her behavior by many people from inside and outside the social system in which he or she works.

One cannot doubt that whenever risk for the leader or the group is involved, the outcome is stress. The way in which one endures stress probably has an effect on one's characteristic manner of behaving, which is called *style*.

Style

It is a rare individual who assumes the role of leader in each of the social systems in which one participates. An individual may be an aggressive, innovative leader of a civic or political group and a passive follower in his or her job group. This may be due to the fact that a person operates at different need levels (see Table 1-1) and requires different satisfactions in the two systems. Also, some individuals simply choose to maintain a low profile because of low needs for ego satisfaction, and this should in no sense be considered a cop-out.

Nevertheless, in any social system in which one accepts a leadership role, an individual is expected to be "authentic" while still exhibiting a relatively consistent behavior pattern called style. Obviously, this style will be different for a person seeking the satisfaction of realizing his or her potential that the style of a person seeking the satisfaction of group praise.

Style is one of several components, then, that distinguish the role of leader from the role of follower.

THE ROLE OF FOLLOWER

Any time that two persons are in interaction and there is reduction of uncertainty on the part of one, or direction of that individual's actions by another, one has led and the other has followed. The role of follower has an attached expectation that the role player will, for whatever reason, allow a leader to make decisions that affect him or to take actions that he would otherwise have to take. The question naturally arises as to why anyone is willing to conform to such an expectation. One of the basic reasons lies in uncertainty.

Effects of Uncertainty

Maturity consists of recognizing and being able to accept one's weaknesses as well as strengths. One starts early in life to distinguish areas in which one knows as much as anyone else, or can perform as well as anyone else, from areas in which someone else is better informed or more proficient. Areas which are not distinguishable either as areas of proficiency or ineptitude leave one in uncertainty.

The reduction of uncertainty is the essence of information. Telling a rational adult her or his name provides no information, because there is no uncertainty to be reduced. However, we are all willing to make instant authorities of others when uncertainty is great enough. If a person is looking for an address in a strange city, one is likely to stop the first passerby to ask directions, disregarding the fact that the "informant" may be equally unfamiliar with the neighborhood! One may even follow completely erroneous directions if the giver sounds convincing!

The role of follower implies an expectation that the person is less certain about what is to be done in a given situation than is another who is or will be designated as leader. The follower's uncertainty may attach to a recognition that someone else has skill or knowledge that she or he does not.

Effects of Skill or Knowledge

A person is likely to experience uncertainty when one recognizes that another possesses a competency or some bit of knowledge, important to group tasks, that one does not.

The specialization and division of labor in technological societies causes many a person to be increasingly responsible for others in his or her own area of competence and dependent upon others in theirs. This is a lesson not yet well learned regarding school personnel, and there are many people who still expect that a school principal be able to do the job of every person in the school, and do it better. Yet some of those same people would instantly see the absurdity of expecting a university president to be able to perform all jobs in his institution!

The role requires that the follower acknowledge that in areas such as obtaining and allocating resources that will help him or her, or in getting people to work cooperatively, or in integrating the aims of the educational agency with the aims of other agencies, there are individuals who have specialized skill and knowledge on which one can rely.

It may be that the follower could develop the skill or acquire knowledge equivalent to that of the accepted leader if she or he had sufficient ego-involvement in the situation.

Effects of Ego-Involvement

The role requires that the follower have less ego-involvement in the outcome of a specific situation than has the leader. If two people have equal ego-involvement, they may vie to be leader. If a patricular matter becomes of sufficient concern, a follower may become an emergent leader for that situation, although normally content to go along with a designated leader who has the potential for satisfying personal and organizational needs.

For most activities of an ongoing nature, the role of follower requires that the individual get his satisfactions from what he is doing in his role. The status and other rewards of the position must provide satisfactions in themselves. If all teachers spent their time aspiring to be principals or superintendents, few learners would be helped.

For several years, behavioral scientists have been concerned about what the traditional role of followers does to people, and have been trying to set new expectations for the role through what is called Organization Development. Although the movement has not yet reached far in education, it is on the horizon, and would-be leaders should be familiar with it.

Possible Modification
Through Organization Development

One of the best explanations of Organization Development (OD) was provided by Randall (1971), who said that the movement assumes people have the capability and motivation to improve their organizational structures and products. It accepts conflicts as inevitable— conflicts among the needs of individuals, groups, and the organization—but advocates open facing and resolution of conflicts. It attempts to make maximum use of human potential. Obviously, such views, if applied to the nonformal and formal agencies of education, could make vast changes in the roles of followers as well as of leaders.

While most of the OD plans now operational are in industry, the *OD Practitioner* is a publication of the NTL Institute for Applied Behavioral Science, and NTL is familiar to many educators.

The OD concept is compatible with our earlier discussions of the needs for flexible organizational structures and for flexible natures among leaders.

SUMMARY

Specific position titles of amazing variety are used to designate persons who are expected to lead in a wide range of nonformal and formal agencies of education. Heaviest emphasis is placed on positions in formal agencies.

Educational positions, as with positions in general, are characterized not only by their degree of permanence, but by the responsibility, status, authority, perquisites, skills, and knowledge required in each.

Observable behavior is related to and dependent on roles and their attendant expectations, with individual behavior being affected by the relative pulls toward individuality and conformity, by value conflicts, and by role conflicts.

The role of leader results from expectations regarding preferred outcomes, taking initiative, administering, risk, stress, and style.

The expectations for the follower are different from those for the leader, and include some relating to reduction of uncertainty, to skill or knowledge required, and to ego involvement. Organization Development is a concept that may bring radical change in the expectations for the roles of follower and leader.

Chapter 2 will discuss how roles are defined by expectations.

SOME SUGGESTED RESOURCES

E. Fromm, *The revolution of hope toward a humanized technology.* New York: Harper & Row, 1968.

D. A. Goslin, *The school in contemporary society.* Glenview, Ill.: Scott, Foresman, 1965.

I. L. Heckman, Human relations in industry. In C. Heyel (Ed.), *The encyclopedia of management.* New York: Van Nostrand Reinhold, 1963. Vol. 1, pp. 287–291.

R. Linton, Concepts of role and status. In T. M. Newcomb and E. L. Hartley (Eds.), *Readings in social psychology.* New York: Holt, Rinehart and Winston, 1947. Originally published in R. Linton, *The cultural background of personality.* Englewood Cliffs, N.J.: Prentice-Hall, 1945.

R. G. Owens, *Organizational behavior in schools.* Englewood Cliffs, N.J.: Prentice-Hall, 1970.

L. G. Seligman, Leadership: political aspects. In D. L. Sills (Ed.), *International encyclopedia of the social sciences.* New York: Macmillan, 1968. Vol. 9, pp. 107–113.

L. F. Urwick, Notes on the theory of organization. In C. Heyel (Ed.), *The encyclopedia of management.* New York: Van Nostrand Reinhold, 1963. Vol. 2, pp. 621–622.

CHAPTER 2

ROLE EXPECTATIONS

*A role has certain normative rights and duties, which we may
call role expectations. When the role incumbent puts these
rights and duties in effect, he is said to be performing in his role.
The expectations define what the actor, whoever he may be,
should or should not do under various circumstances while
occupying the particular role in the social system.*

—Getzels et al.

This chapter will examine the general nature of role expectations,
the relationships that result in expectations, the levels at which expectations are held, the forms in which they are expressed, and the
social forces that define roles through expectations.

THE NATURE OF EXPECTATIONS

For any agency of any social institution, people attempt to: establish
an organizational pattern *to assure some degree of permanency,*
to more or less guarantee that the institution will be maintained;
divide the labor to be performed along hierarchical lines; establish
positions which indicate the particular division of labor—the tasks—
to be performed in each, regardless of *who holds the position;* and
set expectations regarding the behaviors of individuals. Each position-holder, if living up to expectations, attempts to carry out the
tasks of the position, helps to maintain the organization, tries to help
achieve institutional functions and agency goals, assists in maintaining morale, and may try to bring about changes in the institution

or the agency. The individual plays a role, through trying to meet the expectations held for him or her.

Any of the holders of positions in education agencies such as those outlined in Chapter 1 may play their roles better if they understand the manner in which roles are defined by expectations to which sanctions attach, by basic views of humanity, and by cultural effects.

There are open assertions in our society that those who are economically unproductive are largely uneducated and socially alienated persons. Nonproductive behavior that does *not* result from unemployment is a result of failure of the involved individuals to internalize the values that the middle-class majority of society reflects in expectations held for everyone, such as having economically productive skills, recognizing authority, "doing one's part," and "getting along with others." Failure to internalize generally acceptable values results in a failure to meet expectations; failure to meet expectations results in sanctions.

Sanctions as Reciprocals of Expectations

Sanctions consist of rewards or denial or rewards (a punishment), and punishments or obviation of punishment (a kind of reward!), and thus are based in the emotions of hope and fear. Rich[1] provided a model that is useful in understanding the reciprocal nature of expectations and sanctions, as follows:

> Type 1: A is a desirable act—Person X did A.
> Type 2: B is an undesirable act—X did not do B.
> Type 3: C is a desirable act—X did not do C.
> Type 4: D is an undesirable act—X did D.

From this model, it is clear that expectations are expressed in terms of expected conformity according to predetermined standards of desirability-undesirability. Conformity to the standards will be rewarded, while nonconformity will be punished in some fashion. Thus, X would be rewarded for actions of types 1 and 2 and punished for types 3 and 4.

Expectations often are thought of only in terms of desirability, but sanctions really attach to conformity or nonconformity in terms of standards of what is desirable *or* undesirable. An individual's view of standards of desirability or undesirability probably is linked to one's concept of the nature of one's fellow human beings.

Expectations as Views of Humanity

McGregor (1966) polarized the extreme views of humanity in his now-famous *Theory X* and *Theory Y,* but it seems that he was restat-

---

[1] J. M. Rich, Rules, sanctions, and responsibilities. *The Record.* Teachers College, Columbia University, 1967, **69**(1), 37–41.

ing the views espoused much earlier by Thomas Hobbes ("life is mean and competitive") and John Locke ("man is natively cooperative").

THEORY X. The advocates of bureaucracy seem to be largely of the Theory X mind, believing that:

1. The average human being has an inherent dislike of work and will avoid it if he or she can.
2. Because of this human characteristic of dislike of work, most people must be coerced, controlled, directed, and threatened with punishment to get them to put forth adequate effort toward the achievement of organizational objectives.
3. The average human being prefers to be directed, wishes to avoid responsibility, has relatively little ambition, and wants security above all.

THEORY Y. Some people believe that it is possible to have a structure more flexible than that of bureaucracy, among them Theory Y adherents who believe in essence that:

1. The expenditure of physical and mental effort in work is as natural as play or rest.
2. External control and the threat of punishment are not the only means for bringing about effort toward organizational objectives. People will exercise self-direction and self-control in the service of objectives to which they are committed.
3. Commitment to objectives is a function of the rewards associated with their achievement. The most significant of such rewards, for instance, the satisfaction of ego and self-actualization needs, can be direct products of effort directed toward organizational objectives. This has special import for leaders, perhaps.
4. The average human being learns, under proper conditions, not only to accept but to seek responsibility.
5. The capacity to exercise a relatively high degree of imagination, ingenuity, and creativity in the identification of organizational problems is widely distributed in the population.
6. Under the conditions of modern industrial life, the intellectual potentialities of the average human being are only partially utilized.

Theory X managers see their jobs as making individuals responsible for functions and as having to coerce, direct, and threaten those individuals. Theory Y managers, on the other hand, agree, basically, with Marcuse[2] that human beings will not be truly free until they

[2] H. Marcuse, Eros and civilization. Boston: Beacon, 1955.

view their work as a highly desirable recreational activity. They see their jobs as making groups responsible for objectives. They believe that if the members of a group see a goal, they will think together to find ways to accomplish that goal and, left to their own devices, will set about deciding how to proceed. Close supervision may be unnecessary in such groups, and a Theory Y leader strives to develop a structure more flexible than the usual bureaucracy. Few existing agencies of education are organized along Theory Y lines. One of the crying needs for leaders is to get educational agencies so organized. However, even in the most flexible organizations, expectations for individuals are influenced by cultural effects.

Cultural Effects on Expectations
Gardner (1963) said that:

> *Without some grasp of the meaning of his relationship to the whole, it is not easy for the individual to retain a vivid sense of his own capacity to act as an individual, a sure sense of his own dignity and an awareness of his roles and responsibilities. He tends to accept the spectator role and to sink into passivity* [p. 59].

Undoubtedly, one's grasp of the "meaning of his relationship to the whole" results from the effects of the various cultures of which one is a part. In a later section of this chapter, the levels at which expectations are held and the forms in which they are manifest will be discussed. However, it appears that each person becomes basically oriented by his or her cultures as either a *local* or a *cosmopolitan*.

The terms local and cosmopolitan apparently were introduced into this country by Merton (1948), but Gouldner (1963) summarized relevant research and concluded that the organizational identities might be described thus:

> *COSMOPOLITANS—Those low on loyalty to the employing organization, high on commitment to specialized role skills, and likely to use an outer reference group orientation.*
> *LOCALS—Those high on loyalty to the employing organization, low on commitments to specialized role skills, and likely to use an inner reference group orientation* [p. 361].

Abbott (1965) discussed individuals having local and cosmopolitan orientations and concluded that employees whose orientation is basically local may be expected to be amenable to influence by a normative group. When the behavior of a local elicits negative sanctions from the group, the individual tends to question the accuracy of his cognitive orientations and will restructure these orientations to remove the perceived dissonance. The person tends to conform readily to organizational demands and will, eventually, adjust his own level of aspiration so that personal satisfaction can be achieved within the limits of organizationally permissible behavior.

However, an employee whose orientation is basically cosmopolitan may be expected to be less amenable to influence by a group. When his behavior elicits negative sanctions from the group, the cosmopolitan seems to maintain his cognitive orientations but tends to increase his search for alternatives to the course of action proposed by the organization. For some such individuals, the increased search could eventuate in leaving the organization if opportunities are available and if the time and effort already invested in the organization are not too great.

When leaving the organization seems an unacceptable alternative for the cosmopolitan, he or she may remain in it but seek opportunities for satisfaction without conforming to organizational demands. The individual may derive satisfaction from recognition for research and/or publication in a professional field, from activity in professional or trade associations, or from participation in community affairs. In any event, recognition from outside groups is sought as a substitute for recognition which is not forthcoming from doing the job. Individuals of both orientations often work in various relationships in a number of social systems.

RELATIONSHIPS

The manner in which society and the individuals within it set and maintain internal standards for individual performance has been explored by Merton (1948), Riesman (1950), Getzels and Guba (1957), Thelen (1960), Homans (1961), Parsons and Shils (1951), Gouldner (1963), and Abbott (1965), among others. These writers all concluded that there are identifiable relationships among structures, positions, roles, personalities, and behaviors. Such relationships determine the process of social systems.

Relationships in Social Systems

Each individual in an organization is in a perpetual dilemma and often faces value conflicts or personal conflicts because he or she simultaneously is playing roles in each of several social systems, as was discussed earlier. The situation may be summed up by paraphrasing Thelen (1960, pp. 71–72):

1. Each person or group in an organization or society holds expectations for the behavior of other persons and groups.

2. The expectations may be sorted out among networks or systems.
3. Each person belongs simultaneously in several systems, each of which has expectations for one's behavior in that system.
4. The overlapping of systems and expectations generates conflict for the individual because the expectations, which are reflections of values of the various systems, often are not compatible.
5. Value conflicts are felt as conflicts of interest by individuals belonging to the different systems.
6. Persons subject to expectations or value conflicts perceive others as putting pressure on them, and they assume, in action at least, that decisions about them are to be made through the alignments of groups for and against, with the larger pressure decisive.

These role or value conflicts can be very important to one's mental health.

Effect of Relationships on Mental Health

Mental health includes the prevention of mental and emotional disorders; the detection, treatment, and rehabilitation of the mentally ill; and the promotion of positive expectations, including those of self and others. Stress from physical or chemical processes within one's body, or from relationships with other persons in the various social systems within which one interacts, may bring on mental illness.

Situations that reduce the pressures of human relationships and social situations can obviate mental illness. No one expects that a school superintendent or college president should be a clinician, skilled in diagnosis and treatment of mental illness, but it is expected that any leader will know enough about such conditions that he or she will strive to provide a working atmosphere free of the more obvious stress-inducing situations. The individual also needs to be able to recognize danger signals, of which faltering morale is one of the more obvious, while remembering that Utopia is, itself, bad for mental health. An occasional crisis invigorates most normal people.

Relationships and Morale

Morale is a sufficiently precise word to designate the capacity of a group to pull together toward goals that its members accept. Later writers seem not to have improved on Bell (1961), who said there are five prerequisites of morale that should concern us, and all involve expectations. The comments that follow about the five are those of the present writers.

Faith in the leaders. Followers must believe that decisions made and actions taken are better than they could have made/taken on their own.

Faith of members in each other. Unless individuals see the group as doing something for them that they could not do for themselves, or doing it better than they could do by themselves, they lose faith.

Confidence in equitable distribution of awards. If individuals believe that others are being given preferential treatment, group spirit is lost.

Organizational efficiency. The structure must provide adequate communications, distribution of supplies, and the means for carrying out one's responsibilities. The failure of any one of these almost guarantees organizational collapse.

Attention to well-being of group members. An organization must find ways of making its members believe that they matter. One way of doing so is to show solicitude for the mental, emotional, and physical health of its members.

Jay (1971) said that ". . . this shared sense of all belonging to-gether, this shared understanding and recognition of what it is we belong to . . . is the hardest to build and the hardest to de-stroy . . . [p. 283]." Morale definitely is related to expectations, and to the patterns of accommodation that individuals develop in coping with their own and others' expectations.

Patterns of Accommodation to Organizations
Three basic patterns by means of which individuals attempt to cope with expectations were described by Presthus (1962). Essentially they are the following:

UPWARD-MOBILES. Upward-mobiles are the competitors, the status seekers, the pyramid climbers. They expect to and are expected to compete, and they do so. These people seem to be both internally and externally motivated, and they glory in the reciprocal expecta-tions-sanctions relationship, because they have found that they can get at least a fair share of the favorable rewards and they enjoy vying for them.

INDIFFERENTS. Indifferents are self-actualizers, the inner-moti-vated. They join groups only because the groups can help them to do what they want to do, and they refuse to compete for any rewards other than self-chosen ones.

AMBIVALENTS. Ambivalent individuals tend not to know what their motivations are; thus, they sometimes compete for organizational rewards and sometimes strive for the attainment of personal goals. Expectations of other persons *may* be meaningful to them, but there seems to be almost no way of predicting when role demands will be meaningful and when they will not.

Obviously, most leaders come from the ranks of the upward-mobiles, and their jobs are made easier if most of their followers are upward-mobile strivers also. In almost every organization one may find all three patterns of accommodation, and even indifferents in a work organization are affected in their attitudes by their patterns of accommodation to other social systems in which they are more active participants.

Leaders and followers need to be aware of the multiple *levels* at which expectations are held for all members of their organizations and for the organizations themselves, and of the forms in which expectations are manifest.

LEVELS AND MANIFESTATIONS OF EXPECTATIONS
The employee who is uncertain about the expectations held for him is at a disadvantage, to say the least, but imagine the devastating uncertainty regarding one's social worth when one doesn't even have a job! An individual who *is* employed, and who is fortunate enough to be employed in an organization which has written policies, rules, and procedures, still is likely to be unaware of many of the expectations held for him, for those groups of which he is a part, and for the organization.

Human beings can see themselves as reflecting a larger harmony if they understand that there are certain values held by the majority of their society for the universe, the world, the human race, the culture, the nation, the institution, the subculture, the organization, the group, and the role player; that those values are reflected in expectations held at the various levels and are manifest in certain fashions and forms which can be discovered and communicated; and that communication of expectations in the form of *information* is the main and proper concern of the pluralistic agencies of education.

Some of the levels at which expectations are held and the implications that they have for the goals of educational agencies and the roles of individuals are included in the following discussion.

The Supranational Level
Although a sizable conservative minority disagrees, the majority expects that everyone in our nation will learn certain things that transcend national goals, such as: to respect the United Nations, to believe in and work for world law, to show loyalty to the Western rather than the Eastern world, and so on.

At this supranational level, expectations take the forms of universal or natural "laws," principles, traditions, customs, or mores. Thus, we all are subject to laws such as "survival of the fittest," to principles of morality or human decency, and, supposedly, to the Geneva Convention. Some educational goals, such as a striving for world peace and order, also transcend nationalism.

The National Level

As a U.S. citizen or future citizen, one is expected to learn, among other things, that this is the "best" country, we have a Constitution and a set of laws that are a source of pride, a belief in equality is part of the national spirit, national property and pride are to be defended, education provides national hope as well as social mobility, culture is to be transmitted to the next generation, social reform is desirable and essential, the discovery of new knowledge is valued, and so on ad infinitum. One also is expected to be a producer and a consumer within the capitalistic system.

At the national level, normative expectations for other countries are expressed through treaties, pacts, and other agreements. Expectations for the individual citizen of this country are expressed in the Constitution, the federal laws, customs, traditions, mores, and educational goals.

The Social Class Level

At the social class level, expectations are held that one will behave according to one's status; that the basis for stratification depends on what the society sees as important at a particular time; and that judgments regarding class are made informally and unofficially. Class is not a matter of law, and judgments are made on the basis of only a few characteristics. There are both closed and open systems, and mobility occurs largely in the latter. An individual is expected to learn that conditions determining stratification include social change, industrialization, urbanization, ethnic heterogeneity and migration, ideology, popular education, and fertility rates. Berelson and Steiner (1967, pp. 70–89) provided an excellent resume of research findings in these matters.

At the social class level, expectations are exhibited in forms such as the respect and deference accorded others, the attribution of authority, or the seeking of homage from others.

The Ethnic Level

One soon learns, whether by intent or not, that the prevalence of prejudice and discrimination usually relates to race, religion, country of origin, or sex. Any one of these matters can and often does lead to limited relationships and stereotyping on both sides. Certain expectations are held by others for every role player in regard to these matters, although such current norms as "black is beautiful" and "don't tell ethnic jokes" indicate that some self-image building is occurring that sociologists are not yet reporting. Berelson and Steiner (1967) pointed out that:

Everyone comes to "know his place" and to act accordingly, thus reinforcing the very stereotyping with which the process begins. In this way, it becomes difficult to treat people "for themselves," and communication between the groups comes to be superficial, subject to misunderstanding, and highly stylized [p. 100].

Education is expected to overcome or greatly reduce prejudice resulting from ethnic expectations. Role demands at the ethnic level seem to be reflected by behaviors of persons with whom role players interact. The interactors' behaviors may be dichotomized as:

acceptance-rejection (of persons, folkways, or other actions)
equal treatment-discrimination
liking-prejudice
love-hate

The Organization Level

At the level of the organization, the individual is expected to: (1) accept the division of labor and responsibility, (2) make oneself and one's goals subservient to the organization and its goals, (3) participate in organizational decision-making on a rational basis, (4) maintain organizational secrecy, (5) submit to and legitimize authority, (6) seek personal security (but in cooperation with, not at the expense of, peers), and (7) tolerate centralized control. That some expectations are expressed as principles at the social institution level was examined by Mort and Ross (1957):

. . . there is a body of cultural values, relatively stable and universal, that illuminates the behavioral manifestations of all social effort and, in particular, the public provision of educational services.

These cultural values may be called "principles." They are the frequently unverbalized basic arguments for taking this course or that, for behaving in this fashion or some other, for a positive rather than a negative decision on a specific issue.

The authors believe that those distillations of what people think of as "goodness" in the management of public affairs are things that well up from the long history of man's learning to live and work side by side with his fellows.

To some extent these principles are an attempt to describe wisdom. Wisdom can be defined as the drawing off of accurate generalizations from experience. Some old men, sages, have been considered wise because of the accuracy of the generalizations they have drawn from a long lifetime of experience. But compared to the lifetime of one man, how long is the experience of mankind! By deliberate analysis of the tacit anchors to reason that observers of man's institutions through the ages have as-

sumed, perhaps some concentrates of wisdom can provide the substitute for age [p. 33].

Organizational expectations find expression also as regulations, creeds, codes, and rituals. Ritualized behavior, including tradition, is one of the characteristics of institutionalization. Within the particular structure of an institutional agency, expectations at the job level may be further spelled out.

The Job Level

According to Schein (1965), a sketchy outline of expectations at the job level is embodied in "the psychological contract" if the contract is known to the individual and accepted by him. The organization pays him, gives him status and security, and asks him to do work which has been described to him and which he has accepted as his; in return, he gives the company hard work, good performance, and loyalty [p. 44].

At the job level, expectations also may take the form of organization charts, policies, job descriptions, written contracts, rules, procedures, schedules, orientation sessions, and in-service education. Some organizations explicate role demands through orientation and performance evaluations.

The Work Group Level

Within an educational agency there are likely to be smaller work groups. For instance, in a college there are people who work together in departments. In an industrial setting, a special group works with training. In a public school, the work group may be an entire building staff or, if differentiated staffing is effected, the team. In the work group, as at the ethnic level, expectations are mirrored in the reactions of those individuals with whom one interacts— namely, by their acceptance or rejection.

SOCIAL FORCES

Every agency of the educational institution carries out its functions through a social system which is structured around a unity of purpose and an interdependence of its core elements—people. Those people operate within certain constraints on the organization—some of which are self-imposed and some imposed from without.

Every system has inputs, a process, and outputs. If the process is to be changed (and proponents of accountability insist that the process of the schools, at least, *must* be changed), there must be feedback to the system. At all points, expectations for everyone in the organization are operative and they come from people, power structures, physical conditions, legal arrangements, financial needs and resources, "what is," and professionalism. These will be examined in the remainder of this chapter.

People as Social Forces

Since people are encountered both on the job and in larger social settings, they must be considered among those forces that affect positions and roles. Since influences are exerted both by individuals and by groups, both must be considered.

The natures, characteristics, and needs of at least three categories of individuals seem germane to understanding expectations. A position-holder himself, any other position-holder in the same organization, and any person outside the particular organization who exerts either authority or influence over the position-holder all seem certain to affect his role.

The job-related groups, formal and hierarchical in nature, which must be considered as affecting positions and roles include subordinates, organizational peers, and professional peers outside the organization. Each of these groups in its own way affects each position and role in any except the most informal and unstructured organization.

Informal or social job-related groups also may affect positions and roles. The formation of cliques is a phenomenon which has been observed by any organization-watcher, and many individuals have learned, to their sorrow, that cliques can indeed affect positions and roles. The common interest groups found within many organizations, too, can be forces affecting positions and roles. An example is an informal association of teachers interested in applications of data processing to instruction. It is likely that such an association, long continued, would eventually affect the roles of the members. Groups of people meeting together on *any* regular basis, whether it be due to continuing shared interests in art, music, bridge, or the sex life of the African fire-ant, develop expectations for each other.

Job-related groups that meet because of temporary common interests also affect roles. An example would be a "task force" to improve instruction. Such a group, if successful in completing its assignment, may have a lasting effect on a number of positions and roles. Wiles' (1963, p. 190) observations regarding the effects of groups on individual students seem generalizable to nonstudents also, namely: The phase of social climate that an individual feels most is the way one's peers treat one. A sense of belonging and of being wanted is vitally important. Some groups make an inclusive approach: Newcomers are welcomed; many social functions are open to all. Others display exclusiveness: Newcomers must prove themselves; small cliques form which consider themselves superior to others and try to prove it by striving for rules that favor them and for status positions.

Power Structures

Outside groups which influence organizational roles comprise that vague amorphous mass which professors of administration have called the *power structure* when educating past generations of school leaders. Many individuals have faced leadership responsibilities believing that there is a fixed and influential power structure in each community, and that survival depends on being able to identify and secure the support of that structure. Rather than a monolithic "elite" power group that is effective on all issues, it is now believed that there are at least three types of power structures in most communities, as identified by McCarty (1964) and as described below. Kimbrough (1964) identified more than these three, and described how each functions in a public school setting.

FACTIONAL. In a factional power structure, there are two factions, pro and con, and sides are chosen according to the issue, for example, federal aid for parochial schools. The faction that wins is the one which has the most clout with decision-makers. Whichever wins affects the expectations held for many persons.

PLURALISTIC. Sometimes called the *diffused* (see Thelen 1960, pp. 5–8), this structure is seen by Kimbrough (1964) and others as one in which the persons who are influentials vary, depending on the issue. Thus, a board of realtors might be the power structure in a public housing struggle and a taxpayers' union the structure in a tax issue.

INERT. People who are uncommitted may constitute a power structure simply by being apathetic toward issues. School superintendents, community college presidents, and others who have promoted operating millage issues know what a potent force the uncommitted can be.

An estimate of the division of registered voter propensities is shown in Figure 2-1. Whether the estimated percentages are accurate has no effect on the concept of an inert power structure.

Physical Conditions as Social Forces
Physical conditions affect educational roles more than is normally recognized, due to such things as type and size of community, type of neighborhood within the community, climate, topography, roads and streets, size and type of agency, and services and plant facilities available.

TYPE OF COMMUNITY. Anyone familiar with the public schools will immediately be able to think of ways in which the schools are affected by whether the community is rural, suburban, urban, or metropolitan in character. Other agencies of education sometimes have their existence *determined* by the type of community. For example, there are almost no company or proprietary schools in rural or suburban communities, and until very recent years there were relatively few 4H clubs in suburban, urban, or metropolitan settings.

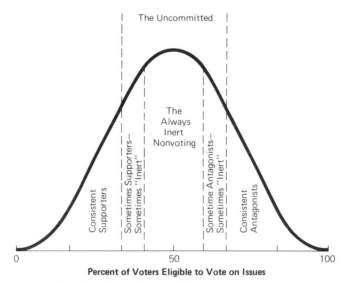

Figure 2-1   *The Inert Power Structure*

SIZE OF COMMUNITY. Given corresponding positions in each of two educational agencies, individuals will find that the roles associated with the positions are vastly different even though the single apparent variable is size of community. Consider, for example, the position of president of a college of 1,000 students. If the college were located in a city of 50,000 population, the positional role would be quite different from what it is if the college is located in a city of 750,000.

NEIGHBORHOOD. The proprietor of a school for beauticians will have a considerably different set of expectations held for her or him if the school is located in a deteriorating industrial neighborhood than if it is established in a thriving, improving, semiresidential neighborhood of the same city. We have long known that teachers in schools located in lower socioeconomic surroundings spend a disproportionate amount of their time on police duties as compared with their peers in middle- or upper-class neighborhoods, and this reflects expectations.

CLIMATE. Climate influences matters such as noon hour activities, care and storage of student clothing, operational aspects such as heating and ventilating, maintenance schedules, and the location of health and physical education classes. Climate conditions complicate or simplify the job of a school bus driver and affect the principal, teachers, and other school employees who are automatically concerned whether the driver does or does not keep his schedule. Weather phenomena are dominant factors in determining the expectations held for the directors of proprietary schools, such as those for heavy-construction equipment operators.

TOPOGRAPHY. Physical features, of course, affect whether students can walk to any kind of school, the laying out of student bus routes, the ease with which anyone who drives an automobile can get to an educational enterprise, the density of population from which an agency can draw students, the linkage of a community to other communities, and the ease of access for service vehicles to a particular site. Topography may be a determining factor in the choice of a site for a particular type of educational agency and certainly will affect the roles of persons responsible for maintenance of the site.

STREETS AND ROADS. The basic nature of a community and the density of its population are controlled to a great extent by the pattern and condition of the streets and roads. The presence or absence of traffic signals, safe crosswalks, and overpasses, plus the frequency of accidents at particular intersections, all affect roles and the expectations held in the agencies of education.

SERVICES AVAILABLE. An experienced public administrator need not be reminded of the effect that the availability of services can have on population. Open land can turn into housing developments with alarming speed when water, sewer, gas, and electric services become available. Developments affect expectations.

SIZE AND TYPE OF AGENCY. Although belaboring the obvious, we might point out that the headmaster of a private school enrolling 350 *boys* has a somewhat different role if he moves to a *coeducational* boarding school enrolling the same number of pupils, and a still different role if he gains employment in a private school enrolling 1600 students. Were one of those institutions to be church affiliated, the headmaster would find his role expectations again changed.

PLANT FACILITIES. Plant refers to all of the physical properties of an agency—the site, developments on the site, buildings, equipment, and furnishings—and points can be made readily to illustrate how any one of the plant elements can affect roles. One striking example is found in certain centers that are maintained for the express purpose of preparing teaching aids and equipment for the instructors in the armed services, where virtually any request of an instructor for a piece of equipment is honored. As a result of such support services, instruction in the armed forces often is far superior to, or ahead of, that in the best of public or private schools. The effects on role demands are obvious.

Legal Arrangements as Social Forces

Almost all aspects of how an agency is organized and financed affect the roles of all persons within it. Among the important aspects of an organization are its legal arrangements. At what level is it institutionalized? For what purposes does it exist? By whom is it licensed? To what regulations is it subject?

LEVEL OF ORGANIZATION. The role of the superintendent of the Air Force Academy certainly is different from that of the superintendent of a local school district, and part of the difference must be ascribed to the fact that the role incumbents are in contact with dissimilar groups of learners. The position of director of the National Union of Christian Schools is certainly different from that of director of an American Overseas Dependents' school. Also, some positions exist only at certain levels because the institutions of which they are a part exist only at those levels. Examples would be the executive secretary of a regional accrediting association who has no counterpart at the state level because there is no such association at the state level, or the executive secretary of a state education association who has no peer at the area or intermediate level because no similar association exists at that level.

PURPOSE. If one asks the question, "Why did it come into being?" about each of the many agencies of education, there is likely to be a different answer for each. Some of the differences in the two superintendents' roles described above undoubtedly lie in the overt purposes of the two institutions. The effects of agency purposes are quite pronounced when one compares the role of principal in a public school to that of principal in a parochial or private school.

ACQUIRED FUNCTIONS. Many agencies now have functions other than those for which they were established. Perhaps the outstanding example is the philanthropic foundations which came into being to help wealthy persons distribute their largesse in worthy (and tax-advantaged!) fashion but which now "persistently affect" education. This covert, and perhaps unintentional, effect of the foundations has brought great changes in the roles of foundation employees and trustees. To cite a different example, the late A. B. Graham, a rural teacher and school superintendent, sought some way for rural children to help themselves and make the most of their not always salubrious environment, and thus established 4H clubs. Now, those clubs endeavor to provide almost unlimited summertime learning activities, many of which have nothing to do with rural environment;

furthermore, many such clubs now exist in other than rural settings, here and in other countries.

BASIS FOR ESTABLISHMENT. Whether a university exists as a result of a state constitutional provision, developed under permissive legislation of the state, is chartered as a nonprofit institution, or is incorporated as a business enterprise, the legal basis for its establishment affects the roles of its status leaders. An accrediting agency which is *required by law* poses different role requirements for its executive secretary or other administrator than does an association of voluntary members. A private or parochial school which exists under permissive state legislation develops role expectations for a given position which differ markedly from those in a public school which is mandatory under laws of the same state.

TARGET POPULATION. A proprietary school which is the only one of its kind in a given geographic territory places requirements on its admissions officer that are different from those of a similar school which is surrounded by competitors. The school which exists to serve and is controlled by a local parish sets up different role expectations from those established by a parochial school of the same size which is ruled as part of a diocesan system. The small city school system which is jealously boycotted by the surrounding rural areas develops roles which are different from those in a city of identical size which has no competition with its neighbors.

Finance as a Social Force
Any individual who has established a mission school can give fervent testimony as to the effects of the source of financial support on roles. Some educators decline flattering proffers of college presidencies in private institutions because it is a demonstrable fact that the major portion of the presidents' time in those institutions must be devoted to fund raising. University presidents or vice-presidents who must spend endless time and effort in lobbying on behalf of state universities often envy their peers in heavily endowed private universities. The superintendent of schools in a local district which has $2,500 of local assessed property valuation per pupil may aspire to a position where the local assessed valuation is $10,000 per pupil, but the incumbent of *that* position probably is eyeing the district that has a valuation of $18,000 per pupil!

One might say, with some degree of accuracy, that the amount of time which an educational leader can devote to the improvement of educational opportunity is directly proportionate to the adequacy of financial support of his or her institution and inversely related to the amount of public support. Finance is a vicious cycle, and one of the saddest spectacles in our society is the school superintendent or college president who is unable to recognize the need for program improvements because she or he is too busy trying to eke out a mere subsistence for the existing program.

The role of each person employed in any educational agency is affected by the learners enrolled in or available to the institution, by the persons who are available to staff it, and by the community resources available to it. For many years, the positions of teachers and principals in the parochial schools have been greatly influenced by low salaries, making the pool of prospects for employment quite limited. Community resources may be unavailable to denominational schools but available to the public schools. The community which can attract or which desires only locals to teach in its schools makes the role of every administrator and every teacher in those schools different from corresponding roles in another community which desires and can attract both locals and cosmopolitans. A proprietary school for teaching the barbering trade develops a different role for its director than does a public vocational and technical school, though both may draw students from the same general age range and the same community.

There is a respectable body of data to indicate that, while the expenditure of more money does not necessarily bring about better education, there is a positive correlation between the investment of funds per learner, over a period of time, and the quality of the educational program. Financial supporters who do not see or are unwilling to recognize this will hold different expectations for their educational leaders than will supporters in communities where the relationship *is* seen and recognized. If the taxpayers of a school district are providing all of the investment for education which they believe to be feasible, expectations will be quite different from those in a community where people are willing to invest more if they can be shown that educational quality will thereby be improved.

"What Is" as a Social Force

Any person who is considering any position of educational leadership must be realistic in assessing all facets of the job and the social setting; also whether one, as an individual, is compatible with the expectations that one finds. Here we only suggest some facets of "what is"—those aspects of the social setting which seem to affect roles and expectations.

LEADER SKILLS REQUIRED. The skills needed by leaders at different hierarchical levels vary widely. Technical skills are needed by persons who are more concerned with things than with either people or ideas; human skills are in greatest demand for those whose primary concern is people; at the upper levels of most organizations, expectations are held that leaders will have a high degree of conceptual skill.

NEEDS. The needs of learners, the needs of staff personnel, and the needs of persons outside the agencies of education all play some part in establishing the expectations held for persons in the agencies' leadership positions.

ETHNIC COMPOSITION. If all members of a group are of the same ethnic background, expectations will be different from those held if the group is an ethnic mixture. Expectations of the typical WASP suburban neighborhood are different from those of a Spanish-American neighborhood. What a female student body expects may be different from what a coeducational student body expects.

SOCIAL CLASS. Class structure often imposes expectations on the roles of educators, and social class seems to be closely and positively correlated with economic class. People likely will be divided into classes on one basis or another for a long time to come, and so long as they are, those in one class will hold expectations for their educational leaders which are different from those of any other class.

ECONOMIC CONDITIONS. Social class implications aside, the type and state of the local economy also affect expectations. People in an agrarian economy hold different expectations from those in an industrial economy; people in a booming economy hold different expectations from those in a depressed economy.

PRESSING PROBLEMS. A college may have as its most pressing problem the need to find a better way of selecting its students; in one public school situation, the problem in most urgent need of attention may be the passage of an operating levy while in another the curriculum may be in dire need of revision. In any situation, the urgent problems are likely to affect the role expectations of people working in the situation.

MORES. There are still some communities where a visit to a local tavern by the public school principal for any reason would bring a demand for his immediate ouster, but few of the people who would take the principal to task would boycott a private school because of a similar action by its proprietor. The principal of an overseas school for dependents of U.S. military personnel who wishes to live in the native community may find virtually impossible conflict between the expectations held by the natives and those of his countrymen.

TRADITIONS. Practices of long standing may acquire the force of law, and more than one administrator has found himself in hot water for flying in the face of them. The practice can be as trivial as excused school absence for students on the first day of hunting season or the bonfire before a college homecoming, but violation of a tradition may bring sanctions upon the violator. Individuals going to work in any educational agency should explore, and inform themselves about, its traditions.

PRESSURES OF TIME. The urgency with which problems must be met, the nonprofessional demands made on a leader's time, and any other pressures of time combine to affect the expectations held for one.

STAFF ADEQUACY. If teachers are scarce, so that a school must have a pupil-teacher ratio of 45:1, the expectations held for teachers and principals are different from those when the ratio is 25:1. The university that uses graduate students to teach undergraduate classes and to grade papers for professors obviously can hold expectations for its professors which are different from those held by a university that does not utilize graduate students in this manner. In a proprietary school having a specialist for each function, there is no expectation that the director be a jack-of-all trades. If a base school in a military establishment is well staffed, the education officer will not need to schedule overly large classes, but his counterpart at another base may be forced to do just that.

Professionalism as a Social Force
While *professionalism* may not be a very exact word, no other is readily apparent to describe one very important group of forces that affect positions and roles. Professionalism accounts, in some measure at least, for the tremendous differences found among educational agencies of the same general type, and it also may account for the lack of regard for education found in huge segments of the population. Discussion of some aspects of professionalism follows.

UNDERSTANDING OF FUNCTIONS. Some understanding of the functions for which an educational agency is responsible is necessary for the public, or for that part of it which comes in contact with the agency or any of its representatives. Understanding must, in most cases, emanate from the employed personnel and be transmitted through the learners. The degree to which understanding is or is not achieved has a great deal to do with the expectations held for all who work in the agency. One of the big difficulties with schools is that the people in them often have no apparent understanding of what the schools are supposed to be doing—they are guilty of the "mindlessness" deplored by Silberman (1970). Thelen (1960) proposed "school burning" as a tongue-in-cheek solution!

The extent to which people understand the overall process of education and the part of it that an agency is expected to perform will have much influence on the expectations held for each person employed by the agency. Those who have a belief that education is more than schooling hold far different expectations than those who have no such belief.

PRESTIGE. The general regard accorded an educational agency affects expectations for individuals within it. A dean in an Ivy League university is expected to behave publicly and to perform his duties differently than is the dean of a college founded last year. The superintendent of schools in a community which holds its schools in high regard is looked at much differently than that same person would be were he or she in a corresponding position in a community where people tolerate the schools only because they are legally required to do so.

QUALITY OF PERSONNEL. An educator considering a new position would do well to determine the quality of the personnel with whom she or he will work. Probably no other indicator could tell one as much about the expectations which the community holds. If personnel already on the job are inept or ill-qualified for their jobs, they are certain to affect the way in which a new leader can perform his, and it is a truism to state that nothing else can make an authority figure look quite so good as can a group of qualified and able colleagues.

CERTIFICATION. While the establishment of certification requirements never can guarantee that the quality of personnel will be improved, it seems both safe and accurate to generalize that one finds higher quality personnel where there are certification standards than where there are none. Thus, an agency which is willing to accept people with no certification, with substandard, or with minimum certification (assuming that certification for that class of personnel is possible), is saying something about the expectations that it holds for its employees. The institutional agency in which all personnel are required to have the highest type of certification available to them is saying something quite different.

IN-SERVICE EDUCATION. The extent to which provisions are made for in-service education of personnel also affects the expectations held for employees. Some agencies are not content to be selective in employment and to demand quality performance and certification, so they make provisions for employees to continue their own education on a regular and formal basis. If no such provisions are made, one may assume either that no further educational expectations are held or that they are considered an individual responsibility.

INTRA-AGENCY RELATIONS. To see how intra-agency relationships affect positions and roles, one need look only at the example of the public schools. Expectations are quite different in a school system having no apparent ties among the programs of elementary, middle or junior, and high schools than in a system where there is complete articulation of all instructional programs, both horizontally and vertically.

PUBLIC RELATIONS. The liaison of an agency with the public and the degree to which the public is involved in the affairs of the agency markedly affect the roles of persons working in it. The director of a proprietary school has expectations held for him only by the students of the school and their parents, while the principal of a parochial school has expectations held by all church members within the parish. But the principal of the public school has expectations held for him or her by every person in the area served by the school!

SUMMARY

Expectations and sanctions have a reciprocal relationship which implies that conformity will be rewarded and nonconformity punished. Expectations are closely related to age-old views of the human race, and show cultural effects.

There are relationships among structures, positions, roles, personalities, and behaviors as social systems function. Those relationships affect and, indeed, determine mental health and morale. They are influenced by the patterns of accommodation of the system's members.

Expectations are held for every individual at the supranational, national, social class, ethnic, organization, job, and work group levels. At each level, expectations are manifested in distinctive and distinguishable forms.

Among the social forces that affect expectations are people, individually and in a variety of groups, including power structures. Physical conditions such as type and size of community, neighborhood, climate, topography, roads and streets, services available, size and type of agency, and services and facilities available all affect expectations. Legal arrangements such as level of organization, purpose, acquired functions, legal structure, and relationship to other agencies are social forces. Financial needs and resources also affect expectations. "What is," as found in leader skills required, ethnic composition, social class, economic conditions, urgent problems, mores, traditions, pressures of time, and adequacy of staff, is a potent social force. Professionalism, as represented by understanding of institutional functions and roles, prestige, quality and certification of personnel, provisions for in-service education, intra-agency relationships, and liaison with the public, is also a social force affecting expectations.

The next chapter will discuss what leaders can do to make expectations known to all members of their organizations.

SOME SUGGESTED RESOURCES

B. Berelson and G. A. Steiner, Groups and organizations. Ch. 4 in *Human behavior* (shorter ed.). New York: Harcourt Brace Jovanovich, 1967. Pp. 53–69.

J. W. Getzels, J. M. Lipham, and R. F. Campbell, Institutional expectations. Ch. 7 in *Educational administration as a social process*. New York: Harper & Row, 1968. Pp. 182–217.

R. K. Merton, Types of influence: Local and cosmopolitan influentials. Ch. 10 in *Social theory and social structure* (2nd ed.). New York: Free Press, 1957. Pp. 387–420.

P. R. Mort and D. H. Ross, The humanitarian considerations in school administration. Ch. 3 in *Principles of school administration* (2nd ed.). New York: McGraw-Hill, 1957. Pp. 33–41.

H. J. Leavitt, *Managerial psychology* (2nd ed.). Chicago: University of Chicago Press, 1964.

H. A. Thelen, *Education and the human quest*. New York: Harper & Row, 1960.

CHAPTER 3

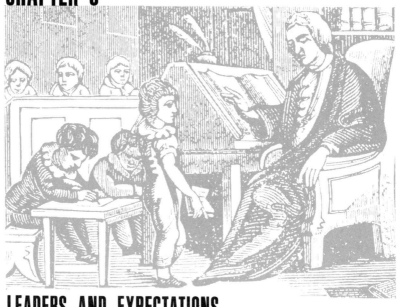

LEADERS AND EXPECTATIONS

> . . . there is the peculiar fact that whenever we encounter the
> unfamiliar, we instantly translate it into the familiar and thereby
> never see the unfamiliar.
>
> People never see their environments. They never know them.
> They always know the preceding one. This stands out loud and
> clear.
>
> —McLuhan

Leaders need to help each member of a social system to translate
the unfamiliar into the familiar—to see his specific social environment and to recognize that the expectations held there for him are
different from but similar to expectations held for him in any other
social systems of which he is or has been a part. To do this, a leader
needs to know how expectations are manifested and the relationship
of positions to roles. These matters were the gist of Chapter 2. This
chapter will examine the relationship of goals to expectations, the
ways to communicate expectations, the reasons for and how to for-
mulate policies, and the way in which all of these constitute a system
of signals.

SIGNALS
The use of signals in regard to expectations was discussed by Simon
(1968):

> The purpose of signals in football, or bidding in bridge, is to
> enable each player in a team to form accurate expectations as

*to what his teammates are going to do, so that he can determine
the proper means for cooperating with them to reach the common
aim. A major purpose of the planning and organizing that pre-
cedes any administrative activity is not merely to put each partici-
pant in the job he can best fill, but to permit each to form accurate expectations as to what the others are going to do [pp.
71–72].*

Purposes of Signals
In lieu of the signals used in football or the bidding ritual in bridge,
people in agencies of education in this country generally use a system of procedures, rules, regulations, and policies to permit each
to form accurate expectations as to what others are going to do.
The degree to which these *signals* are spelled out depends to a
great extent on the degree of sophistication of the social system
and the people in it. Also of help in the forming of accurate expectations as to what the others are going to do are goals and principles—personal, organizational, and societal—yet these are rarely
spelled out. Thus, in this chapter, consideration will be given to the
part that the leader can play in the clarification of expectations.

Necessity for Signals
The necessity for helping the individual understand expectations
held for him or her was highlighted by the paraphrase from Thelen
in Chapter 2. To paraphrase Goslin (1965, pp. 146–147): The development and transmission of specific policies to provide for all of the
conceivable contingencies that are likely to be faced by subordinates and leaders is difficult, even under conditions of face-to-face
interaction over a period of time. Such transmission is a virtual impossibility when given only formal channels of communication and
the necessity for having uniform policy throughout a system. A good
example is found in the very great difficulty experienced in communicating necessary information about standardized tests to teachers
who are expected to administer them and make intelligent use of
scores in a system-wide testing program.

   If educational subsystems are to live up to their responsibilities
to the society, leaders at all levels must do some hard thinking about
two possible alternatives, namely: (1) circumventing formal channels
by facilitating intimate and immediate communication throughout the
system when it is needed, or (2) significantly increasing the autonomy of local units.

   Major tasks facing most educational agencies are: (1) full-scale
reassessment of policies, in order to make sure that they have provided the maximum potential for flexibility and innovation, and (2)
professionalization of the instructor role consistent with external demands for "accountability."

   Thus, one can see that the provision and dissemination of procedures, rules, and policies of the magnitude needed to signal the role expectations for all of the persons in any agency of education is a large order indeed. However, signals are necessary to the structuring of relationships.

Structuring Relationships Through Signals

Whether flexible or rigid, temporary or permanent, the informal structures within any formal organization are important because of the parts that they play in information flow and in the distribution of influence and power. The signals sent and received structure all interpersonal relationships.

In a formal, enduring structure, relationships and interactions tend to be rigid and generally are of a continuing nature. Unfortunately, the norm in educational agencies has been to develop a manual or handbook for instructors and/or other employees in which procedures, rules, policies, laws, and—sometimes—principles, are mixed together in an indiscriminate potpourri. That persons new to the institution often are confused by such manuals is quite understandable. Yet, a handbook could, if properly developed, help to reduce uncertainty and provide a measure of security for a social system's members.

Providing Security Through Signals

Individuals who are faced with tasks to be responsible for are more comfortable and less anxious if expectations are known to them in some detail. They can be more certain of the correctness of their actions and, once the tasks are completed, they can rest easily knowing that they have done what was expected of them. It is standard practice for organizations to develop and to disseminate directions for handling recurrent situations such as ordering supplies, completing reports, developing budgetary requests, and scheduling activities; thus, the needs of individuals are served.

Persons in most positions find their work much simplified if everyday tasks are routine and of a repeated nature so that they can be handled in a standardized fashion. The organization which develops and disseminates statements of expectations regarding as many situations as possible thus "kills two birds with one stone," by alleviating the personal anxieties of subordinates while making it possible for superordinates to standardize task procedures.

Stating expectations helps to build the strength, faith in purpose, vigor, and cohesion which are the "apparatus of permanence" and the elements of organizational survival. Unfortunately, however, spelling out expectations sometimes has adverse effects.

Possible Adverse Effects of Signals

It is possible that the signals used for clarification of expectations may have unanticipated effects, such as taking away individual initiative, causing inefficiency, lowering morale, or reducing organizational flexibility.

An individual faced with particular tasks which must be done precisely within deadlines is apt to suffer a loss of morale. The reaction to the expectation of having to submit a periodic report is likely to be, "Oh, no! Not again!" Anyone who has been a part of an organizational setting, regardless of how salubrious the climate, is almost certain to recognize the symptom, if not the situation.

Any social system in which expectations are standardized runs the risk of having the expectations met in an inefficient manner. Organizations which have incentive systems for suggestions from employees can attest to the fact that many of the most valuable suggestions received are those which *change* the expectations held for certain individuals or groups.

Closely coupled to possible inefficiency of operation is the possible loss of individual initiative. If an organization can tolerate allowing people to perform their tasks in their own ways, it may discover methods of performing some tasks which can be temporarily standardized to the benefit of all concerned—and without the incentive of monetary or other rewards. Any time that task performance is standardized by the imposition of a prescribed procedure or other form of expectation, without provision for periodic reconsiderations, serendipity may be sacrificed.

The signals utilized to make expectations known to the members of a social system should start with clear statements of goals, both organizational and individual, but generally they do not.

GOALS

Many businesses and educational agencies today make much of *objectives* and *management by objectives.* Evaluation and accountability require that there be some kind of judgment about the progress that has been made in terms of pre-set standards. An individual who engages in self-assessment also looks at what he has done or is doing as compared to what he set out to do. Pre-set standards are goals or objectives. Goals are seldom mentioned in many agencies of education. Yet goals are related to values, and values determine what the society or the individual expects educational agencies to accomplish.

Values as the Basis of Goals

Most contemporary sociologists define values somewhat like this: "Values are culturally based social judgments of what is important with respect to an individual's interactions with people and the nonhuman environment." Social values are both finite and infinite, and exist at many different levels.

The individual absorbs values from his or her earliest childhood. Each member of a social system finds that other people in it attempt to influence him, as he attempts to influence them. Chapter 2 emphasized that expectations are the reflections of values, expressed in myriad forms. To the extent that a person finds significant others—persons whose approval is meaningful to him—at a given societal level, it is likely that he accepts the values at that level in terms of *expectations held for him.*

The values which guide one's conduct may be his own individual values, those of family or friends, those of work associates, those of a particular community, or those of the society at large. Most of us use a combination of values from these sources, along *with what we now believe to be fact,* to guide our actions. According to Wheelis (1958), we always rely on institutional (nonprovable) values as being more significant than instrumental (provable) values.

As has been stated, a person affiliates with a social system because one sees possibilities that it can do something for him that he could not do himself, or can do something better than he could do alone. Thus, an individual becomes a member of an educational agency because he wants to do *something*—earn a living, be of service to others, gain acceptance—for which the agency offers him need-satisfiers that he could not otherwise have as a lone individual. To the extent that the system makes good on that promise, a person accepts organizational values and expectations. His goals, he hopes, will be achieved in the fulfillment of organizational goals, and this affects his philosophy.

Philosophy Related to Goals

Philosophy, to the individual, is not a vague amorphous set of beliefs to be argued about in academic circles. Philosophy, to him, is that accumulation of values—social judgments of what is important"—that has visceral impact on what he does with respect to *his* interactions with people and his nonhuman environment. He may hold values for the behavior of others that differ from those he holds for his own behavior. He may speak of what others "should" do, and thus exhibit the values that he holds for them; what he *does* exhibits the values that he holds for himself.

A leader needs to know what values individuals within a social system hold in common, because to that extent their expectations may be mutual. She or he also needs to know what individuals may do that they will not tolerate others doing!

Values and philosophy are important, then, in establishing a given goal. Objectives are important in getting to it.

Objectives: Steps Toward Goals

Objectives are way stations between values and goals. They are actions which individuals see that they or others might take to achieve certain goals. However, persons may set their objectives, perform the actions indicated by them, and then discover that they are no nearer the goal than when they started. Perhaps the following allegory will explain:

A, B, and C each has determined that job "success" is his individual goal. All are writers and each has determined that success may be achieved through working for the Sonic School of Journalism, so all apply to it and all are employed there. Thus, they share some common values.

A decides that to achieve success he must make a lot of money, be recognized as "the best," and get fame outside his discipline. B wants only to be cooperative and make a decent living. C wants to be known as an individualist and to have students come to Sonic because he is there.

Time passes. A writes a best-selling novel, is awarded a plaque as best instructor of the year, and sells movie rights to the novel at a figure that gets him national headlines. B is known as Mr. Congeniality, and plugs along getting his annual salary increments. C is known as "brilliant but eccentric," and there is no middle ground—people revere him or hate him—but he has a coterie of faculty and students who follow him and bask at his feet wherever he goes.

Who has achieved success? Who has accomplished his objectives?

But suppose that one of the three finds that he is not happy, that he doesn't yet "feel" successful? Or suppose that C feels impelled to make snide remarks about B trying to proselyte some followers of C?

Perhaps it is evident that goals, values, philosophies, and objectives are all, to a very great extent, individual matters, as are judgments as to accomplishment. Yet, expectations have something to do with all of them, and it is in settings not much different from Sonic School of Journalism that educators (*not* just public school teachers and administrators) are facing insistent demands for *accountability*.

Accountability and Goals

Accountability is not something new; only the word and the persistent current emphasis on it are new. While a whole later chapter will be devoted to accountability, enough discussion is provided here to indicate the relationship of accountability to expectations.

When "the school" was *the* agency of the educational institution and when the overt function of the school was to teach boys and girls to read and write, accountability was an easy matter. Particularly with early-day subscription schools, as with private schools today, parents who did not like the results being achieved could withdraw their children and their financial support. Everyone involved knew what the school was supposed to be doing and could tell whether it was being done.

Compulsory attendance laws, ever more complicated curricula, and a plethora of "schools" destroyed the ease of holding *the* school accountable. Many educational agencies today (many public and private schools included) have no clearly stated goals, no clearly identified measures of performance, and few defined means of determining learner status.

Performance measured against goals—preset standards-*expectations*—is what accountability is all about. Every educational leader needs to get agreement of all persons involved as to the goals his or her agency is expected to strive for and the measures of performance to be used. "Performance contractors" do that. Can other agencies do less?

Getting Agreement on Goals

As many as possible of the written expressions of expectations should be collected in a manual or handbook for the guidance of all. However, each of the types of expressions should be carefully defined, each type should be printed on its own color-coded paper, and the whole should be meticulously organized and indexed.

The suggested steps which follow may be useful guidelines for persons faced with the necessity for establishing a manual or handbook to clarify for individuals the expectations that others hold for them.

1. Define all terms concisely, so that they are clearly distinguished one from another.
2. Get organized. Determine who is to participate and the responsibilities each is to have. Set a time schedule, and provide time for participants to work.
3. Determine those areas in which you think there should be consistency of actions or decisions in your organization.
4. Organize the areas in which statements are to be made in some kind of numerically codified order.
5. Determine what now exists. Examine minutes, file copies of state codes, administrative bulletins, directives, and handbooks. Rigorously sift those items which can give consistency to actions or decision-making.
6. Analyze each existing statement for clarity, consistency, and completeness. A statement which attempts to govern in detail every action of an employee represents an unrealistic effort to put the social system into a strait jacket.
7. Fill in the gaps in the outline. Make policies or rules or establish procedures where none exist—if they are essential to understanding expectations.
8. Reconcile conflicts and ambiguities. Careful cross-indexing (see step 11) can help.
9. Put all statements in clear-cut, understandable language.
10. Make provisions for automatic and periodic review, changes, and additions.

11. Index and cross-index the entire work carefully and methodically.
12. Publish and distribute copies. Each employee should have a copy and there should be an ample supply of extras. New additions to the staff alone will require many additional copies over a period of years, and people do lose things.

BE PATIENT—BE PREPARED TO SPEND THE AWESOME AMOUNT OF TIME THAT IS REQUIRED TO DO A GOOD JOB.

EXPRESSION OF EXPECTATIONS

A number of the many forms in which expectations can be manifested were mentioned in Chapter 2, along with numerous levels at which expectations are held. In the formal, enduring organization that characterizes most educational agencies, the most common written forms in which expectations are expressed are laws, principles, regulations, charts, policies, job descriptions, contracts, schedules, rules, procedures, and memos.

Laws, charts, job descriptions, contracts, schedules, and memos all seem to be readily understood when they exist. Because the other written forms seem to be less well understood, they are discussed here.

Principles as Expectations

In answering "Why?" for any sound policy, rule, or regulation, one should come face to face with a principle. Statements of principle inextricably interweave facts and values. However, the interweaving does nothing to detract from the worth of principles. A principle is, by definition, a "settled rule of action, a governing law of conduct," and many of our actions are governed as much by mores and values as they are by data-established facts.

Principles are the form in which expectations are expressed at many levels, but many people do not understand what they are. How is it possible to condense human values held as expectations into principles? Principles are widely accepted general guides to actions, and are axiomatic, but what makes them so? A view at considerable variance with the "knowledge explosion" cliché was expressed by Halle (1963):

> . . . even with the development of modern science the increase in significant knowledge had been virtually imperceptible. For one thing, new knowledge generally takes the place of old, rather than adding to the sum. When our society began to teach that the earth moved around the sun it stopped teaching that the sun moved around the earth, and the burden was not increased. For another, knowledge that has been long established lends itself to sententious expression. To a schoolboy of Hellenistic

times the idea that the earth was a sphere might have been so strange that it would have taken an elaborate effort of pedagogy to teach it, and a hard mental effort to learn it. But it came in time to seem obvious. The teacher could, at last, communicate it in a few words. So knowledge tends to shake down and become compact, taking up no more room than it had before [p. 107].

So it is with principles, including principles of humanity. When we began to teach "love thy neighbor," we gave up teaching "an eye for an eye," and it "came in time to seem obvious."

Numerous books have had the title of *Principles of School Administration,* and the reader can judge whether they are aptly named. The present authors are not yet ready to tackle *Principles of Educational Leadership,* but there perhaps are some *principles of learning* and some *principles of human relations* which the members of an educational agency can agree to use as guides to common expectations. We do not agree with defeatists who say that until there is a complete and "objective" set of principles we can do little about using *any* principles in helping people to understand the expectations held for them.

We do believe that there are *some* principles which are "settled" for certain individuals, some for certain institutions, and some for certain "social settings." Individuals need to learn how to identify their personally "settled" principles and how to find job situations and social settings in which the principles held by other persons are compatible with their own.

We suggest that unless an individual or a group can find "a settled rule of action, a governing law of conduct" which unquestionably is the reason behind a policy, a rule, a procedure, a regulation—or a law—then the statement in question either should not be promulgated or, if already in effect, should be repealed. Most handbooks would, if submitted to this test, be considerably reduced in size.

Principles and policies are used in flexible organizations to give consistency to decision-making while allowing decision-makers to exercise individual discretion.

Policies as Expectations

Policies are needed for two kinds of situations, namely when decisions that are similar in nature are to be made (1) by more than one person, or (2) by one person on a repeating basis. Decisions of this kind often affect the capability of the organization to produce—in other words they affect goals or objectives. Leaders need to be able to clearly distinguish policies from other statements of expectations and to develop policies.

Unless policies are consciously and systematically developed and disseminated, at least four potential dangers exist: (1) people within an organization may not know what is expected of them, (2) some individuals may be subject to discrimination at the hands of others, (3) undesirable policy may develop through precedent when decisions must be made, and (4) decision-making may be quite inconsistent.

A policy may, and perhaps should, originate with any person who will be affected by it when, or if ever, it is officially adopted. Policies are nearly always, if formally adopted, adopted by the topmost figures in the authority hierarchy. In most agencies of education, this means that policy is adopted by the board of education, the board of trustees, or other governing body. However, policy is not always formally adopted, and even when it is it may be thrown into an indiscriminate handbook where it is almost impossible to locate and pull together. Sometimes, policy exists even though it is unwritten. Sometimes written policy exists only in discrete entries in the minutes of the governing body. Sometimes a single authority figure writes and disseminates to subordinates statements which he calls policy but which are, in fact, rules.

Rules as Expectations

Rules are made by persons in superordinate positions and are intended to apply to subordinates. Administrators make rules for instructors; instructors make rules for learners; learners in superordinate positions—such as student council members, monitors, and safety patrolmen—tend to make rules for other learners if allowed to do so. Rules usually are made to structure relationships, to substitute for personal authority, to reduce the need for supervision, or to give security.

The division of labor in an organization is usually effected in such a manner as to achieve a hierarchical ordering of positions. In order for each person to understand the specialized role which accompanies his position, to know the limits of his responsibility and authority, and to know to whom he is to report and who is to report to him, most organizations resort to rules.

In most organizations, it is impossible for a given individual to personally supervise all of the personnel, the activities, and the situations over which he has nominal authority. Rules may be developed, then, to decentralize authority, to legitimize it, or to allow bargaining.

SURROGATE AUTHORITY. A rule places in the hands of each of the persons to whom it applies a small bit of the authority of the person or body that imposed the rule, thus decentralizing authority. Even laws are a means of decentralizing authority, as evidenced by the legality of a citizen's arrest. While decentralization of authority often has a salutary effect, there is no assurance that the effect will be of this nature. The child who says, "I'm going to tell!" when a rule is broken is simply recognizing that she or he possesses, at least temporarily, a bit of the authority embodied in the rule. Adults who refuse to "become involved" when a law—even a criminal law—is being broken are abrogating authority which they could invoke.

LEGITIMIZATION OF AUTHORITY. A rule legitimizes authority, and the individual who will argue when a superordinate says "That is the rule" is rare indeed. Few people question a rule or where it came from, and those who do are likely to "get the book thrown at them" regardless of whether the applier of the rule is an immediate superordinate or the authority figure who established the rule.

BARGAINING VALUE. Rules substitute for personal authority in at least one way, and that is by allowing the person who is expected to enforce the rule to use it for bargaining purposes. For example, a principal may say to a habitually tardy teacher, "We will forget about your tardiness this time if you will just be sure to get your report in on Friday." The teacher may be happy to meet her part of such a bargain in order to avoid sanctions that might otherwise be invoked against her; the principal may be happy because it allows him to get a report on time when lateness of the report might be held against *him,* and the superintendent who made the rule about tardiness may be none the wiser!

Perhaps one of the most wide spread symptoms of malaise in life in this country today is that which Anderson (1966) identified as the "anxiety-conformity-approval" syndrome. It is observable almost daily in most situations, and most of us exhibit it at times. The anxiety comes from one wondering whether he is conforming to the expectations held for him and thereby gaining the approval of his superiors, or whether he may be falling short in some ways and thereby making himself subject to censure or worse. Some persons actually welcome a surfeit of rules because they feel that they can be reasonably secure and certain of approval so long as they are conforming to all of the rules.

AS INHIBITORS. Anderson (1966) developed a number of interesting hypotheses about the possible effects of rules in inhibiting the behavior of individuals. In general, the inhibitions suggested are of six kinds, but the author emphasized that the hypotheses had not been researched. He said that rules may: (1) tend to displace goals, (2) bring resistance to change, (3) result in "legalism" in direct ratio to their numbers, (4) reinforce apathy on the part of subordinates, (5) encourage lack of commitment, and (6) result in development and pervasiveness of informal "action" groups.

It is possible in bureaucratic organizations for the emphasis on rigid adherence to rules to become so pronounced that conforming behavior ultimately may interfere with the achievement of institutional goals. This situation is particularly deplorable in schools, where all should be striving "to help each individual learn to the limits of his potential," but usually are, instead, rewarding conformity to rules on the part of both students and teachers. Far too often, the condition extends also to principals, superintendents, and other nominal leaders. In many, many schools those who wish to get ahead learn early to stick to the rules and regulations. Need-satisfactions and avoidance of negative sanctions often depend on conformity, and thus rules which are intended as means become ends instead.

NUMBER OF RULES. Anderson also speculated that the number of rules varies directly with: (1) the size of the organization, (2) the "routinizability" of the tasks to be performed, (3) the likelihood of outside pressure and influence, and (4) the dependence on outside resources. Thus, one would expect a large organization to have more rules than a small one; an organization in which all of the tasks are routine to have far more rules than one in which there are few routine tasks and no two jobs are alike; a public university to have more rules than a private one; and a private one which depends on an annual fund drive to have more than a permanently endowed one. Sheer numbers of rules in educational institutions of like size might, if Anderson's hypotheses are correct, tell a great deal about which has a greater commitment to individualized instruction!

Anderson further hypothesized that the number of rules to be found in organizations vary inversely with: (1) the specificity of organizational goals, (2) the perceptions which superiors have of the competence of subordinates, (3) the perceived commitment of subordinates, (4) the reliability of measures of performance available to the group, and (5) the amount of direct supervision given. He also posited an inverse relationship between the number of rules protecting organization members from outside influence and the degree of dependence of the institution on outside support! These hypotheses appear to be in urgent need of research, but are so "common sensical" that a person who is considering a position of leadership in an educational agency should think twice if it seems to have an inordinate number of rules. Furthermore, any leader should ponder the implications of the hypotheses well before she or he devises or allows others to devise new rules. Carlson (1972) made cogent comment about the "successor," the person new to a position of leadership, and his rule-making propensity.

GUIDELINES. Rules either imply or overtly state sanctions which will be imposed on persons who do not conform. Any experienced organization member or parent will recognize that there are at least three guidelines which should be strictly observed if rules are to be promulgated, namely:

1. Make no rule unless the sanctions which are to accompany noncomformity *can be imposed.*
2. Make no rule unless those who have the power to impose sanctions for nonconformity *have every intention of imposing them* in an impartial manner.
3. Make no rule for an isolated or nonrecurrent situation.

It undoubtedly is true that most educational agencies have rules which do not conform to these guidelines, and that most have far too many rules. Perhaps it would be good *policy* for each agency periodically to wipe the slate clean of all rules and start over, developing only such rules as seem to be absolutely demanded by present needs. Rules can help to communicate expectations, but they usually inhibit behavior unnecessarily. The same may be true of regulations.

Regulations as Expectations
Regulations and rules are alike in that both are prescribed guides for conduct, action, or usage and both at least imply some sanctions for nonconformity. The threat of sanctions may even be overt and specified in detail. Regulations differ from rules in that the former are imposed from outside the affected agency, and the latter from within. Furthermore, regulations often pertain not only to a particular agency but to all like it. Regulations of educational institutions are usually found in the provisions of state constitutions, in statutory law, in case law, and in administrative fiat. An organization may find it expedient to repeat regulations in handbooks for personnel simply because the regulations would not otherwise be readily accessible for scrutiny.

In some instances, a university may establish its own regulations relating to all of its colleges, or a school system may develop regulations affecting all attendance centers within it. Regulations and procedures are similar in some respects.

Procedures as Expectations
Procedures almost always consist of directions for handling certain recurrent situations within an organization. Normally, they are developed by persons in superordinate positions in a hierarchy to direct those in subordinate positions. For example, in a community college, a department head spells out for instructors the manner in which they are to ask for supplies and other materials, the forms to be used, the time and place of submission of requests, etc. The purposes for spelling out such details are that properly delineated pro-

cedures can (1) alleviate anxiety and (2) help to ritualize the behavior necessary to the performance of routine tasks.

Procedures as described here are not quite the same as either rules or regulations, but the purpose of all three forms of statements is to aid in the communication of expectations.

COMMUNICATION

Often, individuals have only been exposed to communications about expectations held for them; they have not been *informed.* No doubts have been removed, no uncertainty allayed.

Much has been written in recent years in regard to communication and the ways in which it may be affected by numerous variables. Knowledge about communication is even beginning to "shake down and become compact," and we know that communication can be oral, written, or nonverbal. Hall (1959) developed the idea, and others have stressed the importance, of "the silent language" to the educational leader. Fast (1970) provided a popularized version of "body language" and Birdwhistell (1968) provided an excellent summary of the developing science of kinesics. All of the communications forms can aid in providing information. Communication will be discussed in detail in Chapter 9, but we are interested here in its use for informing people about the expectations held for them.

Informing Through Communication

A number of researchers have investigated the selective perception and comprehension of persons on the receiving end of communications—whether the receiver sees, reads, feels, or hears as the sender intends. Since there apparently are indisputable relationships of certain variables, it would appear that, regardless of how good the efforts made to communicate them, expectations held for the individual will be perceived by him or her only to the extent that (1) the communication reduces his uncertainty, (2) authority is attributed by the receiver to the sender, and (3) expectations accord with his or her predispositions.

Findings of communications research may be useful in trying to determine the motivations of various persons, but more research is needed. We hypothesize here that: (1) attribution of authority to agencies of society may be in direct proportion to one's comprehension and internalization of communications from people in those agencies, (2) one's acceptance of social values is directly dependent on the "significant others" who hold these values, (3) one's perception of significant others relates to one's own perceived needs, and (4) being held to expectations regarding standards for performance does not necessarily destroy self-reliance. If these hypotheses should be verified, a leader might then be able to anticipate or predict the level at or the conditions under which a given individual might fail to conform to expectations held for her or him.

We believe that McLuhan (1964) is correct in his esoteric analysis of communication. All of us *are* immersed in, "massaged" by, fed on, assaulted by the media of communication which themselves are messages. Society cannot expect individuals to conform to the set of values that it verbalizes to them while visibly *informing* them that it rewards an antithetical set! What we do speaks so loudly that he cannot hear what we say. We say that we are against the slum dweller's poverty, his hunger, his rats, his powerlessness, and his unemployment—but he experiences those realities year after stretching year. We say that we are against vice and lawlessness, but vice-lords prosper and the lawless go free, while we incarcerate the Valjeans of our society. We say that we reward those who live up to society's expectations and punish those who do not, but con- formists go without luxuries while looters acquire theirs with impu- nity. We say we value honesty and service to humanity, but a presti- gious sports or other entertainment figure may "earn" more for a single brief (and often obviously insincere or dishonest) spot com- mercial or testimonial than a social worker is paid in a year.

The educational leader needs to make certain that what people are doing is not drowning out what they are saying to each other about expectations. All must know what is expected.

Knowing what is Expected
All communication in an organization is based on shared assump- tions about behavior, ritual, and goals and on a shared understand- ing of how the organization functions. Individuals who do not share the group concepts of right and wrong ways to behave are out of place. Each must know what the right and wrong ways are, and knowing is achieved through communicating expectations. Each indi- vidual must also know whether the degree to which she or he is conforming to expectations is acceptable to those about her or him.

For many years, personnel managers in industry have been re- marking that most persons who are fired do not lack job skills, but lack skills for getting along with people. Some may not know the expectations held for them, some may not have found significant others in the work environment, and some may not have had feed- back regarding their effectiveness—their ratio of performance to expectations.

Educational leaders need to make certain that followers know the expectations held for them and that they have feedback regard- ing their performance. Leaders can utilize both formal and informal communications systems to achieve this, but many of them seem to be unaware that informal systems even exist.

Formal Systems of Communication
It was mentioned earlier in this chapter that written forms in which expectations are expressed include principles, laws, charts, policies,

job descriptions, contracts, schedules, rules, and procedures. Most organizations also utilize unwritten forms, still through formal communications channels. These include orientation sessions, rituals, stereotypes, and oral instruction or direction.

Positive feedback to the individual in the formal systems may be either formal or informal, in the form of a letter, a word of commendation, an award, a pat on the back, a nod of approval, or an "evaluation." Negative feedback ranges from a lifted eyebrow to a reprimand, a conference, or a pink slip.

The *grapevine* is outside the formal communications channels. It refers to informal systems of communication, and is not to be ignored or taken lightly.

Informal Systems of Communication
According to Anderson (1966):

> *Informal groups arise spontaneously within organizations and are based upon person relationships. Usually they represent attempts to control the behavior of members of the group and the conditions under which they work. They include patterns of expression, status systems, sanction and reward systems not provided for in the formal organizational structure. Behavior of these groups is centered about the specific problems and goals that are relevant to the particular subdivision of the organization [p. 28].*

The patterns of expression, status systems, sanction and reward systems are all forms used for communicating expectations. Anderson explained why they come into being in almost any formal organization.

> *. . . it would be expected that where attempts are made to highly structure behavior and to impersonalize relationships within an organization, there will arise informal systems based on personal relationships to countermand the formal, rigid, impersonal system, to allow the individual to maintain some control over his working environment, and to maintain his self-respect. It is suggested that the development and pervasiveness of this formal system will be a function of the rules prescribing and limiting behavior within the formal framework of the organization [p. 30].*

While the reasons for the development of informal forms of communication, as described above, are agreed to by the present authors, we find "rules" too limiting and conclude that the development and pervasiveness of informal systems of communication are a function of the several forms used by the formal organization for prescribing or proscribing behavior.

One way of allowing some autonomy to people in fulfilling objectives is to have less communication through regulations, rules, and procedures and more through well-developed policies based on principles.

DEVELOPING POLICIES

It was stated earlier that the chief function of policies is to give consistency to decision-making, thus reducing uncertainty. Simon (1957) attributed to Barnard a profound observation regarding the complexity of organizational decision-making:

> It should be perfectly apparent that almost no decision made in an organization is the task of a single individual. Even though the final responsibility for taking a particular action rests with some definite person, we shall always find, in studying the manner in which this decision was reached, that its various components can be traced through the formal and informal channels of communication to many individuals who have participated in forming its premises. When all of these components have been identified, it may appear that the contribution of the individual who made the formal decision was a minor one, indeed [p. 221].

Reasons for Policies

In order that there may be consistency in decision-making, that people involved in decision-making may operate from at least some of the same premises, that individuals may know what is expected of them, that individuals may know the bounds of discretion allowed them, that the "anxiety-conformity-approval" syndrome referred to earlier may be minimized—organizations need to develop policies. At the very least, policy should be established to give consistency to decision-making, and should thus indicate the responsibilities and the limits of discretion of those who will be engaged repeatedly in making recurrent kinds of decisions.

Previously, people in education referred to *personnel policy,* and the first policies developed in most organizations appear to have dealt with such matters as appointments, promotions, salaries, and tenure. However, in recent years more and more organizations have found need for policies in an increasing number of areas. Some have well-developed policies covering virtually all areas of their operations. At least three "services" aimed at giving guidance to public schools in the development of policies have marketed voluminous guides. A spate of articles in periodicals and chapters in recent books deal with the subject of policies and few of them confine their discussion to personnel policies. However, personnel policies—those relating to people and their activities—continue to be a major concern of all who work for organizations, and properly so.

The changing times in education make it doubly important that leaders, particularly in schools, be thoroughly conversant with personnel policies. With the advent of "professional negotiations," certain policies are being written into the master contracts of teachers' and instructors' groups with increasing frequency. While many of these policies have to do with such traditional areas of personnel as tenure, working conditions, and salaries, increasing numbers of them pertain to a wide variety of conditions.

Inclusion of policies in master contracts may pose a real dilemma for the serious-minded people-oriented educational leader. Historically and traditionally such leaders have found themselves trying to secure for individuals certain rights allowed them by adopted policies. How does a leader attempt to secure for an individual a right *allowed* her or him by policy but *delegated* or *given* by the individual to a group of his peers?

Criteria for Policies

There are a number of criteria which a policy should meet if it is to be judged "good" and worthy of inclusion in an officially adopted code. A policy should relate to the organization's capacity to produce and it should be *flexible,* in that it should not prescribe exact ways of proceeding or give answers for all situations. Unless a statement allows a decision-maker some discretion, it more than likely is a rule rather than a policy.

COMPLETENESS. It is essential that a policy statement be *complete,* but we have just inveighed against having a policy be either prescriptive or proscriptive. It is essential that the statement be complete enough to embody answers to all of the questions which will follow in the section headed Policy Content.

CONCISENESS. A policy must be *concise.* The primary purpose of any policy or rule is to communicate to certain people the expectations that other people hold for them. A basic tenet of communication is that the message must be as brief as possible to transmit the essentials.

CLARITY. Clear expression of ideas is essential. People looking for statements of the expectations held for them or for other persons with whom they have regular and professional contact do not want to spend their time clearing verbal underbrush.

PRECISION. Communication of expectations needs to be *unambiguous.* Policy statements which leave large areas of doubt in the minds of those who are supposed to receive guidance from them do not really inform. Neither do those which give two or more meanings to the statements.

MODIFIABILITY. Policy statements should be *easy to change,* because the expectations held for people change, often as the result of changed conditions. Policies which are printed and bound tightly together are difficult to change. For this reason, all statements of expectations should be arranged in a numerically codified order indicating general relationships only, rather than on sequentially numbered pages; any section likely to need revision should be typed or printed on a page by itself; and all pages in the handbook should be loose-leaf.

Policy Content

Workshop experience with people actually developing tentative policies for their own situations indicates that satisfactory results can be achieved by asking participants to make certain that they have answered the traditional questions used in journalistic reporting. Thus, a complete policy statement should clearly indicate *who* is to make decisions, *who* is to be guided by the policy, *what* the situation is for which guidance is intended, *where* the decision is likely to be needed, and *when* the situation may be encountered.

It will be noted that the preceding paragraph makes no mention of the questions of *how* and *why*. That the question "why" should lead to a principle has already been discussed. It is our belief that statements of *how* a policy is to be implemented are, by definition of the terms, either rules or procedures. It is conceded that the individual who is to receive guidance from a policy often needs to know the procedure, also, as a vital part of the expectations held for her or him. Whether the procedure should be included within the policy statement is a moot point. Our personal preference is for keeping statements of procedure separate from statements of policy, due to a belief that most persons have far more frequent need for the statements of procedures than for the statements of policies.

Any individual in an organization should be able to examine its handbook for areas in which *decisions that affect him or her* are made repeatedly by the same individual or by different individuals. The person should feel free to suggest improvements or to ask for development of policies in those areas where none now exist.

SUMMARY

An educational leader needs to help people see their social environment. To do this, one must understand the purposes of and necessity for group signals; they structure relationships and provide security. One should understand the relationship of expectations to goals, values, philosophy, objectives, and accountability.

It is imperative that a leader be able to distinguish rules, regulations, requirements, policies, procedures, principles, and laws. It is important that the leader understand how these statements can be transmitted through the formal and informal communications channels in his or her organization. The leader must understand and help others to understand expectations as delineated by rules, regulations, requirements, policies, procedures, principles, and laws.

Perhaps most important and least emphasized is the need for the leader to understand that an over abundance of restrictions on the behavior of people may be detrimental to the organization's goals. Most organizations probably need more and better-developed policies and fewer of the other kinds of statements of expectations.

In the next chapter, there will be an examination of organizations as institutional agencies.

SOME SUGGESTED RESOURCES

J. G. Anderson, *Bureaucracy in education.* Baltimore, Md.: John Hopkins Press, 1968.

R. O. Carlson, Performance in office: Successors and their policies. Ch. 7 in *Superintendents: Careers and performance.* Columbus, Ohio: Merrill, 1972. Pp. 89–105.

H. Levinson, Reciprocation: the relationship between man and organization. *Administrative Science Quarterly,* 1965, 9 (March), 370–390.

P. R. Mort and D. H. Ross, A series of basic principles expressing the common sense of the culture. Ch. 2 in *Principles of school administration.* New York: McGraw-Hill, 1957. Pp. 17–30.

H. A. Simon, Loyalties and organizational identification, and The anatomy of organization. Chs. 10 and 11 in *Administrative behavior* (2nd ed.). New York: Macmillan, 1957. Pp. 109–247.

CHAPTER 4

ORGANIZATIONS AS INSTITUTIONAL AGENCIES

The organizations with which we are concerned may be defined as large, fairly permanent social systems designed to achieve limited objectives through the co-ordinated activities of their members.

—R. Presthus

Any institution must have a *structure*. In a structure, the presence or absence of significant others may be the key to individuals being willing to interact and behave in prescribed ways. The structure or framework in which people interact in order to perpetuate a shared pattern of living constitutes an organization, and an organization is an agency of a social institution. An agency, itself, develops many institutionalized beliefs and practices. This chapter explores these ideas.

ORGANIZATIONS

The word "organization," to the minds of many, conjures visions of giant factories, stiff-necked boards of directors, and endless red tape. As this anecdote illustrates, organization may have other guises:

I was appraising some rural property in northern California when I came upon a commune, an abandoned farm where a group of young people were "doing their thing." A bearded youth was cultivating a row of beans. A young woman softly strummed her guitar. A pleasant-looking man was painting an ancient barn.

> *I struck up a conversation with the barn painter and found him affable and articulate. "We seek total freedom here," he told me. "We are trying to escape the clock-oriented, regimented life-style of modern society."*
>
> *At this point we were interrupted by the ringing of an old-fashioned school bell. The bearded gardener dropped his hoe and sauntered off in the direction of the bell. The guitar player stopped her strumming and followed.*
>
> *"You'll have to excuse me now," said my new friend. "That bell means it's ten o'clock and we all have to meet at the house to get our work assignments for the day."*[1]

Even the most informal, most protesting, way of life results in some organization. Organizations are the agencies—the medium—through which institutions perpetuate values.

People collect into and work in groups in order to accomplish those things which they cannot do alone, or to accomplish them better than they could do alone. The organization of groups varies tremendously, but even an informal group has a loose organization. All organizations have some characteristics in common.

Characteristics

All organizations have these five common characteristics, according to Hicks (1972) and others: (1) they involve people, (2) the people interact, (3) interactions are to some degree ordered and prescribed, (4) each individual sees the organization as in some way helping her or him, and (5) the interactions help to achieve some joint objectives that are related to individual goals. An organization has certain core elements in addition to these characteristics.

CORE ELEMENTS. Hicks (1972) indicated that humans, interacting purposefully, are the *core elements* of any organization. The formal organization is dependent on people who find in it rewarding work, status, vigorous activity in the company of their peers, a channel for aggressive instincts, and an identity. The core elements of the organization need certain working elements also.

WORKING ELEMENTS. A leader must be fully aware of the resources available to that portion of the organization's functioning for which he or she is responsible. Those resources are *working elements* of the organization, and may be either human or nonhuman.

People are resources to the extent of their ability *to do* necessary tasks, *to influence* others, and *to use concepts.* Human resources

[1] R. A. Moss, Life in These United States. *The Reader's Digest,* September 1972, pp. 76–77.

of a school or college are the learners for whom learning opportunities are provided, the faculty who help learners, and the staff people (aides, secretaries, administrators, counselors, custodians, cooks, bus drivers, etc.) who provide supportive services to the other groups.

Nonhuman resources necessary to every organization include materials, facilities, and a means of interacting with some elements of the larger society. For example, some of the materials necessary to the functioning of a school include books, films, tapes, paper, pencils, and chalk. Facilities needed include a building, furniture, chalkboards, projectors, screens, tape recorders, and the like. Without some interaction with the larger society, there is no way of knowing whether the service provided by the school is satisfactory. However, because of interaction with the larger society, some survival elements must be built into every organization.

SURVIVAL ELEMENTS. In order to survive, the elements of strength, faith in purpose, vigor, and cohesion must be built into or acquired by an organization. The organization must develop an "apparatus of permanence" (Jay, 1971, p. 260) to keep it from being destroyed by outside enemies, torn apart by internal strife, rotting away through vitiation of individual energies, or simply falling apart as common bonds come unglued.

The apparatus of permanence is achieved through a series of multilevel, overlapping, interlocking social systems. That apparatus is complicated by the fact that, while each individual in an organization is a member of one or more of its internal social systems, she or he simultaneously is a member of other social systems outside the organization.

As Social Systems

The key elements that characterize all systems are unity and interdependence. Digestive system, circulatory system, plumbing system, sewer system, system of roads, school system, distribution system, computer system, and so on ad infinitum—in each system there is a unity of purpose and an interdependence of parts necessary to its functioning. A social system consists of parts (people) who are interdependent. The actions of one affect others. If an individual is to be useful to an organization, one must have a feeling of *belongingness* and must feel that the rewards an organization makes possible are "worth it" to him.

If an organization is to operate as an entity, every individual must feel that he or she belongs not only to a department or building, but to the total organization. A good communication system is a medium that transmits a picture of the social system. The picture is composed of, first, addition to identity. Even a badge or pin has "powerful magic" if it represents a status that one values. Second, the picture includes how individuals are treated, and this is learned both through formal channels and the grapevine. Third, the shared pattern of living—the social system—provides satisfaction, and the central faith must be one in which each individual can believe. He or she must share the doctrine, rituals, awareness of purpose and of limits, folkways, and special jargon. Regardless of level, one's superordinate—"the old man"—must merit one's respect.

Even more important to the individual than the above is the system of payments, promotions, bonuses, and seniority available to her or him. A group member who believes that the deck is stacked so that he can't "make it" as well as the next will never feel that he belongs.

However, as Goslin (1965) noted:

> The distinction between social system and organization is by no means a sharp one, since it is obvious that organizational characteristics have a very great influence on the informal social structure of the group and vice versa. System (or social structure) almost never entirely precedes formal organization, although in expressive groups (groups that exist primarily or wholly for the enjoyment of their members and have no goal beyond this) a relatively well-defined set of role relationships (a social system as we have defined it) may exist without any formal organization being introduced. On the other hand, a table of organization and a set of procedures for decision-making, recruitment, communication, and the like may be established for some groups prior to the selection of any personnel. In such a case formal organizational characteristics obviously exist prior to the development of any specific role relationship among the members. The resulting social system to a great extent reflects the formal organization, although informal relationships can be expected to have a modifying impact [p. 132].

Every social system has a structure for making the relationships of its members known.

STRUCTURES

The structure of an organization can be informal or formal, flexible or rigid, temporary or enduring, specified or unspecified. Our concern here is primarily with the formal, enduring, specified structure. The rigid structure is of interest because of its prevalence among educational agencies; the flexible is of concern because of its promise. We have a secondary concern with informal structures, or interacting groups, within formal organizations, and some cognizance is taken of discrete, informal, unspecified structures. It is the belief of the present writers that the process of leadership is little different in the informal than in the formal.

TABLE 4-1
EXAMPLES OF INFORMAL STRUCTURES

	LOCATION OF INFORMAL STRUCTURES	
GROUP CHARACTERISTICS	INSIDE A FORMAL ORGANIZATION	OUTSIDE A FORMAL ORGANIZATION
Flexible	Lunch partners	A fishing party
Semirigid	A company bowling team	A bridge club
Rigid	The board of directors	A family

Informal

Some examples of informal structures, or organizations, as shown in Table 4-1, may be helpful in understanding distinctions and in relating the informal structure to formal organizations. From Table 4-1 it may be seen that flexibility-rigidity pertains to the degree of choice that a group member has in regard to the persons with whom she or he interacts in the structure.

The temporary-permanent quality of a structure is determined by whether the interacting members change from day to day or week to week or whether they remain unchanged for months on end.

Whether flexible or rigid, temporary or permanent, the informal structures within the formal organization are important because of the part that they play in: (1) information flow and (2) the distribution of influence and power.

For every formal organization, there are one or more informal structures. The informal, while not easy to recognize or to chart on paper, may be as important to the functioning of the enterprise as is the formal. The organization is dependent on human relationships, and these are likely to be considerably different in the informal than in the formal, even though relationships in both are structured.

Undoubtedly an analysis of daily contacts experienced by each individual in an organization or a department would reveal many contacts, both within the organization and in outside social relationships, in which agency business was transacted without any apparent connection to the formal organization chart. However, understanding the social milieu in which educational leaders function depends in large measure on understanding enduring formal structures.

Formal

Every formal structure develops an apparatus of permanence, consisting of the elements of strength, faith in organizational purpose, vigor, and cohesion; these are also the elements of survival. Most current formal organizations involve hierarchy.

HIERARCHY. Both formal and informal organizations consist of people who interact in prescribed and proscribed ways to achieve goals and individual objectives related to those goals. The chunk of responsibility assigned an individual by prescription and limited by proscription defines his or her position. Among the characteristics of a position is *status,* and where there is status there is *hierarchy.* Status is not abolished by moving from an elitist to an egalitarian system; the differences between the lowest and the highest position are only reduced.

A hierarchical chart is always in the form of an isosceles triangle. The less the responsibility, the more people found at that level and the broader that portion of the triangle. As the amount of *responsibility for the performance of the group increases,* the triangle narrows toward the apex. The individual or the few at the top have the greatest responsibility for group performance.

People, though, don't always or often conform to lines on charts. They insist on acting like human beings, and communication lines are sometimes short-circuited between friends or severed between rivals for power. Also, as staff specialists are introduced in an organization they play havoc with chart lines that are supposed to show responsibility and communication.

Nowhere are lines more distinctly drawn (on the charts) nor more numerous than on the chart of a bureaucracy. Most school and college organizations have followed the bureaucratic model.

BUREAUCRACY. Bell's (1961) discussion of bureaucracy and his historical account tracing back to Max Weber seem typical of the views of contemporary sociologists: ". . . the advantages of bureaucracies far outweigh their disadvantages. Moreover, no other presently known form of social organization is capable of coordinating and integrating the high degree of specialization required to support our way of life [p. 317]."

Some who have examined bureaucracy are challenging this type of statement. Characteristics that are labeled essential depend on the labeler, but Bell's list will serve our purposes if we add one characteristic from Presthus (1962) that many sociologists seem to overlook. These eight characteristics constitute potent arguments for those who maintain that the day of bureaucracy is over.

According to Bell (1961, pp. 319–328), except as indicated, the essential characteristics of a bureaucracy are the following.

1. *Division of labor and responsibility.* Allocation of responsibility is an essential characteristic of any organizational structure, its *raison d'être.*

2. *Downgrading of the individual.* Controversy regarding whether the individual needs, or is capable of, upgrading or downgrading is at least as old as theology, and perhaps as old as man himself. The present authors believe that the resistance of educated people

to being downgraded as individuals is spelling the doom of bureaucracy, particularly in schools and colleges.

3. *Rational decision-making.* Smith (1969, pp. 370 ff.) and Simon (1957, pp. 61–78) spoke eloquently to the assumption that if relevant facts can be ascertained, truth will prevail. Simon provided cogent arguments that man is a rational animal only on infrequent and self-serving occasions. Certainly it is doubtful that bureaucracy assures rationality of decisions.

4. *Secrecy.* Secrecy is part of the apparatus of permanence and people in almost every profession insist that laymen do not possess the secret knowledge upon which professional decisions must be made. Those in schools and other agencies of education are no exception. The absurd extremes to which secrecy flourishes in a bureaucracy is exemplified by the dozens of classified stamps placed on innocuous materials by some branches of the federal government. Jay (1971) said that bureaucratic corporations burnish their image by "selective disclosure of favorable information [p. 300]." Governments, schools, and colleges do likewise.

5. *Submission to authority.* A bureaucrat may raise objections to an order that he considers wrong, but if he is overruled he is expected to carry out the order with enthusiasm and *to never raise that same objection again.*

6. *Security for members.* Regular pay with periodic increases, life tenure, and freedom from the capriciousness of superordinates supposedly characterize the bureaucratic organization. Together, they provide a security for which many individuals are willing to sell their birthright of freedom of thought and action. Bell (1961, pp. 325–326) pointed out the difficulties to be expected in instituting a true merit system in a school setting, because such a system threatens the individual security of some persons.

7. *Centralized control.* One of the chief sources of power is control of the means of production. A comptroller or business manager can soon stifle the most creative and promising employee by denying requests for means. Of course, it is to the official's benefit to deny, since his or her own achievement is likely to be measured by holding dollar costs down. This situation has caused real problems in schools and colleges, and in recent years there have been attempts to decentralize control through instituting program budgets.

8. *Oligarchy.* Presthus (1962) pointed out that "the assignment of authority and status along hierarchical lines means that the conditions of participation in big formal organizations are determined by a minority [p. 39]." When a minority rules for its own benefit, an oligarchy exists. Such a structure seems more prevalent in large bureaucracies than in small; more frequent in industrial than in political (or educational) organizations; and more due to control of means than to ownership of resources.

The need for the organizational skills of certain officials, the hierarchy of control, the size of specialized groups, and the difficulties of communication, when coupled with desire for power by the few and apathy of the many, "cause" oligarchy. Presthus (1962, p. 49) said that oligarchic behaviors appear in academic and professional associations, in labor unions, corporations, and universities.

An individual's willingness to be subservient to a bureaucracy, or even to be a part of its oligarchy, depends to some extent on one's belief in and expectations for one's fellow human beings, which may be related to the type of formal structure in which one works.

TYPES. It is rare that a school or college can set a pattern of organization which will remain unchanged, but there are concepts of organization which may help to understand what is being done, and perhaps help leaders to develop structures more flexible than those in current usage.

The types of organization most frequently charted on paper are all hierarchical in nature and the very word "organization" means one of five bureaucratic types to most individuals. The *line* organization is one which assumes a direct line of responsibility, authority, control, and communication between any two positions, one of which is always superior and the other subordinate. A direct line extends from the highest position in the organization to the lowest. The closest thing to this in education is an instructional department with *no* staff specialists.

In the *line and staff* organization, a direct line of responsibility, authority, control, and communication is maintained among those responsible for the teaching function, but there are other persons who serve specific support functions *without having authority over line personnel.* Examples are a college department which has a secretary and a graphics specialist or a school with secretaries, clerks, and custodians.

The *functional organization,* originally advocated by Frederick W. Taylor, "the father of scientific management," is now of historical interest only. In this plan, the staff specialist was to have authority, control, and responsibility for his or her particular specialized function. Practice revealed that the idea was impractical because each worker had as many bosses as there were functions connected with his job and, as a result, he did not know to whom he was responsible! For example, a teacher in this type of organization would be responsible to a principal for such things as pupil records and reports, to a curriculum supervisor for teaching methods, to a graphics specialist for certain materials, to an equipment specialist for any machine used, and to a custodian for room and building care.

In the *line and functional* staff plan, the line relationship is maintained but staff assistants or staff departments are given responsibility and authority over their specialties *only.* Thus, a personnel director might have authority over employment, a curriculum coordinator over teaching content, and a business manager over accounting, but disagreements would be settled by a line officer. This type exists in many public school districts and in most colleges.

In the fifth hierarchical type, the *line, functional staff, and committee,* the organization adds committees for special duties while otherwise functioning as described in the fourth type. This type is often found in universities, where the standing committees may be called councils. It is illustrated in Figure 4-1, and attention is invited to the intricacy and overlap depicted. It should be noted that the administration council in this illustration is comprised of those individuals whose position titles are indicated by asterisks.

Flexible

Opposed to the bureaucratic leader, who sees people below him in the hierarchy as instruments with which to carry out his or her job, is the leader who sees groups and individuals as responsible for objectives. Those who have the latter point of view often work with "job enlargement" and "organization development" concepts in trying to develop flexible structures that provide enterprising responses to change. Many people are insisting that individuals within agencies of education be responsible for objectives, and this necessitates structures more flexible than the usual bureaucracy.

A remarkable tale of the Inca civilization, "The Almost Perfect Decision-Making Device" (*Input,* 1968), illustrated the dangers of inflexibility. This extraordinarily advanced empire fell to 180 tired Spaniards because their marvelous system of communication had no provisions for dealing with the unexpected! A curious collection of knotted cords (in which color, size, type, and location of knots made possible infinite message combinations) served for record-keeping for 16 million subjects in a 380,000 square-mile domain—nearly five hundred years ago! The knotted device, called a quipu (pronounced "kee-poo"), transmitted raw information to the capital city of Cuzco and returned orders to the field. People were organized by groups of ten families, ten groups of ten, and so on in a *precise pyramidal hierarchy!* But the quipu could not warn of invaders nor inform about unanticipated events. Most modern bureaucracies are similarly handicapped, and only a flexible organization can provide for response to change.

A fascinating hypothesis that if people are brought together in "ten groups" and given stimulating and demanding group goals, a leader will emerge and the basic responsive organization will be formed was advanced by Jay (1971, pp. 66–78). He explored the idea of the tribal group, fixing its maximum limit at about five hundred members [p. 134]. He speculated that managing a hundred thousand people is almost impossible, but managing two hundred tribes of some five hundred members each is quite possible. One possibility

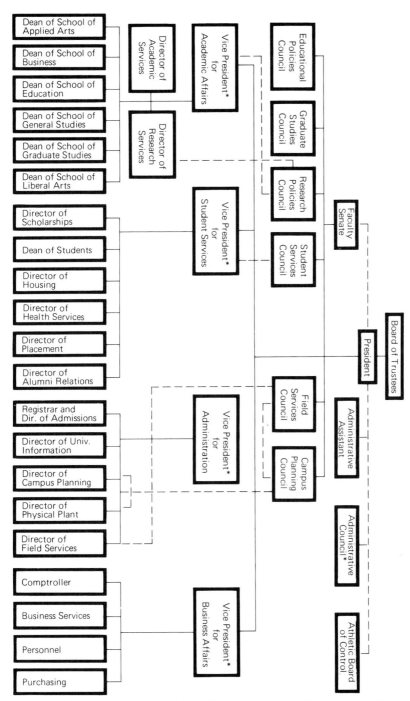

Figure 4-1 A Theoretical Line, Staff, and Functional Committee Organization

for those persons whose shrill chorus is demanding educational accountability would be to look to a flexible structure based on the ten group and the tribe.

In recent years there has been great emphasis on trying to find structures that would allow people to work together as peers, with no set of responsibilities valued more than any other set. One highly touted form that is purported to do this is the "task force" organization. In theory, in this form of structure, no status attaches to anyone until a particular problem needs to be solved. Then, the person with the most expertise (is that not a de facto status?) in the problem area gathers about him two or three assistants (no status here implied?), each with his or her own area of specialization in some facet of the problem, each of those then gathers others who have the needed skills (*still* no status?), and they all proceed to interact until the problem is solved. The team then dissolves, and a new team forms when a new problem begs for solution!

The patent absurdity of the claim for total task force organization becomes vivid if one asks the questions: What relates the organization to the larger society? Who gives it purpose? Who identifies problems and marks them for solution? Who decides who is most expert, and on what basis? Who determines when a problem is solved?

The task force structure of organization is a farce as a "substitute" for hierarchy. Ad hoc groups disband after the specific task has been accomplished and, therefore, are anathema to the "apparatus of permanence" necessary to an organization. However, Berkley (1971) suggested a modification that may make the task force structure feasible. He joined Bennis and Slater (1968) in their view that some structure more nearly approximating democracy than any now extant is inevitable, and in his compelling chapter on "The Crumbling Pyramid," gave this description:

> *The new organizational form does not display the smooth compactness of the bureaucratic pyramid. . . . It is perhaps best visualized as a squishy, uneven circle within which clusters of small units, like amoeba, constantly form and reform. At the center there is a more or less stationary cluster which is connected by lines to all the others. However, the center cluster, while it may more or less stay in the same general position within the circle, also undergoes changes in shape from time to time. Furthermore, there is no single unit at the exact center of even this center cluster, and the lines that come into this central cluster from all the others do not all terminate at the same point but at various units within it.*
>
> *. . . we notice two other distinctive features. First, there are not only lines connecting the floating clusters with the center one, but there are also many lines connecting these clusters with*

one another. Secondly, these lines, whether they connect floating clusters with the central one or with one another, are never pulled taut. They show considerable slackness, thus enabling the floating clusters to move around pretty much as they please.
        . . . we see an organization consisting of small groups engaged in specific tasks. For the most part, these task forces are made up of staff specialists and professional line personnel. . . . As the task on which any group is working is completed, the task force dissolves with its members joining new groups that are constantly forming. The center cluster consists of management along with various support services which the task forces utilize as they feel the need. But management is now multi-headed, hence there is no subunit in the exact center [pp. 24–25.]

Some of the alternative schools operating in 1974 had structures approximating this description. Leaders in all of the agencies of education would do well to consider structures which leave people relatively free to achieve agreed-on objectives. Let us examine the diversity of those agencies.

AGENCIES OF EDUCATION
Chapter 1 pointed out that there is an educational institution which, like the other major social institutions, has numerous agencies charged with responsibility for its functions. However, at least three misconceptions regarding these agencies are rife in society today.

Common Misconceptions
The first of the common misconceptions is that *the school* (an agency of the institution) can be equated to the *educational institution.* Thelen (1960) spoke tartly to this:

The false belief that the school is the community's sole educative agency leads to a rather seriocomic state of affairs: every group or individual with any kind of vested interest in education immediately gets out its snickersnee and goes out after the schools! Service clubs, religious groups, merchants, police safety squads, charitable institutions needing pennies, colleges wanting students—not to mention the 100 percent Americans, the regional chauvinists, and the foundations with pet notions about education [pp. 54–55].

Furthermore, so long as we persist in the false belief that the school (including the college and the university) is society's only educative agency we will continue to condemn to lives of failure and feelings of worthlessness those people who fail to fit the mold of the school. We have no wish to halt the search of the schools for better means of reaching and teaching more people, but the whole society needs to understand that people can learn and are learning outside "the school" as well as in it, and that there are many ways of getting an education—some without having an instructor!

A second common misconception is the result of a long-held but limited view of education as a prevocational activity of the young—an activity which terminates at an age somewhere between the late teens and the early twenties, depending on the occupation for which the individual is preparing.

The age of technology is bringing a realization that education is a process in which every person must engage himself throughout one's lifetime, that occupational information and skills are but a small part of the total education to be acquired, and that more than increased income is to be found in education. The journalist Mayer (1961) pointed out the obvious: ". . . there is something sickening about the spectacle of a society which can reach children's minds only through their stomachs or their vanities [p. 131]."

The third common misconception is that "the school" can be solely responsible for those functions which society has demanded of the *educational institution.* One needs only examine those functions to see the impossibility of this.

Functions
Functions for which the educational institution, through its many agencies, has overt responsibility include:

1. *Transmitting the culture.* This was, originally, the responsibility of the family, the church, the artisans, the craft workers, and the tradespeople.

2. *Social reform.* Reform can occur either through force or through persuasion and rationality. If the latter are to prevail, education is essential.

3. *Discovering new knowledge.* Each individual is supposed to be free to explore, to find his or her own truth.

4. *Rehabilitation.* Remolding individuals is a manifest responsibility—to help those who have erred against their fellow human beings and those who feel, for one reason or another, that they are less than whole people.

5. *Making children into adults.* European countries, about 400 years ago, came to regard childhood as a special period of life, and the child's world of fairy stories, games, toys, and special books for learning was invented. So was the school, as a distinct agency for helping the child to learn values and judgment, to gain information, to become an adult. As humanitarian concerns and a steadily shortening work-life took children out of agriculture, industry, and

the trades, there was concomitant concern that they learn salable skills prior to induction into the labor force! Responsibility for teaching skills passed from the family, tribe, or "master" to other agencies.

6. *Using leisure time.* That every adult learn to use his ever-increasing nonwork time in ways not inimical to society has become a must.

7. *Individualization.* The Judeo-Christian professed belief in the dignity and worth of the individual required society to help him develop his uniqueness and to discover who he is.

Those functions for which the educational institution presently has secondary responsibility include:

1. *Baby sitting.* When children could no longer go into the fields or the factories with their elders and some agency had to keep them occupied, the task fell to the schools because of the Puritan ethic that "the devil finds work for idle hands." Hence, compulsory school attendance. This function is doubly important since many families now have both parents employed outside the home.

2. *Teaching sexuality.* Whereas the home once taught boys to be boys and girls to be girls, this responsibility has now been abrogated and has been seized by the advertising world. If sexuality is to be purposefully and objectively taught, it seems to be up to formal educational agencies. It remains to be seen whether the unisex movement is a passing fad.

3. *Providing a courting ground.* This responsibility developed since most families no longer have the intimate kinds of interaction provided by husking bees, barn raisings, etc. Often, there are few community activities in contemporary life and for many families the church is no longer a focus of major social activity. Thus, for boy to meet girl and for nature to take its inevitable course to assure precreation, new meeting grounds are essential.

4. *Controlling the labor supply.* The function of withholding the young from the labor market until about the age of twenty-two or so, in order to assure more jobs for those who are older, is of comparatively recent origin. Education also has the functions of assuring that there are enough people with the proper skills to get society's work done, of retraining as necessary, and of assuring that the older worker learns something that will make him continue to feel useful when he or she is ejected from the work force at an ever-earlier age.

5. *Providing a sense of purpose.* This evident responsibility of the religious and domestic institutions is partially shared by the educational institution.

6. *Relating the individual to society.* The school needs to share with the family in helping each child to learn: (1) how groups respond to him, (2) where he stands in regard to others in terms of achieved or ascribed status, (3) whether he prefers to and can lead or must be led, (4) how to gain friends, (5) ways of relieving frustra-

tion, (6) the limits of logic and rationality, and (7) the need for a society built on and led by average persons.

7. *Teaching kinship.* A family responsibility that often falls to the school by default is teaching about family relationships: that groups of some permanency include both sexes, protect the young, care for the aged, provide siblings, hold incest taboo, and are kind to child bearers; that labors are divided; that such groups are essentially monogamous; and that cross-cultural marriages are exceptionally difficult.

8. *Allocating influence and power.* This recently assumed responsibility of educational agencies, particularly in a technological education-oriented society, is shared with the political institution, but education *does* play a part.

9. *Relating to the physical environment.* This function probably is closely related to finding a sense of purpose. From earliest recorded times, human beings have searched for explanations of their relationships to their environment, and most agencies of education have the function of aiding this search.

10. *Teaching the importance of standards.* This, as a responsibility, was discussed in Chapter 1.

Perhaps all except (7) of the above listed functions of educational agencies could be subsumed under the function of "socializing the individual." Even though the agencies of education do not have precisely the same functions, they do have certain elements in common.

Elements

If an organization is to carry on, on behalf of individuals or of the society, activities that will help or affect what individuals learn for certain purposes (and this is the definition of an educational agency), certain elements seem essential to its structure. First of all, it must include *learners.* Second, it must include *persons* who are *to help learners.* Some *purposes for learning* also must be apparent, and they should be examined from the viewpoints of society, of the learner, and of the agency itself. Purposes generally indicate what is to be learned and why. *Facilities* also are essential, as are *resources,* and a social *structure* within which people can interact. Some *communication with the outside* is the last of the common elements.

When these elements of an educational agency are used as criteria for whether a particular organization is an agency of education, horizons extend far beyond "the school." If an educational leader is to function effectively, he must be able to conceive *all* of the agencies and how the agency that employs him fits into the overall pattern. To hold such concepts, some understanding of the sources of information available to learners is essential.

Sources of Information[2]
The following catalog of the information sources available to any learner, regardless of age, may seem overly simplified, but the categories do not appear to be affected by one's belief as to what constitutes education. The sources are:

1. One's own explorations (*action*), in an environment either natural or of human origin, in the form of
   —direct experience, either at play or at work
   —purposeful study and observation
2. *Interaction* with other people or *reaction* to their recorded images in
   a. Informal relationships with
      —peers
      —persons of more experience (parents, friends, neighbors, etc.)
      —persons of less experience
   b. Formal relationships with those individuals whom society imposes upon the learner for the express purpose of imparting information to her or him (teachers, master craftsmen, etc.)
3. *Reaction* to the ideas of people as recorded in
   —printed or written words
   —symbols, charts, diagrams, statistical tables, etc.
   —artifacts
   —pictorial illustrations
   —voice recordings

Rather than consider "the school" the sole educative agency, one needs to look at the entire gamut of agencies through which learners can utilize these sources of information. Thelen (1960) spoke also to this:

> It is no doubt as flattering to the egos of schoolmen as it is relieving to the anxieties of parents to believe that schools educate our children. Nothing, of course, could be further from the case. The school, like the meat market, pool hall, church, and streetcar company, contributes something to the education of children, no doubt, but one would be hard put to know just what, how important it is, how central in the student's life, and how much it contributes to the overall development that we refer to as education. In our society it is the community's responsibility to educate its

---

[2] Some of the material in the remainder of this chapter is adapted from H. Boles, *The 3Rs and the new religion.* Midland, Mich.: Pendell, 1973, and from M. F. Seay (Ed.), *Community education: An emerging concept.* Midland, Mich.: Pendell, 1974.

> *children; and in fact, the community does educate its children—*
> *one way or another. Our pious assumption that the educational*
> *job is done entirely by the schools is patently false as judged*
> *by our knowledge of what really goes on* [p. 54].

The actual agencies of education are very numerous, and are of three distinct types.

Types

There are three basic types of agencies of education: informal, non-formal, and formal. While our concern is largely for persons who hold leader positions in formal organizations, those persons need to understand all three types and comprehend their pervasiveness.

INFORMAL. There are several agencies of society which, while they may provide no formal instruction, provide opportunities for an individual to learn, and are thus educational agencies in the broad meaning of that term. A recapitulation of these may help in seeing the total scope of education. Most of them have been considered agencies for educating *children,* but most of them *could* provide opportunities for anyone, regardless of age, who has a mind that is trying to reduce uncertainties.

1. *The self.* Pestalozzi, Dewey, and others who advocated "learning by doing" brought about an awareness that the self is important to learning, and the schools have taken some recognition of this fact in the recent trend toward providing for independent study. The self is, of course, the educative agency used by the laboratory researcher—and by the infant who must feel, bite, and taste everything that she or he can see or touch.

2. *The family.* In the home, the family serves as an agency of education. *What* and *how* the family teaches in contemporary U.S. life are quite different from what is learned in many societies or from what was learned in ours in an earlier era, but there can be no question but that the family, regardless of its composition, is an agency of education.

3. *Social groups.* An individual learns, albeit informally, from playmates, whether they vary from time to time or consist of a regular "gang"—in clubs, at dances, or at skating, swimming, pizza, bridge, or cocktail parties.

4. *Neighborhood haunts.* In a social group or alone, in a secluded sylvan retreat or in the middle of a busy street, the individual is learning *something.*

5. *Occupational groups.* From the time when a child was "bound out" or apprenticed to a master to learn a trade, up to and including the present apprenticeship or professional internship for adults, it has been recognized that a neophyte learns from those who are more experienced than he or she at a particular skill or trade. One

also learns other things from the same people during coffee breaks, at work, or over lunch.

6. *Personal media.* Although not often mentioned, personal communications media—media serving one or a few individuals—also serve as agencies of education. Media such as conversation, question-answer, photographs, color slides, scrapbooks, diaries, letters, family documents, and individual learning systems all can have tremendous impact on the learning of individuals.

NONFORMAL. A useful distinction, separating nonformal education from both informal and formal, was made by Paulston (1972), who defined the nonformal

> . . . *as structured, systematic, nonschool educational and training activities of relatively short duration in which sponsoring agencies seek concrete behavioral changes in fairly distinct target populations. It is, in sum, education that does not advance one to a higher level of the hierarchical formal school system* [*p. ix*].

Agencies of nonformal education, by this definition, abound in our society, and include the following.

1. *Mass media.* Certainly advertisements are "structured, systematic, nonschool . . . activities of relatively short duration in which sponsoring agencies seek concrete behavioral changes in fairly distinct target populations." Perhaps the same is true of all media messages aimed at large segments of the population. Thus, books, newspapers, magazines, church services, political and civic meetings, records, tapes, radio, television, billboards, and signs of all sizes and descriptions may be considered agencies of nonformal education.

2. *Church schools.* Church school groups, whether of the "daily vacation" or the year-round type, provide learning opportunities for countless individuals of widely varying age levels.

3. *Youth-serving groups.* Many groups have been organized for young people of varying ages, and each has, either overtly or covertly, one or more specific aims for which it provides learning opportunities. The list is extensive, and varies from community to community, but typical of the groups which reach large numbers of people are Scouts, Little League, Rocket Football, 4H clubs, and YMCA–YWCA. Overall, there are some 250 such organizations on a national scale (Paulston, 1972).

4. *Armed forces.* For centuries, nations have armed certain of their citizens and have taught them to use arms. Increasingly, the service branches have turned to providing education of an ever-broadening nature on both required and elective bases. Clark and Sloan concluded after their study of *Classrooms in the Military* (1964) that, in peacetime, the average serviceman often spends 80

to 85 percent of his waking hours in educational endeavors. They also reported that at that time more than one million servicemen all over the world were studying over 2500 USAFI courses. Cohen (1967) showed total enrollments in the armed forces classes expanding from one million in 1967 to a projected three million in 1970, and leveling off there.

5. *Special governmental programs.* At least from the time of the Freedmen's Bureau just following the Civil War; through the C.C.C., N.Y.A., and F.E.R.A. of the Depression; to and including the Peace Corps, Job Corps, Work-Study, O.E.O., VISTA, and similar programs, the federal government has provided numerous learning opportunities often not directly connected with "the school."

6. *Government schools.* There are literally hundreds of schools that are operated either directly or indirectly by various departments, bureaus, and special agencies of the federal government. Examples are the Indian schools run by the Bureau of Indian Affairs; schools for law enforcement officers, provided by the FBI; and the school for meteorologists under the auspices of the U.S. Weather Bureau.

7. *Civic and cultural centers.* Citizenship schools, art centers, museums, theaters, libraries, and concert halls are among the centers serving educational purposes.

8. *Social organizations.* Many organizations have functions which provide opportunities for people to learn something for a specific purpose. Thus, all are educative agencies. They range from fraternal organizations to service clubs, to professional organizations, to labor and credit unions, to penal institutions, ameliorative associations (*e.g.,* American Cancer Society, Goodwill Industries, Salvation Army, etc.), and to governmental welfare organizations.

9. *Company schools.* Industry pioneered the trend for organizations to educate their employees by setting up "training programs" to provide individuals with specific job skills. Cohen (1967) projected an enrollment of 12 million in company schools for 1970 and a whopping 17.5 million for 1974! He also projected *additional* 1974 enrollments of 18.1 million in "professional and technical training" and 6 million in "on-the-job training."

10. *Special-needs schools.* Most people are not even aware of the schools which have been developed to meet peculiar and pressing needs in certain industries and occupations, and which are controlled by no one company. Since no catalog of them appears to exist at the present time, it is not possible to indicate the entire gamut which they cover, but perhaps two examples will suffice to indicate their variety. Poultry raisers cooperated to provide a "school" in which the exotic art of chicken sexing is taught, and graduates of the relatively short course earn more than do most public school teachers! A school which trains jet pilots for airlines has a long waiting list of persons willing and presumably able to pay the shockingly dear tuition for this highly specialized training.

11. *Proprietary schools.* Almost any employee of the public schools would be amazed at the extent and variety of the listings to be found under "Schools" in the yellow pages of the telephone directory of any sizable community. Clark and Sloan's (1966) discussion of *Schools on Main Street* included both proprietary and special-needs schools.

12. *Correspondence Schools.* Cohen (1967) reported that enrollments in correspondence schools rose from 1 million in 1940 to 2.4 million in 1965, and projected enrollments of 2.8 million for 1970 and 3.2 million for 1974. Although Pfeiffer and Sabers (1970) reported some dismal statistics regarding attrition in and completion of such courses, many learners continue to utilize these agencies.

FORMAL. Every modern society has designated some agencies specifically for transmitting knowledge to its younger members, and has thus institutionalized education. In a society such as ours, there are numerous agencies, each of which is charged *by some segment of society* with this responsibility, but we commonly have recognized only those that are formal in nature, such as the following.

1. *The school.* Once, the school consisted of the "common" or "grammar" school, which taught the 3 Rs to a privileged few for a few months in each of one or two years. Today, every child is required to attend, and the school is in session for at least five days per week, and nine months per year, with some serious discussion of and experimentation with extending the school day, the school week, and the school year. Many schools offer adult classes, and there is a burgeoning movement for community education programs, some of which fall in the nonformal category. There are also some area vocational schools as offshoots of the public schools. Increasingly, both informal and nonformal agencies of education are being considered as alternatives to the school, as Saxe (1972) indicated.

2. *Alternative and free schools.* According to Newsweek,[3] in early 1973 there were 900 privately financed free or alternative schools operating in at least 39 states, plus somewhere between 400 and 1000 alternative schools being run by public school systems. These must be classed as agencies of formal education since the learners who attend them undoubtedly will be accepted by other units of the hierarchical system. As a *Newsweek* article[4] pointed out, the big difference between this and earlier reform movements is that learners, parents, and teachers are deciding—on an unprecedented scale—for themselves what is best. Graubard (1973) analyzed the reasons for disaffection with the public schools, and it seems clear

[3] Schools with a difference. *Newsweek,* 1973, **81**(17), 113.
[4] Ibid., p. 114.

that either the public schools must change or face increasing competition from the alternative and free school movement.

3. *Vocational and technical institutes.* Numerous vocational and technical institutes exist, and they usually enroll learners at the post-secondary level. Whether they are agencies of formal or nonformal education is a moot point, since few of the "graduates" advance to a higher level of the hierarchical formal school system. However, since it is possible, in most cases, for them to do so, we have chosen to classify the institutes as formal agencies.

3. *Community and junior colleges.* The junior college concept seems to be waning while that of the community college is expanding, but there are still numbers of both. Several states now have systems of junior or community colleges so extensive that virtually any citizen of the state is within reasonable, if not easy, commuting distance.

4. *Four-year colleges.* Although plagued by financial and enrollment ills because so many of them are private and lack substantial endowments, the four-year colleges still abound and are recognized as necessary components of our traditional pluralistic system of education.

5. *Universities and graduate colleges.* Most universities in this country consist of a graduate college plus several other colleges, but there are some graduate colleges that exist independently of universities. Together, the universities and graduate colleges comprise the capstone of formal education. Here, too, though, alternatives are under consideration that mix the informal and the nonformal, as Coyne and Hebert (1972) indicated.

The agencies of formal education are generally recognized as public, parochial, independent, or private, depending upon their sponsorship.

SPONSORSHIP OF AGENCIES

There are many reasons for the sponsorship of the numerous agencies of education. One needs to consider the purposes served, the levels at which the agencies are organized, and the sources of their support if one is to begin to understand sponsorship.

Purposes

Educational agencies serve at least three different groups of purposes: those of society, those of the agencies themselves, and those of learners.

PURPOSES OF SOCIETY. Society expects that, among them, the various agencies of education will carry out the functions of the educational institution; namely, transmitting the culture, social reform, discovering new knowledge, rehabilitation, making children into adults, individualization, babysitting, teaching sexuality, providing a courting ground, controlling the labor supply, relating the individual to society, teaching kinship, allocating influence and power, and relating the individual to one's physical environment.

PURPOSES OF AGENCIES. If one examines the purposes of educational agencies from the agencies' point of view, they seem to include:

Carrying Out Institutionalized Functions Prescribed by Society. Examples of agencies having this purpose are public schools and colleges.

Meeting Special-purpose Needs of Some Segment of Society. Examples of agencies having this purpose include parochial schools, church-related colleges, and the occupation-related schools described earlier.

Meeting Individuals' Needs. Public, private, and parochial schools, as well as most legitimate proprietary schools, serve this purpose to some degree.

Diffusing Propaganda. Propaganda as used here refers to the spread of doctrines, and this is a purpose of diverse agencies exemplified by church sects, advertisers, the American Legion, the news media, Common Cause, and the service academies. Agencies with this purpose are interested primarily in providing or affecting *what* the individual learns.

Profit-making. This is a purpose of most legitimate proprietary schools, and many owners recognize that it can be accomplished only by meeting individuals' needs also. "Fly-by-night" schools have only the profit purpose.

Regulation. This is a purpose of some agencies which provide *no* learning opportunities and only regulate those who do, through various forms of accreditation. A regional association such as the North Central Association of Secondary Schools and Colleges and a State Board of Cosmetology would be examples of such agencies.

PURPOSES OF LEARNERS. The purposes for which learners patronize the multitude of agencies of education are quite varied, and include:

Meeting Legal Requirements. If truth were told, this is the lone reason for many children and youths being in some schools.

Becoming More Socialized. Society provides many powerful compulsions for individuals to accept values held in common by others; to the extent that individuals do so, they accept the purpose of becoming more socialized.

Becoming More Individualized. To the extent that one wishes to foster his uniqueness and learn who he is, he accepts this purpose.

Reducing Personal Uncertainties. The individual who accepts this purpose needs no external motivations, and has found "the joy of learning."

Enjoyment. Those who have experienced exhilaration or the sense of power that comes just from *knowing* may patronize agencies which can help them to know.

Inspiration or Self-renewal. Some learners seek agencies that can lift melancholy, reduce despair, or provide new or renewed sense of purpose.

Some agencies of the educational institution exist for the purposes of society, some for their own purposes, some for the purposes of learners, some for two of these, and some for all three. The levels at which they are organized may be of help in understanding their sponsorship.

Levels of Organization
Some educational agencies are organized at a single level, some at several levels.

LOCAL. At the local level are public, parochial, private, proprietary, and company schools; private colleges; radio and television stations; jails; and newspapers.

AREA. At the area level (larger than local, smaller than state) are intermediate or county public school systems, diocesan parochial school units, some vocational schools, and some community colleges.

STATE. At the state level are found several types of special schools, penal institutions, colleges and universities, state departments of education (usually regulating public *and* private schools), some private and parochial school units, most examining boards, and most *compulsory* accrediting agencies.

REGIONAL. Accrediting agencies which provide services for those agencies who seek them voluntarily usually are organized on a regional, multistate, basis; for example, the Southern Association of Colleges and Secondary Schools and the North Central Association mentioned earlier.

NATIONAL. At the national level there are the many government schools, some correspondence and other proprietary schools, some company schools, testing services, most parochial schools, and, of course, the U.S. Office of Education (USOE).

INTERNATIONAL. Some agencies which have educational, sometimes along with other, purposes are international in scope. These include UNESCO, the International Red Cross, international labor unions, YM-YWCA, scouting, and some service clubs. All of these except UNESCO have national units also.

Sources of Support
A vital question in sponsorship of agencies is finance: "Who pays?" Agencies are in perpetual competition for dollars and all appear to get their finances from one or a combination of the following sources.

TAXES. Property taxes have been used to support public elementary or common schools since about 1832 and to support public secondary schools since about 1874. Community colleges, state universities, and state and local schools for the handicapped all engage in political activity and compete for tax dollars. All of the national government schools and many libraries and museums also derive support in whole or in part from this source. The many court cases pending in 1974 made it apparent that numerous states will soon undertake sweeping tax reforms.

TUITION AND FEES. Most private, parochial, and proprietary schools and colleges charge tuition, fees, or both. Most state colleges and universities in recent years have had to resort to using tuition or fees to supplement tax fund allocations. Many museums, galleries, and concert halls also charge fees.

ENDOWMENTS. Endowed funds have been and continue to be of considerable help in the support of many colleges and universities, both public and private. Some libraries and museums also benefit.

MEMBERSHIP OR ADMISSION FEES. Individual charges are the principal source of support for many unions, concert halls, galleries, and museums.

VOLUNTARY CONTRIBUTIONS. Donations from friends and patrons keep numerous private and parochial schools, libraries, theaters, galleries, and concert halls going.

PRODUCT SALES. Sales revenues support most book publishers, most of the educational programs in industry and business, test publishers, and most manufacturers of learning systems. Sales are of considerable help to newspapers and magazines, along with advertising fees.

ADVERTISING FEES. Fees charged advertisers are the chief source of support for radio and television stations, and a major source for newspapers and magazines.

COORDINATION OF AGENCIES

Inasmuch as even the smallest community has a wide variety of agencies that can be used by learners, it behooves educational leaders to get the agencies coordinated. Furthermore, since agencies inevitably engage in political and economic struggles for the allocation of resources, it would be wise to try to avoid waste of resources and *unnecessary* duplication, as the present writers are in no way suggesting the abolition of our pluralistic system of agencies.

The Norm

The norm is that no one in a given community has any catalog or other tangible evidence of all of its existing agencies. The one attempt, up to the present writing, of even conceptualizing and calling attention to the plethora of agencies is the *Yellow Pages of Learning Resources* (Wurman, 1972). The pathetic waste that results from lack of coordination is exemplified, in many cities, by school playgrounds that stand vacant during summer months while city recreation directors scrounge for funds and staff to provide playgrounds. Also exemplifying the norm are Boys' Clubs and Scout troops that desperately seek facilities while school buildings stand vacant many hours of every day, and the school-based adult classes that hunt for enrollees while YMCA, YWCA, or similar classes *of the same type* have unfilled seats. In order to help obviate such conditions, some school districts have turned to Community School programs.

Community Schools

Community School programs attempt to use the school facilities for more hours of the day than those required by the regular instructional program. They often provide classes for persons of nonschool age and recreational activities for those of preschool, school, and post-school ages.

Programs that reach beyond the instructional program and the 9:00 to 3:00 day have been tried in many places, and many have continued for several years with varying degrees of success. The schools of Flint, Michigan, have operated such programs since the 1930s, with the enthusiastic support of the Mott Foundation, and they yearly attract hundreds of visitors from throughout the United States and numerous foreign countries. Many other systems have instituted programs based on the Flint model, and some go further by attempting to make their schools all things to all people. At the opposite pole are critics of the schools whom we are characterizing here as de-schoolers.

The De-Schoolers
In full cry at the heels of school teachers, administrators, and board members are a variety of critics led by those who would abolish schools entirely. Critics of the schools are not new on the educational scene, but de-schoolers are. Men such as Reimer (1971) and Illich (1971) insist that schools do not carry out the functions entrusted to them and should be totally abolished, with their responsibilities being taken over by other agencies. Holt (1972) has now joined them, along with Coyne and Hebert (1972).

Close behind these leaders are contingencies that bay for accountability, for performance contracting, for alternative schools, or for the choices permitted by a voucher system. All the critics have some justified criticisms of the schools, but few of them have constructive plans for carrying out all of the institutionalized functions of education. Among those who do are some of the leaders in the Community Education movement.

Community Education
One purpose of Community School adherents is to provide programs that use school buildings for more than the daytime instructional program. Some few Community School directors have been and are guilty of trying to organize classes and activities for this purpose alone, without regard for the needs and wishes of local residents. Sometimes this action is understandable, if the only criterion for the director's accomplishment is how many people he or she gets into the building.

By contrast, the Community Education movement centers in the belief that any community should use all of its educational agencies to foster individuality while helping individuals to recognize their commonality; to help all its citizens learn to identify and solve common problems. Community Education has its origins many years ago in such diverse localities as Appalachia, Florida, New England, and Michigan's Upper Peninsula, as well as in Flint, Michigan. Sometimes in concert with and sometimes discrete from Community Schools, it has spread and engulfed many communities. Through the National Community School Education Association and the National Center for Community Education, the movement enjoyed unprecedented growth in the early 1970s. The editors of *Phi Delta Kappan* saw fit to devote their entire November 1972 issue to the movement, and numerous books have been written about it.

Community Education stands staunchly between the "school is all" and the "De-Schooled Society" poles. Its adherents would use every agency, of which the school is an important one, to help all of the people to learn, but no one can presume to speak for all of Community Education.

SUMMARY

Social institutions function through agencies, each of which has a structure, or pattern of organization. Organizations can be formal or informal, but the formal are more important to our present considerations. Formal organizations have characteristics, core elements, working elements, and survival elements in which social systems are involved. A formal organization involves a hierarchy which, in educational agencies, generally has been bureaucratic in nature.

A structure more flexible than bureaucracy is necessary if educational agencies are to be responsive to change, and a flexible structure depends on the size of its groups and the motivations of its people.

There are at least three general misconceptions about the agencies of education, but the agencies' functions, elements, sources of information, and types are identifiable. It probably is useful, in trying to understand agencies, to analyze their sponsorship according to purposes, levels of organization, and sources of support.

Educationally, economically, and politically, the coordination of agencies is desirable, but it seldom is achieved at present. In this regard, Community Education provides a middle ground between the "School is All" and the "De-Schooled Society" extremes.

In Chapter 5 there will be an exploration of the social institutions that organizations represent and how those institutions reflect social change.

SOME SUGGESTED RESOURCES

G. E. Berkley, *The administrative revolution.* Englewood Cilffs, N.J.: Prentice-Hall, 1971.

A. H. Halsey, Educational organization. In D. L. Sills (Ed.), *International encyclopedia of the social sciences.* New York: Macmillan, 1968. Vol. 4, pp. 525–532.

H. G. Hicks, What is an organization? In *The management of organizations.* New York: McGraw-Hill, 1972.

A. Jay, The instruments of corporate identity. In *Corporation man.* New York: Random House, 1971. Pp. 273–284.

R. Presthus, The bureaucratic model. Chapter 2 in *The organizational society.* New York: Vintage, 1962. Pp. 27–58.

H. A. Thelen, Society: The house that Jack lives in. Chapter 4 in *Education and the human quest.* New York: Harper & Row, 1960. Pp. 54–73.

CHAPTER 5

SOCIAL INSTITUTIONS AND CHANGE

> *Sociologists study institutions to learn (1) why they were established, (2) how they function, (3) how persons carry out their roles in institutions, and (4) how institutions serve the needs of individuals.*
>
> *—Rose*

An educational leader needs to study institutions to learn: (1) why there is an educational institution, (2) how its functions are differentiated from those of other social institutions, (3) the variety and types of educational agencies, (4) the *institutionalized practices* that exist in various educational agencies, and (5) how institutions affect one's role. This chapter is addressed to these needs.[1]

DEFINITIONS
Every society has many and varied institutions, but the term "institution" is used so loosely and with such varied meanings that agreement on a definition seems essential.

Dictionary Definition
According to Webster, an institution is "that which is instituted, as: (a) an established practice, law, custom, etc., (b) an established

---

[1] Portions of this chapter were adapted from H. W. Boles & M. F. Seay, Institutions, communities, and the agencies of community education. Ch. 3 in M. F. Seay (Ed.), *Community education: A developing concept.* Midland, Mich.: Pendell, 1974. Pp. 47–81.

society or corporation; an establishment, esp. one of a public character; a foundation, as, a charitable institution; also, the building or buildings used by such organization."

Common Usage
If it is said that a public figure spent some time in a mental institution, one knows that the word "institution" indicates a specific *type of place.* If an article states that the institution of penology needs drastic overhaul, it is clear that the reference is to a *total philosophical idea and the agencies responsible for it.* A comment that Wall Street represents the financial institution is generally interpreted to mean that a specific type of agency is representative of certain *transactions.*

When the University of Notre Dame is mentioned as an institution that almost invariably fields a good football squad, it is evident that institution in this case means a particular *establishment.* Savings and loan associations are said to be a part of the institution of banking, and thus institution is equated with particular *practices.*

Most adults cope with these and other uses of the word "institution" without a second thought as to its ambiguity. Yet, if one were asked whether it is learning, education, schooling, teaching, instructing, or training that our society has institutionalized, most would be hard put to reply. Indeed, most educators do not know, because they have never thought seriously about the matter, and few have any criteria by which to judge. To find such criteria, it may be helpful to look at the sociologists' definition of *social institutions.*

According to Sociologists
Eisenstadt (1968) has stated:

> *Social institutions are usually conceived of as the basic focuses of social organization, common to all societies and dealing with some of the basic universal problems of ordered social life. Three basic aspects of institutions are emphasized. First, the patterns of behavior which are regulated by institutions ["institutionalized"] deal with some perennial, basic problems of any society. Second, institutions involve the regulation of behavior of individuals in society according to some definite, continuous, and organized patterns. Finally, these patterns involve a definite normative ordering and regulations: that is, regulation is upheld by norms and by sanctions which are legitimized by these norms [p. 409].*

Institutions constitute a part of the basic definition of society and are essential to the existence of order in a society. In one of the best discussions of institutions in the educational literature, Getzels et al. (1968, pp. 56–59) said that institutions are (1) purposive, (2) peopled, (3) structured, (4) normative, and (5) sanction-bearing. If one takes as criteria for an institution the regulation of individual behavior, the ritualization of that behavior, and the existence of norms to which sanctions are attached, four facts become evident that are not evident in the definition: (1) the matter of values is involved, otherwise norms could not exist; (2) the term institution is used to refer to (a) general patterns of expectations for social behavior and (b) individual groups in which this behavior is embodied; (3) there is great overlap of responsibility among institutions; and (4) any major social institution functions through one or more agencies.

Usage Herein
As used herein, institution means an established practice, law, or custom to which sufficient value is attached that attempts are made to assure its perpetuation. An institution by this definition seems to meet all of the sociologists' criteria. The general patterns of expectations for social behavior are also accommodated by this definition.

By this definition, the sandlot version of baseball is institutionalized, the garage sale of the suburbs is an institution, and the negotiation of contracts by teachers' groups is an institutionalized practice in many states. The instructor-student relationship and many other practices that are common to all educational agencies are institutions.

Sociologists list from five to ten spheres of influence that exist in most societies, in each of which regulative principles tend to organize the activities of individuals into definite patterns. Each sphere is a social institution, and the chief ones are the domestic, the economic, the educational, the political, and the religious. Some persons substitute either the occult or the scientific for the religious institution, depending on the individual and the culture.

The functions for which these basic institutions are said to have responsibility vary in number from seven or eight to twenty or more. Some of the more important functions, along with the present writers' judgment of responsibilities which specific institutions have for them in U.S. society today, are shown in Table 5-1.

An examination of Table 5-1 reveals that the institutions have a wide variety of primary as well as subordinate functions. Responsibility for major societal functions is usually shared by several agencies representing overlapping institutions, and some further consideration of functions and agencies is therefore necessary.

FUNCTIONS AND AGENCIES
Each social institution has one or more functions for which it came into existence, but it may serve also some secondary function or

TABLE 5-1
SOCIAL INSTITUTIONS AND THEIR FUNCTIONS

SOCIETAL FUNCTION	INSTITUTION AND RESPONSIBILITY				
	DOMESTIC	ECONOMIC	EDUCATIONAL	POLITICAL	RELIGIOUS
Produce new members	1				
Individualize each member	1		1		2
Give each member a sense of purpose	2		3		1
Relate each member to society	1		2		3
Maintain order in the society				1	
Distribute influence and power		2	3	1	
Produce and distribute goods, services, and satisfactions		1			
Relate each member to the physical environment	2		3		1
Teach kinship	1		3		2

Key: 1—indicates primary responsibility for a function.
2 or 3—indicates secondary or tertiary responsibility for a function.

functions. As an example, the domestic institution developed to beget new members, but also serves the functions of cultural transmission, individualizing new members, relating each new member to the interactions of society, teaching one's kinship to other individuals, and giving the new member a sense of purpose.

Some sociologists refer to manifest and latent functions of institutions. We prefer to consider all things done for a society as institutional functions, with *responsibility* being primary (clearly evident) for one certain institution and secondary or tertiary (concomitant) for others. This may become clearer through reexamination of Table 5-1.

We can think of few instances in which a function is the primary responsibility of more than one institution. However, two or even three institutions may share secondary or tertiary responsibility for a function. No one institution has the lone responsibility of preserving the cultural heritage, but all have some responsibility. Elaboration of the functions of each major social institution helps to identify responsible agencies.

Among the agencies which help to transmit our cultural heritage are local, county, state, and national organizations and societies. Also, museums exist to preserve and show everything from general collections (for example, the Smithsonian Institution and Greenfield Village) to specialized collections such as in the Museum of Natural History, the Museum of Science and Industry, the various Halls of Fame, many art museums, children's museums, site museums (such as Gettysburg Battlefield), and folk museums (such as colonial Williamsburg). Other agencies include libraries; societies for the preservation of architectural classics; theaters of the dance or drama; as well as art, film, and photographic studios.

The Domestic Institution
The domestic institution has only a single agency, the family or human couple, that represents it in one of the four functions (Table 5-1) for which it has primary responsibility, namely, procreation.

Other functions for which the family has primary responsibility are the socialization of the child, the teaching of his or her kinship to other people, and relating the child to the larger society. Functions for which the family has secondary responsibility include giving the child a sense of purpose, helping one to learn the biological functions of one's body, and helping one relate to one's physical environment. Other institutions share responsibilities for some of these functions.

Any of the functions of the domestic institution except procreation sometimes is taken over by an agency such as the foster family, the single parent, the extended family, a child-care center, an orphanage, the church, a gang, or a commune.

The Economic Institution
According to Merrill (1969), the function of the economic institution is to provide physical subsistence for a society. This includes "activities leading to the production, processing, distribution, and consumption of the goods and services [p. 259]."

Due to the unprecedented amounts of leisure time resulting from technology, many modern societies have developed demands for activities that provide satisfactions for people which can hardly be classed either as goods or services. For example, passive entertainment such as movies and sporting events or active recreational activities such as boating or bicycling provide satisfactions to large numbers of people on a take-it or leave-it basis. Services, on the other hand, are required by individuals or small groups; for example, medical or dental service, service on motor vehicles, or those services necessary to the maintenance and repair of home appliances.

Then the economic institution has primary responsibility for the production and consumption of goods, services, and satisfactions. It has secondary responsibility for processing and distributing, since production is worthless without these. Among the major institutions, the economic is unique in that for its *primary* function, *responsibility is not shared by any other institution.*

The agencies of production include independent artisans, family-type production units, and corporations; agencies for processing range from the farm where on-the-job agricultural processing of livestock feed occurs, up to and including the most sophisticated assembly line; agencies for distribution include sales departments and agents and the wide array of wholesale and retail outlets. The agencies of consumption range from family pets and those animals used for food, through individual human beings, families, processors, distributors, and other manufacturers. The entire transportation (of goods) industry is an agency of the distribution function, as is the Merchant Marine.

Many financial agencies serve the economic institution as adjuncts to the activities of production, processing, distributing, and consuming. These include securities and commodities exchanges, brokers, banks, clearing houses, savings and loan associations, and credit card and other finance companies.

The Educational Institution
Every society has a more or less elaborate process for transmitting the cultural heritage from one generation to the next. In this society, basic responsibility for this function historically has been divided between the agencies of the family and the church. In comparatively recent times, the school was developed as an agency to share this responsibility. At about the same time, according to Plumb (1972), childhood was institutionalized. In the minds of many people in this country, the two concepts have blended into a belief that the educational institution has only one agency, *the school,* which has the function of making children into adults. This belief has brought many, often conflicting, demands on the school. The view must be changed by educational leaders, even though it is held by many persons who work in or support the schools today.

The educational institution is impaled on the horns of a seemingly impossible dilemma. Whether its activities are conducted by parents, tradespeople, teachers, or clerics, one evident responsibility is to hand on the accumulated folkways, mores, values, skills, and institutions of the existing society to the next generation. This function is conservative, provides for the socialization of individuals, and sometimes develops reactionaries.

In primitive societies, children attempt to be like their parents in every respect. However, our society, among others, places value on the worth and dignity of the individual, and encourages his or her uniqueness. The educational institution thus has a responsibility to help him search for his own truth. This function is liberal, and sometimes develops radicals.

From this dilemma, incessant controversy emerges. Should education preserve the status quo or should it seek new truth? Should it prescribe behavior or advocate total freedom? Is it an agency of social control or of social reform? Does it mold public opinion, or does it follow public opinion? Should it serve to confer status or should it make all equal?

Perhaps one way out of the dilemma is through understanding the functions of the educational institution and recognizing the myriad agencies, of which the school is but one, through which the institution functions. These were examined in Chapter 4.

The Political Institution
It is interesting that Linton (1936), in cataloging the common elements found by anthropologists in all of the societies studied up to that time, listed some form of *governance* among them. Apparently there are universal needs for maintaining order, setting the boundaries of society, controlling and using force, according prestige, and controlling and using natural resources. The distribution and exercise of power are the province of the political institution.

The original concept was to have the local government (town or township in this country) do for people those things which they could not do for themselves. Then county or state governments were to do what local governments could not, and the federal to do what the states could not.

Subagencies within the government had rather clear-cut responsibilities for institutional functions. Legislative and executive bodies and courts were to fix the tolerable behavior boundaries for members of society. Militia, armies, navies, and air forces were to control and use force. Prestige was to be accorded through the subtle controls of folkways and mores. Special departments or divisions of state and national governments were to control the use of resources. Health and fire departments were to provide for health and safety, and police were to maintain order.

But there have been fundamental changes in the structure of society in this country and in many others. A massive shift of control has occurred. In 1969, Merrill (p. 254) indicated some of the transfers of responsibility, from other institutions to the government, which were then apparent:

1. *From the Family* [Domestic Institution]
   a. Physical protection of the home
   b. Economic support of the unemployed
   c. Care of the sick
   d. Treatment of the insane
   e. Custody of the aged
   f. Support of widows and orphans
   g. Formal education of children

  2. *From the Economic Institution*
     a. Fixing of prices
     b. Manipulation of credit
     c. Settlement of labor-capital disputes
     d. Regulation of securities and commodities exchanges
     e. Guarantee of bank savings
     f. Production of electricity
     g. Subsidization of recreation
  3. *From the Church* [Religious Institution]
     a. Education of children
     b. Regulation of conditions for marriage
     c. Jurisdiction over divorce
     d. Establishment of grounds for annulment of marriage
     e. Provision of secular over canon law
     f. Maintenance of poor relief

Further transfers obviously have occurred since 1969. Whether shifts of control occur because the people seek them or because of apathy is a moot point. The result is "laws" to the effect that "the further removed an agency of government that does something for one, the fewer the 'significant others' that one finds in it. The fewer the 'significant others' that one sees in an agency, the less is its effect on one."

The proliferation of the functions of government has resulted in a proliferation of agencies to carry out those functions. At the federal level alone, in this country, all of the many executive departments have headquarters in Washington, but about 90 of every 100 of their employees work elsewhere. Furthermore, *independent agencies* have developed in the fields of aeronautics and space, atomic energy, banking and finance, civil service, communications, farm credit, home loans, information services, interstate commerce, labor mediation and conciliation, labor relations, power, railroad retirement, science, securities and exchange, selective service, small business, tariffs, trade, and veterans affairs.[2]

Proliferation of the agencies of government causes alarm on the part of those who accept the stereotype of "all bureaucracy is evil and inefficient" and who fear that the government bureaucracy is enhancing its own power at the expense of the common citizen. What is happening to bureaucratic forms and functions is of particular interest to educational leaders.

The Religious Institution
The religious institution in our society carries out its functions through the agencies of the church, the family, the school, and the

---

[2] "United States, Government of," *World book encyclopedia,* 1972, v. 20, p. 78.

cult. Those functions for which the institution clearly has responsibility are: transmitting its own subcultural heritage, giving each member a sense of purpose, and relating each member to his or her physical environment. A secondary responsibility is the teaching of kinship, although in some sects this is considered primary.

Religion varies from one society and one period to another. In our society, many functions have been transferred from religion to other institutions and back again, and in certain societies the religious institution has dominated all the others.

In our own and other societies, there are many persons who look to *science* for the functions of giving meaning to life, explaining the relationship of human beings to their physical environment, transmitting its own subculture, and teaching kinship. People who perceive a scientific institution that is competing with the religious institution for the same functions have posed special problems for educational leaders in this country since the days of the Scopes trial.

All of the social institutions require some kind of structure if norms are to be developed.

STRUCTURE

For any agency to exist, it must have structure. Structure, according to Sumner (1906) is ". . . a framework, or apparatus, or perhaps only a number of functionaries set to cooperate in prescribed ways at a certain conjunction [p. 53]." Today, we call that structure "organization." Understanding of ethos, values, significant others, ritual behavior, and the question of legitimacy is essential to understanding of social organization.

Ethos

Each cultural system has a cluster of characteristics, called *ethos,* that distinguishes it from other cultural systems. Those characteristics include values, practices, and individual behaviors. There is a distinctive ethos in a national culture, the subculture of a street gang, or a motorcycle club. Indeed, there is a cluster of characteristics that distinguishes the culture of the Occident from that of the Orient, so ethos exists even at the supranational level.

Ethos requires consensus of members of the cultural system in regard to mores, or norms. When a majority of system members reach the point where a particular value is no longer (or never was) sufficiently important to regulate behavior, that characteristic is discarded. The classic example from the culture of the United States is the repeal of Prohibition. There simply was not consensus on the value of banning sales and consumption of alcoholic beverages; mores did, in fact, sanction their use. Other examples of what happens when consensus is lacking are rife in contemporary life: the changing patterns in sexual practices, in public attire, in head and facial hair styles, in attitudes toward abortion, and in the push for legalization of marijuana. Often, when statutes lack the sanction of mores and cannot be or are not changed, the legal sanctions are widely ignored. Examples are the persons who exceed automobile speed limits or walk against "Don't Walk" signal lights. Behavior becomes highly individualized and the ritual aspect disintegrates when rules or laws are not enforced. Thus, the ethos changes because ethos depends on individuals holding *shared* values.

The Question of Values

An idea, practice, or belief must be valued by an individual or a group if it is to be continued. The child who repeatedly engages in play with an imaginary playmate—or with real playmates—must find sufficient satisfaction in the activity to wish to repeat it, or she or he will choose another activity instead. The same is true of the adolescent who takes drugs or the adult who engages in volunteer hospital work. Collectively and individually, the members of a chess club must derive sufficient satisfaction from playing chess to spend time doing that rather than in some other activity. If the time comes when they no longer care that much, the club will disintegrate.

A society must care enough, individually and collectively, about having the young learn what the elders know to make provisions for learning activities. Importance must attach to having others experience the satisfactions that we have experienced or we will make no provision for the creation and preservation of artifacts such as sculpture and paintings. Repetition and perpetuation require effort, loyalty, and commitment; people devote effort and give loyalty or commitment only to what they value for some reason. It does not really matter whether they are aware of the reason.

In addition to ethos and values, another factor of great importance to the structure of social institutions has to do with where significant others may be found.

Significant Others

To any person, another person with whom he interacts in some structure, whose approval is meaningful to him, is a *significant other*. Every person who functions in society is a part of several cultural systems simultaneously. In each, one's behavior is to some degree regulated by overlapping institutions. The degree to which one feels loyal to a particular institutional agency depends on how many significant others one perceives in it.

For example, each child is born into a family, which is *the* agency of *the* domestic institution. As he grows and learns, he usually accepts and takes as his own the family values. All family members are "significant others" so long as their approval is meaningful. As the child acquires neighborhood (but nonfamily) playmates and acquaintances, some of them become significant others.

As his or her horizons are extended, the child comes in contact with and may become a part of the school, the church, and probably some of the general cultural agencies, such as museums or libraries. By the time that the child reaches adulthood, she or he has been in some way a part of the systems of government and the economy. It is hypothesized here that the degree to which an individual feels loyal to a particular system is directly proportional to the significant others in one's life. Thus, a child who feels little acceptance or approval in the home but much acceptance in a gang may feel much closer and more loyal to the latter.

Regardless of level, there must be organization—structure that gives form and substance to the interactions of people—for every institutional agency that the individual experiences. An organization may be formal or informal, but it will to some degree regulate the behavior of all individuals in it, and ritual behavior is a fourth essential of the structure of any organization.

Ritual Behavior

Every institution requires individual behavior that is learned and patterned. Behavior becomes ritualized when it is associated with values, is memorized, and is performed as habitual. The individual engaging in ritual behavior rarely considers its meaning, and one does not have to grope for words if words are to be recited, as in singing the national anthem or in reciting multiplication tables.

The older a social institution, such as religion, the more solemn and elaborate its prescribed ritual behaviors, and this truism extends to professions. The more an individual's behavior becomes ritualized, the less chance there will be for nonconformity to occur.

Every institution sets certain limits on behavior which its members must accept if they are to share in the reward system. So long as the behavior of an individual stays within those limits, it is either rewarded or unpunished. Thus, institution-demanded behavior is conforming behavior.

Ritual behavior results from a division of labor and of the rewards among those who comprise the structure of a specific institutional agency. Thus, there is always a hierarchy in such structures, and various terms are used to designate relative statuses—management-labor, leader-follower, boss-worker, superordinate-subordinate, superior-inferior (the latter term seldom, if ever, is used in "democratic" societies). Each term is used to help specify the behavior expected according to an individual's status in an organization or informal group.

Another facet of structure is legitimacy.

Legitimacy

The values and behavioral norms of a particular social structure generally are considered legitimate by those persons within it. If someone does not consider them legitimate, he confronts one of three situations. He continues in the organization and faces severe inner turmoil because of value conflict, he changes the norms if he can, or he gets out—if group sanctions will let him out.

Whether those in an outside cultural system legitimize a particular organization often is unimportant to the organization's members. A teenager who gets no approval from a moralistic family may feel quite loyal to a club and thus legitimize the club's right to demand that he or she shoplift, use drugs, or engage in promiscuous sexual activity as a condition of membership. Behavior considered nonconforming by the family thus is conforming behavior to the club members.

An adult who feels remote from the agencies of the political and economic institutions of his society may legitimize in his mind the values of a "business family" that makes him welcome, even though its activities involve corruption, extortion, or even murder. The sanctions of an agency which contains many significant others are more desired/feared by the individual than are those of a less approving agency. It is because of the combination of significant others and legitimization of authority that peer pressures exert such profound influences.

The structure of social institutions and their agencies is of importance to persons interested or involved in social change, as school principals, superintendents, college officials, and other educational leaders must be.

SOCIAL CHANGE

Any significant change in the structure of society is social change. In an earlier section of this chapter, several mentions were made of shifts of responsibility from one institution to another. Anyone who believes that the structure of society is fixed and permanent might try to make his or her own analysis of structure today and make it again five years from now. Comparison of the two might show little change, but that there would be no change seems improbable, given human nature.

Nature

Most sociologists consider the main types of social change to be those: (1) related to changes in numbers and variety of positions and social roles, (2) concerning responsibilities attached to positions, (3) leading to new ways of organizing social activities, and (4) involving redistribution of facilities and such rewards as power, education, income, and respect.

The concept of change is implicit in the concept of interaction within social structures. In its most concrete form, societal change means that the present generation is engaging in activities that differ from those of preceding generations. The persons who comprise the complex network of patterned relationships in which they participate to varying degrees all act, interact, and react differently from time to time—or from day to day. No normally functioning person ever engages totally in unvarying ritualized behaviors. Automatons, robots, and computers always do; normal humans, never.

Social institutions change, the structure of their agencies changes, the positions within a particular structure change, the holders of positions change, the person in a particular position changes. Statuses and roles change. All of these changes, collectively, constitute social change.

Desirability

Whether or how rapidly social change occurs depends on how well pleased people are with things as they are. People in some communities seem pleased with their customs and struggle to perpetuate them, shielding their young from "contaminating" influences. At the opposite extreme are the revolutionaries of the world who seek change for the sake of change, but seldom have constructive alternatives to propose; the "Yippie" cult of the late 1960s, with its "Revolution for the Hell of it," is representative.

Inevitability

Whether or how rapidly change occurs depends, too, on whether people will devote effort to causing or preventing it, or whether they are apathetic. By their nature, institutions impose limits on the behavior of individuals. They exist for that reason. When an institution gives up a function for which it has been responsible, some other institution usually assumes or is given the function by the society, as was illustrated earlier. When there is a vital function for which no agency assumes responsibility, limits sometimes disappear. Limits on elements of the social structure also disappear sometimes, as Halle (1963) indicated:

> Pluvis said he could sum up the evolution of our society in a
> phrase: the disappearance of limits. The limits on the size of
> our communities disappear, so that our cities spread and multiply
> their cells without control. The same thing happens to our gov-
> ernments, which go on growing even after their growth has re-
> duced them to floundering helplessness, like dinosaurs in a
> swamp. It happens to our population when the limits that disease
> and the food supply have set to its growth are removed. It hap-
> pens to our weapons of war when the chemical limits on their
> potential power is removed. It happens to the jurisdiction of gov-
> ernment when the limits of natural law disappear from among
> us. It happens to musical composition when the limits set by
> traditional scales and harmonies disappear; and to art when the
> limits set up by the requirements of representation
> disappear. . . .

> *The consequence, to Pluvis' . . . mind, was the proliferation of disorder and the collapse of harmony, since order and harmony represent systems of limits. . . .*
>
> *Once, Pluvis said, where we didn't have limits we used to invent them . . . [pp. 93–94].*

Social change is inevitable in any society, because of its very nature. It is inevitable when vested interests deliberately plan change and people at large either support it or care so little that they do not oppose it. Much unplanned social change also is inevitable, particularly in areas where there are no limits or the limits are disappearing.

Perhaps a function for which the educational institution must have responsibility henceforth is teaching the necessity for limits.

Planned or Unplanned

In proposing that we go "beyond freedom and dignity," Skinner (1971) went further than any other contemporary in suggesting planned social change—further in terms of the long-range and pervasive nature of the proposed change. Proponents of certain planned and purposeful changes have always been vocal, and there are many on the contemporary scene. Many proposed changes are issues, each with its protagonists and antagonists, and in most cases it is not yet clear which side will win the perennial tugs-of-war. Some such issues are legalized abortion, sex education in schools, legalized drug usage, euthanasia, eugenics, government aid to nonpublic schools, busing to achieve racial integration, and conservationist ecology.

Social change is brought about by people through their social institutions or one or more of the institutional agencies. Any proposed change is a threat to persons whose interactions would be affected and may be resisted for that reason alone. Early advocates of the school being an agency of social change, such as George Counts and Harold Rugg, suffered much abuse for their views. Indeed, as recently as 1951, Rugg's appearance on the campus of Ohio State University set off a furor about his publicly stated views that got national press coverage. It resulted in a board of trustees' screening policy intended to keep "subversives" off campus! Yet, at this writing, the several boards of education of metropolitan Detroit are under court mandate to achieve racial balance on an unprecedented geographic and numerical scale, and in dozens of other cities, thousands of school children are being bused away from neighborhood schools for the same purpose. Schools now *are* agents of social change, by court mandate, since courts have taken on the responsibility of legislating as well as adjudicating.

Change not deliberately planned will nevertheless come whenever pressures become strong enough. Supreme Court Justice William

O. Douglas[3] made that point chillingly succinct in regard to government when he said, "There are only two choices: A police state in which all dissent is suppressed or rigidly controlled; or a society where law is responsive to human needs [p. 92]."

The changes that Justice Douglas advocated (pp. 92–94) do not seem radical of themselves:

1. . . . there must be created an adult unrest against inequities and injustices in the present system.
2. . . . we must make the Pentagon totally subordinate in our lives.
3. The poor and disadvantaged must have lawyers to represent them. . . .
4. Laws must be revised so as to eliminate their bias against the poor.
5. Hearings must be made available so that the important decisions of federal agencies may be exposed to public criticism before they are put into effect.
6. The food program must be drastically revised so that its primary purpose is to feed the hungry rather than to make the corporate farmer rich.
7. A public sector for employment must be created that extends to meaningful and valuable work.
8. The universities should be completely freed from CIA and from Pentagon control, through grants of money or otherwise.
9. Its [the university's] curriculum should teach change, not the status quo.
10. . . . equality of opportunity has, in practice, not yet been achieved. There are many, many steps still necessary. The secret is continuous progress.

It is difficult to see how this manifesto is subversive. However, it advocates planned change; thus, it threatened some people and there was serious and impassioned talk of impeaching its author.

Change in human interaction sometimes results from constructive suggestion and planning, and sometimes from unplanned and difficult-to-control crowd action. Sociologists often make clear and useful distinctions between "the acting crowd" and "the expressive crowd" and between the goals of the two. School principals and superintendents, and college presidents, as well as government officials, need to understand those distinctions.

Reciprocity
Since social institutions are represented by structures through which humans interact, the concept of reciprocity within and among institutional roles has face validity. Reciprocity is inherent in the definition

[3] W. O. Douglas, *Points of rebellion.* New York: Vintage Books, 1970.

of interaction. When two people or institutions interact, one acts and the other reacts. When a woman starts to play a role in an economic agency, her role in the family changes, of necessity. When the child was no longer needed in an economic role, his role in the educational institution changed. When the production of goods moved from the family or tribe to the factory, family or tribal and corporation roles changed. When responsibilities of state or national governments increase or expand, those of local communities contract, disappear, or move into new areas. When common problems are solved or disappear, the focus must change to new problems or the sense of community is lost.

COMMUNITY

To both sociologist and layperson, the term "community" means things held in common—things ranging from real estate to beliefs and customs. A community means a set of people who have many elements in common. There are many communities in the larger society, usually based on ethnic considerations of country of origin, race, religion, or sex. Thus, we speak of the Italian or Greek community, the black community, the Jewish community, or the female community.

Definition

Many other definitions are possible, but the one that we choose to use here is: a community is a geographic clustering of people that makes possible human interaction in solving problems of concern to all. In rural areas, the clustering may be by townships, or even by counties in sparsely populated areas. Clustering also may be by villages or towns. In the metropolitan setting, clustering may be by ghetto, neighborhood, or suburb.

Reasons for Communities

Coleman (1966a, p. 674) attributed to Tönnies this list of important activities that usually require human interaction for their completion:

> work
> education of children
> religiously related activities
> organized leisure activities
> unorganized social play of children
> voluntary activities for charitable or other purposes
> treatment of sickness, birth, death
> buying and selling of property
> buying consumable goods (food, etc.)
> saving and borrowing money
> maintenance of physical facilities (roads, sewers, water, light)
> protection from fire
> protection from criminal acts

These activities, in short, bring about *shared patterns of living*— cultures or subcultures. Many of the activities are necessary to carrying out institutionalized functions of the larger society. Some of the activities, and the agencies which provide them, themselves become institutionalized. The sandlot baseball example used earlier is a form of institutionalized activity that provides unorganized social play for children.

Reasons for Disorganization

There are at least eight reasons why clusters of people, close enough in geographic proximity to act, sometimes *do not* act as a community. They are: (1) the really meaningful problems that can muster the all-out energies of people have been solved, (2) the people may perceive no common problem, (3) there may be no persons willing to lead in problem solution, (4) the individual energy required for collective efforts may be greater than the people are willing to invest, (5) there is collective effort, but two or more subgroups are pulling in different directions, (6) the structures necessary for collective efforts may not exist, (7) needed resources may be unavailable, and (8) the goals sought may be recognized as unattainable.

If one lives in an established community, the problems that can mobilize the all-out efforts of people may have been already solved. There may be in existence schools, fire departments, police, and departments of public utilities. It is difficult to get as worked up about litter in the street as about getting the community's first and only hospital. This is particularly true with the high degree of mobility found in the population today. People sometimes do not stay in one place long enough to learn the nature of its pressing problems.

A geographic cluster consisting of people of all age strata, from newlyweds through retirees, may not perceive any common problems. The childless young may be concerned about tennis courts and swimming pools, the young marrieds about schools, the middle-aged about crime in the streets, and the retirees about lower taxes.

Leaders are always in short supply. It takes commitment and "joyously enduring stress,"[4] for one to stick his neck out and say, "Here is a cause in which I believe. Who will follow me?" When all of the several social systems in which a person functioned were concentric, centered about the place where one lived, the sense of affiliation was stronger, and leaders were much easier to find. Now, many men and women with leader propensities earn their living miles from their bedroom communities.

Coleman's tale (1966a, p. 680) of the hotel cornice bricks about to fall illustrates that the consequences of each person's action or

---

[4] H. E. Sponberg, in an address to The Michigan Association of School Administrators Conference, Cobo Hall, Detroit, September 1965.

inaction must somehow be felt by him if he is to make the effort required to take action:

> *Suppose there are some bricks loose in the cornice of a hotel, and I see them from my hotel room. These bricks could fall, injuring or killing a passer-by on the sidewalk below. If action is to take place, I, out of concern for the passer-by or the hotel, must report this to the desk clerk, the desk clerk must report it to the manager, and the manager must call a brick-layer to have the loose bricks repaired. All this is no simple matter, for it requires a chain of organization: from me to the desk clerk to the manager to the repairman. Each person in this chain must be sufficiently motivated to carry out his particular action, or there is effectively no organization.*

The witnesses in the infamous Genovese murder case, and others who "don't want to get involved," simply cannot see enough "what's in it for me?" to make the effort worthwhile.

Factional fights in which there is plenty of collective energy, but all of it devoted to "us against them" struggles, abound in almost every community. Lots of adrenaline flows but few problems get tackled, and fewer yet get solved, because of wasted energy.

If existing structures for human interaction cannot provide, or cannot be perceived as providing, for resolution of a particular problem, that problem is likely to go unsolved. Inertia sets in, because it requires awesome energy to initiate and bring to fruition a new structure, or to compete for scarce resources.

Effects on the Educational Institution

When social problems go unsolved or when there is lack of "community" among geographically close clusters of people, the educational institution often becomes the whipping-boy of society. Going back at least to the Franco-Prussian War, and following every war since, the losing side has invariably said, "If only our men had been better educated, we would have won." This was true even of the Cold War of the 1950s. After Sputnik I, the tired cliché was the same, and *the schools, as the only generally recognized agency of the educational institution,* were charged with the "defeat." The school curriculum was beefed-up with more mathematics, more science, more foreign languages.

Social institutions have much to do with the social climate in which educational agencies function. The structures necessitated by those agencies constitute the social milieu in which educational leaders lead or fail to lead.

SUMMARY

An institution is a practice, custom, or law to which sufficient value is attached that attempts are made to assure its perpetuation. The social institutions found in this and many other societies are the domestic, economic, educational, political, and religious. Responsibility for functions desired from an institution may be primary or secondary, and may be the province of one or several agencies of that institution.

Each institution has a structure in which ethos, significant others, and ritual behavior are important. Legitimization may be localized in the institution and its members, sometimes without regard for the larger society.

Social change may result from planning or from chance, but change should be viewed as both desirable and inevitable. There is a reciprocity among social institutions and among individual roles within them, and change that results in new responsibilities for one subtracts responsibilities from another.

Common problems are the focus when people form community structures. Disorganization is likely to occur when no common problems are perceived, when leaders are lacking, when energy called for seems unlikely to be sufficiently rewarded, or is dissipated in power struggles, or when new structures or resources are needed. When there is disorganization, or lack of community, education often is blamed.

Section Two of this book will be devoted to the role of the educational leader as she or he functions in the social milieu described in this first section.

SOME SUGGESTED RESOURCES

J. H. Chilcott, N. C. Greenberg, and H. B. Wilson, *Readings in the socio-cultural foundations of education.* Belmont, Calif.: Wadsworth, 1968.

B. R. Clark, The study of educational systems. In D. L. Sills (Ed.), *International encyclopedia of the social sciences.* New York: Macmillan, 1968. V. 4, pp. 509–516.

J. S. Coleman, Community disorganization. In B. K. Merton and R. A. Nisbet (Eds.). *Contemporary social problems* (2nd ed.) New York: Harcourt Brace Jovanovich, 1966. Pp. 670–722.

S. N. Eisenstadt, Social institutions: The concept. In D. L. Sills (Ed.), *International encyclopedia of the social sciences.* New York: Macmillan, 1968, Vol. 14, pp. 409–421.

W. R. Lassey (Ed.), *Leadership and social change.* Iowa City: University Associates Press, 1971.

S. D. Sieber and D. E. Wilder (Eds.), *The school in society: Studies in the sociology of education.* New York: Free Press. 1973. Part II, Socialization and learning, Pp. 41–146. Part III, School as a formal organization, Pp. 149–236. Part IV, School-community relations, Pp. 363–438.

H. Zuckerman, Social change. In *The world book encyclopedia,* 1972. Vol. 18, pp. 448d–448e.

SECTION TWO
ROLE OF THE LEADER

> *Research findings to date suggest, then, that it is more fruitful*
> *to consider leadership as a relationship between the leader and*
> *the situation than as a universal pattern of characteristics*
> *possessed by certain people.*
>
> —McGregor

This section will examine the role of the leader, giving specific attention to leaders and the process of leadership, the situations in which
leadership can and cannot be found, the interactions that occur
when someone is leading, the communication that implements
leadership, and the accountability of those who work in education,
including leaders.

CHAPTER 6

LEADERS AND LEADERSHIP

. . . the good leader may sometimes give the impression that he is a rather stupid fellow, an arbitrary functionary, a mere channel of communication, and a filcher of ideas. . . . He has to be stupid enough to listen a great deal, he certainly must arbitrate . . . and he has to be at times a mere center of communication.

—Barnard

The leader has to be stupid enough to learn the expectations that people hold for his organization, for each other, and for him. He must be arbitrary enough to make his own expectations known to others, and he must try to get people to meet the legitimate expectations which are held for them. In doing these things, the leader is serving as a communications clearing house.

This chapter will discuss the leader's job in terms of who leads, what leadership is, why we have leaders, when leaders function, where they function, and how they function.[1]

WHO LEADS?

A status leader in an educational agency is expected to be able to impart a "contagion to perform" (Zaleznik, 1966, pp. 3–4). He is

[1] Portions of this chapter were adapted from H. W. Boles & M. F. Seay, Community education leadership: A theory. Ch. 4 in M. F. Seay (Ed.), *Community education: A developing concept.* Midland, Mich.: Pendell, 1974. Pp. 85–116.

an executive by definition, in that he is ". . . responsible for a con-tribution that materially affects the capacity of the organization to perform and to obtain results [Drucker, 1967, p. 5]." One is by no means the only leader or the only producer of ideas, but the role expectations held for that person may differ from those held for any-one else in the organization. They have to do with the bases for leading.

Bases for Leading
Some of the relationships that are important to the status leader's role, regardless of his or her job title, concern: (1) one's effect on the capability of the organization to produce, (2) the sometimes con-flicting dependence-independence urges of individuals, and (3) the interwoven purposes of society, the organization, and the persons within the organization. All of these relate to the reasons why most people, at certain times and in certain situations, are willing to legiti-mize the right of certain others to make decisions that we would otherwise have to make or to take actions that we would otherwise have to take. The others to whom we defer may be either status leaders or emergent leaders. A leader's relationship to followers is always an acknowledged authority relationship, even though the acknowledgement may be either subconscious or conscious.

The *most common reason* for one person acknowledging the authority of another lies in the second's possession of the means for satisfying the needs or wants of the first. In a military academy, Instructor A will legitimize the right of Director B to do certain things if B can provide a job that A wants, can get him increased pay or other benefits, or can make possible his promotion. In an informal group, C will accept decision-making or action-taking on the part of D if the decision or action will provide some benefit desired by C, such as group approval, opportunity to engage in some desired activity, or a chance to meet significant others. More discussion of control of means follows later in this chapter under When Leaders Function.

A *second basis* for one individual being able to lead another lies in their relative degrees of uncertainty about a matter. If two persons are lost in a forest, the one who has no idea which way to turn will defer to the one who does. Whether the leader's hunch is correct becomes significant only after the expenditure of time and effort with no results (getting out of the forest) to show!

A *third basis* for legitimization of the leader lies in the relative ego-involvement of individuals. If the members of a group are inter-acting and doing their jobs, inertia will carry them along unless some unusual force is brought into play. Thus, if one member (whether he be a status leader or an emergent leader) feels strongly that he wants to make a change, he may be able to influence the direction of the group. He injects a *preferred outcome*—something that he thinks will result from his intervention and likely would not result without it. Status leaders are expected to have preferred outcomes.

Status Leaders

In and for every educational agency, many persons and groups hold expectations that help to determine who leads.

SOCIETY'S EXPECTATIONS. The larger society holds expectations that a business college will fulfill certain functions as an agency of education. Those executives who determine the course of the college hold expectations that personnel will produce and that certain staff members will be more responsible than others for that production. Those who are producing expect to learn what they are supposed to accomplish and what they can expect in return.

DEMAND FOR EXPERTISE. One of the tenets on which any modern organization is built is that tasks and responsibilities will be divided among positions and that each position will be filled by a person who can do its allotted tasks well. Thus, there are institutional expectations that expertise is desirable and will be used, and these also help to determine who leads.

ADAPTABILITY. An *apparatus of permanence* is necessary for any organization, as was mentioned in an earlier chapter. In a dynamic organization, that apparatus provides for change. The buggy manufacturer who converted to automobile parts persisted while his unyielding competitor did not. In every organization, certain individuals are more adaptable to change, more willing to assume the risks and tolerate the stresses of change, than are others. The needs for change, too, help to determine who leads.

STATUS. The fact that status attaches to any position in an organization helps to determine who leads. Leading is an expectation for certain positions in a hierarchy, but not for others. Anyone who occupies a high status position without doing any leading probably will have limited tenure. Anyone in a low status position who takes initiative in certain situations will be an emergent leader in those situations. If one persistently takes initiative, one likely will be considered for a higher status position—unless the individual poses a threat to those who might make such a decision!

Emergent Leaders

Many of those who lead in certain situations are not holders of positions having high status in the organization. Gibb (1958) said that who leads is determined by the situation or problem at hand, and so different persons lead at different times. Sommerville (1971) said that the role of the status leader is to create a climate where person-alities who are influential can gain support for significant change.

ADVOCACY. It follows that an emergent leader relies on personal authority rather than positional authority, but she or he must know enough about the idea or situation to be a persuasive advocate. The goal or preferred outcome may be one's own, provided by some other person in the organization whose status is irrelevant, or be that of the status leader. The emergent leader simply comes forth to champion a cause in which he believes or in which he has some other interest. He may see it as being good for the organization, good for his status leader, good for certain colleagues, or good for him.

USING EXPERTISE. The wise status leader does not slap down or attempt to repress emergent leaders within the organization unless the causes they are advocating are inimical to the organization's purposes, or to him personally. It is generally recognized that one of the marks of leadership that is both effective and efficient is the utilization of individuals' expertise. If that expertise involves leading in specialized facets of the overall organizational tasks, the status leader's job is made easier by utilizing all of the expertise available. It is a common misconception that only the status leader leads, and some persons resent all status leaders because of that misconception.

Regardless of whether an individual is a status leader or an emergent leader, one does the job through communications. The ulti-mate aim, and the measure of whether a leader is doing his job, is whether he is influencing others.

People Who Influence Others
In his "Keys to Leadership," Stoops (1963) presented lists of twenty "Do's" and six "Don'ts" for leaders, all intended to assist in influenc-ing other persons. Gibb (1968) discussed various theories of leader-ship and the leader's role in terms of intended influence. By our definition (see Glossary), influence is a relationship in which one individual affects the thoughts, attitudes, or behavior of another.

REDUCING UNCERTAINTY. Cartwright and Zander (1953) said that the two main functions of a leader are: (1) helping the group to find the machinery or means to a goal already agreed upon, and (2) help-ing to decide on a goal that is satisfactory, in that the group can pursue it. Thus, the leader influences the group by reducing group uncertainty. The leader also influences by reassuring individuals. As Ginzberg (1966, p. 115) said, "This is a hostile world [as viewed by many], and many individuals feel their insecurity acutely." Leaders influence them by making them feel more secure.

AUTHORITY. Weber (1922) opined that groups are formed because of material interests, the need for feelings of affinity, and the need for authority (a special form of influence) in social relations. Obviously, people are influenced by considerations relating to their material well-being and by their feelings of affinity. The measure of authority is found in the probability that a given command with a specific content will be obeyed by a given group of persons—the ultimate, perhaps, in influence.

SKILLS. Numerous writers have described the skills that leaders must utilize. Katz (1955) categorized them as technical, human, and conceptual, and contended that a person's ability to influence others lies in what one can *do* rather than what one *is*. Taylor (1962, pp. 98–99) listed twenty-six skills among his "factors extracted from executive experience." Bellows, Gilson, and Odiorne (1962) devoted an entire book to the skills needed by executives, and indicated in it that a leader is primarily an initiator and a decision-maker.

WHAT IS LEADERSHIP?
Taylor (1962, pp. 3–16) concluded that leadership is people, and that we don't know much about leadership because we don't know much about people. He continued:

> . . . it also becomes evident that just as we do not require a perfect definition of gravity to be able effectively to slide things down a chute—or of love to be concerned for our children; or of magnetism to build a compass that works; or of memory to recollect—we need not wait for The Compleat Explanation of Leadership to put to practical use that which we do know that is useful [p. 18].

Definition of Leadership
The present authors do not have the "Compleat Explanation of Leadership" but a definition is offered that should help a leader to do his job and should help others to understand his job. Leadership is a process in which an individual takes initiative to assist a group to move toward production goals that are acceptable, to maintain the group, and to dispose of those needs of individuals within the group that impelled them to join it.

INTERACTION. For the process of leadership to occur, there must always be a group of persons (two or more) in interaction. Gibb (1958) stated that leadership is always (1) relative to a situation, (2) directed toward some goal, (3) a process of mutual stimulation, and (4) a *social interaction.* The present authors largely agree, having reservations only about whether there is always mutual stimulation.

TYPES OF ACTION. The leader's job is always done in a *social exchange* setting, and a more intensive discussion of this is given in Chapter 8. However, that job, and the *leadership process,* always involve the actions of leading and of administering. Both types of actions must be taken by someone in an organization, although not always by the status leader. Even the leader who performs both usually does not perform them in equal degree or with equal skill.

ACTIONS OF LEADING. The activities of leading have to do with innovation and change. Sommerville (1972) said that leaders who fail to influence needed change contribute to their organizations' stagnation. Goldman (1969) reported a disquieting revelation of the lack of leadership on the part of a group of school administrators. Ginzberg (1966, p. 121) said the successful leader ". . . must know how to administer; he has the responsibility for keeping the organization on an even keel, solvent, and free from discord. A great leader must also have vision. He must use his power not only to control the present but to mold the future." Litchfield (1956) presented the proposition that there are certain administrative actions that one must engage in regardless of the type of organization in which he is employed. We believe the same to be true of the actions of leading. Thus, we are in effect saying that we believe the process of leadership and the job of the leader to be unchanged regardless of the structural context. Koontz (1968) and others have supported this thesis.

Further discussion of the actions of both leading and administering appears later in this chapter in the section Why Have Leaders?

Why Others Accept Leaders

The leadership process can occur only when the leader-follower relationship is established. If two teenagers are ice-skating together and decide to go inside to get warm, it has to be because one suggests, in some fashion, and the other agrees. The authority of one—the right to make decisions or to take actions that affect the other—must be recognized by the second or there will be no movement toward a common goal. If the second decides to stay on the ice, no leadership has occurred and no authority is recognized. The basis for presumed authority is really of no consequence unless the authority is legitimized by the follower.

Many a status leader has been chagrined by trying to exercise the nominal authority of his position only to find it ignored by those whom he would have follow him!

ACHIEVING GROUP GOALS. The leader's job has to include assuring that the goals toward which she or he wants the group to move are accepted by group members. One also must ascertain that one's authority is acknowledged. If he has power, he may simply impose sanctions in order to get his way. The leader's authority may be ascribed, because of the position that he or she holds. Authority may also be achieved through rational appeal, or demonstrated skill. It is our hypothesis that leaders are accepted only when their authority is acknowledged, either openly or tacitly. The acknowledgement may range from grateful accord to grudging—or even surly—submission, but it must occur.

Behaviors in the Leadership Process

The leader's job and his understanding of the leadership process require that the leader be able to understand and interpret his own and others' behavior. Understanding and interpretation may be aided by considering the dimensions of observable behavior illustrated in Figure 3-1 and described in Chapter 3. For every individual, role expectations combine with the need-dispositions to cause one to act as she or he does. The resultant actions provide the actor with a sense of either satisfaction or frustration, and one's reactions with others indicate which one is experiencing. Of course, the leader is viewed more charitably by followers who experience relative satisfaction than by those who are frustrated, and the leader's job is tolerable only so long as he himself is experiencing relative satisfaction.

An intriguing view of the leader in relation to a work group was presented by Graves (1966). He described seven levels of human existence, each representing a combination of motivation and value system, and stressed that the leader must be cognizant of followers' behavior levels and needs. Anderson (1973) built on the work of Graves to investigate the styles and effectiveness of school superintendents.

An Example of Leadership

We are of the opinion that the leadership process, even in a simple situation, involves four distinct and identifiable phases, namely:

— Goals are set that are acceptable to group members, in that they can be achieved.
— A leader is chosen or emerges through group members legitimizing an individual to make decisions or to take actions that affect all.
— The means for achieving goals are agreed upon.
— Group members set limits of the leader's authority.

To illustrate, suppose that a parochial school principal suggests to a few fellow principals that they make sweeping curriculum reforms. Those who agree have accepted a goal. The initiator or some other is designated to decide when, and in what form, changes will be made, although suggestions may come from several persons. Authority has been legitimized, even though the proposed changes may be considered illegitimate by the church society! The leader wants to just make the changes without informing the superintendent, but group members veto this as being too risky. Limits have then been set on the leader's authority which he can overcome only if he can force the others to accept his plan (an exercise of power!). Simultaneously, the range of acceptable means has been narrowed, although the means have not yet been agreed upon. If someone else can now suggest a *means* that is satisfactory to the group, he may become the emergent leader—or the previously designated leader may utilize his idea.

Leaders both conform to group norms and yet frequently alter them, or try to, by an exercise of influence. If a leader tries to go beyond the limits established for him, he is likely to be deserted or expelled from the group, as Knickerbocker (1948) so cogently described. The limits set for one individual are not necessarily the same as the limits for any other member of the group. Hollander (1958, 1967) has done research in reasons for differentiated expectancies, and concluded that the leader's job requires that he understand the expectations held for him. In Hollander's terminology, the leader must understand how much "idiosyncrasy credit" he has with the group. Anderson (1967) used the term "social credit" for a similar idea.

WHY HAVE LEADERS?

The question of why people, in many instances not only willingly but eagerly, legitimize others to make decisions or to take actions that affect them is indeed a rational one. It seems particularly interesting in a democratic society. To understand the phenomenon, we must look at the coping behaviors of individuals, at routine and ritual vs. situations of change, and at what happens when problems arise.

The Anomaly of Leaders in a Democracy

The leadership process requires a relationship in which one role clearly has more status than another. As was described in Chapter 1, status has to do with regard and other rewards. In the most informal of groups, the individual who, occasionally, emerges as a leader usually is held in higher regard than one who never has followers even on a temporary basis.

If all situations were routine, there might be no need for people to behave in other than ritual fashion. Life is uncomplicated when situations are similar to those experienced previously, because we can behave as we did then, and can expect the response from our environment to be the same. Any social institution specifies ritual behaviors so that people within its agencies hold similar expectations for each other.

However, in Chapter 5 we discussed social change, whether planned or unplanned, at the institutional level. It was pointed out that change causes people to feel threatened and anxious. Whether a proposed change is in the self, in a social system of which one is a part, in a cultural system, or in an institution, the effects of threat and anxiety are felt.

Even though no change is planned, unplanned change occurs. It, too, has the effect of inducing anxiety and threat. It often arrives in unexpected forms, and the earlier example of what happened to the Inca civilization illustrates the dangers when there are no provisions for communicating or handling the unexpected. The job of leading requires handling the unexpected, helping others to accommodate to unplanned change, and implementing planned change, or innovation.

Innovation
Among those who maintain that leaders must be implementers of planned change are three stalwarts of school administration, Campbell, Lipham, and Lonsdale. Campbell (1971) averred that the administrator must originate action for others if he or she is to be also a leader. Lipham (1964) viewed leading (innovating) as the antithesis of administering (maintaining). Lonsdale (1964) carefully stressed the two facets of the leader's job—leading and administering.

DEFINITION. Innovation is a process by which new outputs, or techniques that affect those outputs, are introduced into a social system (Nelson, 1968). Innovation results in new capability for the system, and it includes more than invention. It can include finding a new source of students; a managerial concept such as team teaching; the reallocation of resources into machine time rather than human labor, as in Computer Assisted Instruction; or an organizational concept such as continuous student progress. It includes, but is not limited to, the "filching of ideas" advocated by Barnard (1946). Hägerstrand (1968) hypothesized that innovative individuals are attracted to areas that use their talents, and that "centers of innovation" are thus created, and there is some evidence of this in some of the free and alternative schools as well as in certain "lighthouse" school districts.

Berelson and Steiner (1964, pp. 613–619) reported that numerous researchers have found that innovation *is* possible, and they listed several significant propositions regarding it. Coch and French (1948) reported some guidelines for innovators suggested by their research in industry, and these were reiterated in the film *Overcoming Resistance to Change* (1962).

RESISTANCE. That there is resistance, often massive, to change is indisputable. Change seems to threaten people, and as mentioned earlier, can induce anxiety or stress. A leader must know how to minimize resistance to change. Such resistance can be diagnosed, and must be, for the leader's well-being. The risks that the leader always experiences are magnified when changes are resisted and the causes remain unidentified.

An individual may be a capable administrator, in the sense of maintaining the status quo, without giving thought to innovation. The administrator who does give thought to innovation and is able to implement it becomes a leader. The innovative group member may become an emergent leader. The wise status leader makes use of this and other coping behaviors of individuals in the solution of group and individual problems.

Problem Solving

When change occurs unexpectedly, when a situation needs changing and settled routines are not adequate to produce the change, or when change occurs that evokes doubt and uncertainty, problems for the organization occur.

A problem is a deviation from some pre-set standard of performance; an *imbalance between what should be and what is* happening. A problem can be either urgent or not pressing, temporary or long range. It can be trivial or of great consequence. It can affect one individual, several, or all of the members of an organization or unit. The job of leading includes handling problems. Emery (1970) included solving problems as one of five major areas of concern to "The Compleat Manager."

Livingston (1971) said that one of the greatest weaknesses In the preparation of managers has been the failure to teach them how to *identify* problems. However, many leaders who identify problems either do not solve them, try ineffective "solutions," or take actions that actually magnify the problems. Kepner and Tregoe (1965) described and have conducted workshops on how to "specify" a problem. The leader needs to be able to specify a consequential problem, analyze it (see Glossary), find alternatives, consider the possible consequences of each alternative, choose the "best" alternative, and implement it with action.

To solve problems intelligently, the leader needs to understand the behaviors that he or she and others use to cope with situations and problems. Leaders are needed to help others to cope.

Helping Others to Cope

When individuals encounter situations they can respond with either approach strategies, avoidance strategies, or accommodation mechanisms.

APPROACH STRATEGIES. Approach strategies, successfully completed, usually lead to satisfaction as a need-disposition. Such strategies include adapting routine or ritual to the situation, choosing a "solution" that seems adequate for handling the situation and implementing it, considering alternatives and selecting the "best," seeking help from another person, or asking a group (the ubiquitous committee!) to consider alternatives and recommend a course of action. In using these strategies, one may persuade, cajole, or coerce others depending on style and power differentials. Bass, in his staggering compendium on leadership (1960), said:

> Members with ability relevant to solving the group's problems (but not too much ability) are likely to persuade others success-fully. . . . Members, by virtue of their position [sic] or personal attributes, may also have the power to reward or punish others directly. The promise of reward or threat of punishment can be used to coerce others successfully. When the promise or threat is made to come from the group or is used in limited restrictive ways, the leadership is permissive. But both coercion and permis-sion require power [p. 36].

AVOIDANCE STRATEGIES. Avoidance strategies are forms of need-disposition that result from situations in which individuals feel frus-trated. Those strategies include flight, either physical or psychologi-cal—in the form of withdrawal into fantasy, substitute activity, or drug use; head-in-sand, or "ignore it and it will go away"; and passing the buck. Flight is an extreme form of coping, and either physical or psychological flight from the problems of an organization is not possible, on a sustained basis, for one who wishes to retain a position in the organization. The head-in-sand technique undoubt-edly works for some individuals with some situations, and could per-haps be used to advantage more often than it is. However, there are some situations and some problems that just do not vanish re-gardless of how long one waits. When the buck is passed, it must eventually stop somewhere and that usually is with the designated leader.

Leaders often can help those individuals who are using either approach or avoidance strategies in coping with the situations they encounter, but some persons use neither, resorting instead to accom-modation mechanisms.

ACCOMMODATION MECHANISMS. A person may develop some psychological mechanism as his need-disposition response mode in situations that he finds unsatisfying or downright frustrating. The mechanism may become the individual's habitual means of accom-modating to the lack of satisfaction if an unsatisfying situation must be faced repeatedly. Symptoms of accommodation, such as apathy, submission, or unaccustomed forgetfulness, should be considered warning signs to the leader, who should know enough about the mechanisms to detect their presence. The forms of such mechanisms will be listed in Chapter 8, in the section on Feedback, as they are among the important dynamics of leadership.

Then group members may cope with problems by following others because it requires less effort, because they are persuaded, or because they have been coerced. A leader makes use of this follower propensity, regardless of his or her personal style.

The leader who possesses power may, if he is not sure of his solution, say, in effect, "Right or wrong, do it my way, or else. . . ." Such an individual usually prides himself on his decision-making ability, and may boast, "I may be wrong, but I'm never in doubt!"

Shopping for solutions—seeking alternatives—may be a joint effort, and it is here that group members may make real contributions. This is one of the times when the leader "has to be stupid enough to listen" and may be "a mere channel of communication, and a filcher of ideas." Systems analysis is a sophisticated means of shopping for solutions, and some systems can be simulated in advance.

Leaders also are needed to resolve conflicts that arise, and ways of doing this will be discussed in Chapter 8.

WHEN LEADERS FUNCTION

One of several writers who stressed that leadership is a functional interaction process among the leader, the group members, and the situation was Adair (1968). He said that the overlapping areas of leader responsibility arc the task, team maintenance, and individual needs. He overlooked innovation. We choose to look at individual needs and innovation in terms of the uncertainty that every individual feels at times, the dependence-independence conflict that is within us all, the differences between leaders' and followers' need-dispositions, and the possession or control of means for satisfying needs.

Conditions of Uncertainty

Leaders function when people are uncertain. Brown (1966) observed that an organization needs no direction when there is but one clear-cut way to go. A leader functions when there are choices to be made by or for a group. Ginzberg (1966, p. 115) said that the leader's goals are always personal. Presthus (1962) pointed out that leaders function when others must be shaken out of complacency. Sexton (1961, p. 233) made an eloquent plea for finding a place for educational reformers because there is a need for their advocacy of causes—even unpopular ones. Leaders function when they have causes to champion. By advocacy, a leader reduces the uncertainty of others who are less sure of personal and organizational direction.

Uncertainty is reduced by the provision of information. We have referred repeatedly to the nature of information. If we say "You are now reading a book," we have provided you, the reader, with no information, because you already knew that. You are *not* completely certain what "educational leadership" is, however, or you would not be reading this book, so it may provide you with information.

Each of us is willing to make another an "instant authority" when our uncertainty is great enough. For example, if one is in a strange city one may ask the first stranger he meets, "Where is the nearest post office?" If the questioned gives the questioner directions which are followed, note that the visitor has:

— set a goal (and *means*—walking or riding—are presumably available)
— chosen a leader, and
— set limits of the leader's authority

all because he or she was uncertain!

When Some Need to be Dependent

Everyone from early childhood faces conflicts in that one strives at times to be independent but at other times seeks individuals who will make decisions or take actions for one. Specialization and division of labor in educational agencies cause each individual to be increasingly responsible for others in one's area of competence. Thus, a leader functions when she or he knows more about the task at hand than do others. This is well illustrated by the fact that most individuals shift from follower role to leader role and back again to follower many times in the ongoing activities of an organization. Most status leaders find themselves taking back seats when it is obvious that someone else knows more about the matter under discussion or the problem being solved.

Leaders function in times of crisis, from the local flood or blizzard to the pressing national emergency. They function when someone is expected to be responsible and they are more willing to accept responsibility than are others. Emergent leaders become visible when status leaders abdicate, fail to act, or lack necessary expertise.

But some individuals seem perpetually to seek dependency status, looking to leaders as surrogate fathers. The status leader's well-being requires that he understand the implications of prolonged dependence, and he should make every effort, short of outright rejection, to discourage such a relationship.

In summarizing the lesson taught by a wonderfully effective allegory, Leavitt (1964) pointed out that:

> *To the extent that dependency yields ready satisfaction of existing needs that one cannot satisfy independently—to that extent one's feelings are likely to be positive, friendly, affectionate, protective, grateful, and one is likely to develop strong social needs. To the extent that dependency does not satisfy, but rather*

frustrates—to that extent one is likely to develop feelings of anger and hostility and to wish more strongly for independence and autonomy, to develop strong egoistic needs [p. 21].

Leaders function when they possess or control the means necessary to satisfy the need-dispositions of others as well as of themselves.

When Need-Dispositions are Served

One of the basic manifestations of an individual's need-dispositions may be seen in his orientation as either local or cosmopolitan (see earlier discussion, pp. 24–25). However, designation of the person as one or the other accomplishes little in terms of distinguishing the need-dispositions of leaders from those of followers, since both leaders and followers may be found among those of both orientations.

Fiedler (1967), Hersey and Blanchard (1969), and Schroeter (1970) all postulated certain beliefs about what constitutes *effective* leader behavior, that is, performance that matches the expectations of followers. Nelson (1969) reported a modest bit of research, with a very limited population, to the effect that leaders, whether liked or less liked, display certain similarities of behavior. We hypothesize that similarities include these need-dispositions:

NEED-DISPOSITIONS

Leaders	Followers
Like to structure their own activities	Like to have their activities structured for them
Take responsibility for themselves and others	Let others take responsibility for them
Enjoy the exercise of authority (or power)	Prefer to submit to authority
Actively advocate "causes"	Involve themselves in others' causes, if active at all
Anticipate others' reactions in given situations	React without analyzing "why"

If these hypotheses bear up under examination, then it would appear that leaders function when they feel strongly enough about preferred outcomes to seize the initiative. Certainly they function when they possess or control the means of need-satisfaction.

Controlling the Means of Need-Satisfaction

One of the most beautifully succinct statements of when leaders function was made by Knickerbocker (1948):

> *To cut through the diverse usage which has been made of the term "leader," we might say that to the extent that any individual succeeds in collecting an actual following, he does so because he controls means.*

The means referred to are, of course, means of need-satisfaction. Some of the means of need-satisfaction which the leader may possess or control include:

In the Formal Organization	**In the Informal Group**
a job	approval
a pay raise	opportunities for social interaction
fringe benefits	access to influential persons
a promotion	skilled assistance
approval	fellowship
improved work conditions	recognition
recognition (title, status)	praise
praise	
tools or other resources	
freedom to perform tasks in one's own way	
security	
a part in decision-making	
improved communication	
a change in interpersonal relationships	
access to learning opportunities	

The effect of the possession or control of means is to get compliance with what the leader wishes. If others believe that he can give or get them what they want, can prevent loss or reduction of their need-satisfiers, or can prevent frustration, they will allow him to function as their leader.

However, every member of a group and every leader has limits to his behavior which the group will not permit him to exceed. Those limits may well depend on the amount of "idiosyncrasy credit" that the individual has (Hollander, 1958; Knight, 1971). Leaders function effectively when they are aware of and accept as legitimate the expectations of group members, yet they sometimes utilize authority and power to change those expectations.

In any case, though, the leader is comparable to a bus driver. He functions when his passengers perceive him as taking them where they want to go. If he changes his destination, those who do not wish to go along either get off, get him to reconsider, or get a new driver.

WHERE LEADERS FUNCTION

Leaders function in situations. Mockler (1971) laid claim to having coined the phrase "situational theory of management," yet acknowledged that the concept is not new. He gave an excellent review of recent writings in management, all of which stressed situational or contingency approaches. Mockler also pointed out that Drucker was using an essentially situational approach as early as 1954!

The situational aspect of leadership was clearly evident in the question by Punch and Ducharme (1972, p. 67); "What kind of leader behavior is most effective with what kind of group for what kind of task?" We will not attempt to answer that question here, but it is sufficient to indicate that leaders function in situations that involve groups—in social systems. The manner in which they function will be explored in Chapter 8.

Social Systems

In Chapter 4 it was pointed out that any system is characterized by unity of purpose and interdependence of parts, and Chapter 5 discussed the implications of the fact that every person has simultaneous membership in a variety of social systems. Leaders, both status and emergent, function in any social system *so long as the system itself is functioning.*

If workers in a factory, for example, deliberately set about slowdown or sabotage of production, unity of purpose is lost and the organization temporarily is not a system. On the other hand, if a group of young people unacquainted with each other set out to organize a summer playground program, they temporarily become a system.

Every system has *inputs,* there is some *process* in which interdependence is essential, and there are one or more *outputs.* If there is to be change to improve or better the system, *feedback* is also a system essential. Feedback relates to whether the output measures up to some pre-set standard.

The *core elements* of an organized educational system are the people who work in it. Barnard (1938) was among the first to view an organization as a social system. The social systems of an educational organization may be found in a classroom, an office, an entire building, an entire campus, or on a network of campuses—as, for example, in California's system of state colleges—or in an entire branch of military service.

At each system level, *inputs* consist of role expectations and individual behaviors. The process is one of social exchange, where each individual gets something in return for something he gives. The *outputs* consist of a service (provision of learning opportunities), maintenance of the organization, and satisfiers of individual needs. Meaningful *feedback,* the purpose of which is to validate or change the process or the inputs, may relate to (1) how satisfactory are the learning opportunities provided, (2) how well organizational needs are being met, or (3) how well the needs of individuals are being met.

It may be apropos to point out here that, at the instructor-student level of social system, the student is a participator in the sense of social exchange, *not* just a bit of human "material" essential to the organization. At this level, the instructor is the status leader, and functions by the same means and in the same manner as leaders in larger social systems!

Leaders function in social systems through the use of influence, authority, or power (or a combination of all three) in the social exchange process. Lerbinger (1965) seems to have originated the idea of influence as currency.

Social Exchange
Each individual in an organization sees it as in some way helping him. Homans (1950) developed the first systematic theory of social behavior as an exchange process. One joins an organization because it can do things that he cannot do alone, or can do them better than he could do alone. One is expected to give effort, performance, and loyalty. He or she expects to get pay, status, and security, and to do a job the parameters of which are known. A leader's job is to get others to do their jobs, to achieve organizational goals which she or he is ever-attempting to improve, and to satisfy individual needs.

In the exchange process, the leader provides direction. He sometimes gives rewards, at other times punishments. The leader tries to achieve conformity to job expectations from others. The currency

TABLE 6-1
THE USE OF SOCIAL EXCHANGE CURRENCY

WHEN THE CURRENCY IS	THE FOLLOWER		THE LEADER	
Influence	Gives:	Some change of action, inaction, or belief	Gets:	Someone to do something he or she desired
	Gets:	Reduction of uncertainty	Gives:	Direction
Authority	Gives:	Someone else the right to make decisions or take actions that affect him or her	Gets:	Legitimization to make certain decisions or take certain actions
	Gets:	Relief from responsibility	Gives:	Direction
Power	Gives:	Obedience or conformity	Gets:	Conformity to her or his wishes
	Gets:	Reward or punishment	Gives:	Direction *and* reward or punishment

that he uses consists of influence, authority, or power, as illustrated in Table 6-1. There are, however, limits within which he must function.

Limits on Leaders
Leaders function within limits prescribed for them. Limits sometimes are prescribed by superordinates, and the same or different limits are validated by peers and followers.

Earlier in this chapter, we suggested that there are four distinct and identifiable phases of the leadership process, namely: (1) goals are set that are acceptable to group members in that they are achievable, (2) a leader's authority is legitimized, (3) the means for goal achievement are agreed upon, and (4) limits of the leader's authority are fixed.

GOAL LIMITS. The ratification of goals is, itself, a limitation. Once ratified, goals cannot be changed unless group members reratify. The means for getting them to do that will be discussed in the section How Leaders Lead.

The amount and extent of authority that followers are willing to grant to a leader depend on both the leader and the situation.

PERSONAL LIMITS. It is well known and easily observable that in almost any group, the limits of behavior tolerated for one individual may be quite different than those for another. Hollander (1958) hypothesized that each group member has group-awarded idiosyncrasy credit that can be accumulated and then "spent in idiosyncratic behavior before group sanctions are applied." He speculated that credit accumulates according to:

— the individual's performance on group tasks
— his group-approved characteristics (even though they may be task-irrelevant)
— the recency of past idiosyncratic behavior
— the length of time the person has been a member of the group.

To combine all of these in one illustration, let us imagine two members of the same group. The first does his job well, is enthusiastic and outgoing, is a "straight arrow," and has been in the organization for ten years. The second barely meets minimal job requirements, is a surly "loner," is repeatedly on the carpet for nonconforming behavior, and has been in the organization for six months. Now, suppose that both commit the same offense. With which will the group be more severe? Or look at it another way. Suppose both are *appointed* department heads in the same organization, and that they agree to make certain changes in both departments. Which will find the changes easier to implement? Leaders function within the limits of their group-accorded idiosyncrasy credit.

SITUATIONAL LIMITS. There could be situational limits which bear on idiosyncrasy credit. If a hunting party became lost in the Canadian north woods, individuals might willingly follow for many painful miles an acknowledged woodsman who would not be trusted for directions to the nearest pharmacy back home! Leaders function within situational limits.

If the situation is one in which the leader can exhibit competence, he will be able to make a deposit to his banked idiosyncrasy credit. Any situation that shows his incompetence will result in a withdrawal of credit. When the balance is exhausted, group sanctions will be imposed.

However, an abundance of credits only allows an individual to display idiosyncratic credit if he or she chooses; it does not automatically make one a leader.

HOW LEADERS LEAD
Leaders lead by influencing others. Knickerbocker (1948) said there are four methods of doing this: force, paternalism, bargaining, and the provision of mutual means. He said the appointed leader is not free to choose among them, that his method is prescribed by the

policies of the organization. Frank (1954) discussed the dynamics in his *How to Be a Modern Leader.* The U.S. Military Academy, in the two-volume set *Military Leadership,* joined theories relating traits, situational effects, and group dynamics to explain the phenomenon of how leaders lead. Drucker (1967) said that leaders exercise right over might. Many writers have taken the approach that leaders lead through rational appeal to followers. That is a normative approach, and ours is a bit different.

It is evident from reading about leaders throughout history that some have indeed influenced followers by rational means, but many, many others have successfully used emotional means. Influence can result from either.

The Currency of Exchange Used

We said earlier that the leader uses the currency of influence, authority, and power in his social exchange with others. Let us consider some examples.

INFLUENCE. Influence is a relationship in which one individual affects the thoughts or attitudes of another. The reader of this book may conceivably be influenced by it. If his thoughts are affected by the logic of our arguments, the influence is rational. If his pulse is quickened because his emotions are appealed to—if, for example, he sees a way to utilize some insight in exploiting others for his own gain—then the influence is emotional. The influence of a John Dewey was rational, while that of a Max Rafferty is largely emotional.

AUTHORITY. Authority is another form of influence, and it, too, comes in botn guises. Authority is a relationship in which one person accepts as reasonable the unquestioned right of another or a group to make decisions or take actions that affect him. If the reason for legitimization is due to what the leader *is* or can *do,* the authority is rational. If the acceptance is based in what the follower feels for the leader or what the latter represents, the authority is emotional. Thus, the individual who obeys the policeman out of recognition that he can protect cedes to him rational authority. The professor who sees a colleague as a father figure may grant to him authority that is emotional in nature.

POWER. Still another form of influence, and of authority, is power. It is a relationship in which one individual can impose sanctions on another. Since sanctions involve hope or fear, there is always an emotional element in power. It is difficult to perceive of power as having a purely rational basis.

Leading Through Communicating

Communication is a process through which an individual receives a sense impression of another. Leaders lead by communicating. There is no way that influence, authority, or power can be utilized without some form of communication.

There must be a *system* in order for communication to occur. There must be unity of purpose and interdependence of parts. The input is a message originated by a sender, the process is transmittal from one to another (a medium), the output is a message to a receiver, and feedback indicates whether it has been received, the intended meaning given it, and its purpose served. The interdependent parts are sender, message, medium, receiver, and feedback. If any one of them is missing, the system cannot function properly.

Many educational leaders try to lead by utilizing only one-way communication. For many purposes, it will not work. Without feedback, there is no way of knowing:

1. Did the message get to its intended receiver? Did it get lost? Did the medium break down?
2. Did the medium allow "high fidelity" reproduction of the signal? Was it obscured or changed by "static" somewhere?
3. Was the signal attended? Is the purpose of the message being served, fretted about, or ignored? Did the message automatically go into "File 13" because it neither induced nor reduced uncertainty in the receiver?

Communication is the basis for perception.

Effects of Perception

The leader leads by understanding perception—his own and others'. He learns that everyone has a *perceptual screen* through which he filters all sensory stimuli. No sensory stimulus is ever identical for any two individuals.

The importance of perception has been recognized for years—certainly since the days of the Hawthorne experiments. It was the perception that others cared about what they were doing that caused Hawthorne plant workers to be more productive. Roethlisberger (1968) has been particularly concerned with the effects of perception on communication. He stated that it is the situation to which words refer that is important to the receiver, not the words themselves. A touch, a motion, a posture, an artifact, words, time, color, or space—any of these has meaning only as individuals give it meaning.

Sherif (1967) and others have noted that as people work together over time their perceptions and interpretations tend to become more and more alike. Leaders lead by learning the effects that individuals' perceptual screens have on what they see as system inputs, as the social exchange process, as system outputs, and as the communications network.

At best, a leader faces risk. He can reduce it by understanding perception.

Risk as a Concomitant

Leaders lead by exposing themselves to risk. They continue to lead by knowing how much risk they can afford. The leader new to a situation may have little idiosyncrasy credit. If a superintendent was appointed, his authority may not as yet be legitimized by subordinates. If he has little or no power and his position is important to him, he cannot afford to take much risk. If, on the other hand, he was elected chairman of a committee and he does not care whether he maintains that role or not, he perhaps can afford a high degree of risk.

Byrd (1971) related the matter of how much risk managers can afford to take to their power bases. He also provided a ten-item checklist by means of which a manager could assess the strength of his power base which could easily be adapted for use by an educational leader.

Twelve "functions of managing" were identified by Brown (R. E., 1966), and there are elements of risk in each. For example, the first was "Purposes and Objectives," and it is apparent that if the leader has preferred outcomes of his own, there is the risk that followers will not accept them. If the leader is a "filcher of ideas," the same risk may exist, plus the risk that the leader could become known as a person who never had an idea of his own. Whatever their source, purposes and objectives are a potential for risk until they are accepted by a group.

Leaders lead by recognizing that risk "comes with the territory." We said earlier that both influence and authority have components of rationality, while power does not. One of the greatest sources of risk lies in a leader's assumption of social rationality. Only recently have behavioral scientists begun to examine this assumption; that if ". . . scientists could ascertain relevant facts, the truth would prevail [Smith, 1969, p. 370]." Smith suggested that there are four "indispensable ingredients of rationality, each acquired through childhood socialization." Obviously, many persons have not acquired the optimum in childhood socialization and we are left with the frightening realization that many persons lack the "indispensable ingredients" of rationality. Indeed, Simon (1957, pp. 61–78), for one, said that the assumption is unfounded and that man is not a rational animal except on infrequent and self-serving occasions. If these men are correct, as we believe them to be, then more leaders lead by appealing to emotions than by appealing to rationality.

Leaders lead by assuming responsibility, and responsibility is attended by risk. Ginzberg (1966) said:

> *For the top executive, the sharing of responsibility is impossi-*
> *ble. He must make his decisions, change them if necessary, but*
> *he must live with them. If his calculations go awry he cannot*
> *place the blame on others. Nor has he anything to gain by pass-*
> *ing the buck, for failure leaves him vulnerable. If a general loses*
> *a campaign, or a high command loses a war, they have lost it*
> *and must suffer the consequences no matter who else has failed.*
> *Even the master propagandist, Hitler, was unable to shift the*
> *blame for Germany's defeat in World War I [sic] from Ludendorff*
> *and the high command to labor and the bourgeoisie [p. 115].*

Leaders lead by behaving in characteristic fashions called *style.*

Leader Style

The matter of style has been of considerable interest to behavioral scientists in recent years. We will give it fuller treatment in Chapter 11, but will here consider some elements which seem to affect, if not determine, style. These are hypotheses only, and have not been tested.

SOURCE OF AUTHORITY. What one perceives as the source of his authority seems to affect his style. If he views his authority as a concomitant of his status, he is likely to be *autocratic.* If he sees authority as something given him by superordinates, he will act in *bureaucratic fashion.* If authority is perceived as legitimization by subordinates, the leader may be *democratic.* If he sees authority as resulting from the manipulation of people's emotions, he may be *demogogic.* If authority is seen as a rare commodity genetically endowed for the benefit of self and friends, he may be *oligarchic.* If it is believed to be due to privileged information, to be used in bargaining situations, he probably will be *paternalistic.* If authority is perceived as coming from logic and fact, or as an attribute of skills he can demonstrate, its user may be *rationalistic.* If authority comes from a power greater than man, then the leader may be *theocratic* in approach.

Style is a characteristic manner of behaving, and probably no one behaves in characteristic fashion at all times, in all of his social systems, or in all situations. However, we believe that the perceived sources and uses of influence, authority, and power do affect how leaders lead.

MODE OF COMMUNICATION. We further hypothesize that the leader's perceptions of these matters will be reflected in his choice of modes of communication and the purposes for which he communicates. For example, the autocrat probably uses one-way paper communication for the purpose of getting compliance or conformity. The democratic stylist may utilize two-way or many-way face-to-face communication to assure constant reaffirmation of his authority.

AUTHENTICITY. Whatever the style, a leader leads by being authentic. Most writers aver that authenticity is a word difficult to define and a state impossible to describe. The concept will be discussed in some detail in Chapter 12.

SUMMARY

The leader's role always involves expectations regarding an authority relationship, and reasons for acknowledgement include possession or control of means, relative degree of uncertainty, and ego-involvement.

In our society, leaders may lead either because of relative status in an organization or because personal authority helps one to be an emergent leader in certain situations. "Good" status leaders often utilize the talents of emergent leaders to supplement their own. Both types function through influencing others. The skills necessary to influence others have been widely discussed and are in the process of being identified.

Leadership is a process of social interaction or exchange, in which each person gives certain things for something in return. In the interaction, someone (perhaps the leader) administers (maintains the status quo) and leaders innovate and try to meet individuals' needs. While some writers have seen the activities as mutually exclusive, they cannot be, and all occur in organizations where the leadership process transpires.

Acceptance of leaders depends on a legitimization of authority, which can have any of several bases.

A leader must be able to understand and interpret observable behavior, and there are many bases for doing this. The leadership process, however, *always* includes

— the acceptance of group goals
— the legitimization of authority
— agreement on means of achieving goals
— the setting of limits of authority.

Leaders function and indeed are necessary, even in a democratic society, because:

— not all situations can be handled by routine, ritualized behavior
— change is inevitable
— change brings problems
— the coping behaviors of individuals vary greatly.

Leaders function when individuals face uncertainties, when others prefer to be dependent and they wish to be independent, and in times of crisis. However, prolonged and forced dependency can have frustrating and fearsome effects, even on the most passive individuals. Leaders function also when their need-dispositions are reciprocals of those of followers or when they possess or control the means of need-satisfaction.

Leaders function in social systems in special situations, and always within group-set limits.

Leaders lead others through the use of influence, authority, or power. There are emotional components of all three of these "denominations" of social exchange currency, and rational components of the first two. Leaders lead by using both types of components. Either type is exercised only through a communication system, in which perception plays a vital part. Risk attends the process of leadership, but style and authenticity are the essence.

SOME SUGGESTED RESOURCES

J. Adair, *Training for leadership.* London: McDonald & Co., 1968.

B. M. Bass, *Leadership, psychology and organizational behavior.* New York: Harper & Row, 1960.

P. Drucker, *The effective executive.* New York: Harper & Row, 1967.

F. E. Fiedler, *Theory of leadership effectiveness.* New York: McGraw-Hill, 1967.

C. A. Gibb, Leadership: Psychological aspects. In D. L. Sills (Ed.) *International encyclopedia of the social sciences.* New York: Macmillan, 1968. Vol. 9, pp. 91–100.

E. Ginzberg, Leaders and leadership. Ch. 9 in *The development of human resources.* New Pork: McGraw-Hill, 1966. Pp. 109–121.

A. W. Halpin, *Theory and research in administration.* New York: Macmillan, 1966. Pp. 253–279.

Overcoming resistance to change (film). Beverly Hills, Calif.: Roundtable, 1962.

A. Zaleznik, *The human dilemmas of leadership.* New York: Harper & Row, 1966.

CHAPTER 7

THE LOCUS OF LEADERSHIP

> But if leadership is anything determinate, we should know
> how to distinguish its presence from its absence; similarly, if
> there are some social situations that especially require
> leadership, we should know how to tell them apart from other
> social situations.
>
> —Selznick

If leadership is a process comprised of actions of leading and of
administering, then leadership occurs where the essentials of leading and of administering are present and does not occur where some
of those essentials are missing. The process can occur only where
there are people whose motivations impel them to lead, since leadership is *expected* of persons who hold positions of headship in all
of the myriad agencies of education.

The actions of *leading* constitute one vital part of the leadership
process, but certain essentials must exist if the actions are to occur.
The actions aim at the goals of *innovating* and *meeting individuals'
needs*.

ESSENTIALS FOR LEADING

A group will allow an individual to lead if he or she is perceived
as contributing significantly to a particular situation, according to
Wiles (1967). Individuals have differing functional capabilities, and
thus a particular relationship (differential ranking, or status) is one
of the essentials for leading.

Status

An individual must enjoy a particular status in a group if one is to influence other group members. That status is usually accorded an individual because of one's possession or control of means for achieving goals or satisfying the needs of individuals. Innovation in group tasks and need-satisfaction of individuals in a group require that most or all of the other group members submit to the influence of one or a few.

The most common reason for submitting to influence is that an individual has the authority of position, or wields power. However, status often is accorded an individual because he or she has a personal influence or authority, even without power. More about authority follows, but status cannot exist without some kind of structure.

Structure

People form groups to do those things they cannot do alone, or to do them better than could be done alone. Groups, or social systems, function through structure, which is the second essential for leading.

Informal groups have a looser structuralization than do formal organizations, but some structure still is necessary. Leaders function in informal social systems in much the same fashion as in formal, and in either the would-be leader must have a status within the system that allows him or her to influence others.

In formal groups, structure is likely to take the form of rigid organization, even though flexible organization might serve as well or better for most situations. The person with status sufficient to influence is likely to be a person designated as an administrator, and to appear higher in the hierarchy than those whom he influences. Nevertheless, as was pointed out in Chapter 4, there is an informal organization within every formal organization which may greatly affect patterns of influence.

All of the educational agencies previously discussed (except for *the self*) whether informal, nonformal, or formal, have some degree of structure. Leadership can and does occur in all of them, although Hughes and Hughes (1973) raised some serious generalized questions about past and present *school* leaders, charging ineptitude at the local level, power-grabbing by the states, congressional shifts in policy, and fierce internal disputes at the USOE. Subsequent cutbacks of federal funds by former president Richard Nixon posed further problems for would-be school leaders.

Research with a limited population sample, as reported by Nelson (1969), supported the assumption that in a group some individuals tend to become leaders and others to become followers, thus giving structure to groups. It seems that these tendencies either cause or result from the group process of social exchange, depending on one's point of view. Tessin (1972) substantiated this in a university setting.

Social Exchange

The process in which all groups engage is a form of social exchange in which the currency of influence, authority, and power is used, as was discussed in Chapter 6. Kimbrough (1968) is among the several writers who aver that leadership is a phenomenon growing out of the dynamics of social systems and cannot occur outside such systems. Social exchange is the third essential for leading, as no one can either bring about change or meet the needs of others unless she or he can give something to the group and get something different in return. The process must admit of a certain amount of flexibility.

Flexibility

If the structure is so rigid that no modification can be made, or if the process of social exchange is so ritualized that no deviations are possible, the leadership process cannot occur, because leadership implies and demands innovation and change. Thus, at least a degree of flexibility is a requirement for leading. The leader himself must be somewhat flexible, too, and any individual who is not will be unable to lead a dynamic organization. He will not be able to countenance change for himself, for other group members, or for the organization.

The second vital part of the leadership process is found in the actions of *administering,* namely, those aimed at the goals of *production* (the provision of learning opportunities) and *maintaining the organization.* Thus, a place in which leadership can occur must provide the essentials for both leading and administering. Leadership also requires that individuals with certain need-dispositions and motivations be present, and its exercise is *expected* of certain position-holders in organizational settings.

ESSENTIALS FOR ADMINISTERING

The actions of administering in a public agency (or *managing* in an agency in a private sector) are those of *producing* and of *maintaining the organization.* Producing in a school or college means providing learning opportunities. Maintaining the organization requires maintaining qualified personnel and resources and coordinating them sufficiently to provide learning opportunities. Either set of actions requires recognition by all social system members that certain of them have the unquestioned right to make some decisions or take some actions that affect all. This is recognition of authority or power. Authority or power then is an essential wherever administration is to occur. McDavid and Harari (1968) made the point that social power is essential to leadership, although their definitions are a bit different from ours.

Basis for Authority or Power

Influence is a relationship between persons and, as such, can be either subtle and unrecognized or overt. Its basis can be either rational or emotional in nature, as was pointed out in Chapter 6. Influence maybe a concomitant of administering, but it is not an essential.

Authority is always recognized, either openly or tacitly. Thus, it is a relationship between persons, not an attribute of one. If the reason for recognition is because of what the authority figure *is* or *can do,* the basis for authority is rational. If recognition is because of what one *feels* about the authority figure or what he represents, the basis is emotional. With either basis, the authority relationship is an essential for administering.

Power always involves the capability of one individual to impose sanctions on another, and the emotions of hope or fear. Thus, its basis is emotional in nature. Power *is* a personal attribute, and often accompanies authority, although power sometimes exists without authority (as, for example, when one individual has a weapon and another does not, or when a policeman can extort money for "protection" from arrest). In neither case is power an essential of administering, although it often reinforces the authority which *is* essential.

Positional Authority

As early as 1922, Weber was describing two types of legal-rational authority. Positional authority has been in the conceptual realm of most persons from their first acquaintance with an organization in which statuses were differentiated, and the idea was explicated in admirable detail by Barnard (1938).

Sergiovanni and Carver (1973, pp. 154–174) discussed "Authority and the School Executive," in reference to the positional authority of the school principal. Clear and Seager (1971) reported on "The Legitimacy of Administrative Influence [sic, i.e., authority] as Perceived by Selected Groups." Positional authority is an essential for administering, and it flows downward from the top through all levels of an organization. It always exists where there is a hierarchy of positions, although it may be more or less nominal unless supplemented by personal authority.

Personal Authority

The ascribed right of an individual to make decisions or to take actions that affect others is recognized as authentic by subordinates only if they find in the positional authority figure: (1) a credible basis for personal authority, or (2) a power capability.

Personal authority flows upward from followers to an acknowledged leader, giving him a particular status within the group. Thus, personal authority is an essential not only for administering, but for leading. It may have either a physical or a psychological basis. Authority stems from such physical qualities as blood ("royal lines"), appearance, voice, skin color, size, strength, skill, and tone or quality of voice. Contrived appearance, as represented by war paint, cosmetics, or the garb of religious, military, or academic figures may also contribute to or confirm personal authority or serve as the badge of positional authority.

A credible psychological basis for authority may be found in an emotional regard based on admiration, affection or liking, or love; on identification with a cause, an organization, or a familiar figure; on moral integrity; or on persuasive ability. The latter is of particular importance in the matter of *advocacy,* a discussion of which follows later in this chapter. Regard also may be due to such rational factors as demonstrated physical or intellectual ability or knowledge, commitment or dedication to a cuase ("the true believer"), commitment to an organization ("the organization man"), to courage, to social prestige or status, to professional accomplishment, or simply to demonstrated willingness to assume responsibility.

Less credible psychological bases for personal authority lie in such attributes as personality, name (Roosevelt, Taft, Kennedy, Rockefeller, or Ford, for example), wealth, or notoriety.

Power
Power is a relationship in which one individual has the capability to impose sanctions on another. Power often accompanies positional authority, and thus flows downward in organizations. However, Plachy (1973) exemplified the view of many in his article "Leader Power Requires the Consent of Followers," in opining that recognized personal authority must reinforce positional authority if a leader is to have maximum power in today's organizational climate. He pointed out that rebellion usually is not against authority per se, but against the way authority is used. Knickerbocker's (1948) statement of the four methods which a leader may use for directing activities of people included force, paternalism, bargaining, and mutual means. Some element of power exists in each.

The distribution of control [power] in organizations was found by Smith and Tannenbaum (1963) to be relevant to organizational effectiveness and to positive member attitudes. Another Tannenbaum (1963) suggested that authority is delegated to a leader by those who follow because of some benefit or punishment which rests on acceptance of that authority. This we would call power. Coercive power is not an essential for administering if positional authority is sufficiently reinforced by personal authority. Such power *is* an essential if personal authority is lacking. Byrd (1971) said that one derives authority from the organization; from his peers, who set limits on his authority; and from himself, when he assumes responsibility. He suggested that an individual could assess one's power base by examining the factors of company friendship, personal traits, confidence, opportunity, information, expertise, status, seniority, proprietorship, and interpersonal skills. We perceive proprietorship as a vital component of power, but all of the other factors as components of authority.

"Social power" was conceived by French and Raven (1959) as having five bases, which they called: (1) reward power, (2) coercive power, (3) legitimate power, (4) referent power, and (5) expert power. The terms seem self-explanatory, but in our context "expert power" would be seen as personal authority. All authority and any power short of absolute power must operate within group-conceded limits.

Limits

A final essential for administering is that the actions taken or decisions made by the administrator be confined within certain limits.

Among the limits are those imposed on the individual himself by the group, as discussed by Hollander (1958) in his concept of idiosyncrasy credit (see Chapter 6). It seems evident that groups do impose limits that vary with the individual, and for an administrator those limits are established through consideration of his performance on group-relevant tasks, his group-approved characteristics, the recency of his past idiosyncractic behavior, the length of his association with the group, and the amount of authority accorded him. Knight (1971) confirmed the existence of such limits in his sample of community colleges.

An administrator can extend his limits for deciding and acting on behalf of others by extending his authority. This means that promotion to a higher status position is one possible avenue, but he also can extend his personal authority through strategies such as improving his competence, knowledge, or dedication; showing more courage; or taking on more responsibility. There can be little doubt that these modes often lead to increased positional authority.

The second set of limits for administering has to do with goals and objectives. If the aims of the administrator are not in accord with those of the group: (1) one or the other must be able to dominate, (2) there must be compromises, or (3) they must agree on the new aims that please both. The coming to agreement on goals and objectives for administering is a moral imperative in our society, as Bartky (1953) indicated. Agreement has to do with the means used to achieve ends rather than with ends themselves, and Bartky argued eloquently that, with educated people, persuasion is a morally legitimate means while coercion or manipulation is not.

Institutional limits comprise a third set of limits on administering, and they are of three types. Society imposed some limits on all agencies when it institutionalized the concept of education. A particular educational agency, such as a four-year liberal arts college, establishes further limits when it decides which educational functions it will undertake. Most agencies operate under boards of control, and each board sets still more restrictive limits through its adoption and modification of policies.

If the motivations of all individuals in a training department, a boarding school, or other educational agency are such that everyone wishes to depend on someone else, then the leadership process cannot occur. An examination of motivations may indicate certain groups in which the necessary propensity for leading may be found.

MOTIVATIONS

People and relationships with people constitute the *means* that one uses for the satisfaction of his needs, as was pointed out by Knickerbocker (1948). Combining with other people allows one to do things that one could not do alone, or to do them better than one could do alone. Others possess or control money, knowledge, skills, or tools that one does not have. The individual then attempts to establish a relationship which will allow him to trade his time, knowledge, and/or skills for a share of the resources possessed or controlled by others. The needs of individuals may be widely different, and the means of their satisfaction certainly are different in most organizations—even in the simple commune described in Chapter 4. Kimbrough (1968) defined an organization as "any cooperative system in which people are able to communicate with each other and are willing to contribute action toward a conscious common purpose [p. 14]." The motivation of each person is to find a means of satisfying some need that she or he has.

Both avoidance needs and approach needs as felt by professionals in education were discussed by Sergiovanni and Carver (1973). They also reviewed a study by Sergiovanni (1967) of the applicability of Herzberg's "Motivation-Hygiene Theory" to people working in schools, in which it was found that the greatest satisfiers, from a percentage standpoint, were *achievement, recognition,* and *responsibility.* The dissatisfiers, rank-ordered by percent of appearance, were: student relations, peer relations, school policy and administration, technical supervision, and incidents in personal life. All of these have implications for the leadership process.

We believe that competent instructors in any agency at any level of education are themselves leaders who perform the same functions in the same manner and for the same reasons as do their own leaders. The classroom group, albeit formed involuntarily at the elementary or secondary level, is formed (at least in theory) to do for the individual something that he cannot do for himself, or to do it better than he can do alone.

We now need individuals who will replicate Sergiovanni's study in other schools and in other agencies of education. We also need studies of the applicability of the "Motivation-Hygiene Theory" to students at various levels. Perhaps most of them have needs, too, which can be satisfied by achievement, recognition, and responsibility. No doubt there are other students with needs which require other satisfiers, however. If the student studies were done, there might at long last be some basis for meaningful teacher evaluation, and for accountability. Teachers and other leaders have been told for generations that they must *motivate,* and arguments have proliferated over whether motivation could best be done by example, precept, exhortation, persuasion, or reinforcement. Psychology has a long history of attempts to identify structures of personality and units of motivation. That struggle is continuing, and perhaps the behavioral sciences will yet find a way to give the word motivation specificity and precision. There is little doubt that communication and perception are the keys to motivation, because it is only through them that uncertainty can be reduced.

Motivation and Information

The leadership process occurs wherever people are motivated through having their uncertainties reduced. The principal satisfiers—achievement, recognition, and responsibility—all help in some way to reduce the uncertainties of the recipients.

The editor (Sills, 1968) and publishers of the *International Encyclopedia of the Social Sciences* saw fit to devote a whopping 79-page section to "Communication." Insofar as a communication receiver is concerned, the purpose of most communications regarding his part in a group effort—regardless of subject, sender, message content, or medium—is to decrease his uncertainty regarding his own performance. Whatever personal interpretation he gives a message will depend on whether he sees it as providing *information for him*—in the decrease-of-uncertainty sense.

The leader sometimes may stir lethargic persons or static organizations by creating uncertainty. However, she or he ultimately motivates by providing information that *reduces* their uncertainties.

There is reason to believe that certain individuals have predispositions toward those needs that we have identified with leaders, while others have quite different predispositions.

Predispositions

An individual's predispositions are important to what he perceives, and this is particularly true of social or person perception. His previous experience and his needs, desires, wishes, and interests help to determine what an observer wants to see or not to see. Getzels et al. (1968, pp. 310–315) stated that individual predispositions consist of attitudes, beliefs, and values that have been handled through assimilation, rationalization, simplification (into either-or dichotomies or dogma), or accentuation.

Indirect expression of unconscious motives, in the forms of repression, unacknowledgement, rationalization, projection, and reaction-formation were discussed by Berelsen and Steiner (1964, pp. 279–286), and these, too, may be parts of one's predispositions of *unconscious* need-dispositions. These authors concluded: "In summary, and in general, behavior, attitudes, and feelings are not always what they seem to be—not what they seem to be to an observer and not even what they seem to be to the actor himself. What a man does, why he does it, and what he thinks or feels at the time he is doing it are related, but not always in a simple straight-forward, conscious way [p. 286]." Such knowledge can be valuable to leaders, and undoubtedly the predispositions of the persons in a social system affect their self-perceptions and their perceptions of others.

One way of looking at predispositions is through categorizing people. Categorizing group members is a method of showing relationships among social system variables, but it results in stereotyping. A stereotype describes a group of people without describing anyone in the group. Thus, it injects risks of inaccuracy, of prejudice, and of dehumanizing individuals. Taylor (1962, p. 67), in discussing the stereotype effect, pointed out that in-depth studies refute conceptual typecasting and show instead that: (1) any normal person can successfully perform many different jobs, (2) while people in given occupations do tend to have certain things in common, the characteristics popularly attributed to them do not necessarily exist, and (3) certain apparent common-to-the-job characteristics seem to *develop on the job,* as the consequence of experience and association, but do not necessarily or commonly exist as predispositions.

Nevertheless, stereotyping may be useful in predicting behavior and in providing proper satisfiers, so the following are suggested as some possible stereotypes of people according to their predispositions or orientations, which may help in understanding motivations, including the motivation to lead.

Cosmopolitans—Locals

A previously mentioned stereotype, that a person is either a cosmopolitan or a local, may be one of the more useful. Individuals' perception is affected by assumed similarity to themselves of an observed person, and leaders and would-be leaders might find significance in determining whether they and their followers are locals or cosmopolitans by orientation or predisposition. Merton (1957) appears to have introduced these terms into considerations of social theory and structure in this country. The local person's interest is confined to his own home community and is parochial in nature. By contrast, the cosmopolitan regards himself as an integral part of the world. In Merton's (1948–1949) study, numerous rather basic differences were found.

Gouldner (1957) identified four types of locals—the dedicated, the true bureaucrats, the homeguard, and the elders; and two types of cosmopolitans—the outsiders and the empire builders. Each of these types is briefly described below. It is difficult to examine these types in a nonevaluative way as each of us has prejudices which cause him to favor some types over others.

LOCALS: THE DEDICATED. The dedicated are the "true believers" who identify with and support the distinctive ideology—the belief system—of the school, college, or other agency. They are deeply committed to this ideology and are concerned that those within the system support it, believing that community agreement is more important than the acceptance of individual differences. They would prefer that others hired have value systems similar to theirs.

LOCALS: THE TRUE BUREAUCRATS True bureaucrats are inclined to oppose bargaining or other militant units on the grounds that they are "outside" organizations or are controlled by "outsiders." True bureaucrats are distinguished from dedicated locals in that they are oriented to the community and its people rather than to the educational agency itself. They are not advocates of internal consensus and are willing to risk conflict in order to bring about organizational adjustment.

Gouldner suggested that, generally, locals of the true bureaucrat type seek to accomplish organizational goals by installing more authoritarian and *formal* regulations to control the behavior of others. Locals who lead may be true bureaucrats.

LOCALS: THE HOMEGUARD. The homeguard members have the least amount of specialization among organization members, have little or no advanced college work, attend few professional meetings, and typically are not involved in curriculum development or other professional activities. Many are graduates of the local high school or of schools in neighboring districts. This group is predominantly female and often includes wives of men who are "prominent" contributors to the educational agency. They generally have personal reasons for sticking with and expressing loyalty to the system. Few leaders are found among them.

LOCALS: THE ELDERS. Elders, as their name implies, have the largest share of tenure in the system and are committed to stay with it indefinitely. Some arrived at this commitment willingly, while others found that, as the years slipped by, employment visibility to other institutions diminished. Gouldner suggested that elders are oriented either: (1) to an informal peer group, those as old as themselves and those who came into the organization about the same time as they did, or (2) to a special or earlier time period. Their leading potential is limited.

COSMOPOLITANS: THE OUTSIDERS. Outsiders are those who have little loyalty to the system and do not intend to stay permanently.

They are willing to leave for more money, better positions, or more prestige. They are not particularly close to students on a social basis, but may be interested in students who relate to their specialties. They are relatively infrequent or low-intensity participants in terms of faculty friendships and group interaction; they wield little influence and show no overt interest in increasing their influence efforts.

Outsiders are more committed to their professional skills than to any one agency. They look toward outside reference groups and to colleagues elsewhere for intellectual and professional stimulation. When they serve as leaders they may have difficulty attracting followers.

COSMOPOLITANS: THE EMPIRE BUILDERS. Empire builders enjoy high professional visibility outside the local system and thus feel less dependent on the system for economic reasons or for satisfaction of their other needs. While relatively satisfied with his present situation, the Empire builder remains on the lookout for a better position elsewhere, and often complains that maintenance demands (community activities and the like) are too heavy and distract him from his professional work.

Empire builders, particularly in colleges, are committed to their specific *academic departments,* especially in the physical sciences and the creative arts, and have a strong pull toward increased departmental autonomy. The situations in which they lead are thus limited.

As pointed out by Sergiovanni and Carver (1973), cosmopolitans are generally more difficult to accommodate within present educational structures than are locals, but providing meaningful outlets for their need-expressions may harvest unique benefits derived from the experiences and professional know-how that they offer. Many schools and small colleges have tended to seek, encourage, and reward local orientations in employees primarily because locals are more easily pleased and more malleable in terms of administrative directions. Cosmopolitans, on the other hand, often are vocal, resentful, demanding, and self-exerting and often bring conflict. Cosmopolitans are more likely to become locals as the years go by than are locals to become cosmopolitans. Educational reformers nearly always are cosmopolitans.

Goal-Oriented—Task-Oriented

A second stereotype closely related to the cosmopolitan—local is the goal-oriented—task-oriented. The tendencies of persons of the two extremes were clearly differentiated by Hughes (1965), as shown in Table 7-1.

Most educational agencies suffer from what Silberman (1970) characterized as "mindlessness," particularly in regard to defining

TABLE 7-1
TENDENCIES OF THE GOAL-ORIENTED VS.
THE TASK-ORIENTED PERSON

GOAL-ORIENTED INDIVIDUAL	TASK-ORIENTED INDIVIDUAL
1. Seeks feedback and knowledge of results. Wants evaluation of own performance. Wants concrete feedback.	1. Avoids feedback and evaluation. Seeks approval rather than performance evaluation.
2. Considers money a standard of achievement rather than an incentive to work harder.	2. Is directly influenced in job performance by money incentives. Work varies accordingly.
3. Seeks personal responsibility for work if goal achievement is possible.	3. Avoids personal responsibility regardless of opportunities for success.
4. Performs best on jobs that can be improved. Prefers opportunity for creativity.	4. Prefers routine nonimprovable jobs. Obtains no satisfaction from creativity.
5. Seeks goals with moderate risks.	5. Seeks goals with either very low or very high risks.
6. Obtains achievement satisfaction from solving difficult problems.	6. Obtains satisfaction not from problem solving so much as from finishing a task.
7. Has high drive and physical energy directed toward goals.	7. May or may not have high drive. Energies are not goal-directed.
8. Initiates actions. Perceives suggestions as interference.	8. Follows others' directions. Receptive to suggestions.
9. Adjusts level of aspiration to realities of success and failure.	9. Maintains high or low level of aspiration regardless of success or failure.

Reprinted by permission of the publisher from C. L. Hughes, *Goal setting: Key to individual and organizational effectiveness.* New York: American Management Association, Inc., 1965, p. 38.

and clarifying goals. It seems apparent that clarification of goals is essential to the goal-oriented individual, while specification of tasks satisfies his opposite number.

Individuals—Conformists
A third means of categorizing individuals is in the extent to which they tend to be unique individuals as opposed to conformists. Each

person is born unique, but all of one's experiences with others tend to make one more like them. The mature adult focuses on establishing awareness, in himself and others, that he is unique, while conforming in many ways in order to make his contribution and to have his needs met through one or more groups. At one extreme is the artist, and at the other the military man. As Zaleznik (1966) pointed out, "The complete merger of his identity within any social structure results in a gradual loss of feeling and responsibility [p. 237]. Examples of complete merger may be found in an Eichmann, a Calley, or any of the several tragic figures in the infamous Watergate affair.

As Zaleznik (1966) also described, the problem of self-esteem may be seen by examining the polarity of giving and getting, of controlling and being controlled, of competing and cooperating, and of producing and facilitating. The adult individual needs to assume responsibility and to learn to exercise choice if he is to have self-esteem. Some may do that by an overall showing of individuality, others by generally conforming. Conformists seem to be more generally accepted as leaders—except in great causes.

Dependents—Independents
Every individual must learn to strike a balance between his conflicting wishes for independence and for being dependent on those who are in positions of authority over him. According to Zaleznik (1966), "studies of conflicts underlying the outbreak of ulcers show the presence of marked unconscious wishes for passive dependency [p. 19]. Yet, as was pointed out in Chapter 6, some individuals seem perpetually to seek dependency, even though prolonged dependency, particularly where one has no choice but to be dependent, can be deleterious to the personality. Dependency that yields satisfactions is self-reinforcing; dependency that frustrates fosters strong *independence* needs. Leaders would seem to be more prevalent among independents.

Upward-Mobiles—Indifferents—Ambivalents
The fact that individuals adapt to organizational expectations in various ways has been noted by numerous writers. Among them was Presthus (1962), who used the terms upward-mobiles, indifferents, and ambivalents to describe various types of adapters. This classification, too, may be used as a stereotype for categorizing individuals so as to predict their behavior and to try to provide satisfiers for them. A brief description of each of the three types was given in Chapter 2 and this particular stereotype is discussed in some detail in Chapter 11, since it is thought to have particular relevance to leader type. Hence, it is not described here. However, we would hypothesize that there are more leaders to be found among upward-mobiles than among indifferents and ambivalents combined.

Theory X—Theory Y

The way in which an individual appears to view human beings can also be used for purposes of stereotyping him. The opposing views formulated by McGregor, known as Theory X and Theory Y, were sketched in Chapter 2, and thus are not repeated here. Leaders may be of either orientation.

Whether a particular stereotype, either one of those outlined here or some other, may be useful to the reader may be judged by whether (1) he can "find" himself in one of the descriptions, and (2) he can understand the nature of the satisfactions needed by each of the described types.

SUMMARY

The locus of leadership is in, but not confined to, administrative positions in formal agencies. Influence or authority, status, structure, social exchange, and a modicum of flexibility are essentials for leading; authority or power and operating within limits are essentials for administering.

Leader persuasiveness and language mastery are extremely important, and can be used to extend the limits within which leadership can occur.

Motivations and the reduction of uncertainty can be somewhat understood through stereotyping (despite inherent dangers). Stereotyping also can be used as a means of predicting behavior and providing need-satisfactions for individuals. Possibly useful stereotypes include cosmopolitans—locals, goal-oriented—task-oriented, individuals—conformists, dependents—independents, upward-mobiles—indifferents—ambivalents, and Theory X—Theory Y. Usefulness of stereotypes for the reader can be determined by whether he can find descriptions of himself in the general descriptions. Some research regarding students and teacher motivations is sorely needed inasmuch as teachers, instructors, counselors, and coaches are among the position-holders who are expected to lead.

Chapter 8 will examine the dynamics of the leadership process—who does what, with which, to or for whom—to make it occur. Again, leader persuasiveness and language mastery will be highlighted.

SOME SUGGESTED RESOURCES

H. H. Albers, The problem of stagnation, p. 585, and Managerial and operating efficiency, pp. 255–256, in *Principles of management: A modern approach.* New York: Wiley, 1964.

P. M. Blau, Strategic leniency and authority. In R. T. Golembiewski and F. Gibson (Eds.), *Managerial behavior and organization demands: Management as a linking of levels of interaction.* Skokie, Ill.: Rand McNally, 1967. Pp. 153–156.

F. Herzberg, The motivation-hygiene concept and problems of manpower. In R. T. Golembiewski and F. Gibson (Eds.), *Managerial behavior and* *organization demands: Management as a linking of levels of interaction.* Skokie, Ill.: Rand McNally, 1967. Pp. 106–114.

J. W. McDavid and H. Harari, Leadership and social power. Pp. 348–366 in *Social Psychology.* New York: Harper & Row, 1968.

D. P. Nelson, Similarities and differences among leaders and followers. In C. R. Gibb (Ed.), *Leadership.* Baltimore, Md.: Penguin, 1969, Pp. 307–314.

L. C. Schroeter, Behavior patterns in *Organizational élan.* Washington: American Management Association, Inc., 1970. Pp. 27–33.

P. Selznick, *Leadership in administration.* New York: Harper & Row, 1957.

A. S. Tannenbaum, Leadership: Sociological aspects. In D. L. Sills (Ed.), *International encyclopedia of the social sciences.* New York: Macmillan, 1968. Vol. 9, pp. 101–106.

R. Tannenbaum, The nature of authority. In M. D. Richards and W. A. Nielander (Eds.), *Readings in management.* New Rochelle, N.Y.: Southwestern, 1963. Pp. 708–714.

J. W. Taylor, Leadership in potential—who has it? In *How to select and develop leaders.* New York: McGraw-Hill, 1962. Pp. 53–93.

CHAPTER 8

THE DYNAMICS OF LEADERSHIP

Leadership is always a group phenomenon. Consideration of the ideal of leadership thus invites a good look at human relations.

—Zahn

Three historical views have considered leadership as a positional attribute, as a personal characteristic, and as a category of behavior. In earlier chapters, we have tried to develop a fourth view, namely that:

— Leadership is a process, and is *not* a category of behavior; it is not a prerogative of any individual due to personality or position, nor is it a collectivity of persons.
— Leaders achieve positions by appointment, capability, election, force, knowledge, inheritance, or ownership, depending on what basis, or bases, each has for influence, authority, or power.
— Leading is an expectation for certain persons holding administrative positions in formal organizations.
— The process of leadership and the actions of leading can occur only in social systems.

In this chapter, these ideas will be expanded and others added to explain the phenomenon of leadership. By our definition, *leadership is a process in which an individual takes initiative to assist a group to move toward production goals that are acceptable, to main-*

tain the group, and to dispose of these needs of individuals that impelled them to join it. This chapter will consider social system function, the actions of leading, actions of administering, and some of the effects of perception on leader behavior.

SOCIAL SYSTEM INTERACTION
Every social system consists of individuals bound together by some *unity of purpose and interdependence.* Each puts something into the system and each gets something in return.

Inputs
inputs of an educational social system may be considered as expectations and need-dispositions.

EXPECTATIONS. Expectations are held by every system member—the leader, his peers, his superordinates, and his subordinates. Fiedler (1967) said that ". . . it follows [from this theory] that we can improve group or organizational performance either by changing the leader to fit the situation or by changing the situation to fit the leader [p. 247]." Either change automatically changes the expectation inputs of every system member. However, every member continues to expect that in return for the time and effort that he gives he will have a job, periodic pay raises, fringe benefits, promotions (few of which are available in traditionally structured schools), approval, recognition, praise, improved work conditions, tools or other resources, freedom to perform tasks in his own way, and security. For each individual, some of these are more important than others.

In addition to expectations held by social system members, inputs to the social system include expectations of the society at large, of groups outside the particular system, and of individuals who are not system members. Many others have pointed out that there are *opinion leaders* in any community whose expectations are important to the schools and other educational agencies of the community.

That expectations held for young children in school affect their behavior has been well established. Rosenthal (1973) reported that a series of both laboratory and field studies show about the same proportion of significant results from controlled experimentation with adolescents and adults regarding the effects of expectations. Furthermore, it has been established that different tones of voice, with *no change in words,* can convey the expectations held. Would-be leaders need to read the findings of such studies and ponder their significance for learners as well as the adults who work together in educational agencies.

NEED-DISPOSITIONS. The conditioned responses of individuals within the system are added inputs to the system. Again, every individual—whether leader, peer, superordinate, or subordinate—has unique need-dispositions. He behaves as he does because he expects certain reactions to that behavior. It is conceivable that need-dispositions of individuals outside the system also affect its functioning, but for present purposes the need-dispositions of those who constitute the system's *core elements* are considered as system inputs.

Process

The basic process of social systems is social exchange, in which individuals give such things as time, talent, and commitment or changes of attitude, belief, or action in exchange for expected satisfiers of the need levels at which they are functioning (see Table 1-1, p. 9). Those who do not find satisfaction experience frustration. Satisfactions and frustrations thus are outcomes of the process, and will be discussed in the next section of this chapter.

The contingencies of the exchange process make leadership situational in nature. According to Fiedler (1967) and Gibb (1958, 1968), the significant contingencies of: (1) the psychological togetherness of the leader and subordinates, (2) the structure of the task at a given time, and (3) the positional power of the designated leader determine *who leads* in any given situation. Hersey and Blanchard (1972) presented a "life cycle theory" which suggested that the length of life of an organized group may be a fourth determining factor.

Regardless of who leads, these observable behaviors always occur:

— goals are set or tacitly agreed to.
— the leader is either given responsibility (through appointment, election, ownership, or default), assumes it in the absence of a designated leader, or seizes it from the designated leader.
— means of achieving the goals are agreed upon.
— limits of the leader's authority are set, either overtly or covertly, unless he has unlimited *power.*

The exchange process is complicated, in some systems, including those of schools and colleges, by the *working elements,* other than system members, required for the system to function. *Learners* are introduced, so each teacher or instructor then becomes the leader of a subsystem. *Resources,* in the form of supporting staff, space, time, equipment, tools, and monies, are needed and the process is either facilitated or hindered by whether they are supplied. The process, however, whether in the total system or any of the subsystems, is one of exchange among people.

In the exchange process, each individual is trying to influence others in order that he may gain satisfactions of his needs. He influences most who communicates best, and communication is thus vital to all, but it is most vital to the leader. Skill in communication is so essential to the leader that the entire next chapter will be devoted to the subject.

The social system process, overall, must utilize the people in the system to convert the inputs to outputs.

Outputs
The outputs resulting from the interaction process in a successful educational agency are the provision of learning opportunities, organization maintenance, need-satisfaction of individuals, and innovation.

PRODUCTION. For learning opportunities to be produced, emphasis must be placed on learner-centered goals and on the means by which learners can achieve those goals. In all too many schools, colleges, teacher-preparation agencies, and trainer-training programs, the emphasis has been on instructor goals and behaviors.

ORGANIZATION MAINTENANCE. If an organization is to continue in operation and carry out the functions for which it was established, learning, coordination, group solidarity, and feedback all are essential. Individuals must learn about goals, about the tasks at hand, how to work together, and how to improve social system functioning, according to Miles (1959). Coordination of individual efforts toward achieving group goals requires stimulating each individual to do his part in the group enterprise and obviating, resolving, or utilizing conflicts. Group solidarity requires a supportive leader-follower relationship, high-level interaction skills, and feedback. Feedback will be discussed separately.

NEED-SATISFACTIONS. Satisfiers for individuals' needs are necessary for organizational continuance and, as was discussed earlier, Theory X leaders do not worry about this output; they threaten and coerce individuals, and fire any who express too much dissatisfaction. Such practices could result in having to bring in and orient inordinate numbers of new personnel, with deleterious impact on both production and group maintenance.

INNOVATION. Change may be either an output or a byproduct of a social system. Deliberate innovation for purposes of increasing the capability of the system may be undertaken for any of several reasons, but most innovation should result from feedback.

Feedback
Feedback is essential to any system that must continue over long periods of time. Outputs can be changed only through getting feedback that results in changed inputs or process.

EXTERNAL. In an educational agency, the provision of learning opportunities is a service provided for learners who are external to the social system. Learners are not core elements of the producing system, and the degree of success that they experience, in and as a result of their learning opportunities, is viewed by many persons outside the system. It is only through feedback that the ideas of learners and of those who financially support the system can be utilized to improve the process and the product. Yet educators generally have not sought feedback on any organized basis and have not welcomed that which was given gratuitously. If change in a system is effected for any reason, further external feedback is needed to indicate how the change is perceived by those who are not parts of the system.

INTERNAL. Feedback from within the system is necessary if one is interested in knowing how system members perceive each other, the leader, the production, the efforts to maintain the organization, the extent to which their needs are being satisfied, any innovations that may be attempted, or the lack of innovation.

In "Managing the Educated," Drucker (1959, p. 147) proposed that we need an information and decision system—an organization based on judgment, knowledge, and expectations—rather than an organization based on principles of authority and responsibility. Levinson (1973) supported the idea. At present, there is no way of knowing whether such a system might serve education better than do current organizational structures.

LEADER'S NEED. It is only through feedback, internal and external, that a leader can tell whether he is succeeding or failing, whether he is communicating, or whether system members are following or drifting away. An administrator who makes no pretense of leading still needs feedback to ascertain people's perceptions of how well the agency is doing in providing its service and the extent to which he, as administrator, is perceived as doing his job of maintaining the organization.

Either an administrator or a leader should be able to recognize and should be concerned about feedback in the form of psychological mechanisms such as sublimation, increased effort, identification, compensation, reinterpretation, rationalization, attention-getting, reaction-formation, projection, repression, and regression. Hicks (1972, pp. 141–148) described these in simple terms and indicated that they range from the relatively constructive to the relatively destructive. Evidence of any of them, however, may be an indication that the behaver is not having his needs met.

Figure 8-1 illustrates the types of actions that constitute the leadership process and the goals of each. A discussion of "who does what, with which, to whom" follows.

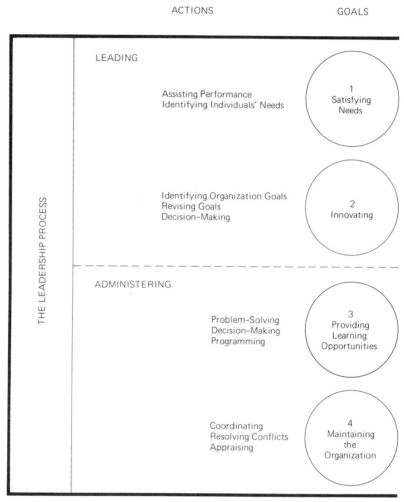

Figure 8-1 *The Leadership Process in Education*

Who Does What

A goal is amorphous, in that often it cannot be pursued until "caught." It cannot be firmly grasped, turned over, examined, and dissected. However, people can agree on goals, such as those shown in Figure 8-1, and can allocate responsibilities and tasks to be done which, when sufficient in scope and when completed, are assumed to indicate goal achievement. The responsibilities and tasks, when stated in terms of observable activity, are *behavioral objectives*.

THE ADMINISTRATOR. An administrator is responsible for those objectives that lead to goal 3, providing learning opportunities. He also is responsible for those objectives that lead to goal 4, maintaining the organization.

Any administrator has a continuing relationship with his role. If a school principal is a administrator only, with no leader skills, he uses the authority of his headship position to hold people to those goals for which he is responsible. He uses that authority by resorting to communications skills, which may be used in any of the modes that will be described in Chapter 9.

THE LEADER. A leader has responsibility for those objectives that accommodate goal 2, innovation, and goal 1, meeting the needs of individuals.

Leaders exercise personal authority, backed up by whatever positional authority they have, by providing for interaction of involved persons and by utilizing communications skills in discharging responsibilities. The role of leader may shift from person to person as the situation changes, or one person may play the role in various ways depending on the developmental stage of the group with which he is working, as Hersey and Blanchard (1972) described.

Lipham (1964) contended that leading and administering are antithetical—that an individual cannot be change agent and, at the same time, maintain the status quo. The present writers disagree, although they believe that the functions need not, necessarily, be combined in one individual. So long as both kinds of actions are carried out by *someone* in an organization, the leadership process will occur.

The real danger to an educational agency comes when circumstances combine to cause an imbalance in the human or financial resources devoted to the four goals. The most common imbalance occurs when all available human resources have to be marshalled to maintain the organization—as when there are prolonged court suits over busing in the schools or when there are student disruptions on a college campus—so that for long periods there is no one who has time to strive for other goals. An equivalent phenomenon was noted when, in 1973, the Watergate affair brought executive functioning of the federal government to a virtual standstill!

THE SUBORDINATE OR FOLLOWER. An educational subordinate gives time, talent, effort, and commitment to the activities of an organization, and the activities must, in some fashion, meet the needs of administrators and leaders. Each individual hopes to receive in return some of the satisfiers of his needs, and it is his leader's responsibility to see that he does.

Some of the actions of leading which are necessary to successful functioning of schools and colleges are listed in the following section.

LEADING

There are actions which principals, headmasters, superintendents, directors, coordinators, supervisors, chairpersons, deans, presidents, and others in positions of headship in educational agencies must take if they are to be recognized as leading. Some individuals may be suited to, or choose to, perform only these actions, leaving administering to others. Others may both lead and administer. Far too many in such positions administer only; then someone else in the organization must perform the actions of leading or the leadership process does not occur.

The actions of leading are considered here according to the two major organizational goals which they are intended to achieve (see Figure 8-1).

Satisfying Needs

As has been reiterated, teachers, instructors, and other educational staff members join particular groups because of what they expect the groups to do *for them.* Their goals and needs must be identified and their performance assisted.

IDENTIFYING INDIVIDUALS' NEEDS. If individual needs are to be met, even partially, it is necessary that their leader be concerned about identifying each individual's personal goals. Actions such as the following can help:

— Discuss with each individual his or her needs, wants, and problems.
— Observe carefully for symptoms of satisfaction or dissatisfaction.
— Communicate at all levels (see Chapter 9).
— Solicit overt feedback.
— Identify and utilize the expertise and ideas of each person.
— Identify any and all indicators of what each person expects from the group.

ASSISTING PERFORMANCE. Of course, the performance of individual staff members is of concern to the educational leader. How well one performs depends on the interplay of need-dispositions and the role expectations that present him or her with opportunities or constraints. Some actions that a leader can take to maximize that interplay include:

— showing the individual how his or her goals can be achieved through group goals
— ensuring that expectations are known and understood
— determining work relationships that satisfy or frustrate
— finding out how people think they are being treated

— learning what the job is doing to the person's self-esteem
— applying the likely effects of proposed innovations to the specific individual and making certain that he or she understands them
— reducing uncertainties regarding acceptability of performance by giving constructive feedback
— recognizing signs of frustration (accommodation patterns such as submission, apathy, and forgetfulness, in addition to the psychological mechanisms listed earlier as forms of feedback)
— utilizing abilities (including leading abilities) of each person
— providing tools and materials necessary to task performance
— providing the rewards an individual expects.

Innovating

"All change is a miracle to contemplate; but it is a miracle which is taking place every instant," according to Thoreau. The actions which educational leaders can take to help others to realize the truth of this maxim include, but are not limited to, these:

— Listen to others' ideas.
— Borrow from other organizations those ideas that fit.
— Combine others' ideas in new ways.
— Imagine ways to improve the organization's operation.
— Solicit feedback regarding problems.
— Specify what, where, when, and how much deviation there
— Identify strategic problems (see Delbecq, 1971).
  is from the expected norm.
— Determine what the problem *is not.*
— Develop as many alternative courses of action as possible.
— Classify "must" and "want" objectives, according to importance.
— Score each possible alternative against objections.
— Consider possible adverse consequences of the "best" alternative.
— Plan to control the effects of a decision before they bring new problems.
— Invent programs to implement decisions.

The actions of a leader help innovation to develop through the progressive stages of possibility, probability, inevitability, imminence, and existence (see Carkhuff, 1971). Some further kinds of specific actions related to innovation pertain to identification of organization goals, goal revision, and the making of critical decisions.

IDENTIFYING ORGANIZATION GOALS. The goals of an organization constitute planning premises, but they are more often assumed than spelled out. To help staff members understand them, a principal or department head can perform actions such as:

— discussing what the group is trying to accomplish
— diagnosing present organization needs
— forecasting future needs and conditions which are likely to bear upon them
— agreeing on actions to be taken
— involving others in these matters.

Since leaders have preferred outcomes, some revision of existing goals may be necessary at times.

REVISING GOALS. Goal revision, or substitution of new goals for old, is a particularly sensitive form of innovation. New goals may develop from individuals within the system, from a group within the system, from social or political forces outside, or from the leader's imagination. The leader always has a preferred outcome that he is advocating—something that he hopes will eventuate that might not occur if he does not intervene. Thus, he needs to have mastery of language, particularly the skills of persuasion. He uses the actions of selling, namely:

— involves people in decisions that will affect them
— stresses desirability of progress and growth
— shows what a proposed change will do for the system and the individual
— demonstrates that the goal is attainable
— invites questions and objections and deals with them honestly
— recognizes symptoms of resistance
— analyzes causes of resistance
— considers altering own views or offers new arguments.

It may sometimes be efficacious to utilize emotional appeal, although it should be noted that Bartky (1953) and Golembiewski (1965) raised questions about the morality of such action when dealing with educated people who can function at the rational level in decision-making.

DECISION-MAKING. Although they lack empirical verification, Jay (1971) presented intriguing ideas regarding the need for and use of groups of various sizes and differing composition in the making of those decisions that are important to an organization—those decisions that Selznick (1957) called "critical." Such decisions in schools and colleges affect the capacity of the organization to provide learning opportunities.

The sizes and types of groups needed, according to Jay, will be discussed in Chapter 9, as the primary purpose of each group is to achieve a different communication pattern.

Some of the specific actions of leading that can expedite the making of critical decisions include:

— involving people in those critical decisions that will affect them (*not* in all decisions)
— establishing objectives
— utilizing any special information that group members possess
— structuring a group of the proper people and size to make the needed decision
— identifying the political and economic forces that may be operative in the situation
— determining the consideration that must be given to political and economic forces
— delimiting any delegation of authority
— giving the group an explicit charge, detailing time and other constraints, establishing limits on discretion, and stating when, by whom, and how the decision will be implemented.

Decision-making is also a major part of the actions of administering.

ADMINISTERING
An administrator is a person who puts into effect the policies and rules of an organized group. Once a group is organized even the temporary leader becomes an administrator. As such, he or someone to whom the responsibility is delegated engages in a series of actions that have long been identified as the *administrative process.* Many writers have discussed the process and their terms for the steps in it have been almost as numerous as the writings. While the steps have generally been considered in relation to formal organizations, they often apply almost equally as well to informal groups or temporary situations. The following are the present writers' choices of steps, divided according to the goals to which they most directly relate. All rely on communication, which is therefore not included as a separate step.

Providing Learning Opportunities
Of course, almost all educators make hundreds of decisions in their daily lives, and many a decision relates to a deviation from some pre-set standard of performance. As long as the actions of learners and the persons who help them occur within the limits of the shared expectations of group members, no one in the group will perceive problems, and everyone can get on with the provision of learning opportunities. When problems do occur, they usually must be solved.

PROBLEM-SOLVING. When a problem occurs, an individual is often able to deal with it by adapting his or her usual routine to it or by following established patterns of behavior. When this kind of coping is not adequate, an administrator often helps individuals to solve problems and sometimes he or she must solve the problems with which others are unable to cope. So long as the prob'ems concern keeping the group functioning or keeping the organization running efficiently, the decisions made are largely of the type Selznick (1957) labeled "routine"; however, when the problems involve the capacity of the organization to produce, the decisions to be made become "critical."

The pre-set standards held for a faculty of a college may be the dean's own, those established by his immediate superordinates, those of the faculty at large, those of a particular group, or those imposed by a larger or more influential social system. Usually, the functional standards which an administrator uses to guide his behavior are a mixture of expectations from all five origins, and they are representative of past experience. Standards, then, are "shoulds"— established expectations—and so long as individual actions, group interaction, and equipment performance are within established expectations, an administrator usually will perceive no problem. If others wish to convince him that a problem exists, they must make him aware that there has been some deviation from his own standards of performance.

When an administrator is convinced that a nonroutine problem does exist, he may find himself in a stressful situation, and some individuals jump to hasty or apparent conclusions because of the stress. A decision based on a faulty conclusion, though, not only may fail to solve the problem, but actually may compound it. It is to avoid just such situations that Kepner and Tregoe (1965) have been dramatically teaching managers in business and industry to "specify the problem" and to analyze it with care and in an organized manner, as was suggested earlier in this chapter.

After a problem is analyzed, a solution may be implemented by making a decision.

DECISION-MAKING. Only after a problem is thoroughly understood can the administrator judiciously select from among possible alternatives, which selection constitutes decision-making. There is a great deal of misunderstanding about this matter, and the fantastic hardware available through technology has led some writers to make overly enthusiastic predictions about machine-made decisions. Some advocates of computer programming and operations research have indicated that all one needs to do is to put all the available data pertinent to a problem into a computer and let it sort out the "best" answer. Unfortunately, problem solution is not that easy, as oftentimes the administrator does not possess and cannot acquire all of the information necessary for a wise decision.

Some of the specific actions required of a leader in making critical decisions were discussed under Leading and the same actions are necessary in administering, but considerable doubt has been cast on the feasibility of making the "best" decision, even when all considered alternatives are possible. In the first place, not all administrators are capable of inventing or elaborating actions not already in their repertories, so the "best" possible solution to a problem may not occur to anyone, and thus may not even be represented among the suggested alternatives. Furthermore, March and Simon (1958) suggested that most people, in most situations, follow the practice of *satisficing*—they find a solution that appears adequate for the problem at hand, rather than the optimum solution, and then quit looking for alternatives. Decision-making is a tough job.

THE TOUGHEST JOB IN THE WORLD
It can be more fatiguing than a day of stonecutting . . .
It can be more nerve wracking than a day of heart surgery . . .
It can bring success, happiness, death . . .
In today's security-conscious society, fewer people want to
tackle it . . .
It's not a job for those who are afraid to fail . . .
It's not a job for the reckless, who can be dangerous . . .
It invites ridicule, criticism and unpopularity . . .
But without it the world stands still . . .
It is the lonely, precarious job of making decisions.[1]

There can be no doubt that administering includes the lonely, precarious job of making decisions. Even so, an administrator must follow the making of any but the most routine decision with a series of other actions, the first of which is programing.

PROGRAMING. If a decision that has been made is to have effects, someone must take some further actions regarding it. Upon analysis, they may be seen to include:

1. Planning the work to be done to achieve goals.
   a. Determining the tasks that must be done.
   b. Organizing the tasks into meaningful patterns.
   c. Apportioning tasks among people.
   d. Fixing responsibility for task accomplishment.
2. Selecting and organizing personnel.
   a. Setting standards for personnel who are to participate.

[1] Author unknown. In *U.S. Motors News.* Milford, Conn.: U.S. Electrical Motors, date unknown.

  b. Recruiting qualified people for the tasks.
  c. Selecting the most able people from among recruits.
  d. Organizing those selected for efficient task performance.
3. Assigning and orienting personnel.
  a. Assigning positions.
  b. Explaining role demands and interpersonal relations.
  c. Clarifying expectations as to results and responsibility.
  d. Clarifying channels of communication.
4. Arranging for housing, equipment, and supplies, if called for.
  a. Establishing physical layout and relationships.
  b. Instructing personnel regarding operation of equipment.
  c. Explaining procedures.
5. Arranging budget, if necessary.
  a. Assuring that financing is based on the job to be done.
  b. Arranging an efficient plan of expenditures.
  c. Assuring a source of income sufficient to allow the expenditures that are planned.
  d. Accounting for the funds appropriated to the purpose.

Maintaining the Organization

To maintain the organization, the administrator must engage in actions of coordinating, utilizing conflict, and appraising.

COORDINATING. The coordinating portion of the "administrative process" appears to include these actions:

1. Reviewing goals.
  a. Determining what the job is that is to be done.
  b. Checking who is to perform the tasks.
  c. Adapting the behavior of individuals to the group plan.
2. Getting people and any required *facilities* together.
  a. Assuring that people are properly located in facilities containing the necessary equipment, whether all of these were previously *programed* or not (this requires feedback).
  b. Learning from people, through feedback, what *things* they require, in addition to or in exchange for those originally *programed*, to get their jobs done.
  c. Securing the necessary *things.*
  d. Assuring delivery of the *things* to the proper *people* at the proper *time.*
3. Setting standards of performance.
  a. Establishing standards.
  b. Assuring that standards are understood.
  c. Assuring that individual responsibilities for achieving standards are understood.

4. Product specification.
   a. Specifying quality—establishing performance criteria for learners, tolerances, materials, sequence of operations, etc.
   b. Specifying schedules—quantities and times.
   c. Specifying unit costs that are allowable.

Social ailments often are manifested in conflicts. While some conflict is required for growth, and learning to resolve conflict seems important to personality development, conflict can interfere with or impede efforts to integrate the activities of an organization. Maintaining the organization must include obviating, removing, or resolving those conflicts which could endanger organizational continuance.

UTILIZING CONFLICTS. Before conflict can be constructively dealt with, there must first be a diagnosis that conflict exists. Knowledge about the following seven variables was suggested by Deutsch (1965) as essential to understanding any conflict between any two parties at most conflict levels:

— The characteristics of the parties in conflict
— Their prior relationship to one another
— The nature of the issue giving rise to the conflict
— The social environment in which the conflict occurs
— The interested audiences to the conflict
— The strategy and tactics employed by the parties in conflict
— The consequences of the conflict to each of the participants and to other interested parties.

Conflicts can be resolved only by: (1) domination of one party over the other, (2) compromise, or (3) integration, as was stated by Follett (1926). It should be noted that strategies (1) and (2) are competitive, while (3) is cooperative. Obviously, in the domination strategy, the dominator "wins" and his opponent "loses," while in the compromise strategy both parties to the conflict "win"—but both also "lose."

The following dynamics for the leader attempting integrative resolution of conflict were suggested by Schmidt and Tannenbaum (1960):

— Listen with understanding rather than evaluation.
— Clarify the nature of the conflict.
— Recognize and accept the feelings of the individuals involved.
— Indicate who will ultimately make a decision.
— Suggest procedures and ground rules.
— Give primary attention to maintaining relationships between disputants.

— Create appropriate conditions for communication between disputants.
— Suggest procedures to facilitate problem solving.

The administrator should know what collective behavior is and why it exists, as it often symptomizes another type of conflict, resolution of which is essential to organization maintenance.

COLLECTIVE BEHAVIOR. According to Merrill (1969), collective behavior is the behavior of associated individuals under circumstances for which their own prior habits do not adequately prepare them. It, as exhibited by the "acting crowd" [pp. 378–380] or the "expressive crowd" [pp. 380–382], is marked by the emotions of affection, of fear, of rage, or of hatred, and is not to be taken lightly. Collective behavior of a crowd represents conflict at the highest level, and the "crowd" which exhibits it is not to be confused with a "group." Crowd collective behavior often results in the abandonment of ordinary controls for limited periods, and usually should be dealt with by the duly constituted authority of the society rather than by an individual. An "acting crowd" can be truly ominous, as was learned in many campus and high school confrontations in the late 1960s. Because collective behavior is both the cause and the effect of social change, the administrator must be prepared to experience it. For centuries, demagogues and chauvinists have exploited collective behavior, usually for political or religious ends, but in the 1930s industry began to experience it and in the late 1960s collective behavior concentrated also in the educational and political arenas. Some administrators have constructively channeled collective behavior by helping the crowd to fix on the desirability of superordinate goals, one of the best strategies for coping with conflict of any nature.

The value of the administrative process may be determined by appraisal.

APPRAISING. The process of estimating the value of what has been done is essential to the overall administrative process, and it, too, can be broken into a series of smaller actions, which include:

1. Identifying evidence.
    a. Selecting criteria (objectives) for determining goal achievement.
    b. Determining what constitutes *observable* evidence that the selected criteria are or are not being met.
2. Recording evidence.
    a. Determining who will record evidence.
    b. Determining the form of the records required.

      c. Providing the necessary record forms.
      d. Instructing the recorders.
      e. Determining who will review evidence.
   3. Interpreting evidence.
      a. Reviewing the recorded evidence.
      b. Deciding whether the recorded evidence provides the desired information.
      c. Selecting and ordering facts of significance.
      d. Presenting evidence to the appropriate decision-makers.
   4. "Quality control."
      a. Determining whether each individual is meeting his responsibilities in terms of the group plan and goals.
      b. Determining whether overall results are meeting pre-set standards.
      c. Making adjustments as necessary to assure that standards *are* met.

Actions included in the administrative process are seen in many ways depending on one's perception.

PERCEPTION

In introducing their excellent inventory and discussion of research findings in regard to perception, Berelson and Steiner (1964) said:

> *How people come to know and interpret their world is fundamental to the understanding of human behavior, since behavior, as distinct from sheer motion, is action that takes the environment into account.*
>
> *Two basic starting points are: (1) all knowledge of the world depends on the senses and their stimulation, but (2) the facts of raw sensory data are insufficient to produce or to explain the coherent picture of the world as experienced by the normal adult. The first of these statements is axiomatic: a philosophical assumption not empirically verifiable but certainly not contradicted by any known facts. The second is an empirical finding that will be documented at length in these pages. Indeed, the study of perception Is largely the study of what must be added to and subtracted from raw sensory input to produce our picture of the world [p. 87].*

Most of the following discussion of perception not directly attributed to others is based on the Berelson and Steiner summary.

The Perceptual Screen

Each individual has a unique *perceptual screen* through which he filters everything that he observes. Thus, it appears that perception may affect what an individual member may "see" as inputs of a social system, as the process that transpires there, and as the outputs from the process. No two people have the same perception, but the perception of every social system member is important. According to Hochberg (1968), "The study of perception is the attempt to understand those aspects of observations of the world of things and people that depend on the nature of the observer [p. 527].

OBSERVATION. Before any stimulus of a sensory organ will be "received" by an individual, he must be aware of it. *Observation* is necessary for one to become aware of sensory stimuli, but many potential stimuli go unnoticed by most people. This is *nonobservation,* and no perception results. In *malobservation,* an individual is aware of a stimulus, but interpretation is quite different from reality. If memory is involved, it may be faulty in regard to the original stimulus.

Extrasensory perception, hypnosis, and certain drugs seem to offer potential avenues for extending what is known about observation. It may be that the widespread disagreement about such purported exotic visual stimuli as "unidentified flying objects" is due, at least in part, to the inadequacy of habits of observation and means of interpretation.

A number of propositions and corollaries relating to sensory stimuli in humans seem to be research-supported. Hochberg (1968) indicated that the contrast and constancy of color, spatial direction and motion, shape, distance, people, and social events are among the stimuli that are capable of producing awareness in most individual human beings.

SELECTION OF STIMULI. Even that small portion of the possible sensory stimuli that becomes part of an individual's experience is selected by the individual, and is not a random sample. The three major factors that seem to determine selection are:

1. Intensity or quality of stimuli
2. Anticipation of familiar things
3. The degree to which one needs or wants what the stimuli suggest.

In regard to motives, it seems established that the stronger the need, the greater the tendency to ignore irrelevant elements; awareness of unwanted stimuli is decreased; the tendency to be open to some experiences and to shut out others extends to the sense organs (at least to the eye), and is not under conscious awareness of control.

ORGANIZATION. Many researchers have reported studies that indicate that the perceiver organizes the stimuli of his senses in terms of: figure and ground; grouping as to proximity, similarity, or continuity; seeing parts as if they were together as whole, continuous figures, with gaps (if any) filled in; "good" figures in terms of similarity, continuity, proximity, closure, symmetry, etc.; and minor differences within figures ironed out—all organized on the basis of his prior experience and motives. This tendency to organize stimuli accounts for most "optical illusions" and aftereffects.

INTERPRETATION AND JUDGMENT. Because of the facts that: (1) there may be no discernible relationship between sensory input and the stimulus represented, (2) a simple object can produce a variety of stimuli when observed from various viewpoints, or (3) different objects can produce the same stimuli, the individual is required to make instantaneous, and often unconscious, interpretations. The propositions and corollaries relating to ambiguity of stimuli are worthy of study by any person who expects to influence others. The importance of *familiarity* and *expectations* to interpretation and judgment can hardly be doubted, and thus both are of concern to educational leaders.

There is a difference, between individuals, of awareness and interpretation of a stimulus because of the nature of fact. Reality *is*—it exists. However, facts are aspects of a situation selected by an individual from reality as being relevant to a particular problem of which he is aware. Even assuming that two individuals start with a common problem, it is likely that they will select at least some different facts from reality because of their *predispositions.*

PREDISPOSITIONS. Almost invariably we interpret our present experiences in accordance with our own interests, attitudes, hopes, and expectations—in other words, in accordance with our predispositions.

Observation tests a hypothesis, and the individual is looking for facts that will support his point of view, so he may be inclined to overlook facts that negate it. How many "research" reports are ever published that discredit the original hypothesis? An individual's predispositions are important to his selective perception, and this is particularly true of social or person perception. Previous experience and needs, desires, wishes, and interests help to determine what a teacher wants to see or not to see in a superintendent, or an instructor in a college president. Getzels et al. (1968, pp. 310–315) stated that individual predispositions consist of attitudes, beliefs, and values that have been handled by assimilation, rationalization, simplification (into either-or dichotomies or dogma), or accentuation.

Berelson and Steiner (1964, pp. 279–286) discussed indirect expression of unconscious motives, in the forms of repression, unacknowledgement, rationalization, projection, and reaction-formation, and these, too, may be parts of one's predispositions or unconscious need-dispositions. Behavior, attitudes, and feelings are not always what they seem to be, either to an observer or to the actor himself. What one does, why he does it, and what he thinks or feels at the time he is doing it are related, but not always in a straightforward conscious way. Such knowledge can be valuable to leaders, as undoubtedly the predispositions of the persons in a social system affect their self-perceptions and their perceptions of others, thus affecting what they perceive to be the inputs of the social system.

Predisposition is especially significant in regard to communication, and Hovland et al. (1953) indicated that the individual's predispositions are affected by his mental ability, his operational need levels, his ability to handle conflicts, his depth of conviction and emotional attachment to present opinion, and his feelings of uncertainty. He may interpret the urgency that a particular message has for him in terms of his predispositions, and those predispositions may include one or more of the psychological mechanisms listed earlier.

Social Perception

According to Tagiuri (1968, p. 560), "Person perception concerns the study of processes by which we come to know and think about other persons, their characteristics, qualities, and inner states. This area has been variously named social perception, person cognition, inter-personal perception, connaissance d'autri. . . ." Further, he stated (pp. 560–567) that situation cues are utilized jointly with stimuli from people, and that both are affected by the characteristics of the perceiver. Among the characteristics that affect cues and stimuli are sex; assumed similarity of the person observed to the observer; observer's liking for and status relative to the person perceived; attributed intentionality of the observed's actions (was the cause internal or external?); stereotyping of the observed individual as to sex, age, ethnic membership, nationality, occupation, etc.; and some base-line judgments (e.g.,—how mean is a mean dean?). These matters may well be of concern to anyone who is interested in how others perceive him or why he perceives others as he does.

Communication, then, is the indispensable tool for starting or ending interpersonal exchange and will be considered in some detail in Chapter 9. However, the effects that perception can have on communication, and thus on perceived social system process and outputs, are significant, and should not be overlooked.

The perceptions which followers have of a leader also affect their perceptions of the amount of risk involved for the organization or for them as individuals when a leader proposes changes.

Perceptual Deprivation

For many years and in many cultures, observers have noted that persons in virtual or total isolation for prolonged periods (such as in solitary penal or prisoner-of-war confinement) often exhibit such effects as disorientation, delusions, or hallucinations (Zubek, 1968).

Sometimes the effects are accompanied by emotional and cognitive disturbances.

Since World War II, there has been increased interest in the matter of perceptual deprivation in the United States, because of the alleged "brainwashing" and "confessions" of some of our servicemen and because of the development of space and underseas exploration programs in which individuals sometimes experience prolonged isolation.

Two principal methods have been employed by researchers. In one pattern, there is an attempt at total *sensory deprivation.* In the second method, the aim is *perceptual deprivation.* Both forms have been determined to be stressful, but a wider variety of measures is impaired by perceptual than by sensory deprivation. There are measurable physiological changes in individuals deprived in either fashion.

Educational leaders, in agencies where tasks to be performed are so routinized as to deprive individuals of many "normal" stimuli (such as when a teacher repeats certain content time and again), undoubtedly should be concerned about the effects of deprivation both on group production and on the deprived individuals. The more technological advances there are in society, and the more limited the stimuli available to individuals in educational environments become, the larger the problem is apt to grow.

Success or Failure?

Throughout the literature of school administration, management, and leadership, there are questions that are conspicuous by their absence, such as: What does an administrative head do when he realizes that his "followers" are not following? What indicators are there of leader success or failure? What are the causes and cures of failure? Although disturbing, such questions must be faced.

SIGNS OF SUCCESS. The responsible person can be assured that the actions of leading are being satisfactorily performed if most staff members are happy in their work, he personally is respected (or even liked!), and innovations are a regular part of life. Barnard (1938) said that an executive was *efficient* when individual needs were fulfilled.

The responsible executive may feel content about the actions of administering if the appraisal step of the administrative process indicates that learning opportunities are being provided and used, there is not an inordinate number of problems, needed decisions are being made and implemented, individuals' efforts reflect coordination, conflicts are being resolved, collective behavior inimical to the organization is not occurring, and there is periodic appraisal of group accomplishments. Barnard (1938) said that such conditions are indicators of executive *effectiveness.* Any signs of either inefficiency or ineffectiveness should, of course, be viewed with alarm, but not panic!

POINT OF VIEW. However, the present writers wish to suggest a somewhat different approach to efficiency and effectiveness, and to highlight the effect of perception on both.

Efficiency we define as the ratio between benefits and costs, or $Ec = B/C$. Then, from a follower's (or a learner's) point of view, a leader is efficient if the benefits to the follower (or learner) are in proportion to his costs in time, energy expended, and frustration. The parent taxpayer will have a different point of view, and the nonparent taxpayer still another.

Effectiveness we define as the ratio between expectations and performance, or $Ev = P/Ex$. Again, from a follower's point of view, a leader is effective if he is performing at the level and in the manner in which he is expected to perform. A dean will be viewed differently by the president or a trustee than he will by a faculty member.

Obviously, because of the perceptual screen through which everyone filters the stimuli that impinge on him, no two persons are going to have exactly the same views of either a leader's efficiency or his effectiveness. Neither will his own view exactly coincide with that of anyone else.

WHAT CAN BE DONE. Any leader can structure the feedback mechanism so that he learns periodically how he is viewed, in regard to both efficiency and effectiveness, by staff, learners, board of control, and financially supporting constituents. If the feedback is generally favorable, he can proceed as before. If a plurality of responses indicates negative perception in either area, he can: (1) try to change his mode of operation to improve his dynamics of leadership, (2) try to change people's perception, (3) institute a comanager system to share responsibility with a person whose interests and abilities complement his own, (4) resolve to "tough it out" until fired, or (5) resign.

The alternative which a leader chooses probably is related to his *authenticity,* which will be discussed in a later chapter.

SUMMARY

The dynamics of leadership occur only in interactions among the members of a social system. Inputs to the system include the expectations of individuals within the system, individuals outside the system, and certain groups, also outside the system. Inputs also include the need-dispositions of system members. In the process of social exchange, communication effects the exchange of such resources as time, talent, commitment, and effort for certain rewards or satisfactions. The outputs of the system are need-satisfactions, the provision of learning opportunities, organization maintenance, and, sometimes, innovation. Feedback is essential to knowing the presence and extent of each of the outputs, and often results in further innovation. In the process, each individual uses whatever resources he or she has, one or more individuals perform actions of leading, one or more the actions of administering, and one or more the actions of following.

In leading, the responsible individual has specific behavioral objectives which, if performed at least adequately, are expected to lead to the goals of satisfying individuals' needs and innovating. Innovating requires attention to bringing general change, but also to identifying organization goals, revising goals, and making critical decisions.

Administering consists of the actions of problem-solving, decision-making, and programing, all aimed at providing learning opportunities. Maintenance of the organization is achieved through the actions of coordinating, resolving conflicts, and appraising.

Perception is vital to the dynamics of leadership inasmuch as everyone has a perceptual screen through which he or she filters all sensory stimuli. That screen is particularly important in social perception, or perception of other people. Leaders need to be concerned about jobs that become so routine or are performed in such ritual fashion as to deprive the performers of a vital array of stimuli. It is only through feedback regarding others' perceptions that a leader can know if she or he is succeeding.

In Chapter 9, the vital subject of communication will be explored, especially its connection to the dynamics of leadership.

SOME SUGGESTED RESOURCES

C. G. Browne and T. S. Cohn, Leadership and change. Ch. 1 in *The study of leadership.* Danville, Ill.: Interstate, 1958, Pp. 417–422.

R. R. Carkhuff, *The development of human resources.* New York: Holt, Rinehart & Winston, 1971.

F. E. Fiedler, *Theory of leadership effectiveness.* New York: McGraw-Hill, 1967.

J. R. P. French and B. Raven, The bases of social power. In D. Cartwright (Ed.), *Studies in social power.* Ann Arbor, Mich.: Institute for Social Research, 1959. Pp. 150–167.

C. A. Gibb, Leadership: Psychological aspects. In D. L. Sills (Ed.) *International encyclopedia of the social sciences.* New York: Macmillan, 1968. Vol. 9, pp. 91–100.

P. Hersey and K. H. Blanchard, *Management of organizational behavior* (2nd ed.). Englewood Cliffs, N.J.: Prentice-Hall, 1972.

H. H. Hicks, Interpersonal behavior. Ch. 9. In *The management of organizations: A systems and human resources approach* (2nd ed.). New York: McGraw-Hill, 1972. Pp. 138–155.

J. P. Lipham, Leadership and administration. *Behavioral science and educational administration,* 63rd yearbook of NSSE, Part II. Chicago: University of Chicago Press, 1964. Pp. 119–141.

E. M. Rogers and F. F. Shoemaker, Adopter categories. Ch. 5 in *Communication of innovations.* New York: Free Press, 1971. Pp. 174–196.

L. J. Rubin (Ed.), *Frontiers in school leadership.* Chicago: Rand McNally, 1970.

H. L. Sisk, Leadership patterns. Ch. 16 in *Management and organization* (2nd ed.). Cincinnati, Ohio: South-Western, 1973.

CHAPTER 9

COMMUNICATION

We communicate to influence—to affect with intent.
—Berlo

The present writers hope to communicate in this chapter—to influence the reader—to affect him, with the avowed intent of having the reader understand that communication is a means, not an end; that much of what is known about communication can help the educational leader to achieve the ends he seeks and for which he is responsible.

This chapter will present a discussion of the nature of communication and the necessity for feedback. Emphasis will be placed on the skills needed by educational leaders if they are to communicate, on the uses they have for communication, on the purposes for which they communicate, and on some of the sources of "noise" that may interfere with communication.

THE NATURE OF COMMUNICATION

By the Glossary definition, communication is "a process through which an individual receives a sense impression of another." It is recognized that one may receive sense impressions from nature, but the communication discussed here is that which occurs between and among human beings, individually and in groups.

If communication is deliberate, one individual, through selective perception, attributes meaning to something about himself, his thoughts, or some aspect of his environment and then tries to convey his attributed meaning to one or more other individuals. However, many of the messages received from or about an individual are not intentionally "sent" by him, and even when he is consciously "sending," the receiver may be picking up unintended messages on channels of which the sender is unaware. For example, a director of industrial training may be orally assuring one of the trainers that he is doing a fine job. But the trainer may be reading disapproval or insincerity in the tone of voice, and saying to himself, "You think I'm not as smart as you." Which message will most influence the receiver depends on many variables relating to the sender, the message, the medium used, the environment, and the receiver.

In addition to other variables, there is always an "and," as Fabun (1968) noted.

"And—"

One cannot attach meaning to an event or interaction until one is aware that it is going on. Thus, to be realistic, every attempt at using words to communicate should begin with ". . . and," to acknowledge the recognition that something preceded the matter about which we are communicating, and end with "and . . . ," to acknowledge awareness that nothing ever really ends.

" . . . and" any discussion of the nature of communication must include principles and research findings regarding the variables of message sender, message, medium, receiver, environment, and feedback, "and. . . ."

The Sender

The person who originates or is the souce of a message is but one of many variables affecting the nature of communication. Still, it seems essential to consider what is known from research about this variable, the skills needed, and the intent of the sender.

PRINCIPLES AND FINDINGS. Characteristics of the individual sender are among the variables that affect the nature of communication. The following list of generalizations relating to "source variables" within the message sender was generated by Rogers and Svenning (1969) from conventional wisdom and from findings of then-current research. Their statements have been paraphrased in most instances.

1. Attitude change in an advocated direction is more likely to occur when the sender is perceived as highly credible, as expert (note the need for personal authority), and as trustworthy.
2. The motivation to seek and accept advice or direction from credible senders is increased when receivers feel uncertainties that they need to reduce.

3. When a sender arouses anger or resentment, the receiver's attitudes tend to be unfavorable toward the sender and the groups, goals, or enterprises with which he is identified.
4. Receivers are favorable toward messages from senders whom they perceive as being similar to themselves.
5. The greater the differences between sender and receiver, the greater the barrier to communication.
6. Empathic ability on the part of the sender is a key to communication.
7. When sender and receiver can communicate despite being dissimilar, their beliefs and attitudes become similar.

Credibility may be more important to the communication sender than some lack of skill unless that lack is acute. Undoubtedly credibility, authenticity, and idiosyncracy credit are all closely related.

The games that people play, and must play, in negotiation have serious erosive and corrosive effects on the credibility of the communicators for both sides. It is probable that the adversary relationship inherent in negotiations arrangements precludes the possibility for open channels of communication and ultimately diminishes the potentials of organization leaders to provide positive direction or change.

School superintendents and college presidents should avoid being cast in the role of negotiators in these days of faculty and staff negotiation. Conflicts are being negotiated, and they usually are resolved through domination of one side over the other or by compromise, either of which affects communication for other purposes.

SKILLS NEEDED. A message sender needs certain skills for preparing to send messages, other skills for encoding messages, and still different skills for decoding any messages received. Few of the skills are learned adequately in the usual public school and college programs. Most communication skills require specific and conscious attention if their development is to reach the level necessary for leading and administering.

In preparing messages, one needs to be skilled in using whatever learning facilities are available to one and adept at locating and using various sources of information. A community college president, for example, needs skills in using written or oral reports, computer printouts, statistical data, and many other facilities and tools. He needs to be able to find who in the organization, what references, or what reports can provide the kinds of information and supportive arguments that will be relevant to students, staff, board members, and paying constituents.

In encoding messages, the community college president or other educational leader must be proficient in the use of words. He must be able to select the most precise for his meanings, spell them, make them legible, use them grammatically, and anticipate their effects on others. He must be able to arrange words correctly and effectively in speaking and in writing. He must be able to interpret his and others' thoughts so they are intelligible for and compelling to the people with whom he works. He must be skilled in the selection of the most appropriate of the various modes in which messages can be transmitted and in the anticipation of effects of these modes.

When a communicator is both heard and seen, some imprecision in word choice, arrangement, grammatical construction, and pronunciation may be overlooked if the person has enough credibility or if other cues outweigh the mistakes. Nevertheless, in situations using both seeing and hearing channels, pronunciation, gesturing, inflections, pitch quality of voice, mode of phrasing, dynamism, and facial expressions all affect the message and its interpretation.

To decode messages sent by someone else, an educational leader must be able to listen to or read the messages and he must be able to interpret their meanings in terms of what the senders intended them to express—to truly understand what he hears, sees, and reads. There has been much emphasis on the improvement of reading skills in recent years, but listening is taught in few places and in most of those places it is taught at the university, not at preschool or early elementary school levels. Interpretation—particularly of body postures, movements, and use of space—is a skill that probably has been self-taught if it has been acquired at all.

ATTITUDES. Any message sender has definite feelings toward himself, toward the content of his messages, and toward his intended receivers, and those feelings affect the modes and media that he uses. A director of management development who is very confident of his abilities and the programs he advocates will communicate much differently than one who is diffident or who doubts that a proposal will be effective. Feelings toward content are particularly important in advocacy, of which leaders must be masters. A Theory X department head who "talks down to" or threatens faculty members will certainly communicate in different fashion than an elected chairman who is a true believer in Theory Y.

KNOWLEDGE LEVEL. What one knows by way of communication skills and theory certainly will help to determine what and how one will communicate, but knowledge of subject matter is an even more important determinant. It has been said, "You don't know it if you can't explain it to others," and that statement is almost certainly true if the sender has basic communication skills.

SOCIOCULTURAL SYSTEM. Everyone operates within the constraints of his need-dispositions, as we have stressed repeatedly.

Both the inherited characteristics of the individual and the socialization process to which he has been subjected combine to give him a unique personality, of which values are a basic ingredient. The individual then is called on to perform various roles in a number of social systems, and each system arose out of a particular culture or subculture, with its built-in values, as was indicated in Figure 1-1. When the sociocultural system from which a person came differs from that in which he is called upon to perform, his ability to communicate is affected—sometimes in drastic fashion.

INTENT. A school principal, superintendent, coordinator, director, or other educational leader needs to understand the intent of each message that she or he originates. That intent usually is to reinforce present behavior, to change behavior, to increase knowledge, or to form or change attitudes of the message receivers. To achieve his intent, he must secure the attention, regard, translation, comprehension, and action of one or more receivers. Attention is gained through being viewed as an authority figure; regard, on the other hand, requires that one possess both credibility (authority) and trustworthiness (authenticity). For followers to translate his messages correctly, they must have the same skills for decoding that the leader needs, and it is his responsibility to see that he and they have those skills in sufficient measure. To comprehend a message, the receiver must attach the same meanings to the symbols used (words, more often than not) as stimuli as did the message sender. This requires that the sender select well-understood symbols when encoding. If a message receiver is to take action, the message must have significance for him—it must somehow reduce his uncertainty about any sanctions for or against him that may ensue.

The Message

Characteristics of the message, too, have been found to affect the nature of communication, and the generalizations compiled by Rogers and Svenning (1969) from their research are considered here, along with the forms that messages may take and the modes in which they may be cast.

PRINCIPLES AND FINDINGS. Some generalized findings in regard to message variables are:

1. People need to be prepared for messages which are likely to evoke emotional responses.
2. People tend to ignore the further content of a message that rouses intense feelings of anxiety.
3. A one-sided presentation is more effective than a two-sided if:
   a. the receiver already agrees with the sender or
   b. the receiver is not later exposed to counter-propaganda.

4. A two-sided presentation of an issue is more effective than a one-sided if:
   a. the receiver initially disagrees with the sender or
   b. the receiver is later exposed to counter-propaganda.
5. If the receiver is likely to have little interest in a message, the major arguments should be presented first.
6. Persuasive logical arguments influence those of high intelligence more than those of low intelligence.
7. Persuasive messages which rely on unsupported, false, illogical, or irrelevant arguments influence those of high intelligence less than those of low intelligence.
8. Messages that appeal to more than one of the senses influence more than do those that appeal to one sense only.

FORM. We are accustomed to thinking of messages as consisting of spoken or written words, and words are indeed the symbols used in speaking and writing. Those words are, themselves, composed of mini-symbols consisting of syllables for spoken words and letters for written words. One must be skilled in the arrangements of the mini-symbols if he is to communicate, as illustrated by the rearrangement of the letters *perquisites* in this fashion: *prerequisites,* which totally changes the meaning. Words themselves have different meanings for different persons and in different arrangements. In addition to words, other symbols used in communication are human artifacts—illustrations, photographs, diagrams, tables, sculpture, paintings, and many others. The message sender must consider whether symbols that he uses can be understood by his target receivers.

In recent years, there has been much attention to "the silent language," and Birdwhistell (1968) summarized the developing science of *kinesics,* which has to do with messages sent through body postures and movements. Each person attaches his own meaning to pointing, winking, nodding, shrugging, smiling, scowling, and grimacing, or to touching gestures such as a tap on the shoulder, a pat on the head, a slap on the back, or a handshake. Such nonverbal messages may be grossly misunderstood if used across subculture or cultural boundaries, and message senders need to be aware that they are always transmitting on a multichannel system when they are in face-to-face or visually recorded situations.

There also are "languages" of space, time, and color, as described by Fabun (1968), and messages in these languages often are inadvertently "sent" along with intended verbal messages. According to precept 8 in regard to The Message, found earlier in this section, messages are more effective when they appeal to more than one of the senses. However, the message sender should use other forms of messages to reinforce, rather than counteract, his verbal message. Few people have the skill necessary to do that.

Kraai (1973) provided an excellent resume of literature, including the findings of research relating to nonverbal languages, and reported the results of his own experiment in a contrived educational setting. In his study, the effects of *space,* a *symbol* (desk), and *color* (similarity or dissimilarity of skin color between respondent and pictured subject) were controlled variables. He measured the message implicit in pictured situations by having each respondent indicate, on a semantic differential scale, how he felt about a pictured situation into which he projected himself as a staff member having a conference with a school administrator. All three variables were found to affect the perceived message, yet no words were exchanged and there was no face-to-face contact.

MODE. The mode in which a message is phrased can also affect its reception and interpretation. Gordon (1970) indicated 12 "ways" that parents communicate verbally with their children, and all seem to be within the repertoire of leaders. They are arranged here in terms of whether the present writers perceive the modes to be positive, neutral, or negative in terms of *generally* anticipated effects on the message receivers, although it is recognized that those effects sometimes vary with the situation. This sequence represents our judgment, ranging from most desirable to least desirable, for most organizational situations. Items 1 and 4 have been added to Gordon's list.

1. setting an example
2. praising, agreeing
3. reassuring, sympathizing, consoling, supporting
4. using parables, allegories, other verbal illustrations
5. lecturing, teaching, giving logical arguments
6. probing, questioning, integrating
7. interpreting, analyzing, diagnosing
8. withdrawing, distracting, humoring, diverting
9. advising, giving solutions
10. exhorting, moralizing, preaching
11. ordering, directing, commanding
12. judging, criticizing, disagreeing, blaming
13. warning, admonishing, threatening
14. name calling, ridiculing, shameing

Of course, the intent for which a message is being sent needs to be considered, as some modes are much more effective for certain purposes than for others. Much research in this area is needed, but it is apparent that in some of these modes additional messages on nonverbal channels are more likely than in other modes. For example, tone of voice adds a message to the words used in mode 13, but might not do so in mode 5.

The Medium

A message can get from one person to another only through some *medium*. The medium may utilize one or more of at least seven channels, and the one chosen for overt sending often determines the direction (whether there will be further dissemination or feedback) and the reliance or trust that receivers will place in the message. Often, as has been indicated, some channel other than the chosen one may be transmitting a covert message that is either secondary or downright undesirable from the viewpoint of the message sender. Again, these principles and findings are paraphrased from the distillations of Rogers and Svenning (1969).

PRINCIPLES AND FINDINGS

1. Interpersonal channels produce more lasting changes in attitude than do mass media channels.
2. Mass media channels are more effective than interpersonal in creating knowledge and awareness of ideas or in changing lightly held attitudes and beliefs.
3. Interpersonal channels are more effective than mass media in persuading or in changing deeply held attitudes and beliefs.
4. Channels that provide for feedback are more effective than those that do not.
5. Messages from mass media channels often are mediated and interpreted by "opinion leaders" for a larger audience of receivers.

CHANNELS. Whether used interpersonally or to reach masses, the channels available for communication are seeing, hearing, touching, smelling, tasting, time, and silence. Both sight and sound channels are used in face-to-face meetings with individuals or groups. Face-to-face communication nearly always is two-way (or three-way if more than two persons are involved) except in extreme circumstances, such as when a person is "dressed down" and ordered to not talk back. There is built-in provision for feedback, and as a result the face-to-face medium is most likely to be satisfying to the message receiver. Unintended messages may, however, be conveyed on the audio chanel by tone of voice, inflections, or pauses, and on the video channel by facial expressions or gestures. Perhaps it is because these added cues are available that communications in this medium are most genuine and receivers prefer it for communications that directly affect them.

The audio channel is also used with the telephone, and again there is implicit provision for feedback, even on a conference call with multiple receivers. Tape or other types of voice recording media use this same channel, whether with one receiver, several, or a mass. Feedback may be invited, but usually is not. Radio, television, movies, and videotapes are other media using audio or video or both channels, and those media rarely make provision for feedback. When video is used, unintended messages may be conveyed by the space channel or by time (pauses). The audio channel may transmit a message in the form of applause, but educators seldom use this medium either to send or receive in professional settings.

Paper is a widely used medium of communication using the sight channel, and no doubt it often is misused, perhaps because it seems to be the most compelling medium for many persons. Unfortunately, any message committed to paper becomes gospel for many receivers who never stop to consider the legitimacy of the message or the credibility of the sender before citing this "authority." Letters automatically invite response, but bulletins, rules, directives, and memos usually do not. Thus, a message sender often has no way of knowing whether his paper message is received, attended, properly decoded, and interpreted. If uncertainty is increased, anxiety induced, or other emotions aroused by a message on paper, the receiver must take the initiative to respond and request clarification or suffer anxiously in silence. Paper more often than not is a one-way medium, but, as noted earlier under Principles and Findings, the paper medium can serve useful purposes so long as its limitations are understood.

In addition to paper, visual stimuli in the forms of nonword symbols, artifacts, facial expressions, body movements, posture, space, and color constitute the media for seeing, one of the channels of nonverbal communication. The visual channel is the one in which the most investigations have been done and from which kinesics is developing. Educational leaders need to be careful about using ideas from "popular" writings in the field which treat nonverbal communication, particularly "body language," as a parlor game. Nonverbal communication is serious business, particularly for those who are unaware of its implications.

The channel of touching is less used in the organizational setting than are the channels of speaking/hearing and seeing. Probably the most commonly used media of the touch channel, for organization purposes, are a handshake, a tap on the shoulder, a pat on the back, or an arm about the shoulders. In nonorganization interpersonal situations, the touch channel media may include kissing, hugging, feeling, and slapping or otherwise striking. Meanings of those messages differ not only from subculture to subculture, but from person to person. Sometimes meaning differs for a touch receiver as contrasted with meaning for a person who experiences the message only on the seeing channel.

The channels of smelling and tasting probably transmit messages only at the interpersonal level in the organizational setting (except in certain industries), with little use being made of them for formal communication purposes.

Time seems to stand alone as a channel of nonverbal communication in the sense that rarely are its messages received on a secondary channel. Even space requires visual cues. Time *may* utilize visual cues, but it does not have to. For example, the individual who is "ahead of time" for every appointment "says" something quite different from the one who is "on time." One who keeps a group or an individual waiting says something else, and one who does not show at all for a scheduled appointment sends yet a different message.

A university president may notify individual faculty members of their individual salaries for the ensuing year on August 15 (rather than on a legally stipulated date such as July 1), the very earliest time possible after legislative action on the budget, but the wait may be a source of anger and resentment for individuals who experienced the duration as "too long."

Silence constitutes a third channel of nonverbal communication. The leader who says nothing when he is expected to speak, who accepts a committee report without comment or action, or who makes no response to an individual's request, nevertheless sends a message.

RELIABILITY. The amount of reliance on and trust in a medium of communication experienced by message receivers probably is related to: (1) the degree to which the medium and channels reduce uncertainty, (2) the extent to which feedback is invited or welcomed, and (3) the freedom from message-garbling "noise." A memo that raises more doubts than it allays will not be trusted, nor will a directive regarding a matter on which receivers have had no opportunity to express misgivings. A tape recording that has ambiguity in its meaning or shows poor fidelity of tone reproduction will not be accepted as reliable. A face-to-face oral message that uses unfamiliar words or convoluted syntax may express less than certain cues picked up through nonverbal channels.

The Receiver
The nature of communication may be better understood by considering what research has to say about the message receiver, the uses that a receiver has for communication, and the skills needed by the receiver.

PRINCIPLES AND FINDINGS. In the area of variables related to the message receiver, Rogers and Svenning (1969) included these among the most significant findings:

1. Behavioral and opinion conformity by a message receiver are directly related to his motivation to maintain membership in the group.

2. Messages from other group members, particularly those with respect to group norms, are valued highly by a receiver who places high value on group membership.
3. Receivers having high prestige and popularity hold attitudes that conform to group norms and resist external influences contrary to those norms.
4. Influence of counter-norm messages is inversely proportional to the value placed on group membership.
5. Receivers with high-esteem are less readily influenced than those with low self-esteem.
6. Overtly hostile or aggressive receivers are little influenced by persuasive messages.
7. Withdrawing or withdrawn individuals are little influenced by persuasive messages.
8. Participation by a receiver in the making of a decision tends to increase his attempts to help implement it.
9. Communication oriented to the receiver is more successful than that oriented to message or sender.
10. A receiver is more receptive to a message that is consistent with his existing knowledge, attitudes, and beliefs than to one that is not.
11. A receiver selectively perceives and interprets messages in terms of his existing knowledge, attitudes, and beliefs.
12. A receiver tends to selectively retain messages that are consonant with his existing knowledge, attitudes, and beliefs.

USES. The uses that a message receiver has for communication are to receive information, to check on the rationality of expectations held by others in regard to his performance, and to send messages.

If the work of Herzberg (1968) is taken seriously, then one of the greatest uses that a message receiver has for communication is to learn how he is doing. The studies reported by Sergiovanni and Carver (1973), based on Herzberg's work, dealt with teachers in the public schools and, if the findings from that study can be generalized to educators at large, it appears that achievement, recognition, and responsibility are important, in that order. Messages relating to such matters could add greatly to one's identity, both personal and organizational, to sense of opportunity, and to feelings of belongingness, or security. Yet few messages provide such positive reinforcements.

Numerous writers have pointed out that rationality is learned, and that it involves learning the symbols and rules that are important to a particular group and having those rules validated by significant others through a succession of experiences. Communication is necessary both to learning symbols and rules and to validation of them. Furthermore, one sees the constraints imposed on his behavior in terms of how norms manifested by those constraints were developed. If the manner in which norms were developed has no meaning for an individual, then he will see constraints on him as irrational and will not be likely to abide by them. In other words, if the norms were developed entirely without his participation or concurrence, or if constraints render him powerless while giving power to others, he will see them as irrational and thus not binding on him. Communication is essential to an individual's participation in the development of norms, and his acceptance of those norms is dependent on such participation.

SKILLS NEEDED. If a receiver's uncertainties are unrelieved, or if his emotions are otherwise aroused sufficiently, he will become a message sender. He then needs the same communications skills as were described under The Sender. When receiving only, he still needs decoding and interpretation skills.

The Environment
The social environment certainly helps to determine the nature of communication. Whether that environment is found in the formal organization, in the informal, or in a combination of both is immaterial. Some of the statements of wisdom gleaned by Rogers and Svenning (1969) in regard to the environment include these, which are quite similar to findings regarding feedback:

1. Times of stress and uncertainty are especially propitious for the spread of rumors (the old saw that "rumor rushes into a vacuum").
2. Communication in formal organizations tends to be horizontal rather than vertical.
3. Positive rather than negative messages tend to flow upward in formal organizations.
4. Formal channels often serve only to confirm change information already diffused by the grapevine.

Feedback
Of course, the only way in which a message sender can know whether his messages are being attended, regarded, translated, comprehended, and acted upon is through feedback. Often, feedback does not occur unless specifically requested and provided for. Once more we have paraphrased Rogers and Svenning (1969) in listing what appear to be statements of conventional wisdom having research support.

1. Communication that gives a receiver a sense of participation tends to ensure some involvement with the message.
2. Feedback from receiver to sender is essential to the integrity of the message.

3. Communication in the formal organization tends to be downward ("messages go down through a bullhorn, but those that
   go up must pass through a series of almost impenetrable
   filters").
4. In formal organizations, feedback received by the upper
   echelons of the organizational hierarchy tend to be positive
   in content.

THE ADMINISTRATIVE LEADER AND COMMUNICATION

The educational leader who holds an administrative position as principal, superintendent, director, coordinator, president, or other has
four basic uses for communication: giving performance feedback,
changing opinions and attitudes, seeking information, and giving
information.

Giving Performance Feedback

It was mentioned earlier that Sergiovanni and others have done the
only research known to the present writers in investigating Herzberg-
style "motivators" in the public school setting. Studies by Trusty
and Sergiovanni (1966) and Carver and Sergiovanni (1971) were summarized by Sergiovanni and Carver (1973, pp. 60–67). In that summary, it was reported that:

> In each instance . . . respondents completed a thirteen-item
> need deficiency questionnaire modeled after each of five cate-
> gories of a modified version of Abraham Maslow's need hierar-
> chy. The instrument assessed on a seven-point scale the amount
> of need fulfillment available for each of the five categories, as
> well as the amount each respondent felt he needed. The differ-
> ence between actual and desired need fulfillment was computed
> and labeled a "perceived need deficiency [p. 67]."

The rank order of the need levels that resulted from the study
in suburban Rochester, New York, according to age of respondents,
is shown in Table 9-1.

The rank order of the resultant need levels from the suburban
Rochester, New York, study, according to sex of respondents, is
shown in Table 9-2. The table does *not* show something that was
clearly apparent in the figure from which this table was prepared;
namely, *for all levels of need operation except security, the perceived need-deficiency was much greater for male teachers than
for females.*

The levels of need-deficiency reported by Sergiovanni and Carver
(1973, p. 62) in a secondary school study of teachers in Illinois,
showed esteem, self-actualization, autonomy, social, and security
needs in that rank order of deficiency.

These research results are repeated here for two reasons: (1)
educational leaders need to be aware that research, although too

TABLE 9-1
RANK ORDER BY AGE LEVEL OF PERCEIVED NEED DEFICIENCIES
FOR SUBURBAN ROCHESTER, NEW YORK, EDUCATORS

	LEVEL OF NEED				
AGE LEVEL	ESTEEM	SELF-ACTUALIZATION	AUTONOMY	SECURITY	SOCIAL
45 and over	3	1	2	4	5
35–44	1	3	2	4	5
25–34	1	2	3	4	5
20–24	1	2	3	5	4

Source: T. J. Sergiovanni and F. D. Carver, *The new school executive.* New York: Dodd, Mead, 1973, p. 60.

TABLE 9-2
RANK ORDER BY SEX OF PERCEIVED NEED DEFICIENCIES
FOR SUBURBAN ROCHESTER, NEW YORK, EDUCATORS

	LEVEL OF NEED				
SEX	ESTEEM	SELF-ACTUALIZATION	AUTONOMY	SECURITY	SOCIAL
Female	1	2	3	4	5
Male	1	2	3	4	5

Source: T. J. Sergiovanni and F. D. Carver, *The new school executive.* New York: Dodd, Mead, 1973, p. 61.

little, has been done on motivators of persons in public school settings, and that perceived need-deficiency seems to vary with age level and with sex of respondents, and (2) the studies emphasize that individuals need communications which provide positive reinforcement, particularly in the areas of esteem and self-actualization. It may be that in many situations deficiencies are not as great as individuals perceive them to be, but no or few reassuring messages come down from higher levels of the hierarchy in the form of feedback about performance. Often, such feedback as is provided is negative (and usually trivial) in nature.

Changing Opinions and Attitudes
To change one's own opinions or attitudes is difficult, but infinitely easier than changing the opinions or attitudes of others. Either is accomplished only through communication.

Many of the actions of both leading and administering (see Figure 8-1, p. 158) necessitate changing some of the opinions, attitudes, or behaviors of some of the persons in an organization. That is what influence is, and we all communicate to influence. We have mentioned before the opinions of men such as Bartky, Golembiewski, and Drucker to the effect that when dealing with educated people persuasion is the only moral means of influence. Rokeach (1971) described research which indicated that it is possible to change a person's values by arousing feelings of self-dissatisfaction, but he, too, mentioned the grave ethical questions that are involved in such an approach.

Quite a lot is known about persuasion, as that is the basis for the art of selling. An educational leader needs to master the skills of persuasion, and to be able to draw the fine line between persuasion and manipulation. In this regard, a rather subtle, but effective, strategy for changing attitudes has been developed and tested by Watson (1966) in what he calls the "S-P-A" approach. The present writers can testify that it works, sometimes dramatically. In essence, the *structure* (patterned relationships of people) is changed, which automatically brings about a change in *process* (social exchange), which results in a change of *attitude.* An example: In 1953, the present senior author, as superintendent of schools, assigned some black teachers to mixed classrooms when a de facto segregated school was closed and abandoned. This was a most uncommon practice at that time. Among the parents of children assigned to black teachers was one white, radically anti-black couple who threatened to move out of the community rather than have their child taught by a "nigger." The board of education stood firm in backing the assignment and the parents started looking feverishly for a new home. Before a suitable one was found, school was several weeks under way and the parents had discovered that not only was the teacher competent, but she was taking an interest in their son (a problem child for the previous five years!) as a person and he was learning. Before Thanksgiving, the mother was serving as a room mother and the father was openly praising the teacher!

Seeking Information

The administrative leader of a unit of any size has many needs for information. He needs to have his uncertainties reduced about the expectations held by others for him and for each other. He must learn of individuals' concerns and problems, seek individuals' opinions regarding organizational goals, and develop the means to be used to reach such goals.

If there are decisions to be made that depend on *judgment only*, not special information, AND ALL GROUP MEMBERS HAVE HAD EXPERIENCE THAT GIVES THEM A SOUND BASIS FOR MAKING THE JUDGMENT, a wise leader will seek the group judgment and rely on it in preference to his own or any other. One such matter would be in "discovering" problems that are critical to the organization. There are numerous very simple exercises that can be carried out in any group to prove that the average of individual judgments will come closer to fact that will the individual judgments of all but a few group members.

A vital purpose for an administrator seeking information is to get feedback regarding perceptions about decisions he has made and actions he has taken. He may want to seek advance information about decisions to be made or actions that may be taken, or to discover how proposed changes are likely to be received. People need to be involved when change is in the offing, and they may help to point out possible consequences of proposed actions, thus obviating future conflicts or other problems.

However, when in-group pressures operate on the self-image of group members, critical judgment may be seriously impaired, as described under Groupthink in a following section on Noise.

Giving Information
The administrative leader uses communication also for giving information to many individuals and groups about a variety of matters. With ever-increasing emphasis on accountability and evaluation, it is imperative to achieve understanding regarding goals and objectives of any organization. Individuals need to be apprised of the expectations held for them and of how their performances are viewed in terms of effectiveness. Advance notice of preferred outcomes to be advocated and of the urgency of those outcomes is needed. All concerned must be kept posted on anticipated changes and their progression from the possible to the imminent stage. Announcements of decisions made or actions taken, and the reasons therefor, can reduce many uncertainties, calm many fears, and obviate many rumors.

APPLICATIONS OF COMMUNICATION
Administrators in the myriad agencies of education have greater control over those communications that are internal to their agencies than over those that are external, but both are important. Each administrator needs to be aware of the various levels at which interpersonal, intraunit, and interunit communication occur internally, and of the external sources of communication that may be significant to the agency.

Internal
Communication is the essence of organized activity and is the basic process out of which social interaction develops. Neither the leadership process nor any of the actions necessary to it can occur without

internal communication. Influence, authority, or power can be exercised only if the holder is able to communicate. An educational leader not only must be able to communicate with those who are parts of the organization, but he or she must communicate with members of and see that communication occurs among various groups.

STUDENTS. Students are the reason for being of any education agency, and their problems must be discovered and dealt with, their uncertainties reduced, and their opinions heard.

STAFF. Staff people, as both core and working elements of the educational organization, have special needs for communication. Many a school principal is aware of and concerned about teaching staff, but some overlook the fact that support staff (such as secretaries, clerks, aides, custodians, cooks, and others), other principals, and central office staff are additional important components of the communication system.

CLIQUES. In Chapter 4, the point was made that the informal structure of an organization may be as important as or more important than the formal. This is particularly true in regard to communication. Earlier in this chapter, a research finding was described, to the effect that the formal communication often serves only to confirm what the grapevine has already made known. Cliques or clusters of people comprise the grapevine, where individuals described by Likert (1961) as "linking pins" are found perhaps more frequently than in the formal organization. When one person has information of interest to other members of his informal group, he passes it on to them; then a member of that group who is a member of a second informal group carries the message on to that group. The grapevine often can spread information faster than formal channels, and it should not be looked upon as undesirable. It is going to exist, no matter what efforts are made to eliminate it, and the realistic leader learns to use it, checking to see that it does not distort messages into quite different meanings.

OTHER UNITS. In a complex organization, such as a university, a school system, or a chain of business colleges, units function in relationship to other units and to the organization as a whole, not autonomously. Without coordinating communication among deans, principals, or directors there could be no common goals and, in effect, no organization.

External
Leaders in most education agencies must be sensitive to and actively work at communication with a number of external groups, both formal and informal, including board, community, and special-interest groups.

BOARD. While communication directly, on policy matters, with the board of control (board of education, board of trustees, board of regents, for example) is the responsibility of the head administrator, it is the concern of anyone who wishes to function as either a status or emergent leader.

COMMUNITY. Communication with the community is imperative for agencies which depend directly on favorable attitudes of community residents for securing financial support, as public schools or community colleges do. To a lesser extent, it also is necessary for parochial schools seeking nonconstitutent family support or for any private or proprietary school that must recruit its students from the local community.

SPECIAL-PURPOSE GROUPS. Educational leaders have reasons for communicating with a number of groups, each having some special interest. The number and types of such groups depend on the type of agency with which the leader is affiliated, and include examples such as alumni associations, boosters clubs, PTAs, parents clubs, parish members, community power structures, and informal groups of opinion leaders. The special purpose is determined by the group's relationship to the education agency.

PRESSURE GROUPS. Pressure groups usually try to affect the goals of the agency, and either exist or are formed especially for that purpose. An example is "The Friends of the Little Red Schoolhouse" group that functioned in Michigan in the 1950s and 1960s. Other pressure groups exist for more general and often laudable purposes, but still try to get their ideological views adopted by schools or colleges. Examples are the D.A.R., the American Legion, or the John Birch Society. Regardless of an educational leader's personal inclinations toward a particular group, he must communicate with any group that shows an interest in or makes an attempt at influencing any of the purposes of education for which his agency exists.

COMMUNICATING WITH GROUPS

Interpersonal communication is necessary and difficult, but group communication is infinitely more complex. Communication is the essence of an organization, and by necessity much of an educational leader's communication must be to and in groups of various sizes. A casual remark of his may be taken as an order or command by a subordinate and thus be translated into "standard operating procedure" at the lowest levels. The messages going up the channels tend, as we have seen, to be filtered so that only good news and laudatory comments reach the top. Getting reliable feedback becomes a major problem.

Jay (1971) made no claim to being a researcher or to having statistics to support his propositions about the size of groups needed for an effective communications network. The propositions are interesting, nevertheless, and the author was reporting from an impressive background in broadcasting where he had discovered empirical evidence regarding the uses and effectiveness of groups for both internal and external communication. The present writers have adapted his suggestions for communicating with groups of various sizes for application in educational settings.

"Ten Groups"

However far one traces the history and prehistory of the human race, one finds groups: family groups, clans, and tribes, among others. Jay's thesis that a work group of about ten persons (with a minimum of six and a maximum of fifteen) is most effective and efficient in securing morale and group output seems unlikely to be challenged by group dynamics authorities. Whether that size group is a legacy from the days of hunting bands is debatable, but size-effectiveness correlation is not controversial for anyone who has worked with groups.

Whether putting groups together to make decisions will necessarily produce the desired results was sharply questioned by Janis (1973). However, Jay said "ten groups" serve "the needs of corporate digestion and communication [p. 242]" and they are the instruments through which organizational objectives are achieved and goals approached. There are four types of such groups found doing the work in most agencies of education, and all may be what Betz (1973) called "task-process" groups. One type is ad hoc groups, each having a task to perform, the second is the board of control, the third is what in 1974 was known as "the administrative team," and the fourth is a combination of board of control and administrative team. The latter two groups may, by sheer circumstance, be too large to operate as "ten groups" in some education agencies. The organizational purposes served by all "ten groups" are, according to Jay (1971, p. 234): (1) to build and help maintain the communication network, (2) to give a feeling of security, (3) to help sort out status and quasi-territory, and (4) to reaffirm identity and the sense of belonging.

TASK-PROCESS GROUPS. Task-process groups, according to Betz (1973), always have extrapersonal objectives; they are to accomplish a task, complete a project, or produce a product. Classes, committees, task forces, action groups, and staff retreats usually are of this nature. Much of the work of education agencies gets done by such groups. This same writer indicated that "socio-process" groups of six to twenty members are best for achieving such interpersonal objectives as causing examinations of attitudes, values, and beliefs, or for informing and orienting. He suggested "psycho-process" groups of five to ten members for intrapersonal objectives such as modifying behavior by focusing on that behavior in the group. Obviously, most educational leaders will require expert assistance, or will need additional skills themselves, if either of the latter two types of groups is to be a part of their communication networks.

BOARD OF CONTROL. The board of control is the closest that most education agencies come to having the "council of elders" that Jay (1971) said should serve every king by making available to him the accumulated wisdom of the tribe. Would that all boards could be counted on to do that for chief administrators! The king and his council need to communicate "to decide what the job is, and in which direction lies the best hope of survival and success for the whole community." So it is with the superintendent or president and board in deciding for the whole of an educational enterprise.

ADMINISTRATIVE TEAM. A third kind of "ten group" is necessary when action has to be taken in regard to established goals and objectives. In it, "one or more of the king's group discuss with one or more leading princes or dukes the action that must be taken to achieve the objectives the king and his elders have fixed . . . this meeting is the crunch [p. 237]."

The term "administrative team" has been much used in recent years, particularly in public school systems, but it means many things to many people and nothing to some others. The concept was succinctly described by Mansergh[1] thus:

> Basically, the concept refers to the involvement of all levels of management in the planning, implementing, and decision-making process when such activities directly affect their professional responsibilities [p. v].

It is in the administrative-team setting that the "crunch" occurs in education agencies. The team may function as either a task-process or a socio-process group with proper guidance.

BOARD-ADMINISTRATIVE TEAM. The purpose of the fourth type of small group is "make the individual generals look at the whole war, and to give the cabinet of elders an insight into the feelings of the whole army [p. 239]." Such a group, in which the board of control and the administrative team meet together on a regular basis, could be quite beneficial for the purposes described if communica-

---

[1] G. G. Mansergh (Ed.), *Dynamics of management by objectives for school administrators.* Detroit: Metropolitan Detroit Bureau of School Studies, Inc., 1971.

tion is not impeded by the "noise" called *groupthink* (q.v.). This group probably functions in the socio-process mode more often than not, *yet most administrators do not have socio-process skills!*

Groups of 40 to 100

Groups of 40 to 100 persons can serve in having decisions and actions explained, allowing people to ask questions to reduce their uncertainties, and letting the aggrieved air grievances. A meeting of this size group is large enough that everyone realizes it cannot be a general discussion, but not so large as to inhibit those with burning questions. Jay warned against too great status-spread as an inhibitor, and spread can be obviated by convening groups with similar interests for this part of the communication process. Examples are groups such as department personnel, building faculty, a particular support-staff classification, PTA, or students.

The Whole Tribe

The gathering together of the whole tribe, with up to perhaps 500 or 1000 people, serves, to use Jay's own words, as a unique and irreplaceable instrument of communication. The whole tribe is an audience; dialogue is impossible and inviting questions is pointless. Addressing such a group is a unique experience, and it requires experience, confidence, and oratorical skills beyond the ordinary. However:

> It enables the leader . . . to sense the true collective feeling with a certainty that is beyond flattery or politeness or misrepresentation. It enables the whole tribe to decide if the leader is leading them in the right way, and to warn or encourage him collectively without risking personal careers or reputations. Above all, it enables the tribe to make a collective discovery of its identity—what it stands for and what it stands against, what it believes in and is proud of, what it rejects and despises. There is a deep need to know this tribal feeling [pp. 250–251].

The meeting of the whole tribe has exceptional promise but is little used as a communication tool. It should be used with students, faculty and staff, and paying constituents—separately, so as to again minimize status-spread.

NOISE

The concept of "noise" in the sense of factors that distort the quality of a signal was introduced by Shannon and Weaver (1949) in discussing the fidelity of electronic means of communication. Both words, noise, and fidelity are used by writers in the field, and they are reciprocals. Some of the things that help to assure fidelity, or success, of communication have been discussed. Communicators also need to be aware of some of the more common distorters of signals, in order to avoid them.

Sender-Receiver Discrepancies

Skills, attitudes, knowledge level, and sociocultural system were indicated as factors important to both sender and receiver of a particular message. A mismatch in any one of the areas can distort the signal, as indicated by the following illustrations.

SKILLS. Supoose that a chairperson of a science department starts a memo with: "In promulgating your esoteric cogitations and articulating your superficial sentimentalities, beware of platitudinous ponderosity." Few receivers are likely to pursue such jargon to find out that the chairperson is really making a plea to keep communication simple!

ATTITUDES. An apologetic directive is unlikely to have the desired effect on a self-actualized staff member.

KNOWLEDGE LEVEL. Some elementary school principals have been so presumptuous as to send messages about how to teach reading to teachers who are specialists in that field!

SOCIOCULTURAL SYSTEM. Messages from a patrician, Ivy League graduate, college president may be garbled if decoded by technical institute instructors born and reared in the inner city.

Concepts of Communicating

As Rogers and Roethlisberger (1952) pointed out, messages may be distorted by what one perceives communicating to be. If sender A thinks that he is communicating when receiver B agrees with his opinions and ideas while B thinks that he is communicating only when he can express his genuine misgivings about A's ideas, communication cannot occur with any great degree of fidelity.

Inability to Listen

Anyone with normal hearing or a hearing aid can hear the distinctly uttered words of another, but to *listen* so that the speaker's meaning is understood requires a skill that few persons have developed. Inability to listen may be due to such varied causes as lack of skill, tendency to evaluate by approving or disapproving, smouldering resentment of or deference to status differences, or to some other predisposition. Brown and Keller (1973) stressed the effect on listening of those relationships in which there are power differentials.

Impediments

While impediments such as stammering or lisping by a sender may be tolerated quite well by receivers, some other impediments, of which senders may or may not be aware, may not be tolerated at all or may be so severe as to interfere with the intended message. Speech teachers for years warned against falling into the habit of interspersing "uh" frequently, but at the time of this writing the frequent interspersing of "you know," "like," and "I mean" were used, by what seemed to be a majority of the population, with a frequency never approached by the worst "uh-er." Some individuals use these phrases to such excess that they lose communication. Some speakers use finger-jabbing, winking, or other movements or gestures so frequently that they detract from the intended message.

Message Elements
Elements of the message itself which may lead to distortion include content, treatment (medium chosen, channel used, and mode in which cast), and the code or symbols selected.

Instant Familiarity
The new principal (particularly if quite young) who immediately starts calling everyone by first name or nickname, totally disregarding age differences or years spent achieving professional prestige, often flips the "off" switch as far as his receivers are concerned. Salesmen are often taught to immediately get on a first name basis, but with certain customers the practice is likely to lose more sales than it makes.

What Was Your Name?
At the opposite extreme is the individual who can't remember names of the people with whom he works, uses incorrect names, or misspells names in letters or memos. These practices, too, introduce noise that may shut off effective communication.

Lack of Confidence in Research
Another source of noise is found in the lack of confidence that most people have in the findings of research in the social sciences. As an example, many of the findings of communications research reported by Rogers and Svenning in 1969 were included in the 1953 summary by Hovland, Janis, and Kelley. Yet even in 1974 those findings had not been widely accepted, disseminated, or acted upon. Most university programs for the preparation of leaders, regardless of the field in which they are to lead or of the disciplines in which they are prepared, make little or no use of specifics in building communication skills and understandings.

Groupthink
One of the most alarming sources of noise in group communications was identified, given the name of "groupthink," and deliberately given an invidious connotation by classing it in the same order of

words as "doublethink" and the "newspeak" of Orwell's *1984.* Educational leaders need to be aware and beware of it in using groups for decision-making. Why highly intelligent individuals sometimes perform poorly in making decisions when functioning in task-process groups was analyzed by Janis (1973), using as examples Pearl Harbor, escalation in Vietnam, and "a perfect fiasco"—the Bay of Pigs. He came to the startling conclusion that under group conditions there may be a deterioration of mental efficiency, reality testing, and moral judgment, resulting from in-group pressures. Six major defects in decision-making contributed to failures to solve problems adequately in the three illustrative situations, and all six relate to communication: (1) there was no survey of the full range of alternatives available, (2) members failed to reexamine the initial decision for nonobvious drawbacks, (3) courses of action initially judged unsatisfactory were not reexamined, (4) little if any information was sought from experts, (5) selective bias was shown by members interested only in facts and opinions that supported their own preferences, and (6) members spent little time considering possible consequences and planning for contingencies. Members tended to consider loyalty to the group as equated to morality, and clung to group norms and pressures toward uniformity, even when their chosen action was working poorly or unintended consequences disturbed their consciences!

The greater the threat to members' self-esteem the greater their inclination to resort to concurrence seeking at the expense of communication.

SUMMARY

Communication is the essence of any organization. The nature of communication is influenced by the "and"—cognition that other matters preceded and will follow that about which a message is formed—the sender, the message, the medium, the receiver, the environment, and feedback or lack of feedback. There are consistent research findings, most of them known since the 1950s, that could help greatly in becoming better communicators.

Any administrative or status leader needs communication for giving performance feedback, changing opinions and attitudes, seeking information, and giving information. He or she applies communication in a variety of uses with individuals and with groups in both internal and external settings.

Specific groups with which an educational leader must communicate include small groups of four distinct identities: task-process groups, board of control, administrative team, and board-administrative team. There are distinctive purposes for communicating with each which can be served in no other way.

Groups of 40 to 100 persons probably are most effective for explaining decisions and actions, allowing people to ask questions, and airing grievances, but they are not used as much as they should be by most educational leaders. Gatherings of the whole tribe (all of the persons in a particular category) have exceptional promise but also are little used as communication instruments. They serve functions for the leader that can be served in no other way.

Noise consists of any factors that distort the quality of message signals and there are many such factors. Communicators need to learn to avoid or minimize the more obvious of them. While not yet researched in education agencies, groupthink seems to be a crucial noise consideration for individuals who believe in and try to use groups for decision-making.

Chapter 10 will concern accountability, which depends directly on communication.

SOME SUGGESTED RESOURCES

R. L. Applbaum, K. W. E. Anatol, E. R. Hays, O. O. Jenson, R. E. Porter, and J. E. Mandel. *Fundamental concepts in human communication.* San Francisco, Calif.: Canfield Press, 1973.

D. K. Berlo, *Avoiding communication breakdown* (film). BNA Films, 1969.

D. K. Berlo, *Changing attitudes through communication* (film). BNA Films, 1969.

D. K. Berlo, *Communicating management's point of view* (film). BNA Films, 1969.

D. K. Berlo, *Communicating feedback* (film). BNA Films, 1969.

D. K. Berlo, *Meanings are in people* (film). BNA Films, 1969.

D. K. Berlo, *The process of communication.* New York: Holt, Rinehart & Winston, 1960.

R. L. Birdwhistell, Communication. In D. L. Sills (Ed.), *International encyclopedia of the social sciences.* New York: Macmillan, 1968. Vol. 3, pp. 24–28.

C. T. Brown and P. W. Keller, *Monologue to dialogue.* Englewood Cliffs: Prentice-Hall, 1973.

D. Fabun, *Communications: The transfer of meaning* (monograph). Beverly Hills, Calif.: Glencoe Press, 1968.

S. J. Knezevich, Decision making and communication. Ch. 3 in *Administration of public education* (2nd ed.). New York: Harper & Row, 1969. Pp. 58–71.

H. J. Leavitt, Communication: getting information from A into B. Ch. 9 in *Managerial psychology* (2nd ed.). Chicago: University of Chicago Press, 1972. Pp. 114–124.

A. C. Leyton, *The art of communications: Communication in industry.* London: Pitman, 1968.

H. L. Sisk, Communications. Ch. 17 in *Management and organization* (2nd ed.). Cincinnati, Ohio: South-Western, 1973. Pp. 510–540.

L. This, *Communicating within the organization* (monograph) Washington: Leadership Resources, Inc., 1972.

K. Wiles, Supervision is communication. Ch. 4 in *Supervision for better schools* (3rd ed.). Englewood Cliffs, N.J.: Prentice-Hall, 1967. Pp. 51–66.

CHAPTER 10

ACCOUNTABILITY

*. . . educators can be accountable only to the degree that
they share responsibility in educational decision-making
and to the degree that other parties who share this responsibility
—legislators, other government officials, school boards,
parents, students, and taxpayers—also are held accountable.*
NEA Resolution

Accountability is here to stay—if schools are here to stay. Those
educators who expect that demands for accountability will decrease
or disappear when certain state and national figures leave the educational arena are doomed to disappointment and disillusion. People
are at last becoming aware that schools are not serving the learning
needs of individuals well and thus are less than satisfactory for
society.

The term "accountability" is relatively new to schools, but the
concept is not. In an earlier era of education, there was emphasis
on evaluation, but the term has never been understood by most
school people. The questions of who should be evaluated, by whom,
on what basis, and to what purpose have been often raised, seldom
addressed, and never answered. The quondam debate about performance appraisal and the relationship of motivation to such appraisal has sporadically sputtered to life, but each time it has died
away with no resolution of the issues.

Questions are somewhat different now, but the asking is clamor-
ous and the attention is unremitting. Who is responsible (accountable) to whom? For what? Who is to decide? What use is to be

made of whatever data are collected? This chapter will include discussion of reasons for the unprecedented emphasis on accountability, some pros and cons of performance appraisal, some definitions of accountability, including one that seems germane at the present time, the relationship of accountability to the functions of education in this society, and the importance of one's time orientation and point of view to one's concept of accountability.

REASONS FOR EMPHASIS

Events and developments in our national and world lives seem to have converged on the years of the late 1960s and early 1970s. In the Cold War with the Soviet Union, the United States lost the battle, if not the war, when the Russians were first into space with Sputnik I, and the memory still rankles. Technology gave us cybernetics, along with an unprecedented capacity for storing and retrieving data, massaging them, and using them to stimulate systems not yet in existence. Revolutionary social changes in the forms of sexual mores, religious liberalization, minorities' consciousness, family and marriage customs, breaking down of sex stereotypes, birth control, legalized abortion, and a host of others engulfed us. Economic boom and bust turned into spiralling inflation; public school teachers, not a few college faculties, and many supporting-staff groups learned that they possess and can effectively use group power for purposes of negotiating higher salaries in a race with living costs. Formal agencies of education—schools and colleges—discovered belatedly that there are competitors "out there." People who "think systems" appeared everywhere. "Evaluation" took on a new meaning in the context of "program evaluation" related to federally funded school-based projects. All of these events and developments contributed to the emphasis on accountability, and a look at each is in order.

Losing the Battle

Immediately after the successful launch of Sputnik I in October 1957 there were cries of outrage throughout the land. As in the aftermath of previous wars, at least since the Franco-Prussian, citizens on the "losing" side wanted to know why the schools had not done their jobs better. There were immediate demands to beef up school offerings in the areas of mathematics, science, and foreign languages. By 1965, we had not only the new science and the new math, but also the new English and the new social studies, all developed by university professors. As Postman and Weingartner (1973b) described, the phases and mottoes could be identified thus: 1957–1960, getting rid of "frills"; 1960–1965, reconstruction of curriculum; 1965–1970, stop schooling for failure, be humane; 1970–197?, get rid of schools.

At long last, our society has come to realize that a favorite assumption is not valid. Education is *not* synonymous to schooling. Education is a do-it-yourself job in which everyone engages from cradle to crypt, womb to tomb, or conception to resurrection. On the other hand, school, in Postman and Weingartner's (1973a) elegant phrasing, "serves many masters, yields to many constraints, has many items on its agenda, and therefore cannot always concentrate its resources on assisting an individual in educating himself [p. 80]." Demands for accountability are demands for realistic appraisal of what schools and colleges can do—and might do better.

Technology

For years, books and other printed documents were the principal forms in which information was stored. Comparatively recent developments, which new generations will take for granted, include microfilm, microfiche, and computer storage of innumerable bits of information in ferromagnetic or other domains. Furthermore, there are many new indexes and cross-indexes of information, some of them mechanized and electronic in nature. Instant retrieval is now possible. Means for internal control and communication are vastly improved, and feedback mechanisms can be provided to automatically correct errors—if standards are known so that error can be determined.

Once, it would have been a tremendously expensive and laborious process to determine the effectiveness of a certain instructional practice or the efficiency of building utilization. Now, hardware, software, and trained people are available to provide almost any desired information about a school, a school system, or a college. Availability has led to demands that people and tools be used to help determine what universities, colleges, and schools—and the people who work in them—might do better than they are now doing.

Social Issues

A veritable encyclopedia could be written to catalog the social issues of concern to various segments of the U.S. populace. Entries would certainly include, but not be limited to, abortion, aggression, birth control, communication, compulsory school attendance, conservation, consumerism, crime, discipline, drug abuse, ecology, economic policy, equalization of opportunity, euthanasia, family customs, farm prices, foreign relations, ghettos, government controls, heterosexuality and homosexuality, housing, inflation, intelligence factors, justice under the law, knowledge explosion, land use, law and order, marriage and divorce, media use and abuse, minorities' treatment, open housing, penal reform, political ethics, pollution, pornography and obscenity, power differentials, privacy of individuals, quality of products, quotas, racial integration, religious training, respect for others, separation of church and state, sex discrimination, sexual mores, social sensitivity, terrorism, urbanism, venereal disease control, violence, welfare, wiretapping, xenophobia, yellow journalism, and zoning.

Each of these matters is still at issue, with pro and con factions each insisting that the schools should inculcate its particular point of view. Obviously, the schools cannot please everyone. Generally, schools do serve secondary or tertiary functions of the other major social institutions in addition to certain primary functions of the educational institution (see Table 5-1, p. 94). Indeed any school *must* to some extent serve the domestic, economic, political, and religious interests of the group that pays to support it if it is to survive. Company, government, parochial, private, and proprietary schools and colleges usually have easier going than do their public counterparts because the interests of their supporting groups are less diverse.

As of 1974, various school systems were serving as instruments of attempted racial desegregation, by court order. Whether the schools can achieve changes of attitude in the absence of open housing is not yet established. Whether forced busing has positive, neutral, or negative effects on the overall learning of children urgently needs investigation. Nevertheless, there are vociferous demands that the school be responsive and accountable to the interests of a majority of its constituents, and in some cases the "real issue" (Boles, 1970) is whether a strident-voiced minority can impose its view on a majority. The moot question for each community is "For what portion of total education is the school responsible?"

Inflation

Despite government attempts at economic controls, consumers have found that living costs continue to rise so they make periodic demands for pay increases, which then force price increases in other sectors of the economy, bringing another round of demands. With more goods available for purchase and more appeals to buy, people have found an ever-widening gap between their wants and their capacity to satisfy those wants. Educators and others who have services to sell in return for tax dollars have been inept at huckstering when compared to their competitors. The buying public is seeking to be convinced that their tax dollars are being used to provide what they want, rather than being squandered foolishly. It seems a reasonable demand.

Negotiations

There is no question but what the discovery that group power can be used in the bargaining process has brought greatly increased salaries to personnel in some schools and colleges. Even those states which do not yet have mandated negotiations have been affected by developments in those that do. To individuals who earn less than the current salaries of teachers, a system that allows a group to make demands and have them met at public expense makes little sense. Even those individuals whose pay scales are higher than those of the teachers in their communities resent being forced to pay to provide a salary schedule that compensates solely or largely on the basis of education and experience, with little or no consideration of merit. The attitude of most seems to be, "if you are going to force us to pay those salaries, prove to us that you are earning them."

Competition
Educators—or to be more precise, those educators who work in formal agencies of education—have tended to view learning as the exclusive preserve of the schools and colleges. The largely abortive attempts at performance contracting described by Page (1972), based on profit motives, shocked the sensibilities of some school personnel, but they were awakened to the fact that the schools do have competition. Some persons are even more shocked at what they consider sabotage from within by those who have been experimenting with alternative and free schools. Some still refuse to acknowledge that any significant learning can occur in such informal and nonformal agencies as were described in Chapter 4. Some recognize that the nonformal do exist, but look on them with disdain.

Not so the general public. Many individuals know the alternatives available to them for learning what the schools cannot or will not provide, as do some of the people who work in formal agencies. Some are aware of the benefits of this pluralistic system, and seek only to avoid needless overlap and senseless waste of resources. Nevertheless, the voices of both groups add to the demands that each agency be responsive to the interests of the group that provides its financial support. The proposal that each learner of school age be given a voucher which he can use to purchase learning opportunities at any agency of his choice is one of the responses to this demand—and it scares hell out of people who work in traditional schools!

Systems
Robert McNamara is generally credited with having instituted a "Planning-Programming-Budgeting System" (PPBS) when he was Secretary of Defense, and is said to have expressed its purpose as "getting more bang for the buck." Those who are trying to bring PPBS, MBO (Management by Objectives), and similar systems to schools and colleges may be said to be trying to "get more learning for the loot." People who "think systems" view an education agency as an array of people, facilities, and other resources which can be organized and categorized in terms of inputs, activities, and outputs. This analytical perspective focuses on the prime purpose of the system as being the provision of learning opportunities. An agency's

excellence is to be measured by the quality of the learning opportunities it provides, and not until those are defined and described can the "system man" specify in what activities the school or college should engage or what resources are required. This possibility of at long last getting the horse before the cart excites the imagination of some—and adds to the emphasis on accountability.

Evaluation

Evaluation as a word has been in the lexicon of most educators for generations, but there has been little agreement on its meaning and the concept has not been used effectively in looking either at people or programs. However, since the U.S. government started spending greatly increased sums on a variety of education "projects" in the 1950s there have been increasing demands that those projects be evaluated in terms of cost-benefit ratio. As evaluation techniques have been developed, the word has taken on new meaning and Cook (1966), Stufflebeam et al. (1971), and Worthen and Sanders (1973) have managed to elevate and sophisticate the term until it is virtually a discipline in and of itself. People are now being prepared to evaluate not only federally funded projects, but total school and school district programs as well. When it is obvious that program evaluation *can* be done, it adds to the demands for accountability, and reminds that perhaps individual evaluation could be part of the process.

DEFINITIONS

As writers in the area of communications point out, meanings are in people, not in words. As a new word is introduced by someone, it either is rejected by others or is gradually adopted through being used by more and more of the people to whom it is significant. Eventually, it may work its way into that historical repository of meanings, the dictionary, but meanings change more rapidly and frequently than dictionaries do. Thus, dictionaries often do not show the most current meanings of a word and do not indicate much specificity of meaning. The current definitions of accountability are a case in point.

Dictionary

According to Webster's dictionary, accountability is "the quality or state of being accountable." "Accountable" means "subject to giving an account: ANSWERABLE."

The *Dictionary of Education* (Good, 1973) was, at this writing, more contemporary than Webster's in regard to the meaning of accountability, but its entries reflect the confusion of people in the field, despite widespread usage of the term among educators who work in public schools.

> accountability: (*admin.*) *liability for results which have been obtained through the responsible exercise of delegated authority* [*p. 6*].

> accountability, educational: *the theory that teachers and school systems may be held responsible for actual improvement in pupil achievement and that such improvement is measurable through tests of teacher effectiveness constructed by outside agencies* [*pp. 6–7*].
>
> accountability, pupil: *the responsibility for carrying out an obligation or trust to each pupil appropriately assigned to a specific school or school district* [*p. 7*].
>
> testing, accountability: *the attempt to monitor the academic results achieved by teachers in their instructional activities and the social and emotional impact of the school on the pupils through periodic sample testing by outside education experts or with specially constructed tests purchased from education industry firms* [*p. 604*].

Obviously, the term "accountability" is ambiguous at the present time. In the first definition, above, accountability is equated to liability; in the second, it is categorized as a theory; in the third, as a responsibility; and in the fourth, it is said to be an attempt to monitor. Furthermore, in some of the situations where accountability is perceived as an attempt to monitor, the "specially constructed tests" used are not "purchased from education industry firms" but are developed, disseminated, and the results collected and fed back by state departments of education. The system in Michigan is one example. The abortive attempt at National Assessment also is unrecognized in this definition.

At least three nondictionary definitions seem to deserve consideration in attempts to reduce the uncertainty-induced anxiety of people who work in schools. These definitions have the merit of being applicable as concepts in organizations of all kinds, not just in schools.

Accountability as Effectiveness

Even effectiveness is not defined with specificity in the *Dictionary of Education* (Good, 1973):

> teacher effectiveness: (1) *the ability of a teacher to create a meeting and an interaction between the physical, intellectual, and psychological interests of the student and some subject-matter content; the ability of the teacher to relate the learning activities to the developmental process of the learners and to their current and immediate interests and needs;* (2) *teacher behavior whether in a classroom or in relation to his or her faculty group; a basis for decisions as to award of tenure or continuing contract and for determination of worthiness for merit salary increases, though not as yet predictable or measurable by any definite criteria* [*p. 586*].

But teacher effectiveness is not the only effectiveness that is important in schools and in other aspects of education, even if one accepts the jargon-filled definitions above. A clearer and more comprehensive statement would seem to be our earlier definition of effectiveness as the ratio of performance to expectations, or $Ef = P/Ex$. *Accountability* then *is the process of attempting to secure performance commensurate with expectations.* Even then, many questions remain: Are we talking about expectations held for and performance by individuals or entire agencies of education? If for individuals, are those individuals students, instructors, administrators, or members of boards of control? Whether for individuals or agencies, how can expectations be agreed on, explicated, and set up as standards? What measures of performance are to be used?

Acountability as Efficiency

The *Dictionary of Education* (Good, 1973) contains two definitions of efficiency, to wit:

efficiency: *the ability to achieve desired results with economy of time and effort in relation to the amount of work accomplished* [p. 207].

This is not too far removed from our own definition, but there is no mention of dollar costs, and these are certainly of concern to at least some who are clamoring for accountability.

teacher efficiency: *the degree of success of a teacher in performing instructional and other duties specified in his contract and demanded by the nature of his position* [p. 586].

Efficiency is not limited to schools or to teachers, to state the obvious. Our earlier definition of efficiency as the ratio of benefits to cost, or $Ef = B/C$, seems broader and allows for description of all manner of benefits and for any conceivable cost measure, including time, effort, and money. If efficiency is an expectation (and the word is used deliberately here), then *accountability is the process in which benefits are considered in terms of what they cost.* But agreement among those who use this meaning seem no nearer unanimity than for those who adhere to the other. Whose benefits? Measured how? Learner benefits, measured in terms of quantity of learning opportunities provided and taken advantage of, or in terms of quality of opportunity, or both? How are quantity and/or quality to be measured? Benefits to the community or to society? Measured by what scale? Participatory citizenship? Economic productivity? Cost to whom? The learner, measured in time? The instructor, measured in effort? The financial backers, in terms of dollars?

Accountability as Effectance

The term "effectance" seems to have been coined to describe the extent to which an individual's or an organization's performance is both effective and efficient. In formula form, it means that $Ec = P/Ex + B/C$. The coined word has not gained wide acceptance to date, but if both effectiveness and efficiency are important, as the present writers believe them to be, then *accountability is the process of attempting to secure performance commensurate with expectations, and one of the expectations is that benefits will be proportional to costs.* Perhaps the semantic leap to that meaning of accountability can be made, so that whether effectance should be accepted and used becomes an academic question.

If the proposed definition *is* accepted, it then becomes necessary to review the ancient and much-belabored concept of performance appraisal with the avowed intent of updating it and making it respectable.

PERFORMANCE APPRAISAL

Most of the current demands for and moves toward accountability are based on outmoded concepts of performance appraisal and motivation that the leading writers in the social sciences and in management have been urging be discarded for at least two decades. The proposals that have been made for other approaches seem not to be known by educational leaders or unheeded if known. Reasons for this state of affairs might be deduced from the earlier discussion of communication, but the reasons do not really matter unless learning them might bring promise of change. For somewhat less than two decades, occasional voices have been heard to the effect that, if new attitudes toward motivation are to be developed, change in organizational structure is imperative. These voices have not reached the ears of many educators.

Traditional Views of Motivation

A traditional view of motivation has been described inelegantly but graphically, by Herzberg (1968) as KITA—an acronym for "kick in the posterior."

> *If I kick my dog (from the front or back), he will move. And when I want him to move again, what must I do? I must kick him again. Similarly, I can charge a man's battery, and then recharge it, and recharge it again [p. 55].*

A different view, or perhaps the same view in different but still pungent language, was described by Levinson (1973):

> *Frequently, I have asked executives this question? What is the dominant philosophy of motivation in American management?*

Almost invariably, they quickly agree that it is the carrot-and-stick philosophy, reward and punishment. Then I ask them to close their eyes for a moment, and to form a picture in their mind's eye with a carrot at one end and a stick at the other. When they have done so, I then ask them to describe the central image in that picture. Most frequently they respond that the central figure is a jackass [p. 73].

If one believes in the self-fulfilling prophecy and the expectations research of Rosenthal (1973), the conclusions are inevitable. Accustom a person to a kick and he will expect to be kicked repeatedly. Treat a person like a jackass and he will behave like one.

The catalog of KITA personnel practices so far developed as attempts to instill motivation includes reducing time spent at work, spiraling wages, fringe benefits, human relations training, sensitivity training, communications, two-way communication, job participation, and employee counseling, according to Herzberg (1968). He concluded that all have been ineffective and that:

Since KITA results only in short-term movement, it is safe to predict that the cost of these programs will increase steadily and new varieties will be developed as old positive KITA's reach their saturation points [p. 56].

Thus, a new approach to motivation may be necessary.

A "New" Approach to Motivation

As early as 1954, Drucker was proposing management by objectives. In 1957, before he had articulated his Theory X and Theory Y concepts, McGregor was pointing out a "new" approach to motivation:

This approach calls on the subordinate to establish short-term performance goals for himself. The superior enters the process actively only after the subordinate has (a) done a good deal of thinking about his job, (b) made a careful assessment of his own strengths and weaknesses, and (c) formulated some specific plans to accomplish his goals. The superior's role is to help the man relate his self-appraisal, his "targets," and his plans for the ensuing period to the realities of the organization [p. 91].

The same author stressed that we all make judgments, unavoidably, about the performance of others, and that salary and promotion policies cannot be administered without them. The same would be true of tenure. Emphasis, however, should be on the leader's actions of assisting performance, and the new approach should reflect an unwillingness to treat human beings like inanimate objects. When the obviously important needs of an organization come into conflict with convictions about the worth and dignity of the human personality, the latter must prevail unless learners might be damaged thereby.

This somewhat idealistic view has been reiterated in a steady flow of articles and books, all in similar vein, from such writers as McGregor (1960), Odiorne (1961), Kindall and Gatza (1963), Maslow (1965), Herzberg (1959, 1965, 1966, 1968), Bennis and Slater (1968), Berkley (1971), Randall (1971), Bennis (1972), Levinson (1973a and 1973b), Argyris (1973), and Conant (1973). Of these, only Argyris reported any attempts at implementation, and those had disappointing results, but he was optimistic nonetheless, and all of these writers make a convincing case for a concept which in essence is Theory Y. Philosophically, of course, it is based on the "third force" psychology of which Maslow is the acknowledged father. Bennis (1972) pointed out some unanswered criticisms, but did not perceive them as disabling.

Organizational Implications

Attention of readers of this book has already been called to Drucker's (1959) speculations about structural changes needed for managing the educated, and to Bennis and Slater's (1968) arguments that more democaratic structures are inevitable throughout our organizations. In Chapter 4, we quoted Berkley (1971) at some length in his description of structures more flexible than most of those now extant, and mentioned that the structures of some alternative schools approximate his description.

The assumption that a hierarchical structure is both a necessity and a given was highlighted by Bennis (1972), who argued that it is neither. He did not dispute that power and control must somehow be distributed and exercised, but he did argue for structure that fits functions and tasks rather than fitting the traditional model if we are to have new attitudes toward motivation. This is in line with the research findings of Watson (1966), to the effect that if one changes structure, process is automatically changed, and attitude change results.

More recently, Drucker (1973) said:

> . . . the basic principles of effective organization are beginning to emerge. The worker and the work-group need to take responsibility for job design and for work-group structure as well as for the fringe benefits that influence the working community. . . . But it is destructive folly to assume, in the name of creativity, that they do not need knowledge that is generally unavailable to them. . . . management can encourage the achieving worker, make his efforts productive, provide him constant feedback and allow for constant learning that transcends the immediate job [p. 92].

These organizational implications require that educational leaders and the society whose interests are served by the agencies they represent make some conscious and difficult decisions regarding the functions of education and schools before proceeding willy-nilly with vast ideas of accountability supported only by a half-vast rationale.

FUNCTIONS OF EDUCATION AND SCHOOLS
It can hardly be doubted that cultural transmission, considering social change, discovery of new knowledge, and helping individuals in personal development are among the legitimate functions of education in this society. If those functions are not served by education, they are unlikely to be served by any of the other major social institutions.

The question that must be resolved at the national level, however, before accountability can be soundly conceived and meaningful, is "To what extent is the *school* expected to be the agency for accomplishing these functions?" The valiant efforts being made to develop strategies for establishing and changing school goals and objectives in many communities across the land are doomed to ultimate failure until there is a national answer to this question. This is true despite federal funding of a massive, lengthy, and promising effort sponsored by the prestigious Phi Delta Kappa fraternity. Let us explore some of the reasons.

Cultural Transmission
The schools can and do provide opportunities for the young to learn some of the history of our country, its geography, its literature, its crafts and fine arts, its performing arts, its technological development, and its form of government. But does not cultural heritage include the record of both successes and failures, the right of dissent, the inevitability of change, and learning to bring desired change through the use of political and economic power? Must the melting-pot myth be perpetuated in preference to teaching cultural plurality and ethnic pride? In short, is any cultural information that is historical fact legitimate instructional matter, or are the schools to help transmit only selected favorable-to-the-status-quo bits of our culture—a practice for which we castigate other nations? If the school is not to expose some of the sorrier facets of our cultural history, such as our long-callous treatment of minorities and the periodic dehumanizing of individuals, then what education agency will do so? Are we to continue to shout "Communist" or "treason" every time someone points out that we have had failures as well as successes?

Social Change
Earlier in this chapter there was a listing of some of the current social issues in this country. In every pro and con faction related

to every one of those issues, plus innumerable unlisted ones, there are voices of educators, among others, saying that the schools should be responsible for perpetuating that faction's particular bias, and that the schools and their designated leaders should be held accountable if the desired results are not achieved. One of the field readers of an early draft of the manuscript for this book arbitrarily selected five of the listed issues in which he had particular interest and castigated the present writers for not specifying what schools (and particularly principals and superintendents) should do about them! He made no mention of the other issues, as if they were unimportant!

A school principal in Harlem, in a 1970 interview, said that there is pressure on the schools "because Americans ask education to do all the things they used to pray to God for." Indeed they do, and they are asking the impossible, as God probably decided long ago. Not only can the *school* not do everything that everyone wants, all of the agencies of education combined cannot. The school has not been notably successful in providing for social mobility nor in equalizing educational opportunities and the power that supposedly results therefrom. Madison Avenue has been very successful at teaching people a variety of wants, but the school has been positively inept at increasing individuals' capacities for acquiring economic goods, services, and other satisfactions, as the Coleman Report and the Jencks rehash attest. The school's efficacy as a court-mandated agency of racial integration is still an open question.

The national issue that must be resolved before realistic educational goals can be set at the community level is whether the school is to be held accountable for social changes that it cannot begin to accomplish. Perhaps it can and should be held accountable for teaching the inevitability and desirability of social change, the nature of current social issues, and the means by which change can be effected.

New Knowledge
A third issue that needs to be resolved at the national level if accountability is to be a viable concept for implementation is whether the discovery of new knowledge is an open or a restricted domain. Are the research laboratories of the universities and the think tanks the only places where new ideas may be had or is exploration to be encouraged universally, including among the very young, in school and nonschool settings? Are all areas open to exploration, or are some taboo? Are some new discoveries to be suppressed because they are inimical to the government establishment or to certain corporate interests that have vital roles in the economy? These are idle questions.

Is the school to be accountable if, either through school instruction, school-sponsored independent study, or school-unconnected analysis, some person develops guidelines that would make a shambles of our present political process? Or suggests and outlines a more appealing form of government? Would we tolerate a present-day Tom Paine, or even a Jefferson? Suppose that a high school scientist, with the frightening (to those of us who are older) sophistication that some now have, develops some process that would put one or more of our major industries out of business. How would the discovery be handled? Is there really academic freedom? In the schools as well as in colleges? For students as well as for faculty?

Purposes of Learners

As long as we have compulsory school attendance, we are demonstrating that the school exists more for the purposes of society than for the purposes of learners. Despite rationalization that "it is for his own good," the fact remains that for a number of those now compelled to attend school, individuals' purposes would be better served if the time were spent somewhere else. Regardless of why the laws were passed initially, we should have learned that we can compel the child to school, but we can't make him learn. The outcome of "The Strangely Significant Case of Peter Doe" (Saretsky, 1973) in California, and of similar ones likely to follow, are being watched with great interest. Is accountability a two-way process? If we compel the child and his parents to be accountable for his presence at school, is the school then accountable for his acquiring the skills that society says he should have? Would the accountability position be more tenable if each school indicated what it believes it can do and learners were then free to attend so long as their purposes were compatible with those of the school? Should not school attendance be a privilege rather than a forced obligation? A voucher system would allow these things, and would make accountability possible, but it might put a lot of public schools out of business.

It may be argued that, even with compulsory attendance, schools can and should structure their goals to make them more compatible with more learners' purposes than they have been in the past. Point conceded. But will there not still be some who are compelled to attend whose purposes would be better served elsewhere? Is it not conceivable that there could be a sizable group of these who might band together in their malcontent and deliberately refuse to cooperate with the school? Is it possible for the school to be accountable for such a group unless the goals and curriculum are totally and absolutely individualized? And is that economically or educationally feasible?

TIME ORIENTATION

It has been said that there are three types of minds; yesterday, today, and tomorrow. Minds of all three types may be discerned among the many people who are clamoring for accountability. All need to be considered if the concept is to be advanced beyond the present state of clumsy fumbling.

Past
Yesterday minds among the critics say that the schools are accountable for everything from the high level of unemployment to the large number of adult illiterates and they would have society recriminate by refusing to fund schools at a level adequate to the demands of today. They see no need for school goals beyond the 3 Rs. Coeval minds among educators cry "unfair" and point to the fact that this society has educated a larger percentage of its population to a higher level of literacy than has ever been accomplished by any other society in recorded history. The former continue to be punitive over conditions that the school cannot now change, and the latter would bask smugly in the glow of self-congratulation. Both see the traditional structure as satisfactory, with only performance lacking.

Present
Today minds among the critics recognize that expectations have changed because demands of individuals and the goals of society and of communities have changed, and insist that school performance has not kept pace. They demand that changes be made now, and that schools acknowledge their shortcomings. Today minds among school people and their school constituents admit to shortcomings and are trying to provide remedies. It is among these people that Lang and Rose[1] found the modest successes that they reported regarding "Community Involvement in Accountability." These groups are trying to bring goal and program changes without changes in traditional school structures.

Future
Critics of the schools who are calling for the schools to take stands on each of the current social issues have tomorrow minds. They worry more about the future than the past or present, recognizing that changes must be made and demanding that the schools help to make them. Among the many educators with tomorrow minds are those who recognize the inevitability and desirability of social change. They are assembling facts and points of view regarding social issues. They are presenting both sides, and they are teaching the means by which change can be accomplished. They are willing to establish goals and be held accountable, personally and institutionally, for performance in these areas, if structures can be changed to bring needed changes in process and in attitudes.

[1] Report made to NCPEA, Bellingham, Washington, August 1973.

EVALUATING PEOPLE AND PROGRAMS

Whether a person or a program is to be evaluated, the questions to be asked seem relatively simple: Who is responsible to whom? For what? What are the standards against which the person or program is to be judged? How is performance to be measured? How are benefits to be measured? What is the measure of cost? Who is to judge whether performance-benefits-cost are up to the desired standards? What is to be done if the standards are not being met in one or more areas? Done by whom? It is when one tries to answer the questions for a specific individual or a particular program that difficulty is encountered, and some present attempts at accountability seem to be trying to provide answers only vaguely related to the basic questions.

Some Examples of Accountability

Most attempts at accountability to date seem to have assumed that accountability is a relationship of an individual to the person next above him in the hierarchy, and that the hierarchy must be preserved. We believe that accountability *can* be implemented in the hierarchy, as illustrated in the following examples, but that the hierarchy does not necessarily have to exist in order to have accountability. Reciprocity always exists, and must be recognized.

THE LEARNER. The learner is responsible to himself, to his teacher or instructor, to his parents or guardian, and to society for learning those things that he wants to learn and those things that he needs to learn to function in society. Standards are to be the goals (ends) set by the national society and the local community, plus the objectives and activities (means) agreed upon by the learner (yes, including the very young) and the teacher. Gronlund (1970) and others have shown how to develop these. Performance is to be measured by criterion-referenced tests and subjective judgments of both learner and teacher, openly discussed. Benefits are to be measured by the learner's own feelings of growth and self-worth. Cost is to be measured in time, effort expended, and frustration experienced (if any). Whether performance-benefits-cost are up to desired standards is to be judged by teacher and learner, and if adjudged inadequate, weaknesses and strengths are to be diagnosed and new efforts made by both parties.

THE TEACHER. The teacher is responsible to himself; to the learner, as indicated above; to the principal; to the community, through the board of education; to the profession; and to society. Responsibility to the learner is for assistance in setting and achieving goals; responsibility to the principal is for doing her or his job; responsibility to the community is to see that its future citizens are prepared with no waste of resources; to the profession for ethical conduct; and to society for seeing that its purposes are achieved. Standards are self-set (and principal-approved) objectives. Benefits are to be measured in learner growth, satisfaction, and feelings of self-worth. Cost is to be measured in time, effort expended, and frustration experienced. If results are adjudged inadequate, weaknesses and strengths are to be diagnosed and new efforts made by both teacher and principal. Society and the community are responsible for setting realistic goals that consider the learner and the teacher, citizens of the community are responsible for providing necessary resources and understanding, the board of education and superintendent are responsible for providing the teacher and his school fair treatment, and the principal is responsible for providing necessary supporting services, understanding, assistance, and leadership.

THE PRINCIPAL. The principal is responsible to the learner and the teacher, as indicated above, and he is also responsible to himself, to the profession, to the school system, and to society. Responsibility to the teacher is for providing necessary supporting services, understanding, assistance, and leadership, as mentioned above; responsibility to the profession is for ethical conduct; to the school system for doing the job for which he or she is being paid; and to society for seeing that its purposes are achieved. Standards are performance objectives and activities set for himself and approved by the superintendent, to assure conformity to overall goals. Benefits are to be measured in terms of learner satisfaction and attempts to help teachers, along with community satisfaction and the principal's own feelings of self-worth. Cost is to be measured in time, effort expended, and frustration experienced (if any). Whether performance-benefits-cost are up to desired standards is to be judged by teachers, principal, and superintendent and, if adjudged inadequate, weaknesses and strengths are to be diagnosed and new efforts made. Society and the community are responsible for setting realistic goals that consider learners, teachers, and the principal; citizens of the community are responsible for providing necessary resources and understanding; the board of education and superintendent for providing the principal and his school fair treatment; and the superintendent is responsible for providing necessary supporting services, understanding, assistance, and leadership.

These analyses are, of necessity, abbreviated, and the list of examples could be much more extensive. However, this should be sufficient to indicate the reciprocal nature of accountability, and we turn now to the steps that are necessary in evaluation of people, which is necessary to the concept of accountability.

Evaluating People
Whether one believes that the performance of people should be judged by self-evaluation or through appraisal by the performer's

superordinate seems to make little difference in the steps involved. However, the steps have not often been spelled out in the literature of education, and those that follow are the present writers' adaptations of ideas stated by McNally (1949 and 1972).

1. *Setting standards.* Society must establish which of the primary functions of education schools are to be held responsible for. Once that is done, these substeps may be accomplished:
   a. Citizens of a given community and the people who work in its schools agree on a dozen or so goals that seem realistic in terms of overall educational functions that the schools are to fulfill.
   b. Objectives are selected by individual in terms of what he can do to work toward those goals, in terms of observable performance or behavior.
   c. Activities are selected that will supposedly allow the individual to exhibit the desired behavior.
   d. Measures of performance, benefits, and costs are agreed upon by the performer and his superordinate.
2. *Recording evidence.* Some kind of record must be kept of pertinent information relating to performance, benefits, and costs, so these substeps become necessary:
   a. The frequency with which behavior is to be observed and evidence recorded is agreed upon.
   b. A decision is made as to who will record evidence.
   c. The form in which evidence is to be recorded is established.
   d. Record forms, if necessary, are provided to the recorder.
   e. Baselines are set, to give consistency to the recorded information.
   f. Agreement is reached as to who will review the recorded information, when, and for what purpose.
3. *Interpreting evidence.* Recorded information is useless unless someone does something with it. If the information is to be of value to the person being evaluated, someone must:
   a. Review the recorded information.
   b. Reconcile the reports if two or more persons have recorded corresponding information.
   c. Select and put in some kind of priority those facts that are considered to have significance.
   d. Decide whether the recorded information indicates a sufficient and unambiguous record of what the person has done.
   e. Discuss the evidence with the person being evaluated (if the process is more than self-evaluation).

4. *Taking action.* The evaluation should result in action, and this requires the following substeps:
   a. Performance, benefits, and cost are compared to the standards agreed upon (see item 1d).
   b. Whether the comparison is favorable or unfavorable to the evaluee, the following actions should be taken:
      (1) Goals are reviewed periodically to see if they are realistic.
      (2) New objectives are set by each individual.
   c. If the comparison is favorable to the evaluee, his or her accomplishment is given recognition, the remaining substeps of item 1 (Setting standards) are accomplished, and the process again goes full cycle.
   d. If the comparison is unfavorable to the evaluee, the person to whom he is responsible tries to help him by:
      (1) Suggesting ways to improve performance in his present assignment.
      (2) Giving him an opportunity to perform in another situation, if possible and necessary.

Evaluating Programs

The accountability concept implies also that the school system should be accountable to its constituents for the programs that it provides, and this requires that programs be evaluated. These statements about program evaluation have been adapted from Stufflebeam (1973) except for additions under 3a(4).

1. Evaluation is assessment of merit.
2. Evaluation is for purposes of:
   a. providing information proactively for decision-making.
   b. providing information after the fact for accountability.
3. Evaluation is accomplished by:
   a. delineating questions to be answered in regard to:
      (1) suitability of goals.
      (2) suitability of program design.
      (3) suitability of individuals' objectives.
      (4) standards to be achieved in terms of:
         (a) individuals' performance.
         (b) overall benefits achieved.
         (c) costs incurred.
   b. obtaining the needed information.
   c. applying the information to answer the designated questions.
4. The evaluation process may be accomplished by:
   a. evaluation departments established within school systems.
   b. contracting with external evaluation agencies.

c. various persons in a school system using "do-it-yourself" kits.
d. consortia of school districts.

Under item 3, the steps listed as necessary are essentially the same as the steps for the evaluation of people.

SUMMARY

Ambiguity, anxiety, and uncertainty exist in regard to accountability of schools and school personnel in today's society in the United States. There are strong and repeated demands for accountability, but little agreement on what it is or what it entails.

Some of the reasons for emphasis on accountability are: losing the "battle" of being the first nation into space, technological developments, the press of a host of social issues in urgent need of resolution, inflation, the advent of negotiations as a means of getting increased salaries, competition from many nonschool education agencies, the training of people who "think systems," and the renewed emphasis on evaluation resulting from the need of the federal government to know whether funded programs are worth their cost.

The mushy and unsatisfying nature of present definitions of accountability requires a new definition, and it is proposed that the only meaningful definition may be "accountability is the process of attempting to secure performance commensurate with expectations, and one of the expectations is that benefits will be proportional to costs." Traditional views of motivation have been unhelpful, but the "new" approach advocated by Maslow, McGregor, and others requires sweeping organizational changes not yet accomplished.

Some major responsibilities of society need resolution in terms of the extent to which the school should be responsible for taking sides on social issues, and for certain primary educational functions. Orientations of individuals as to past, present, or future help to determine their attitudes in regard to accountability.

Once society decides which functions each of its educational agencies is responsible for, accountability *is* possible, but it is a reciprocal process. A person or a program is to be evaluated in terms of whether performance is commensurate with expectations, and one of the expectations is that benefits will be proportional to costs. Program evaluation has greater present acceptance than person evaluation, but most current attempts at accountability require person evaluation, with little attention being given to vital reciprocal relationships.

SOME SUGGESTED RESOURCES

L. H. Browder, (Ed.), *Emerging patterns of administrative accountability.* New York: Hofstra Univ., 1971.

G. V. Glass, The many faces of educational accountability. *Phi Delta Kappan,* 1972, **53**(10), 636–693.

N. E. Gronlund, *Stating behavioral objectives for classroom instruction.* New York: Macmillan, 1970.

L. M. Lessinger and R. W. Tyler, *Accountability in education.* Worthington, Ohio: Charles A. Jones, 1971.

H. M. Levin. A conceptual framework for accountability in education. *School Review,* 1974, **82**(3), 363–391.

G. G. Mansergh, (Ed.) *Dynamics of management by objectives for school administrators.* Detroit, Mich.: Metropolitan Detroit Bureau of School Studies, Inc. 1971.

A. C. Ornstein and H. Talmadge, The rhetoric and the realities of accountability. *Today's Education,* 1973, **62**(6), 70–80.

J. Pfeiffer, *New look at education: Systems analysis in our schools and colleges.* New York: Odyssey Press, 1968.

H. I. Von Haden and J. M. King, *Innovations in education: Their pros and cons.* Worthington, Ohio: Charles A. Jones, 1971.

B. R. Worthen and J. R. Sanders, (Eds.), *Educational evaluation: Theory and practice.* Worthington, Ohio: Charles A. Jones, 1973.

SECTION THREE
THE INDIVIDUAL

People who become leaders tend to be somewhat more intelligent, bigger, more assertive, more talkative than other members of their group. But these traits are far less important than most people think. What most frequently distinguishes the leader from his co-workers is that he knows more about the group task or that he can do it better.

—Fiedler

This section of this book attempts to develop an understanding of the individual who is impelled to be a leader. It explores status and emergent leaders, along with the behavioral styles, communications media, and communications purposes of both types. It also offers an explanation of charisma.

The relationship of personality to the leadership process is examined, along with means and modes of qualifying for leader responsibility. What it takes to lead and the effect of life-style are discussed.

Various forms of self-assessment are considered and some of the instruments presently available to help with the task are cited.

CHAPTER 11

LEADER TYPES AND LEADER STYLES

> *. . . management, administration, executive responsibility, line authority, reporting to immediate superior—all of these are used to hide the unpalatable or shameful fact that there is something called leadership which people, actual named human beings, have to exercise.*
>
> *—Jay*

It is the purpose of this chapter to examine the relationships of *leader types* and *leader styles* to the process of leadership. According to Knickerbocker (1948), the leader-follower relationship is based in symbiosis with the leader utilizing the know-how, technical capability, and performance standards of his followers to achieve his or her organizational goals; followers utilize the need-satisfiers controlled by the leader to satisfy themselves. Therefore, the process is an *interactional* one, as was spelled out in Chapter 6.

It should be clear that leading is not the unique preserve of one individual as she or he functions in a group situation. This latter point may well be one of the most significant perceptions that persons assigned to leader roles could develop, for with this view in the forefront of one's thinking a leader could make optimum use of the talents, capabilities, and potentials of the group members with whom he or she works. *Leadership then is a process which is a function of group interaction and is an outgrowth of the attempts to bring into focus both institutional and personal goals, as well as the means that could enhance the prospects for the achievement of goals.* Lipham (1964), using as a basic source Hemphill's definition, suggested that leadership be defined as "the initiation of a new structure or procedure for accomplishing an organization's goals and objectives [p. 122]." Our foregoing definition varies somewhat from this.

The authors of the present work are responsive to the innovational aspect implied in Lipham's definition, yet believe that leadership so defined may be somewhat restrictive in that it does not take into account the personal goals of an organization's members. It is also believed that personal goals have a profound influence on the development of and directions taken by an educational enterprise. With our own operational definition of leadership as a frame of reference, this chapter on leader types and leader styles was developed.

TYPE AND MANNER OF SELECTION

Individuals may gain positions in which they are expected to lead because of being selected by others either through birthright, appointment, election, or default. Others may obtain leader positions through emerging from the crowd in already functioning groups, or they may build new social systems in which they function as leaders either through accretion of voluntary followers, through force, or through ownership. A person emerging from a group may be considered to have charisma, and may become a status leader. Status does not necessarily depend on the manner in which a leader is selected.

Status Leaders

A company president, a superintendent of schools, the owner of a store, a classroom teacher, a chief of police, a factory owner, a union representative, and a gang leader are all status leaders even though their positions are obtained by radically differing means. Until recent years, most status leaders exercised leadership in an authoritarian manner. However, even in a Theory Y organization which utilizes emergent leader skills and knowledge, the status leader can perform important functions. He can endeavor to set a permissive tone for all under his jurisdiction, thereby encouraging free discussion, contribution, differences of opinion, and *leading by others*—as is necessary during discussion, decision-making, or action. The status leader also may serve as a resource person for certain phases of the work, or aid in coordinating the efforts of group members.

Selection by Others

Status leaders who are selected by others may be selected through birthright, appointment, election, or default, as mentioned above. Such persons may have little or no choice as to whether they accept the positions, they may actively compete to be selected, or they may take over positions that no one else seems to want.

BIRTHRIGHT. Insofar as the present writers can discover, few individuals are born into situations in which they are expected to become educational leaders because of who their parents were. However, the hereditary concept has been a strong one in regard to political leaders and persists in present-day cultures ranging from the largely tradition-and-ceremony of the British monarchy to the "Papa Doc"-to-"Baby Doc" oligarchy of the pseudo-republic of Haiti. The leaders of some of the existing proprietary schools undoubtedly have changed and will change over time through inheritance. Inheritance, as it affects who follows whom as leader, may be of blood lines, of property, or of personality.

APPOINTMENT. Supposedly, appointment is the manner of selection by others that comes closest to guaranteeing that a leader is suited to the demands of a position, and it seems to be the most widely used method of selection in education. Most status leaders in formal and nonformal agencies are appointed by some governing body after position responsibilities are outlined and a search is made for qualified candidates. Examination of paper credentials and interview are usually important parts of the procedure. However, as everyone who has ever been interviewed should be aware, the face-to-face interview communicates infinitely more satisfactorily than reams of paper, and interview impressions often supersede or override paper-recorded information. The would-be leader would be well advised to polish his oral skills—and those human contacts that might get him into interview situations or acquaint him with vacancies for persons of his qualifications.

While we may intellectually and morally deplore the obtaining of positions through "pull" or "connections," the political and economic fact remains that many vacancies are learned of through such sources and many positions gained through such means. The person with local orientation glories in this mode of operation and indeed knows no other, while the cosmopolitan may be forced to utilize it as a political strategy. He or she also may be compelled to obtain certain degrees or certificates that have little or no connection with what he or she knows or can do, in order to be *considered* for appointment!

Though election, ownership, and force are avenues by which some individuals achieve positions as educational leaders in certain proprietary or private schools, the typical route to such opportunities in most public and parochial schools and colleges is by way of appointment. Certainly there are exceptions to this general pattern; for instance: (1) members of boards of trustees usually are elected to their offices, though even here some variations are noted in certain sections of the country with New Jersey, as an example, empowering the mayor and/or the village coucil to appoint members to the local school boards, and (2) department chairpersons in public, parochial, and private schools may be appointed, but more often they are elected to their offices by their peers, with final authority for approval residing with the individual building administrator, the school superintendent, or in some cases confirmation of the assignment by the board of trustees.

ELECTION. Election is usually thought of as the manner of selection for political leaders, but it also is used in varying degrees by a variety of education agencies. A few state superintendents of schools are elected by the general electorate, and most trustees gain office through this means, as do most department chairpersons in colleges. Members of boards of control often conduct their own internal elections for the office of president, and perhaps for other offices. Theoretically, the practice is supposed to give electors a choice, based on candidates' stated positions on issues relating to the productivity of the agency, but often neither the issues nor the candidates' positions are made visible to the constituency. As a result, many an elected official is voted into office on the basis of popularity, general reputation, ethnic characteristics, or even a name with which constituents identify.

DEFAULT. If a designated leader, whether selected by appointment or election, does not perform as he or she is expected to, someone else may become the status leader *whether given a title or not.* More than one school principal or superintendent sits in his or her office shuffling papers and answering telephone calls, perhaps not even acknowledging to himself or herself that someone else is carrying on the vital business of the enterprise and satisfying the needs of group members.

Emergent Leaders
Within established social systems, leaders usually emerge for one of four reasons: (1) there is no designated leader, (2) the designated leader is not doing what group members expect him or her to do, (3) an individual knows more about the matter at hand or can do more to help the group than can any other group member, and (4) the person has a preferred outcome that is so impelling that he or she is willing to use whatever means are available, including force if necessary, to bring it about.

Of all the imperatives of modern educational leadership, probably the most significant is that which is related to *emergent* leaders, for it is through awareness and utilization of the concept of emergent leaders that status leaders have been able not only to maintain the organization but actually to infuse the enterprise with the imagination, vitality, and creativeness necessary for survival. The concept itself has grown out of the democratic practice of making the greatest use of the skills and talents of subordinate members at all levels within the organization. According to the ASCD yearbook (1960):

> . . . *leader behavior exhibited only by people in official positions can never be equal to the task of building an effective organization. Unless leadership emerges from the group, the organizational structure will not be strong enough to maintain itself. A strong and vigorous organization depends for its existence upon the emergence of leaders at all levels of its operation. . . . The vitality of an organization can be measured, in large part at least, by the kinds and amount of leadership that emerge within it [pp. 46–47].*

Consistent with this point of view, the yearbook of the AASA (1963) brought this imperative into sharp focus by pointing out that the demands upon educational leaders "place a premium upon broad knowledge, creative thinking, the capacity for working with and through people to accomplish desired results, adaptability and preparedness for change, resourcefulness and a will to do, and, most of all, a true sense of humility. Where personal limitations impede effective action there must be determination to compensate for these shortcomings [p. 28]." The successful educational leader matches skills on an equal footing and holds his own with the other leaders in the community. To do this, he or she must persuade—not push; lead—not outstrip; skillfully draw forth the powers of staff people; and utilize the full resources of the community.

The above rather strongly suggests that the survival and on-going development of the educational institution will be, in great measure, dependent on the maximum, if not the total, mobilization of society's intellectual and other manpower resources. An examination of the litetrature of educational leadership clearly reveals a continuing thread of concern about the development of emergent leaders.

Status educational leaders have the responsibility to establish the tone or climate in which groups address themselves to the tasks of achieving organizational goals. But in a climate that is conducive to the development of emergent leadership, freedom of expression is encouraged. Any member may lead through a suggestion or an argument, and as suggestions influence the trend of discussion, objections are raised and compromises are suggested. Each of these is a case of shared or emergent leadership. This in no way should suggest that groups of individuals can function without status leaders; it does suggest, however, that the designated head must rely on his or her capabilities as a skilled professional leader rather than on authority that may be vested in him or her as a status leader.

A leader who provides for group formulation of policies and programs of action may achieve desirable ends far better than positional authority ever can. Certainly a climate of permission that encourages discussion, even argumentation, and professional deliberation seems to be necessary for the development of emergent leaders, and within such an environment there are some other specific activities that seem to be helpful as well. The ASCD yearbook (1960, p. 103) suggested the following:

1. Leader actions are encouraged through participation in decentralized decision-making and policy-forming procedures.
2. Leader behavior is encouraged when the number of leader roles is increased by decentralizing administrative and supervisory functions.
3. Public recognition of achievement encourages leader behavior.
4. Providing for growth in confidence and competency in working with other people encourages staff members to participate as leaders.
5. Increasing participative leadership requires that involvement be productive, functional, and accompanied by feelings of respect for all persons, consideration of diverse opinions, kindness, and other positive human qualities of spirit and feelng.

Other Forms of Self-Selection
An individual may select himself or herself to lead through self-anointment or through processes of which he or she is unaware or only vaguely aware. Such leaders may simply emerge from the pack as indicated above, or they may deliberately set out to attract followers through persuasion or manipulation of emotions. Some set up situations in which other people can find the means to satisfy certain of their needs, thus attracting followers much in the manner of the Pied Piper.

ACCRETION OF FOLLOWERS. Whereas emergent leaders come to the fore in existing social systems, some individuals manage to attract followers because of the goals, ideas, or causes they espouse, and thus form new social systems or subsystems in which they function as leaders. Such leaders range from those with the lofty goals of a Gandhi or a Martin Luther King to the aggrieved faculty member circulating a petition to oust the provost. The followers may not even form a social system in the sense of face-to-face interaction.

The frightening ease with which a leader can promulgate even an absurd cause, aided and urged on by a segment of the general public, is evidenced by the following:

In 1959 an organization named SINA, the Society for In-decency to Naked Animals, began to terrorize various virtuous zoo directors with public statements to the effect that taking children to the zoo was like taking them to the burlesque show. . . .

In gratitude for SINA's super-morality, a well-to-do lady from Santa Barbara offered to put $40,000 in SINA's kitty for clothing kittens. Nuts came out of the woodwork seeking to put pants on *squirrels. And behind all this national madness was a "power machine" consisting of a writer, his wife, and his doorman.*

The writer was Alan Abel. The story of his experiences—both hilarious and terrifying (he dominated radio, television, and print media at next to no cost with lies and a poker face which Hitler would have envied)—is now fully exposed in his own book [Abel, 1966].

From a pipe dream by Alan Abel to national acceptance by millions of gullible Americans SINA went unexposed for four years, was the subject of countless magazine and newspaper stories, TV and radio interviews.[1]

Some leaders who set out to accrue followers, such as a Castro or a Cleaver, may also resort to force if that is necessary to accomplish their aims.

OWNERSHIP. Another means of self-selection used by some leaders is owning or controlling means of need-satisfaction to which people are attracted. Some use the direct approach, through establishing profit-motivated chains of schools such as business colleges or beauty academies. Others, such as a Henry Ford, an Andrew Carnegie, a W. K. Kellogg, or a W. Clement Stone make money through other means and then establish foundations having educational purposes largely decided by the founders.

Charismatic Leaders

In contrast to status and emergent leaders, the charismatic leader has received considerably less attention in the literature, yet the type does seem to exist and may be distinctive as well. The charismatic leader is an exceptional individual who seems to have a unique personal power that makes him or her capable of securing the allegiance of large numbers of people. Charisma involves mass psychology rather than group dynamics, and is based on a hypnotic effect on followers. Supernatural qualities often are imputed to the leader by his followers and reinforced by his claim to an indisputable mission which others must rely on him to accomplish.

History is replete with such leader types, yet the charismatic leader usually has received attention with regard to his or her particular leader style rather than as a unique type. Hitler, Mussolini, and Stalin certainly would fall into the charismatic category, yet so would Roosevelt, Eisenhower, and John F. Kennedy. Jesus, most assuredly, had a personal aura and mystique, as did Joan of Arc. One would also have to include evangelists such as Graham, MacPherson, and Father Divine. As is obvious, each in his or her own way was quite different from the others, and it may be difficult to conceive of all of these examples as belonging to the same leader type. Yet, each has or had at least one thing in common with all

[1] *Grand Rapids Press,* July 3, 1966, p. 33.

the others in that each in his or her own way has been able to command, sway, and attract large numbers of followers, some of whom are or would have been willing to go to the gates of Hell and beyond with him or her.

The list could go on almost endlessly, for each generation seemingly has provided us with at least one national or international figure who could be classified as a charismatic leader. But do these persons have more in common than the feature of being able to attract mass followers? The answer is categorically "yes," and some common characteristics are as follows: (1) the charismatic leader is particularly persuasive, (2) he or she has the power to arouse deep emotions in his or her followers, and (3) he or she has a "cause" to espouse. It seems to matter little if persuasiveness is based on glibness; if the leader's emotional life and responsiveness may be a shambles; or if the cause itself may be base and unworthy—the fact remains that some, and oftentimes many, persons are joyfully willing to follow the leader who has charisma.

One might ask: What has all this to do with educational leadership? In partial answer, it may be said that almost always it is charismatic leaders who effect social change, and inevitably with social change comes change in the educational enterprise. Too, education itself has spawned some leaders who fall into the charismatic category; for instance, Dewey at the turn of the century, and later Kilpatrick, Counts, Rugg, Washburne, and Melby. Suffice it to say that education has had its share of charismatic leaders as have the political and religious domains.

With respect to the leader phenomenon, a common plaint heard in a great many educational circles is reminiscent of a popular folk ballad: "Where have all our leaders gone?" This query seems to suggest that there are many educational reformers who are looking for causes to follow and who only need the right leader with the qualifications of persuasiveness and emotional appeal to set them on their ways. It may be disheartening for such potential followers to learn that the chances for the rise of charismatic educational leaders of universal influence are rather slim in our society, as presently organized. Educational agencies are proliferated, responsibility and authority are diffused, and society is increasingly dehumanized—caught up in the web of organization, with its "organization men." It should be noted that charismatic leaders have come from both the status and emergent molds. Thus, it may be that they do *not* represent a distinct type, a matter to which Headlee (1969) spoke:

> . . . *we must concede that* all *who effectively maintain leadership seem to need some measure of charisma. In fact, it is possible that no leader in the sense we understand the term today can function for long on authentic "virtues" alone, and without some charisma to bind and hold his followers, in the manner here described.*

> At the conscious level, this is perhaps no more than chi-
> canery; at the unconscious level there must be some element
> of enormous self-deception since history is full of charismatic
> figures that [sic] had little more than their charisma to offer, and
> every power complex has at least one aspirant to charisma [p.
> 14].

On further investigation, charisma may prove to be a reflection
of particular values that the individual holds and the level of need(s)
at which he is functioning.

Many writers, Tead (1935) among them, have warned against
would-be leaders whose need-dispositions impel them to seek power
for the sake of power, and we have seen firsthand evidence in men
like Ehrlichman and Haldeman. Atkinson and Feather (1966) are
among those who have theorized about and done research on the
need for power as a motivation of leaders.

Charisma is a very useful concept with great significance for
leadership study, and it should not be vulgarized to describe entertainment figures who are merely attractive or popular, as has been
the tendency in recent years.

Status and Style

Whether selected by others, self-selected, or simply recognized as
having charisma, the individual who is expected to lead has a unique
status among those who are his or her subordinates. As was pointed
out earlier, the term "status" connotes the idea of differential ranking
among persons holding various positions within an organization. Invariably, as positions are created, a certain status is ascribed
officially or unofficially to each, and that status extends to the incumbent. The incumbent may diminish or extend the status of the position, depending on his or her idiosyncrasy credit. Authority, powers,
and responsibilities are attached to each position and, consequently,
to the position occupant. However, the fact of occupancy of a status-
leader role does not necessarily make clear to the incumbent the
behaviors that are expected of him. These expectations seem to be
elaborated, in large measure, by persons who hold positions of
higher status, but usually one's peers and subordinates hold expectations for a particular leader as well.

Thus, the behavioral style exhibited by a status leader is, in many
ways, influenced by those who hold superordinate, peer, or subordinate positions. However, style is more strongly influenced, if not determined, by the personality structure that is unique to an individual
functioning within the organization.

HISTORY OF STYLE

The earliest attempts to categorize the characteristic manners in
which leaders behave while attempting to carry out their responsibilities seem to have been made only after we were well into the

twentieth century. Those attempts were little regarded for a considerable period of time but have been renewed in the past two decades by a variety of researchers and writers from a number of academic disciplines.

Origins

The earliest use of the word "style" to describe a characteristic manner of behavior seems to have been by Weber (1922), who categorized styles as traditional, bureaucratic, and charismatic. Incidentally, the word "charisma" seems also to have been introduced by Weber. Weber's assumption apparently was that *style is a personality characteristic rooted in the leader's perception as to the source of his authority.* The traditional style was described as autocratic and perhaps capricious, and the charismatic was considered to have a mystic quality that did not seem to accord with Weber's personal views of what "should be." It seems clear that he preferred, and believed that the future belonged to those who exhibited, the bureaucratic style. His classic outline of administrative functions in a bureaucracy included these:

1. Fixed and official jurisdictional areas which are regularly ordered by rules, laws, or administrative regulations.
2. Principles of hierarchy and levels of graded authority that ensure a firmly ordered system of superordination and subordination in which higher officials supervise lower ones.
3. Administration based upon written documents; the body of officials engaged in handling these documents and files, along with other material apparatus, make up a "bureau" or "office."
4. Administration by full-time officials who are thoroughly and expertly trained.
5. Administration by general rules which are quite stable and comprehensive.

Other Early Attempts

In the early 1930s, research studies by Lewin, Lippitt, and White at the University of Iowa (Lippitt and White, 1947) made use of synthetic styles of behavior used by adults in supervising the activities of children. We say synthetic because the behaviors were not the normal behaviors of the supervisors; they behaved as they were instructed to behave, and the styles were specified as autocratic, democratic, and laissez-faire. These studies seem to have had effects that were illogical, undue, and normative (and in our view, unwise) on many of the later attempts to categorize styles. Indeed, many of the effects still continue today.

We believe the effects of the studies to have been illogical and undue because: (1) the researchers were inducing behaviors that were not the normal behaviors of the supervisors, (2) their findings have been generalized to groups dissimilar in composition and age to the research study groups, (3) a laissez-faire situation utilizes *no* leader style, and (4) the studies were done in a laboratory setting that did not approximate normal group conditions. Why the results had the pervasive normative effects that they did will be examined in the next section of this chapter. As Lane et al. (1967) cogently argued, *any* research on style done in laboratory small groups is essentially irrelevant to other situations because:

1. There are no traditions to affect leader behavior.
2. Laboratory rewards are too small to motivate many persons to the very real and extra effort required for leading.
3. There are no outside pressures affecting the leader as there inevitably are in real life.
4. The size of groups used often is not realistic when compared to the groups encountered in most organizational settings [pp. 320–321].

There is no attempt here to denigrate the work of the early researchers, but that work should be put in perspective and results should not be generalized to groups or situations to which they do not apply. The underlying assumption of these studies seems to have been that supervisor style depends on attitudes that can be accepted or rejected at will, depending on what supervisees find most satisfying, and that is a most questionable assumption when related to what is known about the difficulty encountered in changing attitudes.

The first attempt to relate style to the situation in which a leader functions with a group seems to have been by LaPiere (1938). He discussed fourteen types of situations and implied that there was a distinctive leader style most appropriate for each. He did not develop descriptors for those styles, but his underlying assumption seems to have been that a leader could consciously vary his manner of behaving to fit the situation. That, too, seems questionable except in a very limited range of situations. It should be noted that Lewis Terman wrote in 1904 that leader performance depends on the situation as well as the personality of the leader.

Normative Influences

From the time of Lewin, Lippitt, and White's earliest studies of supervisory style, there has been an implicit notion that leaders "should be" democratic in nature. In the United States, particularly, there have been repeated and at times almost frantic efforts to equate "democratic leadership" with the Protestant ethic. Any other style must, of course, be "wrong" in a nation that prides itself on allowing its citizens the greatest freedom on earth! Furthermore, as Argyris (1957) pointed out, the very idea of a leader-follower hierarchy conflicts with the democratic philosophy.

Fuel was added to the "democratic is right" evangelistic fires by Likert's (1958, 1967) studies, done at the University of Michigan, in which it was ascertained that, for certain groups in certain situations, democratic style indeed was productive and group members had higher morale when supervised under such a style than when subjected to other styles. Killian (1966, pp. 31–36) discussed "Keys to Improved Leadership," but he was assuming that, to improve, a leader's style must be "democratic."

Tead (1935) seems to have stood almost alone in warning that there are some very real weaknesses in the democratic style—and virtually no one seems to have listened to him. As a result, the literature of leadership since the 1930s has been heavily overbalanced with normative prescriptions to the effect that "to be effective, a leader must behave in democratic fashion." This despite overwhelming contradictory evidence from history and from observation of contemporary life! Bennis and Slater (1968) made a convincing case that "democracy is inevitable" in all phases of life and in all human societies. Be that as it may, an adequate discussion of leader style must explain all styles exhibited currently and historically. Certainly not all have been democratic.

NEWER DESCRIPTIONS OF STYLE
Since about 1955, the normative influences have seemed to weaken to some extent and a number of researchers and theoreticians have again been attempting to categorize styles, going far beyond terms such as autocratic and democratic. The approach of each seems to have centered about one of three assumptions, even though those assumptions often were not stated.

Style and Need-Disposition
Some of those who have attempted to describe and investigate style seem to have proceeded from the unstated assumption that *style is a function of the individual's need-dispositions.* In other words, the individual is believed to exhibit the behavior that he or she does because he expects certain consequences of that behavior.

CONSIDERATION-INITIATING STRUCTURE. Among those taking this approach were a group of investigators at Ohio State University who developed the Leadership Behavior Description Questionnaire. Shartle (1956), Stogdill and Coons (1957), and others used the instrument with military, business, and industrial leaders and Halpin (1959) used it with school superintendents. Items in the instrument were related to "consideration," or concern for people, and to "initiating structure," or concern for organizational tasks. The instrument subsequently was used by a number of other investigators in a variety of settings, and underwent several modifications in the process. As reported by Brown (1967), the twelfth version was used with school principals, but the descriptors were virtually unchanged. In most of the studies, "real" behavior was compared to "ideal" behavior.

Reddin (1970), in addition to making his own distinctive contribution which will be discussed later, noted that the terms "task" and "relationships" could be used to describe common threads running through the whole series of Ohio State studies, the style continuum studies done at the University of Michigan Survey Research Center beginning in 1947, and the Bales small-group studies done at Harvard University.

TELLS-SELLS-CONSULTS-JOINS. The "mix" between leader inputs and group member inputs was described in the film, *Styles of Leadership* (Swerdloff, 1961) in terms of four styles: the leader tells, sells, consults, or joins. These styles relate to behaviors of communicating or decision-making, as do the five proposed by Schmidt (1966), namely telling, persuading, consulting, joining, and delegating.

MANAGERIAL GRID. The "Managerial Grid" was developed by Blake and Mouton (1964), and it is supposed to allow the plotting of a leader's behavioral description in terms of his "people" orientation versus his "task" orientation. The grid has a vertical axis and a horizontal axis, each with a scale from 0 to 9. Thus, a leader's behavior propensities can be described by any numerical combination from 0-0 to 9-9.

MOTIVATIONAL VIEWS. Herzberg (1959, 1965, 1966, 1968) intimated that a leader's style can be described according to whether he uses "motivators" or "hygienes" in working with other people. McGregor (1966) implied that a leader's style is determined by whether he views those with whom he works according to Theory X or Theory Y, and Levinson (1973) concurred. Maslow, as early as 1954, was suggesting that a leader's style could be identified by discovering the level(s) of the hierarchy of needs at which he functions.

Style as a Situation Variable

Several other researchers and theorists seem to have started from the premise that *style is a personality characteristic that varies with the situation.*

NOMOTHETIC-IDIOGRAPHIC-TRANSACTIONAL. Getzels and Guba (1957) said that a leader is "nomothetic" to the extent that he is influenced by institutional or organizational expectations and "idiographic" to the extent that he is influenced by personal need-dispositions. Moser (1957) seems to have coined the term "transactional" to describe the style wherein there is the recognition that social system goals must be carried out, and it is obviously necessary to make explicit the roles and demands required to achieve the goals. And, since roles and expectations will be implemented by flesh and blood people with needs to be met, the personalities and need-dispositions of these people must be taken into consideration.

The transactional style is not so simple as appears from just saying that the leader hews to the middle course between what is expected and what is needed. Instead, the aim is to acquire a thorough awareness of the limits and resources of both individuals and institution within which administrative action may occur, with intelligent application of the two as a specific problem may demand. Institutional roles are developed independently of the role incumbents, but they are adapted to the personalities of the individual role occupants. Expectations are defined as sharply as they can be but not so sharply as to prohibit appropriate behaviors in terms of need-dispositions. Role conflicts, personality conflicts, and role-personality conflicts are usually recognized and handled.

No one would deny that the leader who functions in the transactional style will have great demands made on his or her energies, talents, and skills. To carry out the tasks associated with transactional style requires courage, commitment, drive, intelligence, persistence, persuasiveness, the wisdom of a Solomon, and the devotion of a Ruth. Not many leaders are so endowed.

THREE DIMENSIONS. Reddin (1970) identified, clearly described, and claimed to have a valid test for four "basic" styles and eight managerial styles which, he said, relate the personality elements of *task concern* and *people concern* to the *demands of the situation.* His complete 3-D model consists of the four basic styles, four "more effective" managerial styles, and four "less effective" managerial styles [p. 41]. The Reddin book contains the most complete discussion of style explorations known to the present writers.

The four "basic" styles are described by relation to two axes, similar to the Blake-Mouton grid, but each having a scale from 0 to 4 rather than 0 to 9. One axis represents *task orientation* and the other *relationships orientation.*

The "more effective" styles described by Reddin are:

Developer. One who places implicit trust in people. He is primarily concerned with developing the talents of others and providing a work atmosphere conducive to maximizing individual satisfaction. He is effective if the work environment he creates develops in subordinates a commitment to both himself and the job. Even if high production results, his relationships orientation leads him on occasion to put the personal development of others, even though unrelated to production, before short- or long-run organization goals. It should be noted, however, that Drucker (1973) said that a manager who puts the personal needs of the worker before the objective needs of the task is a liar or a poor manager, and that the rare worker who believes him is a fool!

Executive. One who sees his job as maximizing the efforts of others on short- and long-run tasks. He sets high standards for production and performance and recognizes that because of individual differences and expectations he must treat each person differently. His commitment to both task and relationships is evident to all, acting as a powerful motivator. His effectiveness in obtaining results leads naturally to optimum production.

Benevolent Autocrat. One who places implicit trust in himself and is concerned with both the immediate and long-run tasks. He has skill in inducing others to do what he wants them to do without creating enough resentment to lower production. He creates an environment which minimizes aggression toward him and maximizes obedience to his commands.

Bureaucrat. One who is not really interested in either task or relationships but who simply follows the rules and does not let it affect morale. He follows the rules and maintains a mask of interest.

The "iess effective" styles are:

Missionary. One who puts harmony and relationships above other considerations; he is ineffective because the desire to see himself and be seen as a "good person" prevents him from risking any disruption of relationships in getting production.

Compromiser. One who recognizes the advantages of being oriented to both task and relationships, but is incapable of making or unwilling to make sound decisions. Ambivalence and compromise are often used, with the strongest influence in his decision-making being the most recent or heaviest pressure. He minimizes immediate problems rather than maximizing long-term production, and attempts to keep those who can influence his career as happy as possible.

Deserter. One who often displays lack of interest in both task and relationships, and is ineffective because of his lack of interest and his effect on morale. He not only may desert but may hinder the performance of others through intervention or the withholding of information.

MATCHING STYLE AND SITUATION. A leader should learn to recognize his style and then seek situations in which he can effectively use it, according to Fiedler (1967). However, according to him (1969), an individual becomes a leader for any of many reasons, including personality, happenstance, being in the right place at the right time, educational background, and experience. Once in such a position, the leader either becomes task-oriented and *authoritarian* or human-resources oriented and *democratic.* This writer has done perhaps as much research as any other in the matter of style, but it seems that the more he has learned the more frustrated and pessimistic he has become. In 1973 he was saying that the "old" style of leading relied on control while the "new" relies on persuasion, but that both have control and influence on goals, and that the assumption that a leader's effectiveness will improve with increasing influence is incorrect. Fiedler stoutly maintained, with a fair amount of research backing, that regardless of the training in leading that an individual receives, his style must be carefully matched with an appropriate situation. To do otherwise, he averred, might result in counterproductivity. Fiedler does not appear to believe that an individual can choose his style at will.

As indicated earlier, Bennis and Slater (1968) made a good case for their thesis that democracy is inevitable in all types of organizational settings, because of the ever-higher levels of education of the general population. They, therefore, proposed that society should learn to structure organizations purposefully designed to use the democratic style to advantage, a view largely supported by Berkley (1971).

Style and Organizational Accommodation

While not considering style per se, at least two writers have described the ways in which individuals accommodate to organizational expectations. Since the ways describe characteristic manners of behavior, they may be considered styles. The unstated assumption of these writers seems to be that *style is the manner in which one behaves in accommodating to organizational expectations.*

Presthus (1962) pointed out that members within an organization, including leaders, accommodate to situational expectations in one of three ways, which can be described thus:

1. *Upward-mobiles.* These individuals have the most success as organization members, often becoming leaders. The upward-mobile feels friendly toward his superordinates and believes that they are generally sympathetic toward him. He has little difficulty in making decisions in conflict situations because he accepts the organization's values as decisive. He is outgoing and gets along with others, yet regards subordinates with detachment and this leads him to make decisions in terms of the organization rather than the individual. An upward-mobile enjoys organizational life, succeeds at it, and reaps the rewards of status and salary.

2. *Indifferents.* An indifferent refuses to compete for the organization's favors. The indifferent person seems to develop from entering the organization either with high expectations, being unsuccessful, and reacting by turning away from the organization, or with a working lower-class background where he was taught not to expect much from the organization. An indifferent accommodates to organizational demands by doing his work, arriving on time, and leaving on time—and developing his major interests in an extraorganizational manner. His anxieties are minimal because he refuses to become involved in the organizational race for rewards. He separates his

work from the rest of his living. As Presthus said, "He sells his time for a certain number of hours and jealously guards the rest." An indifferent may become a leader more or less by chance, but he seldom progresses far.

3. *Ambivalents.* Ambivalents constitute a small minority which consists of individuals who can neither resist the appeals of power and success nor play the roles required to gain them. An ambivalent finds it hard to get along with authority and cannot play the game. As contrasted with the upward-mobile, the ambivalent places individial friendships above the good of the organization. When confronted with a conflict, he decides in favor of the individual as against the organization. His is, indeed, a miserable lot in the modern large organization.

Though there is the possibility that the accommodations described by Presthus may represent oversimplification of adaptations to bureaucratic structures, they nonetheless point out that individuals with certain styles fare better within the organization than do others. Obviously upward-mobiles receive more of the financial and status rewards available to organizational members, yet they do so at the expense of their subordinates and at the expense of important human values as well. It is interesting to note that an upward-mobil caught up in the web of buraucracy seemingly has little leeway to initiate or to bring about changes that could keep an organization vital and viable. By contrast, the indifferent and the ambivalent have fewer opportunities for leader roles within the organization; the former because he "couldn't care less" and the latter because he cares too deeply about interpersonal relations, at the expense of the organization and its development.

Seven levels used by individuals to accommodate to organization life were described by Graves (1966), who maintained that work standards could best be maintained if the accommodation level of the leader was the same as that of the people with whom she or he works. Thus, each of the seven levels represents style, or characteristic manner of behaving, and is based on the behaver's values in combination with the need level at which he or she is functioning. The seven are described in Table 11-1. A difficulty with Graves' implied styles is that he seems to assume that all followers in an organizational unit will have the same motivational and value systems. This is a very dubious premise in the opinion of the present writers.

Style and Maturity of Followers

That the *style* of a leader, *in terms of task orientation and people orientation, varies with the level of maturity of his followers* was the basic assumption of Hersey and Blanchard (1969) in their "Life Cycle Leadership Theory." In their words, "as the level of maturity of one's followers continues to increase, appropriate leader behavior requires less and less structure (task) but also less and less socio-

TABLE 11-1
LEADER STYLES APPROPRIATE TO CERTAIN TYPES OF FOLLOWERS

TYPE OF FOLLOWERS	FOLLOWERS' MOTIVATIONAL SYSTEM	FOLLOWERS' VALUE SYSTEM	APPROPRIATE LEADER STYLE
Autistic	Physiological	Amoral	Close care and nurturing
Animistic	Survival	Totem and taboo	Simple demonstration; force
Awakening and bright	Order	Constrictive	Moralistic and prescriptive
Aggressive, power-seeking	Mastery	Power	Personal, prescriptive, and hard bargaining
Sociocentric	Belonging	Group-mindedness	Participative, substitutive
Aggressive, individualistic	Self-esteem	Personal	Goal setting, without prescribing means to goals
Pacifistic, individualistic	Information	Cognitive	Acceptance and support

Source: Adapted from Graves, 1966, p. 121.

emotional support (relationships) [p. 29]." Should this thesis be proven, a leader might need to be replaced periodically as followers mature to new levels where their expectations change. However, in the one modest piece of research known by the present writers to have been done on the matter in an educational setting, the theory was neither clearly supported nor rejected (Punch and Ducharme, 1972). The investigators had difficulties with operationally meaningful definitions of "maturity" and "effective leader behavior."

While the present writers agree that flexible organization structures and leaders who exhibit Theory Y convictions are to be desired, particularly in education agencies, they do not believe that the millennium has yet arrived or that it is likely to arrive soon. Nor do they believe that all leaders can perform in transactional style in the interim. They do believe that it is essential to have some explanation for the wide variety of leader styles that can be observed daily in agencies of all of the social institutions, each of which styles seems to be quite effective in certain situations and with certain groups of followers. It is for this purpose that a new proposal is being made in regard to the study of style.

A NEW PROPOSAL

The present writers believe that the study of leader styles might be much more fruitful than anything done to date if investigators were to return to the starting point from which Weber departed, namely to the assumption that *style is a function of the personality and need-dispositions of the performer, and is related to his perceived source of authority.* Herewith are presented basic assumptions, some hypotheses, and some questions that could be used to design meaningful research studies that might give new insights in regard to leader style.

Assumptions

1. Stylized and ritualized patterns of actions constitute behavior style.
2. Every leader has a characteristic manner of behaving which predominates.
3. The basic style of a leader is determined almost entirely by his personality formation and his early socialization, and develops from a combination of his values and the need levels at which he is functioning.
4. One's basic style is modified to some small degree by the group with which and the situation in which one is functioning, but it cannot be consciously altered to some other style without fundamental attitude change.
5. A person's basic style may change over a period of years, but it will be identifiable at any given time in his or her life.
6. Given agreed-on descriptors or definitions, a leader or any other person observing an individual's actions will be able to select those that most nearly describe his or her usual behavior pattern.

Some Hypotheses

HYPOTHESIS 1: Through day-in, day-out observation of a leader's behavior in a work setting, he/she or other observers will be able to indicate which of the following best describes his/her perceived source of authority:

Perceived Source	Style Descriptor
a. capability for rewarding or punishing	autocratic or despotic
b. inheritance; name, property, social status	aristocratic
c. organizational status; rules and regulations	bureaucratic
d. legitimization by groups members	democratic
e. ability to manipulate others emotions	demagogic

Preceived Source (*Continued*)	Style Descriptor (*Continued*)
f. within each individual	idiographic
g. his/her superior abilities	meritocratic
h. a clique to which he/she belongs	oligarchic
i. possession of privileged information	paternalistic
j. logic, fact, research	rationalistic
k. revelation from on high, deltgated to him/her	theocratic
l. both organizational structure and legitimization by group members	transactional

Corollary a. The leader's perceived source of authority is directly related to the manner in which he/she works to get goals of the organization established.

Corollary b. The leader's perceived source of authority is directly related to the manner in which he/she works to discover and introduce new goals for the organization.

Corollary c. The leader's perceived source of authority is directly related to the manner in which he/she works in getting critical-to-the-group decisions made.

Corollary d. The leader's perceived source of authority is directly related to the purposes for which he/she communicates regarding organizational matters.

Corollary e. The leader's perceived source of authority is directly related to the mode of communication used most frequently in regard to organizational matters.

Corollary f. The leader's perceived source of authority is directly related to the medium and the channel used most frequently for business communication.

Corollary g. The leader's perceived source of authority is directly related to the frequency with which he/she invites response to business messages.

Corollary h. The leader's perceived source of authority is closely related to the feelings which he/she engenders in subordinates.

HYPOTHESIS 2: No leader has a single unvarying style to which he/she reports in all situations or with all groups.

Corollary a. Utilization of a variety of styles by a given leader may indicate that he/she clearly perceives or intuitively knows that his/her basis of authority differs with the situation.

Corollary b. Vascillation in style may indicate that the leader is uncertain as to whether he/she has a basis for authority in that situation.

Corollary c. Vascillation in style may indicate that the leader is uncertain as to what kind of authority is appropriate to that situation.

HYPOTHESIS 3: The same leader will be perceived by himself/herself, by various superordinates, and by various subordinates as exhibiting different styles.

Corollary a. Perception of style will be affected by similarity or dissimilarity between leader and observer in terms of such characteristics as:

(1) sex.
(2) age.
(3) skin color.
(4) national origin.
(5) moral-ethic beliefs.

Corollary b. Perception of style will be affected by characteristics of the leader, such as:

(1) age.
(2) general experience.
(3) length of time with the particular group.
(4) sensitivity to other persons.
(5) communication skills.

Corollary c. Perception of style will be affected by characteristics of the subordinate or superordinate observer, such as:

(1) age.
(2) general experience.
(3) length of service as a group member.
(4) sense af obligation to the leader.

Numerous additional hypotheses and corollaries probably could be listed, but perhaps these are sufficient to excite the imaginations of those who are seriously interested in exploring styles of leaders or of individuals who hope to be leaders. Some questions that might help to reveal style may suggest further possibilities.

Revelations of Style

A person seeking to determine whether a particular leader has a characteristic style might look for actions that reveal answers to questions such as these:

1. What does he/she perceive as a basis for whatever authority he/she has?
2. How does he/she determine goals for the group?
3. Does he/she get his/her preferred outcomes for the group (changed goals):

      a. from superordinates?
      b. from imagination (invention, creative synthesis, or theory)?
      c. from group members (creative synthesis)?
      d. by adopting from others (diffusion)?
      e. from research (systematic feedback):
         (1) inside the group?
         (2) outside the group?
         (3) both inside and outside the group?
4. What is the basis for his/her critical-for-the group decisions?
5. For what basic purpose(s) does he/she communicate?
6. In what direction(s) does he/she communicate?
7. What is the nature of his/her messages?
8. What message medium does he/she typically use?

It is believed that if answers to such questions were available, and his or her behavior was consistent, the leader's style could be identified and described, providing that style definitions were stipulated and agreed to, as suggested in hypothesis 1. The hypothesis makes definitions of categories self-evident.

SUMMARY
Leader type refers to the status that a leader enjoys relative to the other members of an organization. A status leader is designated to occupy a superordinate position on an unlimited tenure basis. An emergent leader is one who takes over the leading function in an established social system either: (1) in the absence of a designated leader, (2) because the designated leader is not doing his job, (3) because the emerger knows more or can do more for the group than can the designated leader, or (4) because his preferred outcome is overwhelmingly compelling. Either a status leader or an emergent leader may reach a position of eminence because of being selected by others through birthright, appointment, election, or default. Either also may be self-selected simply through setting out to accrue followers to causes, ideas, or goals, and some individuals may use force. Ownership is another form of self-selection, and may result in the formation of a new social system. Appointment by others is the manner in which most educational leaders are selected.

    Charisma involves more than popular appeal, and either a status leader or an emergent leader may exhibit it. The charismatic leader is extraordinarily persuasive, he arouses deep emotions in followers, and he espouses a cause. There may be some evidence that charisma is related to power-seeking behavior.

    Attempts to describe the characteristic manner in which one behaves, or his style, apparently started with Weber in the 1920s. In the 1930s, LaPiere proposed situational influences as being important to style, and the Lewin, Lippitt, and White studies on supervision of children according to prescribed "styles" had far-reaching and normative effects. There is good reason to question any experiments with style in a laboratory setting.

Later attempts to categorize styles have apparently started with one of four assumptions, namely that style is: (1) a function of the leader's need-dispositions, (2) a personality characteristic that varies with the situation, (3) a manner in which one behaves in accommo-dating to organizational expectations, or (4) a function of the matur-ity level of followers.

A new proposal for the study of style is based on what appears to have been Weber's original assumption: that style is a function of the personality and need-dispositions of the leader, and is related to what he perceives to be the source of his authority. The proposal includes other assumptions, along with some hypotheses and corol-laries, and some questions to which answers should be sought in determining one's style.

The next chapter will be devoted to Leadership and Personality, and efforts will be made to bring into focus the origins and develop-ment of various personality elements as they may apply to leader behavior.

SOME SUGGESTED RESOURCES

W. G. Bennis and P. T. Slater (Eds.), *The temporary society.* New York: Harper & Row, 1968.

R. R. Blake and J. S. Mouton, *The managerial grid.* Houston, Tex.: Gulf, 1964.

C. G. Browne and T. S. Cohn (Eds.), *The study of leadership.* Danville, Ill.: Interstate, 1958.

W. B. Castetter, Leadership influence on personnel behavior. In *The personnel function in educational administration,* New York: Macmillan, 1971. Pp. 30–39.

F. E. Fiedler, Leadership—a new model. In C. A. Gibb (Ed.), *Leadership.* Baltimore, Md.: Penguin, 1969. Pp. 230–241.

A. W. Halpin, *The leadership behavior of school superintendents* (reprinted). Chicago, Ill.: Midwest Administration Center, 1959.

R. Presthus, Big organizations: definitions and dysfunctions. Chapter 1 in *The organizational society.* New York: Vintage, 1962. Pp. 3–26.

W. J. Reddin, Styles. Part 3 of *Managerial Effectiveness.* New York: McGraw-Hill, 1970. Pp. 203–250.

W. H. Schmidt, The leader looks at styles of leadership. 12 pp. monograph in *Looking into leadership executive library.* Washington: Leadership Re-sources, Inc., 1966.

E. Shils, Charisma. In D. L. Sills (Ed.), *International encyclopedia of the social sciences.* New York: Macmillan, 1968. Vol. 2, pp. 386–390.

A. Swerdloff, *Styles of Leadership* (film). Beverly Hills, Calif.: Roundtable Films, 1962.

CHAPTER 12

PERSONALITY AND LEADING

Some people want to lead, must lead, devote their every ounce
of energy to obtaining positions in which they can lead.
Others are content to follow, find security in their dependence
on a leader, in fact would never permit themselves to be
catapulted into a position [sic] of leadership.

—Ginzberg

There is no question but that the demands for quality leaders are
greater today than at any other time in our history. Inevitably, questions must be asked that relate to why some are impelled to be
leaders and others not, the specific qualities of leaders, the sources
of these qualities, and the development of the abilities associated
with leader behavior. It is believed by the authors that a central
element in the development of leader potential and the practice of
educational leadership is the personality of the individual who either
aspires to, or actually has, a leader role.

This chapter will examine the definition of personality, the structure
according to four different categories of theories, some determinants
of performance, value-orientations, the peculiar need-dispositions of
those individuals who seem impelled to lead, some predictors of
success in leading, and the concept of authenticity.

The Encyclopedia of Human Behavior (Goldenson, 1970) said:

> *Personality may be defined as the pattern of characteristics*
> *and ways of behavior which accounts for an individual's unique*
> *adjustments to his total environment; it includes major traits, in-*

terests, values, attitudes, self-image, abilities, behavior patterns, and emotional patterns [p. 945].

This is indeed a complex definition of a complex concept. The same source pointed out that, despite many diverse attempts to encompass the concept within a single theory, there does seem to be general agreement on two points: (1) no individual is born with a ready-made and unalterable personality, and (2) as a personality develops, it achieves some degree of integration or identity. "A person can be recognized from day to day by something more than his appearance alone."

Cattell (1973) was more specific and terse: "The personality of an individual is that which enables us to predict what he will do in a given situation [p. 43]." As a mathematician, he expressed his definition in the equation $R = f(P \cdot S)$, or response is a function of personality and stimulus. The present authors are responsive to this definition, as it accommodates the idea of need-disposition and includes predictability. It may be more meaningful when the structure of personality is considered according to various theories.

STRUCTURE OF PERSONALITY

There have been many attempts to explain personal identity, or the structure of personality. Goldenson (1970) divided them into type theories, trait theories, developmental theories, and dynamic theories. While the present writers might disagree with the particular "bin" into which some theory has been sorted, consideration of the categories may help to understand personality.

Type Theories

Three different bases have been used to classify people into categories in much the same fashion that plants, animals, and minerals are classified. In each, the assumption is that the personality revolves around a dominant characteristic. *Physiology or body chemistry* has been used as a classification basis from the ancient Greek classification of temperaments according to one or another "humors" or body fluids, up to and including recent attempts to sort according to endocrine balance. *Physique or body shape* has been used as a sorting basis from early attempts to use phrenology (conformation of the skull) or physiognomy (facial features), up to and including Kretschmer's body types. Attempts to sort people according to psychological *behaviors* range from Jung's extraverts-introverts through Presthus' upward mobiles-ambivalents-indifferents and Riesman's inner-directed-other-directed. Graves' seven behavioral levels also might be seen in this light.

Trait Theories

Although earlier attempts to find a "set" of traits that would be common to all leaders and would be absent in nonleaders came to naught, there have been recent and continuing attempts to describe individuals in terms of their measurement on a number of scales, each representing a different trait. Some elaboration of two of the major theories may be helpful, since both have been demonstrated to have predictive values, and a test for each is available.

Allport (1968) pointed out that "only very narrow theory, framed so as to exclude most of the contingencies of life, can be put to experimental testing [p. 15]." He also acknowledged that:

> The psychologist first focuses his attention on some limited slice of personality that he wishes to study. He then selects or creates methods appropriate to the empirical testing of his hypothesis that the cleavage he has in mind is a trait (either a dimensional trait or a personal disposition [p. 50]).

Allport chose for his own investigations Spranger's six fundamental dimensions of subjective evaluation—the theoretic, the economic, the aesthetic, social, political, and religious. Working with Vernon, he developed a scale that confronted people with forced choices, and found that they subscribed to all six values, but in widely varying degrees. To achieve a relatively high score on one value on the Allport-Vernon scale, a person must deliberately slight others. Looking backward from a 35-year perspective, Allport concluded that the six "valued directions" had proved measurable, reproducible, consistent, and valid. Other investigators concluded that the test clearly deals with an "evaluative posture toward life that . . . guides specific daily choices over a long expanse of years [Allport, 1968, p. 54]." Allport recognized a "slight" tendency toward covariance between theoretic and aesthetic, economic and political, and social and religious values. He suggested that, in the light of confusing results of the several attempts at factor analysis wherein clusters that emerged were "strange and unnamable, . . . empiricism should submit to rational restraint. The traits as defined are meaningful, reliably measured, and validated. Why submit them to galloping gamesmanship [p. 54]?" He believed that a trait always connotes an enduring tendency of some sort, and did not believe that factor analysis could further develop the "Allport-Vernon-Lindzey Study of Values." Allport's classification included: (1) *cardinal* traits that dominate an individual's whole behavior, (2) *central* traits which cluster to describe an individual's personality fairly completely, and (3) *secondary* traits of a more limited nature not essential to personality description.

Cattell (1973), on the other hand, is imperious in stating that "factor analysis showed that when the raters describe other persons they often unknowingly evaluate the strength of some 20 underlying personality factors [p. 42]." He agrees that, because mental traits are broad patterns rather than specifics, bivariate analyses do not work well except in unrealistic laboratory settings. He maintains that factor analysis allows him to look simultaneously at any number and kind of measures and determine how they reduce to patterns. The Cattell "Sixteen Personality Factor Questionnaire" has two equivalent forms, each of which contains 184 multiple-choice questions, selected by factor analysis, and is claimed to measure 16 primary personality factors and 8 composite secondary factors. Cattell has recognized the problems inherent in introspective questionnaires and has developed a variety of objective tests, in which the person being measured either cannot tell what aspect of his personality is being evaluated or has no way to change the measurement outcome if he does know. Cattell and his colleagues factor-analyzed thousands of responses to more than 2000 objective tests, and concluded that the results supported their previous findings from rater and questionnaire tests. The 16 factors and the basic grid used to display individual or group profiles are shown in Figure 12-1. Cattell himself has indicated a preference for the letter designations (A–Q) of the 16 scales, because of the individual interpretation given to words by each reader, but he admits that the words do convey meaning to persons unfamiliar with the tests. Cattell's classification system includes (1) *source* traits that are constant and steady influencers of behavior, (2) *state* traits that fluctuate with time and situation, and (3) *mood* factors that are very changeable.

If one could accept Cattell's premises, instrumentation, and conclusions, the perennial "nature vs nurture" controversy could be laid to rest. The 16 factor scale purportedly measures both biological and culturally induced traits. For example, those that seem to be largely hereditary are factors B (general intelligence), C (ego strength), F (serious-mindedness), G (superego strength), and I (emotional sensitivity); those strongly influenced by childhood socialization include D (calm-excitable), E (submissive-dominant), and Q (relaxed-tense). Furthermore, since 1960 the factors used have included some that indicate motivations and drives, as determined-through multivariate analysis. While the methods of measuring these are different from and more complicated than the methods used to determine general personality dimensions, the motivational roots, too, reach back into both nature and nurture. "Ergs" seem to be basic biological drives such as sex, fear, parental protectiveness, gregariousness, curiosity, self-assertion, and self-indulgent sensuality. On the other hand, "sentiments" such as respect for self-image, career-sentiment, and conscience are learned and the attitudes that they affect are directed to cultural objects or events. Both ergs and sentiments have a conscious component that shows up in direct measures of attitude and an unconscious component that shows up in indirect measures such as word associations and blood pressure.

Strangely, Goldenson (1970) lauded the Allport theory for its emphasis on individual traits and attention to uniqueness of behavior,

Figure 12-1 *Grid for Sixteen-Factor Profile*
Source: Cattell (1973), p. 44.

then concluded his discussion of Cattell's theory thus:

> *Trait analysis has been criticized on a number of scores. It is essentially an atomistic approach to personality. It yields specific ratings on traits that are emphasized, but these ratings tend to be confined to specific persons [is that bad?] in specific circumstances, and cannot be generalized to other persons [we should hope not!]. Finally, the method can be used to summarize specific responses, but it cannot give a picture of a personality as a whole, or uncover basic principles of personality [why not?]* [p. 951].

Developmental Theories

Some theories stress that human development is a continuous process and hold that the way to understand an individual's need-dispositions is to identify past experiences that cause him to respond as he does. Developmental theories include these general designations: (1) *psychoanalytic* approaches, including that of Freud and that of

Erickson, in which it is assumed that personal identity is achieved through resolving a string of critical problems encountered at different stages of development; (2) *learning* approaches, such as those of Maslow and Rogers that put special stress on cultural conditioning or on rewards and punishments; and (3) *role* approaches which describe personality development in terms of roles such as boy or girl, student, worker, and parent, stressing the effect of cultural norms and the degree of choice in selecting roles.

Dynamic Theories
Psychoanalytic theory examines the individual's present conflicts by describing the interplay between various conscious and unconscious forces in the personality. Thus, psychoanalytic theory is dynamic as well as developmental, in that it examines the interplay of the id, the superego, and the ego. Learning theories and role theories also examine the interplay between the individual's need-dispositions and the role (environmental) demands, so they, too, are *dynamic* as well as *developmental* theories.

Murray (1938) described a holistic developmental theory of personality in which the personality was perceived as the mediator between the individual's needs and the demands of the environment. Although his later writing (1951) indicated considerable change in his thinking and terminology, his original work listed 12 *primary* or "viscerogenic" needs and 28 *secondary* or "psychogenic" needs. Murray and his colleagues created the Thematic Apperception Test (TAT), designed to elicit fantasy responses (inner stimuli) in what is now an accepted projective method.

Figure 12-2 shows the present writers' concept of a dynamic theory of personality that accommodates the ideas of internal and external stimuli, needs, drives, wants, motivations, and need-dispositions, indicating the complexity and large number of variables that result therefrom. It should make clear the reasons why the present authors have been unable to substitute any other term for need-disposition.

Some basic understanding of the term "stimulus" is essential to understanding of the dynamic personality model of Figure 12-2, and we have chosen to use definitions from Goldenson (1970). According to him, *a stimulus is any energy change that excites* activity of *a sense organ;* the physical energy which *excites* the sense organ is a *distal* portion of the stimulus, and the *activity* of the sense organ itself is the *proximal* portion. It seems apparent that the only conditions under which an energy change that excites and activates a sense organ originates entirely *within* the human body are those that produce a change of either electrical or chemical energy of the body. Thus, investigation of truly "internal" stimuli must be very limited indeed, since for most activity of sense organs (proximal stimuli), there must be some external *distal* component of the stimu-

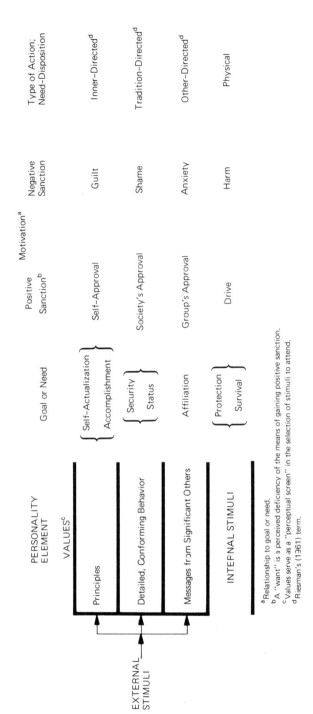

PERSONALITY ELEMENT	Goal or Need	Positive Sanction[b]	Negative Sanction	Type of Action; Need-Disposition
VALUES[c]				
Principles	Self-Actualization / Accomplishment	Self-Approval	Guilt	Inner-Directed[d]
Detailed, Conforming Behavior	Security / Status	Society's Approval	Shame	Tradition-Directed[d]
Messages from Significant Others	Affiliation	Group's Approval	Anxiety	Other-Directed[d]
INTERNAL STIMULI	Protection / Survival	Drive	Harm	Physical

Motivation[a]

EXTERNAL STIMULI

[a] Relationship to goal or need.
[b] A "want" is a perceived deficiency of the means of gaining positive sanction.
[c] Values serve as a "perceptual screen" in the selection of stimuli to attend.
[d] Riesman's (1961) term.

Figure 12-2 *A Dynamic Theory of Personality*

lus. As one considers the vast number of external factors that might trigger activity of a sense organ in combination with those internal factors that might have similar effect, and multiplies each by the number of physiological and psychological needs that an individual has, the number of possible personality variables becomes awesome—indeed infinite. Despite finite limitations of investigation of an infinite number of variables, there can be little doubt that personality *does* affect performance.

Among the dimensions of personality which affect behavior and are exemplary of affective domain learnings, are those related to attitudes, beliefs, feelings, and performance standards. These learnings may be subsumed under the heading of *value-orientations.*

VALUE-ORIENTATIONS
A value is the result of a process comprised of the actions of choosing, prizing, and acting. An individual or a social system freely makes a choice from alternatives (whether aware of all the alternatives available or not), cherishes this choice (is confident of its "rightness" and is willing to or does affirm it publicly), and acts on it (repeatedly, so that it becomes a part of his life-style). Values always look to action, in particular to the selections made by individuals among different possible paths.

A value-orientation was defined by Kluckhohn (1951) as:

*a generalized and organized conception, influencing behavior,
of nature, of man's place in it, of man's relation to man, and
of the desirable and nondesirable as they may relate to man-
environment and interhuman relation.* Such value-orientations
may be held by individuals or, in the abstract-typical form, by
groups. Like values, they vary on the continuum from the explicit
to the implicit [p. 411].

The definition and follow-up statements may be better understood by considering the nature and applicability of value-orientations.

Nature
The nature of value-orientations may be seen in terms of their intent, their content, and their modality, to use Kluckhohn's terms.

INTENT. Goal values, or those that Wheelis (1958) called institutional values, are values which societies and individuals make for themselves; they are "principles," incapable of proof, but unlikely to be disproven. They transcend the evidence at hand. An example is the Occidental cultural belief that the human being has dignity and worth. *Instrumental* values (a term also used by Wheelis) are those which individuals and groups conceive as being means to further ends; they can be validated, measured, redefined, and redirected. The "mix" of institutional and instrumental values that affects an individual's or a group's choice of alternatives, the cherishing of those choices, and the actions that result determine to some extent his or its value-orientation. We hypothesize that the effective educational leader leans more to institutional than to instrumental values.

CONTENT. There are various content classifications of values, such as those used in the Allport-Vernon-Lindzey Study of Values, namely: aesthetic, ecoonmic, political, religious, social, and theoretical. Other psychologists have used designators such as ethical, hedonic, and logical. The content areas of values that affect an individual's or a group's choice of alternatives, the cherishing of those choices, and the actions that result determine to some extent the value-orientation of that individual or group. We hypothesize that effective educational leaders tend toward economic and social value-orientations.

MODALITY. A third determiner of value-orientation is modality of interest and influence, according to such continua as positive-negative, altruistic-hedonic, moral-immoral, logical-illogical, or potential-actual. It is our belief that effective educational leaders tend toward positive, altruistic, moral, logical, actual modalities in value-orientation.

All three of the dimensions mentioned here are indicators of the nature of value-orientation, but there are other dimensions identified by Kluckhohn that concern applicability.

Applicability
Values deal with prescriptions, permissions, and prohibitions. Those values that are regulatory of the behavior of individuals or groups may be considered in terms of their extent, generality, intensity, and explicitness, all of which help to determine value-orientation as to applicability.

EXTENT. The extent to which a value prescribes, permits, or prohibits behavior is significant to one's value-orientation. A value may be idiosyncratic—held by a single individual; cultural—held by a group ranging in size from a few persons to millions; or supposedly held by all of humanity—although it is doubtful that there is a universal value. The level at which an individual or a group recognizes and adopts values helps to distinguish value-orientation, but new values inevitably reflect preexisting values. Individual variability and new situations bring needs for new values.

GENERALITY. The dimension of generality, according to Kluckhohn, concerns whether a value is specific to certain situations or content areas, appropriate only to certain roles, or thematic—applying to a wide variety of situations and diverse areas of a culture.

INTENSITY. The applicability of values may also be examined according to *incidence* of certain dimensions. According to Kluckhohn a person may observe: (1) the degree of striving for the value and the sanctions applied, (2) the strength of "must" or "must not" imperatives, (3) the presence of utopian values which influence the direction of behavior but are considered beyond immediate attainment (although utopian values of one era may become imperative values of a later period, as attested by the adoption, in the 1950s and 60s by both major U.S. political parties of values espoused by Norman Thomas and his fellow socialists in the 1930s), (4) hypothetical values to which some lip service is paid but which have little influence on action, and (5) traditional values which have lost most of their force because of changes in the culture or the immediate situation.

EXPLICITNESS. Choices among alternatives leading to actions often are patterned rather than random, and are attributable to abstract standards of what is aesthetically or morally desirable, or values. If the standards of "ought" or "desirability" are stated verbally by the behavers, they are explicit; if unstated but nevertheless operative, they are implicit. Some standards, of course, range somewhere between these extremes.

Whether a particular person tends to seek situations in which he or she can lead or is content with situations in which he or she must follow would seem to be directly related to the applicability, as well as the nature, of value-orientations as they apply to those situations. However, if his or her personality is to be understood as regards leader proclivity, some additional hypotheses need to be tested.

Some Hypotheses
While some of the following hypotheses apply to people in general, rather than just to those who seem to be impelled to be leaders, some investigation of the hypotheses should help to understand personality, and perhaps differences could be found between the personalities of those who consistently lead and those who are content to follow.

HYPOTHESIS 1. A person's acceptance of societal values is directly proportional to the number and type of socializing agencies with which he or she has had some interaction. Any individual should be able to respond to questions about whether he or she has had occasions to interact with other people in the family, the neighborhood, the church, the school, boy or girl scouts, 4H clubs, church youth groups, YMCA-YWCA, Little League, Rocket Football, Youth Achievement, and a lengthy (but finite) list of other agencies.

HYPOTHESIS 2. A person's acceptance of societal values is directly proportional to the perceived quality of his or her experience in interacting with socializing agencies. Any individual should be able to indicate whether his or her experience with an agency was perceived to be positive, neutral, or negative.

A profile of an individual could then be developed, showing the number of agencies with which he or she has interacted and the perceived quality of the experience with each, and that profile correlated with some measure of the person's values, such as the Allport-Vernon-Lindzey Scale. Both the profiles and the correlations might be useful in understanding personalities of persons ranging from national leaders to criminals.

A "social-experience" score could be developed from the profile by using a scale ranging from minus to plus, as shown in the hypothetical profiles of Figures 12-3 and 12-4. These scores could be used for correlation with some measure of values.

HYPOTHESIS 3. A leader will have significantly higher social-experience and values scores than will a follower.

HYPOTHESIS 4. A known delinquent will have significantly lower social-experience and values scores than will a nondelinquent.

Value-orientations of individuals probably are closely related to need-dispositions, and need-dispositions seem to relate to predictors of success. Both will be discussed in Chapter 14. However, authenticity is one likely predictor of success which is so basic to personality that it deserves to be discussed here as a separate topic.

AUTHENTICITY

According to Bugental (1965), "each of us is like a person who pays blackmail to keep a feared reality from becoming manifest. So paying, we maintain a semblance of peace at increasingly heavy cost to our resources [p. 43]." No one is ever fully authentic, but the less "blackmail" one pays, the more authentic an individual is.

Authenticity should be a concern of everyone inasmuch as one's ability to secure need-satisfactions and to avoid negative sanctions is in direct proportion to his or her perception of reality; high perception of reality seems to be a function of authenticity. Thus, authenticity is of particular concern to educational leaders, despite the fact that several researchers and writers aver that as a word it is difficult to define and that as a concept it is impossible to describe fully or precisely.

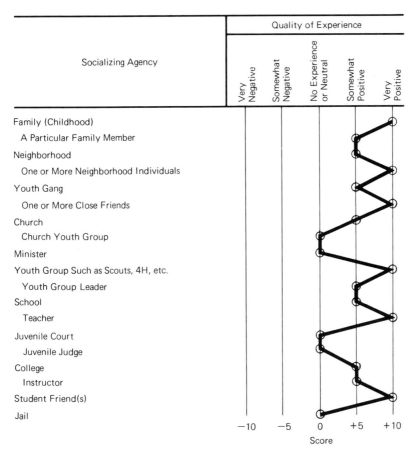

	Quality of Experience				
Socializing Agency	Very Negative	Somewhat Negative	No Experience or Neutral	Somewhat Positive	Very Positive
Family (Childhood)					
A Particular Family Member					
Neighborhood					
One or More Neighborhood Individuals					
Youth Gang					
One or More Close Friends					
Church					
Church Youth Group					
Minister					
Youth Group Such as Scouts, 4H, etc.					
Youth Group Leader					
School					
Teacher					
Juvenile Court					
Juvenile Judge					
College					
Instructor					
Student Friend(s)					
Jail					

−10   −5   0   +5   +10
Score

Figure 12-3 *Hypothetical Profile of an Effective Leader*

Definition

For present purposes, authenticity is defined as that degree of human existence to which one participates in social exchange without negating the cumulative values that he or she has acquired. The more active that one can be in organizational life without caving in to role expectations that violate internal values, while recognizing possible consequences to himself or herself, the more authentic a principal, superintendent, director, coordinator, dean, bursar, registrar, or president becomes. The leader who tends to withdraw from or "adjust" to social exchange rapidly loses authenticity and effectiveness.

Every individual has within himself or herself innate and *conflicting independence-dependence needs.* For most persons, these con-

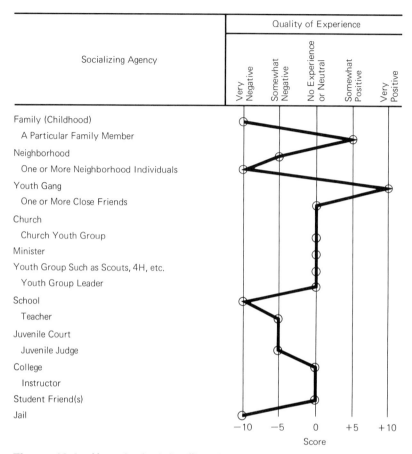

Figure 12-4 *Hypothetical Profile of a Habitual Criminal*

flicting needs require periodic shifting from follower role to leader role or vice versa depending on the situation and the social system, if the person is to be authentic. Thus, permanent assumption of either role by an individual for all of the situations that he or she faces may indicate a very unusual, a very unrealistic, or a very inauthentic individual.

Attributes

The attributes of being authentic consist of: (1) being as fully aware as one can be, (2) choosing alternatives to which to commit effort, devotion, and allegiance, (3) taking responsibility for each choice, knowing that it probably is not the optimum, while recognizing the imperfection of one's awareness and the inherent risk, unmitigated by good intentions [paraphrased from Bugental, 1965, p. 45].

Understanding of Bugental's summary of what he means by authenticity is important to the job of leading;

> authentic awareness . . . confronts the anxieties of being and affirms its own by incorporating these anxieties while yet avoiding their distortion. Man lives in contingency. He can and does take such action without ultimate guideposts of universal value or built-in instincts. And man is in constant relation with his fellows while yet being separate from them [p. 40].

Halpin (1966) called attention to the surprising number and variety of disciplinary allegiances of several individuals who, starting from different points, "found that they were stalking the same deer," that is, authenticity [pp. 210–211].

Ways of Examining

Halpin also proposed that the concept of authenticity could be examined through the subconcepts of the marginal man, the difficulty of cross-cultural interpersonal reaction, and the crisis of identity.

MARGINAL MAN. The marginal man dilemma was referred to by Bugental (1965), although without using the specific terminology: "The too frequent mistake of the person eager for authenticity is to strive subtly and unconsciously for authenticity by renouncing that in which he is still embedded [p. 35]." An example is the teacher who is appointed principal and leans over backward to identify with other principals, denying many of those values that he or she had accumulated as a teacher.

CROSS-CULTURAL REACTION. The difficulty of cross-cultural interpersonal reaction may be seen in the example of a superintendent of schools who is employed in an industrial city but who was born in a white middle-class suburb, educated in its schools, and experienced as a principal there. Authenticity becomes almost impossible for him or her if large segments of the faculty and student bodies in the city are comprised of persons from minority groups and he or she leans over backward to "understand" and be like them.

IDENTITY CRISIS. The crisis of identity may be illustrated by the example of a community college president who is aware that other administrators in his college in some measure share his experience and yet in some measure are separate and apart from him. His ultimate anxiety is the threat of complete isolation, and to it is coupled a continuing anxiety resulting from his sense if loneliness; yet he knows there is a stereotype of behavior for presidents to which is expected to conform. He is expected to heed the adage that "familiarity breeds contempt." Thus, there is no one in his work situation with whom he can identify.

Integrity and Status

Integrity involves whether a person behaves as he knows himself to be. To paraphrase Halpin's (1966, p. 209) illustration: Imagine listening to two principals who, unbeknown to each other, have been fired, but who loudly boast of their successes, putting on an elaborate act to impress each other. We must realize that a situation can be so threatening that persons cannot face up to their inauthenticity, and to condemn them is both unkind and pointless; they are to be pitied, and they need help. Situations of this type reinforce inauthentic behavior, and perception becomes increasingly selective, so that the individual ultimately excludes or illegitimizes response that disagrees with his or her distorted self-image.

To be authentic, a person must have something to be authentic about, according to Halpin (1966). The quest for identity described by Jersild (1952), Wheelis (1958), and others must not be a search for status. When an individual persists in using his status to provide himself with a sense of identity, as many government officials, past and present, have done, his behavior becomes increasingly inauthentic. When the status of an office is used as a protective cloak, the office holder diminishes the possibility of ever being perceived as authentic.

Implications

There are many implications of authenticity for those interested in the personality of leaders. Leaders and would-be leaders must have a sense of identity that does not depend on status, they must have values which are so integral to their natures that they cannot be denied, they must know their cultural prejudices and the limitations that prejudices impose, and they must know how far they can go in trying to be like others without compromising their own standards.

An individual can increase his authenticity by being more open with others or by soliciting information about how he is perceived by them *if* he does not allow himself to try to become something he is not as a result of their response.

In an earlier discussion, it was suggested that one of six needdispositions which seem to be common to all leaders is standing for something, having causes and goals to advocate. This need-disposition, at least, is related to authenticity, and is one of the determinants of performance.

DETERMINANTS OF PERFORMANCE

Performance, of course, results when the individual responds to the demands made on him by his needs and those social systems in which he plays roles. One's performance is, in our view, the sum total of his or her need-dispositions. One of the great concerns of society has to be those individuals whose performance is far below the levels at which others believe they could perform, particularly potential leaders. The leader, too, must be concerned about the underachiever, not only among learners, but also among staff members who are not achieving up to their self-acknowledged potential. For this reason, we have chosen to look at the determinants of performance in terms of "can do" (potential) factors, "will do" (predictability) factors, and "does do" (performance) factors. Robert Burns, of the University of Chicago, is the originator of these designations, to the best of our knowledge. While Ginzberg (1966) did not use these terms in his chapter titled "The Determinants of Performance," he did describe a number of the factors that Burns has long been working with.

"Can Do" Factors

Any leader who is going to lead for sustained periods of time must be concerned about what members of a group can do. Responsible bodies, such as boards of control, must be concerned about what persons whom they are considering for positions of leadership can do. While the studies of personality are not yet far enough advanced to promise that tests or other sources of data can assure infallibility, or even guarantee that one is examining all of the correct factors, it does seem that intelligence affects any individual's overall potential; his aptitudes affect his specific potential; his knowledge, skills, and judgment represent acquired potential; and his record reflects demonstrated potential. Any sources of data about these characteristics should be utilized by any person seeking indicators of another's potential.

However, what one can do on a job may be greatly influenced by the conditions in the environment in which he or she must do that job. Furthermore, the use of a person's record for determining what she or he can do may be misleading. Perhaps he has lacked means of knowing about other situations for which he might be qualified, or perhaps the work he has been assigned to do has been stultifying or has not challenged him sufficiently to elicit his best efforts.

"Will Do" Factors

Despite deficiencies in the information that it may provide, the record of what a person has done or is doing probably is still the best single predictor of what he or she will do. In any but the most mundane job, there should be some indicators of a person's work interests and aspirations, of motivation and drive (and drive here *does* mean physiological energy), of work habits and character traits, of attitudes and values, and of emotional maturity. Among the work habits and character traits would seem necessary for anyone working in any agency of education are stability, industry, perseverance, loyalty, compatibility, acceptance of responsibility, and dedication.

Thus, perhaps what we are saying is that an individual's attitudes, capacity for work, job motivations, preferences, and skills all are important to what the individual will do on a job. All of these may be affected by education and training, and a number of them by one's emotional tone, or what Cattell (1973) has called "mood" factors. Americans have had almost unlimited faith in the educational process as a means of making it possible for people to have social and job mobility. However, Coleman (1966) set off a furor with his findings that: (1) minority group students perform scholastically at lower levels than do white students, and (2) schools exert little influence on student achievement independent of social background. While Jencks et al. (1972) and Mosteller and Moynihan (1972) disagreed with Coleman's methodology, they took his data and did their own analyses. Both groups concluded that economic success is not related to schooling, and this has great implication for would-be leaders.

Another controversy has raged in regard to IQ, which several investigators have found to correlate significantly with leadership. At issue is whether there is a genetic difference in IQ between whites and nonwhites, and in the eye of this storm have been Jensen, Shockley, and Herrnstein. Sanday (1972) pointed out contradictions in their views and indicated the complexity of research that needs to be done on this matter. Meanwhile Ertl (Tracy, 1972) claims the IQ is obsolete and his EI (Ertl Index) is the culture-free wave of the future.

Illich (1971), although without research evidence, has made a damning statement to the effect that our system of schooling teaches everyone to want certain things (including well-paying satisfying jobs) that must, by the nature of economic fact, remain with a privileged few.

These considerations must be kept in mind when examining the "will do" factors of an individual, particularly when his or her record is the basis for that examination.

"Does Do" Factors

An examination of a person's present performance can tell much about one's attitudes, capacity for work, preferences, and skills. But particular care must be exercised in making inferences from such "evidence." One's attitudes might be different in a different environment or with different responsibilities, capacity for work might be vastly different were one faced with more exciting possibilities, preferences may be limited by a restricted range of choices, one may have had no time to seek other possible jobs, family or other factors may have allowed little or no flexibility in terms of place of employment, or one may have skills that his or her present work has never utilized and of which co-workers may be unaware.

In fact, with all three sets of factors mentioned here, it is well to keep in mind that if one could take a cross-section of an individual's personality, using all of the "best" measures currently available, the results would be about as depicted in Figure 12-5. That is to say that all of the methods and instruments can yield only part of the information that might be significant about a particular individual, and after all is said and done there will still remain a large amount that is unknown.

Table 12-1 (pp. 266–267) shows the present writers' judgments about some of the kinds of information that might be sought in evaluating personnel, with some indications of whether the factors are thought to provide information about performance, potential, predictability, or some combination of these. No claims are made as to the comprehensiveness or infallibility of the listing.

With all of the information that might be obtained about a person's performance, potential, and predictability, the fact remains that every individual may exhibit a considerable range of performance, depending on the situation.

Range of Performance

"This fixation on theories about man's nature . . . leaves out the simple point that people, while different, react in one way in one situation and a different way to another," as Drucker (1973, p. 89) said. Ginzberg (1966) suggested that there are at least four reasons for people reacting as they do to situations.

First, the performer's *motivation,* or relationship to one's goal, varies with the situation. An individual certainly will act differently if responding to a drive than if responding merely to a want, because in the first instance one is inner-directed and in the second one is largely, if not entirely, other-directed.

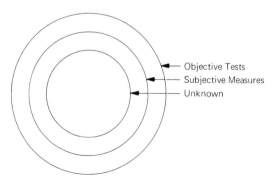

Figure 12-5 *What May Be Learned About an Individual*
Source: Taylor (1962), p. 92.

TABLE 12-1
POSSIBLE PERSONNEL EVALUATION FACTORS

FACTOR AND EXAMPLES	CAN PROVIDE INFORMATION ABOUT		
	DOES DO (PERFORMANCE)	CAN DO (POTENTIAL)	WILL DO (PREDICTABILITY)

APTITUDES
  a. Euduring stress
  b. Tolerating ambiguity
  c. Working with people
  d. Working with things
  e. Working with ideas
  f. Creating
  g. Intelligence
  h. Scholarship
		X	

ATTITUDES
  a. Getting along with others
  b. Loyalty; identification
     with group
  c. Professional ideals; ethics
  d. Self reliance; makes own
     decisions, stands on own feet
  e. Spirit of cooperation
  f. Willingness to take risks
  g. Willingness to work
	X	X	X

CAPACITY FOR WORK
  a. Alertness
  b. Energy, vigor, drive
  c. Health
  d. Industry
	X	X	X

WANTS (Perceived Deficiencies)
  a. Authority
  b. Money
  c. Perfection
  d. Competition
  e. Excellence
  f. Information, learning
  g. Power
  h. Security
  i. Service to others
  j. Status
			X

KNOWLEDGES
  a. Learning theory
  b. Technological; specific,
     job-related
  c. Dynamics of leading
  d. Dynamics of administering
		X	

TABLE 12-1 (concluded)

FACTOR AND EXAMPLES	CAN PROVIDE INFORMATION ABOUT		
	DOES DO (PERFORMANCE)	CAN DO (POTENTIAL)	WILL DO (PREDICTABILITY)
PERSONALITY	X		X
a. Breadth of interests			
b. Emotional control			
c. Dependability			
d. Grooming			
e. Initiative			
f. Manner of bearing			
g. Openmindedness			
h. Poise and maturity			
i. Promptness			
j. Rational-emotional balance			
k. Regard for consequences of actions			
l. Resourcefulness			
m. Self-discipline			
n. Realistic self-image			
o. Sense of humor			
p. Tactfulness			
q. Voice quality			
PREFERENCES	X		X
a. Acceptance of responsibility			
b. Dependence-independence			
c. Perseverance			
d. Stability; maintaining interests and employment			
SKILLS	X	X	X
a. Accuracy			
b. Conversational			
c. General vocabulary			
d. Grammar, pronunciation, spelling			
e. Managing			
f. Organizing			
g. Persuasion			
h. Writing			

Second, the quality—and thus the range—of one's performance often reflects variation in leadership. Depending on who the leaders are, organizational structure, communications procedures, initiation of changes, policy, and many other factors of organizational life may vary, and any one of such variables can affect the performance of every member of the organization.

Third, the way in which people are assigned to jobs and responsibilities within jobs affects performance. A person who feels competent to do tasks which he must do performs them differently from those on which he feels, and is likely to prove himself to be, inept. A person who helps to set his or her own objectives and is then given freedom to accomplish them in his or her own way performs differently than if methods are prescribed and supervision is close and tight.

Fourth, general expectations affect the way one performs, as has been mentioned previously. People tend to behave as they are expected to behave; prophecies tend to fulfill themselves, "the Pygmalion effect lives on."

Perhaps one's value-orientations also affect the range of one's performance. Certainly they are important in attempting to determine whether a given individual's need-dispositions are those of a leader or a follower.

SUMMARY

The definition of personality to which the present authors are responsive is "the personality of an individual is that which enables us to predict what he will do in a given situation." The many theories of the structure of personality can be sorted as to whether they refer to *types, traits, developmental* trends, or *dynamics* interplay. Most developmental theories are dynamic also, and one model depicts interplay of external stimuli, acquired values, physiological needs, and internal stimuli, resulting in goals designated as wants, psychological needs, and drives. The individual's motivations (relationships to goals) are other-directed or inner-directed, but either culminates in a need-disposition.

One's orientation to values refers to the nature or intent, content, and modality of the values involved. Applicability of values to one's life also affects orientation, and relates to the extent, generality, intensity, and explicitness of values. Some hypotheses relating to value-orientation might be tested to gain significant knowledge about the personalities of leaders.

Authenticity is a concept that has developed among investigators from several different disciplines. While difficult to do, it can be defined, and the attributes of being authentic are known. There are at least three ways of examining authenticity, and they relate to, but do not coincide with, integrity and status.

There are many implications of personality and authenticity for would-be educational leaders. Such persons must have a sense of identity that does not depend on status, values so integral to their natures that they cannot be denied, knowledge of their own prejudices and limitations, and standards they are unwilling to compromise.

Determinants of performance consist of "can do," "will do," and "does do" factors, relating to potential, predictable, and actual behavior. It is recognized that even when all possible objective and subjective measures for an individual are used, there remains a vast core of the unknown. Certain determinants may be of signal significance to educational leaders, as there are identifiable reasons for a wide range of performance by a given individual.

The next chapter will discuss some of the seemingly significant characteristics of leaders, giving attention to the influences of heredity and environment, and will suggest some indicators of success in leading.

SOME SUGGESTED RESOURCES

E. E. Baughman, *Personality: The psychological study of the individual.* Englewood Cliffs, N.J.: Prentice-Hall, 1972.

T. Dobzhansky, Differences are not deficits. *Psychology Today,* 1973, **7** (7), 97-8, 100–101.

M. D. Dunnette, Predictors of executive success. In F. R. Wichert and D. E. McFarland (Eds.), *Measuring executive effectiveness.* New York: Appleton, 1967, Pp. 7–48.

J. W. Getzels, J. M. Lipham, and R. F. Campbell, *Educational administration as a social process.* New York: Harper & Row, 1968. Pp. 66–70.

C. A. Gibb, Leadership: Psychological aspects. In D. L. Sills (Ed.), *International encyclopedia of the social sciences.* New York: Macmillan, 1968. Vol. 9, pp. 91–100.

S. Goldberg, *The inevitability of patriarchy.* New York: Morrow, 1973.

A. Jensen, The differences are real. *Psychology Today,* 1973, **7** (7), 80–82, 84, 86.

T. Parsons and E. A. Shils, Personality as a system of action. Ch. 2 in Part 2 of *Toward a general theory of action.* New York: Harper & Row, 1951. Pp. 110–158.

B. Rice, The high cost of thinking the unthinkable. *Psychology Today,* 1973, **7** (7), 89–93.

R. Tannenbaum and S. A. Davis, Values, man and organizations. In National Training Laboratory Institute for Applied Behavioral Science, *Behavioral science and the manager's role.* Washington, D.C.: The Institute, 1969. Pp. 3–24.

CHAPTER 13

SOME CHARACTERISTICS OF LEADERS

If we really understood what made Napoleon and Hitler tick, we would have come close to unraveling the major tangle of the leadership problem. However, we would still be faced with the question of whether Napoleon accomplished what he did because the time was ripe or because he was Napoleon.

—Ginzberg

Thirty-two items were listed Kast and Rosenzweig (1970) as constituting what it takes to lead, and they were subsumed under the headings of: (1) characteristics, (2) behavior, and (3) conditions. Our discussion in this chapter will be limited to some characteristics. The trait approach has been considered unfruitful since Stogdill's 1948 review of the literature.

It may never be possible to determine whether all successful leaders have common characteristics, but there are numerous indicators that leading on a sustained basis requires intelligence, broad interests and abilities, communication and human skills, authenticity, a preferred outcome, drive, and administrative ability. This chapter will be devoted to considering: (1) which of those characteristics seem to be hereditary, (2) which apparently come from nurturing, and (3) some indicators of success.

FACTORS FROM NATURE

The nature vs. nurture controversy is almost as old as psychology. At the risk of opening old wounds or starting new wars, it is suggested here that, of the factors it takes to lead, some come from one source and some from the other. Any individual seems to get at least a basic portion of his intelligence through inheritance, although it may be enhanced or hampered by environment. Any internal stimulus also has to come from something inside the individual, as do physiological or biological needs and drives.

Intelligence

It takes intelligence a little above the average to lead, but numerous researchers have found that superintelligence may only alienate followers. Anyone who is dealing with people very much less intelligent than he or she will have to have unusual amounts of tolerance, humility, empathy, and patience if he or she is not to alienate them. On the other hand, if a would-be leader is mentally inferior to his supposed followers, he will have little or no basis for influence or authority over them. Intelligence somewhat above the average will not automatically make one a leader, but it is necessary to sustain one in a leader position. However, if one easily comprehends and solves complex problems while others are still uncertain as to what the problem is, one may be thought a snob or a "pointy-head" and may be unable to establish rapport. No studies known to the present authors have shown perfect correlation between intelligence and leader success, but Stogdill (1948), Fiedler (1969), and others have concluded that there is some relationship.

Internal Stimuli

Earlier it was pointed out that a stimulus is any energy change that affects a sense organ, and that the conditions within the human body that can excite and activate a sense organ probably are of an electrochemical nature. Such changes apparently can originate entirely within the body, as found in hunger, thirst, anoxia, or the desire for sexual gratification. Whatever triggers those energy changes seems to come from genetic qualities of the person, which we have indicated determine physiological or biological needs.

Physiological Needs

Generally recognized physiological needs (Table 1-1, p. 9) include some which we have classed as survival needs and others we have called protection needs. It is doubtful that it takes any different physiological needs to lead than it does to follow.

SURVIVAL NEEDS. Survival needs include air, food, drink, bodily elimination, sleep, warmth, sexual expression, activity, rest, and sensory stimulation. While survival of the individual may not require sexual expression, survival of the species does. Survival of the individual requires all of the others, although the effects of inactivity and lack of sensory stimulation are only beginning to be understood.

Some internal stimulus often seems to result from one of these needs, producing a *drive for survival* and requiring a physical satisfaction, which becomes a powerful goal for the organism. Individuals so driven have been known to exhibit almost superhuman efforts and strength.

PROTECTION NEEDS. Protection needs have been less examined than survival needs, but they seem to exist in all human beings and include needs for protection from the elements, from enemies, from territorial invasion, and from uncertainty. When one of these needs triggers an internal stimulus another powerful kind of drive results. Thus, one can explain the drive to exploration as resulting from the need to *know*—to have uncertainty reduced. We have not yet found how to fully utilize this need in aiding learning.

If one concedes that the factors of personality that all people acquire through inheritance include intelligence, internal stimuli, and physiological needs one still cannot explain a Napoleon or a Hitler—or an educational leader. Factors that are attributable to nurture, or environment, may help to explain why some individuals lead while others follow, but they do not make the explanation complete.

FACTORS FROM NURTURE
The factors of personality that one seems to acquire from the environment may be said to include values, wants, and psychological needs.

External Stimuli
It appears self-evident that most of the physical energy that impinges upon and excites one's sense organs comes from outside the body. Sensory stimulation is necessary to survival, as experiments in recent years with sensory deprivation have emphasized, and that stimulation comes from the environment. Individuals who have spent long periods in solitary confinement have attested to how very difficult it was to provide such stimulation for themselves. However, external stimuli are available in varying degrees to people in different levels of an organization, and that fact may help to explain why some lead and others do not. Furthermore, the values one has determine to a great extent which external stimuli one will "admit" to his consciousness and which he will not even be aware of.

Values
One is not born with values, they are acquired through learning. An individual learns to make a choice from among alternatives and to cherish his choice as the "right" thing to do, affirming it publicly and acting on it repeatedly so that it becomes a part of his life-style. Obviously the choices one learns to make are affected by choices available in one's environment and to influences experienced very

early in life, including vicarious experiences attained through reading. Values seem to constitute the perceptual screen by means of which only certain stimuli are observed at the conscious level (see Figure 12-2).

Among the things that it seems a person must view as praiseworthy in order to value leading are a commitment to broad, as opposed to narrow, interests; high-level communication and human skills; enough desire for conformity to keep one within limits that are tolerable to the led; acquisition of administrative ability; and appreciation of a leader model. Probably broad interests determine whether one will be a local or a cosmopolitan, place bound or career bound. Skills that are not valued are unlikely to be attained. Certainly one who approaches the social ideal of his or her peers has the advantage when leaders are selected, whatever the means of selection. One who does not value leaders is unlikely to value leading. The external stimuli that are admitted through the perceptual screen of values result in wants and psychological needs.

Psychological Needs

A want is a perceived deficiency of something that an individual believes would lead to a satisfaction that he values. To give examples (see Table 11-1, p. 242), person may feel a deficiency in the approval of others if his need is for feeling loved or wanted at the level of "affiliation," if his need is for praise at the "status" level, or if his need is respect at the "security" level. Thus, the need is the goal and the *want is a perceived means* of achieving the goal. One might avoid considerable anxiety by accepting one's personal world as one consisting of ever-receding goals.

Wants must correlate with needs if authenticity is to be achieved. However, remedying the perceived deficiency may or may not satisfy the need. For example, an individual may perceive that a new car will get him or her the admiration that he or she needs for a feeling of security. If the person gets the new car and is still not admired, he or she feels frustrated and still insecure. The individual may feel a deficiency of self-approval if his or her need is for realization of potential at the "accomplishment" level or for autonomy at the "self-actualization" level.

In the final section of this chapter there will be a discussion of certain need-dispositions that we believe to be common to effective leaders except perhaps for a few in very limited situations. We are hypothesizing that, to *feel* successful, on a sustained basis in a large educational enterprise in our society, a leader must be functioning at either the accomplishment or self-actualization level. A person who wants approval in order to feel accepted may do well in leading a voluntary association but not a university. One who needs praise will find little of it in most leader positions. One who needs freedom from threat will find risk instead if his wants bring him to a position of authority. Such persons probably will not *feel* successful, even if perceived as successful by others.

A second hypothesis is that administrative ability will be valued, and thus developed, only by those functioning at least partially at the "accomplishment" level.

A third and final hypothesis relating to what it takes to lead is that no one ever feels that success has been fully achieved because new psychological needs appear as soon as "lower level" needs are fulfilled.

SUCCESS

Success is a matter of perception, and we have ventured the opinion that one's perceptual screen is one's web of values. Then success, like beauty, is in the eye of the beholder and, for the beholder, it may be amorphous or at least, like goals, ever-receding. If a perceived deficiency is remedied without the need being satisfied, the individual experiences no sense of success. If remedying a perceived deficiency does satisfy the need, success still is ahead on some distant horizon because a new level of need becomes operative. However, a principal, a superintendent, a business manager, a provost, or a chancellor may be perceived as successful by others even though he himself experiences no sweet taste.

It seems reasonable that the success of a leader as perceived by others may be directly related to the amount of his behavior that is seen as acceptable to the group(s) with which he works, his self-concept, his management of time, his handling of stress, and his authenticity.

Acceptable Behavior

Group members inevitably judge the acceptability of the behavior of individuals according to group-held norms. The norms that are particularly proscriptive for a leader probably relate to goal achievement, acceptance of group values, and communication.

GOAL ACHIEVEMENT. Followers seem likely to be most concerned about their own needs, next-most about production, next about organization maintenance, and least about innovation, if one refers to the goals shown in Figure 8-1. Yet many status leaders seem almost oblivious to the needs of individual group members. The rare leader who puts this goal in top priority probably can maintain an enthusiastic following regardless of what he or she does about achieving the other three. However, members of a board of control are likely to be more concerned about production and organization maintenance, or in some cases about innovation. The leader himself, along with learners and those who pay for the educational agency, is likely to focus primarily on innovation, particularly if none has occurred in a long time. Thus, a leader is more likely to be successful if she or he achieves all four goals in some degree than if she or he focuses on one to the exclusion of others.

GROUP-VALUES ACCEPTANCE. The possibility that all culture patterns may be grouped according to dominant, variant, or deviant values was advanced by Kluckhohn (Parsons and Shils, 1951, p. 415). Dominant values were perceived as those held by a majority of a group or by the most powerful elite. Certainly, a leader will be more successful if he accepts the dominant values of the group(s) with which he works than if he does not. If his preferred outcomes conflict with those values, he must either have enough power to impose his will, must work carefully to bank idiosyncrasy credit over a period of time, or must suffer defeat when he tries to achieve his preferred outcomes.

According to Hollander's (1958) notion of idiosyncrasy credit, group-set limits of behavior are not identical for any two members of a group. Behavior is variant so long as it occurs within limits that are *tolerable for that individual;* it becomes deviant when the individual exceeds the limits set for any group members. The leader is likely to be successful if his or her behavior indicates acceptance of dominant values to the extent that his or her behavior is merely variant, not deviant.

COMMUNICATION. There has been repeated emphasis in this book on the leader's need for consummate communications skills. He or she is likely to exhibit acceptable behavior only if he or she solicits and is capable of *listening* to—not just hearing—response and feedback. One needs response to assure that messages are received and feedback to indicate that his or her intended meaning is understood.

Self-Concept

A significant element of an individual's interactions with his social environment is the concept of self. The idea of self-concept certainly is not new, yet a multiplicity of terms has been used in the literature of psychology and education to express such an idea.

Sullivan (1953, p. 373) used the term "self-system" and defined it as "the extensive organization of experience within personality." Sawrey and Telford (1973) referred to this aspect of human personality simply as "the self" and suggested that the self includes more than one's physical being. Later, the same authors interchangeably used "self," "self-concept," and "ego." Kaplan (1959) reported on the dynamic forces in human behavior, using the Freudian term "ego" for self-concept and defining it as "that aspect of mental functioning which organizes and controls perceptions, protects us against unreasonable pleasure-seeking tendencies, and tests reality [p. 236]." Combs and Snygg (1959) referred to the "phenomenal self" which includes "not only a person's physical self, but everything he experiences as 'me' at that instant. [p. 44]." Anderson (1961) utilized the term "self-image" and suggested that this image is "composed of many parts, each . . . conceived of as having both structure and function . . . which include everything that pertains or relates to 'I,' 'me,' or 'my' conceptual thinking [pp. 407–408]." More recently, Coopersmith (1967) wrote of "the antecedents of self-esteem," Diggory (1966) of "self-evaluation," and Branden (1969) of "the psychology of self-esteem." The latter said:

> *The nature of his self-evaluation has profound effects on a man's thinking processes, emotions, desires, values and goals. It is the single most significant key to his behavior. To understand a man psychologically, one must understand the nature and degree of his self-esteem, and the standards by which he judges himself [p. 103].*

Though each of the authors referred to above described essentially the same phenomenon in markedly different terminology, all of them agreed that the "self," as an aspect of personality, is acquired—not ready-made—and that it is essentially a social structure that arises out of social experience. Each author in his analysis also made it clear that the developmental origins of the self-concept are imbedded in the earliest social experiences of individuals and that once the self-concept is established, it has relative durability and permanence. This latter is not to say that the self-concept, once established, cannot be altered, yet it does suggest that *the image one has of oneself is resistant to change.*

One might ask, "What has all this to do with leadership, and particularly educational leadership?" Certainly, such a query is legitimate and, as has already been pointed out in earlier sections of this chapter, there are a number of elements related to the development of desirable personality characteristics for educational leaders. The present writers believe that the core of feelings and attitudes about oneself in great measure guides and directs that person's behavior. There is the further belief that desirable leader personality cannot be developed unless there is an adequate and stable development of the self-concept, and a leader's success is thought to be directly related to his or her self-concept.

Management of Time

The educational leader, particularly the college president or the superintendent of schools, is likely to be successful only if he or she can learn to manage time. If one allows the press of events to compel him and his staff to devote most of the available time to maintaining the organization, then human resources necessary to the achievement of the other three major goals of educational agencies will be unavailable. Drucker (1967) stressed the importance of managing time, and spelled out in some detail how one could learn to do it. It would seem that whether one can manage time is directly related to the need-disposition called "structuring activities" which will be described in the next section of this chapter. The leader must be an organizer and have an awareness of the importance of time if she or he is to be successful.

Mental Health

Of course there are and have been exceptions, yet a leader will more likely be successful if he or she is in a sound state of mental health. Mental health includes the prevention of mental and emotional disorders; the detection, treatment, and rehabilitation of the mentally ill; and the promotion of mental well-being. The ways in which one acts to maintain mental health have not been widely written about, but Levinson (1970) reported a study done by others in which it was concluded that mentally healthy persons behave consistently in five important ways.

1. *Variety of need-gratifications.* A person who is active in at least three or four different social systems may find certain of his or her needs satisfied in one if they are frustrated in another. For example, a school principal who is not finding satisfaction of his needs in his school situation may still retain his emotional balance if he is active in a supportive family, successfully involved in civic affairs, and recognized as useful in some ameliorative agency. The point is to be active in enough social systems that one can be reasonably certain of positive reinforcement in some of them.

2. *Flexibility under stress.* Physicians believe that stress—resulting from pressures in relationships with other persons, from social conditions, or from physical or chemical processes within the body—brings on mental illness. While no designated leader can totally avoid stressful situations or conditions, some persons adapt to such situations or conditions much more readily than others do. A person who can "shift his psychological weight" under stress is less likely to be floored by stress than the person who is stuck with one way of looking at things. Flexibility seems closely related to having a variety of sources of gratification, which may allow one to come at problems from a variety of perspectives.

3. *Realistic self-esteem.* Self-esteem was discussed earlier in this chapter, authenticity was examined in Chapter 12, and realism seems related to both. The mentally healthy individual recognizes and accepts himself; he knows his limitations and his assets, and he likes what he sees without being complacent or smug about it.

4. *Treatment of others.* The mentally healthy leader really cares about what other people feel; he is not so wrapped up in himself that he cannot listen and respond to others as individuals.

5. *Activity and productivity.* Levinson (1970) said something so profound that it bears repeating:

> *Mentally healthy people use their resources in their own behalf and in behalf of others. They do what they do because they like to do it and enjoy using their skills. They do not feel driven to produce in order to prove themselves. They are in charge of their activities; the activities are not in charge of them. When they are chosen for leadership of one sort or another, it is because they have the skills to lead in a given situation, not because they have to exercise power over others. They seek achievement for what they can do, not for what they can be, for when one tries to be something or someone he will never be satisfied with himself even if he achieves that desired goal [p. 19].*

Here then is a model of mental health to which the present authors subscribe. Though attainment may at best be difficult, the reader should not be in doubt as to what is desirable. In essence, what we are trying to say is that for the educational leader—whether in business, industry, the military establishment, in government, or in public or private education—there must be a continuing anticipation of difficult decisions to come, issues that divide, problems that may remain unsolved, and situations that border on the unmanageable. In such times and situations, the inner resources of an individual could be tested to their utmost, and one's psychological survival depends on having resources equal to the test.

Authenticity is a further "predictor of success," but this topic was discussed at length in Chapter 12. It was indicated that authenticity is closely related to value-orientation, and value-orientations of individuals probably are closely related to need-dispositions, and the need-dispositions of leaders seem to follow a pattern.

NEED-DISPOSITIONS OF LEADERS

"Leaders act as they do because they cannot act otherwise," according to Ginzberg (1966, p. 116). We subscribe to the Parsons-Shils notion that any individual behaves in certain manners with respect to objects and persons because he or she expects certain consequences. Freudians would argue that a person's action is due to what is behind one, and Skinnerians would say it is due to conditions in one's present environment. "Third Force" psychologists such as Lewin, Rogers, Maslow, and Combs might argue that the individual is moved by attraction of what is ahead—by an approach drive.

For us, the concept of need-disposition is a rubric under which the ideas of needs, motivations, and drives are all subsumed, as was illustrated in Figure 12-2 (p. 254). Resultant actions, whether Freudian, Skinnerian, or Lewinian in origin, occur because the individual desires certain consequences which he or she expects will eventuate. Obviously, the consequence most desired is need-satisfaction, and when satisfaction does not occur, frustration does. An individual may become so conditioned that she or he simply uses substitute behavior or otherwise accommodates to unsatisfying situations. Leaders, though, seem to generally find satisfactions in what they do. While it may seem that "sometimes in America not much more is needed than arrogance and a sense of audience"[1] for one to be a self-appointed leader, it also seems that every status leader has a high degree of ego-involvement.

Ego-Involvement

Results of research done with several hundred educators in suburban Rochester, New York, and in Illinois were reported by Sergiovanni and Carver (1973). In both situations, the "prepotency" levels of need showed self-esteem needs as highest among Maslow's five basic levels, and we believe this reaction to be typical of educators. Simon (1957) and Zaleznik (1966), among others, have said that leaders must have more than the usual amount of healthy ego. But if one is to take responsibility for leading, one is risking failure and loss of self-esteem. Thus, we believe that a potential leader must believe or feel strongly about a matter if he or she voluntarily incurs such risk—he or she must have real ego-involvement to indulge those need-dispositions which we believe to be common to all leaders.

Havighurst (1972) examined the types of people who are recognized as leaders in education today. Perhaps his categories of "prophets, whiz kids, scholar-scientists, social engineers, and research administrators" say something regarding the ego-involvement of each type.

We will here expand upon the need-dispositions of leaders that were briefly listed in Chapter 6. Each implies intensive ego-involvement.

Structuring Activities

Most educational leaders seem to have organizational ability. They like to set their own and others' time schedules; they enjoy allocating the tasks to be done, coordinating efforts of human beings, and seeking and planning the use of human, financial, and physical resources. They locate, plan for, remodel, coordinate construction of, and schedule the use of facilities and tools necessary to the educational tasks. They generally, depending upon the demands on their time, prefer to do these things themselves rather than have someone else do them. They make or participate in the making of the deci-

[1] Cynthia Buchanan, How the west was conned. *Newsweek,* 1973, **82** (22), 17.

sions as to how policies will be carried out and how learning opportunities will be provided.

Taking Responsibility

Many a leader has achieved visibility—or a promotion—by taking responsibility that her or his role did not call for, doing it only because tasks that she or he thought needed to be done were not being done. Taking uncalled-for responsibility often increases one's personal authority, but it inevitably heightens visibility, which is a potent risk factor. Nevertheless, leaders frequently seem unable to keep from taking uncalled-for responsibility, and the leadership process is enhanced whenever someone *is* willing to do so. Gunther (1971) had some suggestions for those who wish to increase their visibility in the corporate structure. Most would work for educators.

Often a leader or would-be leader who assumes responsibility does so without considering the risk involved. However, risk "comes with the territory." Risk may be due solely to the increased visibility that a leader has, or it may be due to lack of proper skills, failure to make decisions, making the wrong decisions, hasty or excessive action, inaction, or other bad judgment. Some or all of these may result from lack of experience.

Failure to seek alternatives or enough alternatives, taking short-term action on long-term problems, reacting to symptoms instead of ascertaining the problems from which they result, having too much or not enough imagination, exceeding group-set limits, inability to resolve conflict, causing others to feel threatened, improper conceptualization, opposing or capitulating to pressure groups, and prematurity or tardiness of action have all exposed leaders to risk at some time. One of the greatest risks results from making on an ethical-moral basis decisions that must be implemented in a politico-economic context, as described by Davenport (1964). It was proposed by Byrd (1971) that leaders can determine how much risk they can afford to take by evaluating their power base, and a scheme for doing that was presented.

Advocacy

Leadership occurs where people advocate causes. Leaders have preferred outcomes, and press for their accomplishment. Hence, communications skills are of more than usual importance to leaders. Language mastery and articulateness are vital to one who has a cause to espouse. Idiom, cliche, and the vernacular may be adequate for leaders of some groups, but not for educators or other professionals whose constituents use words as their stock in trade. Bartky (1953) said that a school administrator has no right to influence a teacher by any means other than intellectual persuasion; persuasion requires language mastery.

Many of the communications of the educational leader are in

written form, and grammatical gaffes or misspellings erode one's personal authority each time they are viewed by those who know better.

Leaders stand for something; they advocate preferred outcomes, and each has a distant vision of what his or her organization could and should be. They achieve their preferences through communicating. Leaders lead also through understanding others.

Understanding Others

"Whether managers [i.e., leaders] can be taught in the classroom how to cope with human emotions is a moot point. There is little reason to believe that what is now taught in psychology classes, human relations seminars, and sensitivity training programs is of much help to men who are 'mired in the code of rationality' and who lack 'effective empathy' [Livingston, 1971, p. 88]."

Empathy is *not* synonymous with sympathy, despite frequent usage as if it were. According to Webster, empathy is "imaginative projection of one's consciousness into another being." To empathize, one must be able to put himself in the other's boots and *know* how one would feel if he had the same experience as the other. The most bullying autocrat is capable of empathy if he can imagine or has experienced how one feels when he is bullied.

A leader may use persuasion, fear, flattery, rewards, manipulation of aggression or submission drives, emotionalism, or beliefs in the supernatural in getting others to do what one wants. Regardless of the extent of an individual's repertoire for stimulation or of the sophistication of one's communication skills, the strategy chosen will be more effective if one is able to imagine how the recipient will feel about the treatment that he or she receives. Schroeter (1970) made quite a point of this.

The leadership process is found where there are one or more persons who are able to understand how others feel. It also occurs where there are one or more persons who enjoy the use of authority.

Using Authority

"Power corrupts, and absolute power corrupts absolutely" is Lord Acton's widely quoted and accepted maxim. Any person who admits to pleasure in the use of power is immediately suspect. Yet it seems that leaders do enjoy the use of authority, and *must* do so if they are to be effective.

Perhaps the difference lies in the fact that the wielder of power may have achieved the power without regard to merit, may use it capriciously, and may exert it on those who have no choice in the matter; the exerciser of authority, on the other hand, is constrained by the limits of his or her idiosyncracy credit and by the ends and means to which followers will accede.

Nevertheless, most leaders seem to relish the use of authority.

They prefer to take the actions and make the decisions legitimized by groups rather than to have others taking the actions or making the decisions. That the leaders are ceded authority says something about the need-dispositions of other individuals in the group.

SUMMARY

Whether considering Napoleon, Hitler, a university president, a director of training and management development, a commanding officer of a military academy, or some other leader, probably no one knows how much of what the individual does is due to him being who he is, is due to the time at which he functioned or is functioning, or is due to the particular situation.

However, intelligence somewhat above the average of subordinates does seem to be characteristic, and it is the only factor of leadership that seems clearly attributable to heredity, even though it may be modified to some extent by the environment.

Factors clearly attributable to environment include external stimuli, the web of values that comprise an individual's perceptual screen, and psychological needs. It is through these factors that we may account for characteristics such as broad interests, communication and human skills, a modicum of conformity to group norms, and appreciation of leader models. Needs determine goals, and wants are perceived deficiencies in means for achieving those goals. Correlation of wants and needs is essential to authenticity and to an individual's own feeling of success, which is fleeting at best.

Among the elements which may help a leader to be perceived by others as successful, even though she or he does not feel successful, are group-acceptable behavior, self-concept, management of time, and mental health.

Need-dispositions which seem to be characteristic of leaders include ego-involvement, ability to structure and liking for structuring activities of himself or herself and others, taking responsibility beyond the call of duty, advocacy of goals and ideas, understanding others, and enjoyment of the use of authority.

Chapter 14 will consist of consideration of those things an individual may do to qualify himself or herself to lead others.

SOME SUGGESTED RESOURCES

W. Bennis, What went wrong. Ch. 7 in *The leaning ivory tower.* San Francisco, Calif.: Jossey-Bass, 1973. Pp. 129–145.

P. S. Burnham, Role theory and educational administration. In G. Baron and W. Taylor (Eds.), *Educational administration and the social sciences.* London: Athlone, 1969. Pp. 72–91.

R. F. Campbell, E. M. Bridges, J. E. Corbally, R. O. Nystrand, and J. A. Ramseyer, Personal motivations for administrator behavior. Ch. 11 in *Introduction to Educational Administration.* (4th ed.) Boston: Allyn & Bacon, 1971. Pp. 337–361.

R. M. D'Aprix, *How's that again?* Homewood, Ill.: Dow Jones-Irwin, 1971.

J. W. Getzels, J. M. Lipham, and R. F. Campbell, *Educational administration as a social process.* New York: Harper & Row, 1968. Pp. 70–77.

E. Ginzberg, Leaders and leadership. Ch. 9 in *The development of human resources.* New York: McGraw-Hill, 1966. Pp. 109–121.

H. Levinson, *Emotional health in the world of work.* New York: Harper & Row, 1964.

D. G. Mitton, Making the most of your leadership style. *Personnel Administration,* 1970, 33(3), 49–53.

D. Riesman, N. Glazer, and R. Denney, Some types of character and society. Ch. I in *The lonely crowd* (abr. ed.). New Haven, Conn.: Yale University Press, 1961. Pp. 3–36.

J. W. Taylor, Successful leadership—what does it take? Ch. 3 in *How to select and develop leaders.* New York: McGraw-Hill, 1962. Pp. 17–45.

O. Tead, The leader's objectives. In *The art of leadership.* New York: McGraw-Hill, 1935.

CHAPTER 14

QUALIFYING TO LEAD

Leadership calls for decisions; decisions involve responsibility for consequences; and responsibility, a moral habit informed by understanding, is only developed by practical experience.

—Rusk

Undoubtedly would-be leaders are interested in knowing how they may qualify to lead. Is the only way to develop the moral habit of responsibility by means of practical experience, as Dean Rusk stated? This chapter will discuss occupational choice, career patterns of some selected leaders, how one can chart a course to a position of leadership, and ways in which one can prepare himself or herself.

OCCUPATIONAL CHOICE

It should be obvious that a multiplicity of reasons may exist within a given individual as bases for his or her choice of a particular position. Reasons for one's choice of a particular career or profession would be even more complex. Among the numerous writers who have developed theories of career choice is Ginzberg (1966), and the three basic elements of his theory are presented here as being representative. First, the process of occupational choice occurs over a period of from six to more than ten years. Second, each decision is related to one's experience up to that point and influences the future, thus it is basically irreversible; the values to which one is committed likely undergo no basic changes thereafter. Third, occupational choice involves the balancing of numerous subjective ele-

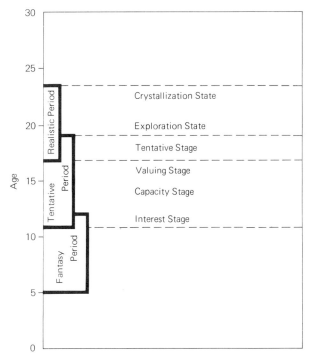

Figure 14-1   *Ages, Periods, and Stages of Occupational Choice*
Source. Ginzberg (1966), pp. 47–54.

ments with real opportunities and limitations and thus the choice is inevitably a compromise among the individual's interests, capacities, and values during the *tentative* stage.

THEORY: AGES, PERIODS, AND STAGES
According to the Ginzberg theory, occupational choice is gradually narrowed down and focused upon during three typical, but sometimes overlapping, periods which are identified with fairly specific age levels. In each period, there are stages of development of choice, these being: (1) fantasy, (2) tentative, and (3) realistic, as shown in Figure 14-1.

During the fantasy period, the individual thinks about occupations in terms of what he or she would like to be. During the tentative period, the necessity of deciding on a future occupation is apparent, but the individual is still thinking in terms of subjective factors: his or her own interests, capacities, and values. In the realistic period, the individual becomes aware that he or she is going to be forced to compromise between what he or she wants on the one hand and what he or she can qualify for and find opportunity for on the other.

Ginzberg, along with other theorists, admit that research needs to be done on the matter of occupational choice. This seems of particular importance to the present writers for three reasons: (1) sociologists have predicted that the average high school graduate of today will change his occupation at least five times during his lifetime, due to new jobs being developed and old ones becoming outmoded; (2) numerous persons, including educators, have been switching occupations in recent years at ages far beyond that at which the crystallization stage is presumed to occur; and (3) some educators, and others, have long been exceptions if there is a pattern to the career choices of most people.

Some Cases

If some readers of this book are now feeling a sense of guilt because they are past the age of the realistic period and the crystallization stage, it may be comforting to look at a few case histories of individuals who did not decide their life's work according to the foregoing theory.

CASE 1 Man, born May 4, 1796, at Franklin, Massachusetts

ca age 25 graduated from Brown University in Law
age 31 elected a member of the Massachusetts state legislature
age 41 gave up law practice to become secretary to Massachusetts State Board of Education, where he made a name for himself as an educational reformer
age 43 founded the first state normal school in Lexington, Mass.
age 52 became a member of the U.S. House of Representatives
age 57 became president of Antioch College
Name—Horace Mann

CASE 2 Man, born February 12, 1809, in what is now Larue County, Kentucky

age 19 flatboat crewman on the Ohio and Mississippi rivers
age 21 farm laborer, rail-splitter, general handyman
age 22 flatboat crewman on the Mississippi River; general-store clerk; soldier in the Black Hawk War
age 23 defeated as a candidate for the Illinois state legislature; partner in a general store, which failed
age 24 postmaster of New Salem, Illinois; deputy surveyor, odd job man
age 25 elected to the lower house of the Illinois General Assembly
age 27 admitted to the bar
age 28 law firm partner

age 31 campaigner for presidential candidate William Henry Harrison

age 35 campaigner for presidential candidate Henry Clay

age 38 elected a member of the U.S. House of Representatives

age 30 was unsuccessful as an applicant for Commissioner of the General Land Office; returned to law practice

age 45 elected to the Illinois legislature, but resigned to run for the U.S. Senate

age 52 became president of the United States

Name—Abraham Lincoln

CASE 3 Woman, born September 6, 1860 in Cedarville, Illinois

ca age 22 graduated from Rockford College; began medical studies in Philadelphia, but had to give them up for heatlh reasons

age 28 founded a settlement house for the immigrant population of Chicago

age 30+ organized civic groups to bring pressure on legislatures and officials

age 42 wrote and lectured on a wide variety of social problems, including child labor, public health, unemployment relief, and social insurance

age 49 became the first woman president of the National Conference of Charities and Corrections, now the National Conference on Social Welfare

age 55 became president of the Women's International League for Peace and Freedom

age 71 shared the Nobel Peace Prize

Name—Jane Addams

CASE 4 Man, born May 8, 1884, in Lamar, Missouri

age 17 timekeeper for a construction crew on the Santa Fe Railroad

age 18 mail room clerk for the *Kansas City Star;* bank clerk and bookkeeper

age 22–33 farmer

age 33 artillery officer in World War I; ran the regimental canteen

age 35 became a partner in a men's clothing store that failed

age 38 county judge of Jackson county, Missouri

age 42 became presiding county judge

age 50 elected to the U.S. Senate

age 60 elected Vice President of the United States

age 61 became President of the United States

age 71 published the first volume of his memoirs

Name—Harry S. Truman

CASE 5 Woman, born 1943, Skokie (?), Illinois

   ca age 18 entered University of Illinois to study occupational
      therapy
   ca age 19 switched to education for the mentally retarded
   ca age 20 changed to journalism
   ca age 21 turned to political writing
   ca age 22 dropped out of law school, became a research assis-
      tant for a semimonthly magazine
   ca age 23 returned to law school
   age 29 received U.S. Department of Justice Special Achievement
      Award
   age 30 was the U.S. Department of Justice attorney involved in
      a spectacular national investigation
   Name—Jill Wine Volner

What do these five cases, and dozens of similar ones that might
be cited, illustrate? Only that: (1) a number of persons, some of
whom have had notable careers, have not conformed to the theory
of occupational choice, and (2) the day of the nonconforming career
chooser is not yet over. Furthermore, the changing times would seem
to increase, rather than decrease, the likelihood of nonconformity.

The Changing Times
Numerous accounts of the early educational history of this country
mention the fact that early schoolteachers often were those who did
not have the skills for, or were physically unsuited for, other occupations. It is doubtful that such individuals chose the occupation of
teaching by going through the stages indicated by theory, or that
their choices were made at the ages representing the various periods. Furthermore, many of the practitioners in the field today, from
classroom teachers to university presidents, could bear testimony
that what they are now doing is not the result of any process that
approximates the theoretical process of occupational choice. While
empirical evidence is needed to support or to deny the idea that
today's educational leaders attained positions through careful and
conscious planning of career patterns, there can be no denial that
the changing times have affected and are affecting choices of people
as to whether they wish to become educators and to aspire to positions of leadership in the profession.
   For many decades, earnest, dedicated people deliberately chose
to teach and among their numbers have always been some who deliberately chose positions of headship in which they were expected
to lead. Nevertheless, the charge has been made repeatedly, and
with some justification, in our opinion, that from the 1930s into the
1960s many people turned to education because of rejection from
other academic programs, because of inability to afford college ex-

cept at the relatively modestly priced teachers colleges, or after having lost enthusiasm for some other curriculum. In our opinion, this condition has been changed. In recent years, more able service-oriented young people have made education their number one preference, but whether this will continue to be true in a declining job market such as prevailed in the early 1970s remains to be seen.

Perhaps we in education have been somewhat myopic. For generations, government officials have demonstrated that an able individual can be taken from one field and given responsibilities in another, where he soon adapts and again does an outstanding job. We have clung to a belief that to be a superintendent of schools, an individual must have been a principal, and a classroom teacher before that. Colleges and universities have been a bit more liberal in their thinking, and have not held that there are career patterns that one must have followed in order to become a dean or a president. Most have held to requirements of having been a professor and having earned a Ph.D. as minimums, but even these have been ignored in some exceptional instances. Little attention has been paid to professional preparation in either administration or leadership at the higher-education level. Training directors in industry and government often have had little or no specific academic preparation, although a number of them appear to have had work and/or administrative experience in public schools.

In 1970, Ohio State University started a National Program in Educational Leadership, with USOE funding, in which they took individuals from noneducation backgrounds into academic programs to prepare them as educational leaders. This and other experiments undoubtedly will be watched with great interest as they may have far-reaching effects on career patterns.

The changing times in no way lessen the importance of or the need for conscious choice by would-be educational leaders, however. Potential educational leaders need to be identified early, encouraged and guided in their development, and they should set their sights and course at an early date if they are to make a maximum contribution.

Importance

Occupational choice is in many ways dependent on an individual's knowledge of the tasks to be performed, the demands that will be held for him or her as a position occupant, plus awareness and understanding of those functions and dimensions which characterize leader behavior. These perceptions are conditioned by the view of self held by an individual.

The importance of occupational choice to the individual cannot be in question and the essential irreversibility of such a choice places a heavy burden upon the individual in terms of insight into self, awareness of personal strengths and weaknesses, recognition of the demands held for persons occupying leadership roles, and cognizance of the difficulties to be encountered in any attempts to bring about change in either the organization or its members. As was pointed out in earlier chapters, the leadership process as it currently is conceived requires leaders who have clarity of perception as to their personal adequacy, who possess deep feelings about the dignity and worth of themselves as well as others, who are open to both experience and change, and who can exhibit confidence as to the rightness of their goals and decisions yet maintain the capacity to entertain intensely humbling doubts about the prospects for being personally fallible. In addition, the lengthy preparation period required and the economic and psychologically costly demands of such preparation make it imperative that individuals determine at an early date whether or not they are suited to the rigors of positions in which they are expected to lead.

CAREER PATTERNS

There seems to be no practical way to learn, in regard to those who currently are leaders in education, what portion of their career patterns have been due to the individuals' specific abilities, to visibility, to timing, to fortuitous circumstance, to influential persons, to specific situations, or to pure chance. That each of those elements has had some effect on most career patterns can hardly be doubted, but there do seem to be some illustrations of *stepping stones* to certain positions, of situations where individuals assumed responsibility and were thereafter given it, of effects of crisis on leader selection, and of individuals having been assigned to too-big shoes and then growing to fit them.

Stepping Stones?

The existence of stepping stones or definite routes to certain positions may be more imagined than real, or more an illustration of what has been than of what is. For example, college presidents, vice-presidents, and provosts seem generally not to have had any stepping stones other than that of a professorship, and some have not taken even that step. The same is true of deans. Directors of training and management development programs in business, industry, government, and the military seem to have been recruited largely from persons already filling other types of positions in those establishments. That a number of those directors had some preparation and experience in education before becoming disenchanted with the schools and seeking employment elsewhere is evident, but we have little reason to believe that many had any formalized preparation in educational administration or leadership except for on-the-job training after being appointed to directorships.

PROFESSORS. At an earlier date, many if not most professors of educational administration had seen experience as public school teachers, principals, or superintendents, or perhaps all of these. Personal observation by the authors indicates that this is not true for a number of faculty members who have been appointed to professorships in recent years.

STATE DEPARTMENTS OF EDUCATION. Routes to positions in state departments of education are by no means clear-cut, although it does seem that for most administrators at this level some experience in teaching and perhaps previous experience as school administrators seem to be general prerequisites.

DIRECTORS AND SUPERVISORS. Directors of special school programs, such as special education, adult education, and community education, seem to be recruited from among teachers in those areas, although there certainly are exceptions. Directors of proprietary schools represent backgrounds so diverse that it is doubtful if there is any identifiable pattern. Supervisors of instruction in public schools sometimes are chosen because they are expert teachers, sometimes because they get along well at helping other people, and sometimes because they can demonstrate both kinds of skills. Perhaps the same is true of supervisors in other areas. Executive directors of teacher associations and unions usually have emerged as leaders from the teachers' ranks. Persons who have full-time positions as directors of youth groups such as YMCA-YWCA represent eclectic experience backgrounds in which no common patterns appear, but a fair number have been recruited from church and education preparation programs.

SCHOOL PRINCIPALS. A typical pattern for a school principal in either a public or private school might be having been a teacher at the level at which the principalship exists (early elementary, middle school, junior high school, vocational school, or high school); service on a school- or district-wide curriculum committee; adviser of one or more student activities (for junior high and high school particularly); department head, counselor, or athletic coach; assistant principal; and principal. Positions as department heads, counselors, and coaches give people visibility and also utilize and test many of the abilities required for higher-level leader positions, so it is not by pure chance that many principals and superintendents are selected from among the holders of such positions.

SUPERINTENDENTS OF SCHOOLS. At least two individuals are personally known to the authors who never taught in classrooms prior to assuming positions as superintendents. Nevertheless, a typical pattern for large-city superintendents would be teaching, principalship (usually secondary), superintendent in a small district or assistant in a medium-sized district, superintendent in a medium-sized district, and superintendent in a large district. One superintendent of a medium-sized district at this writing is known to have been a classroom teacher, an associate professor, a university department head, and then superintendent. He, of course, is atypical.

COMMUNITY COLLEGE PRESIDENTS. At an earlier time, most status leaders in junior or community colleges seem to have been recruited from the ranks of the public schools. However, in 1965 Blocker et al. reported that the percent of community college presidents who had formerly been engaged in public school work had dropped sharply since 1941.[1]

One may conclude that, while there do seem to be stepping stones to certain positions in the public schools and colleges, (1) those steps are not at all obvious for other positions, (2) a fixed path to any position probably is not nearly as definite as has been believed, and (3) there are routes to almost any position in education that do not utilize traditional stepping stones.

Would-be leaders, take heart. Instead of looking for stepping stones, learn whether and how you may qualify for the position to which you aspire.

Ways of Qualifying

Status leaders are either self-anointed, group selected, or appointed by some superordinate individual or group. In most schools, colleges, and industry or government they are appointed. However, there is a strategy that is guaranteed to attract the attenion of superordinates—and probably of peers and subordinates as well—which may work almost as well for the individual who must depend on being chosen by a group or who wishes to be a self-designated leader. It requires that the aspirant declare and demonstrate WAR, meaning willingness, ability, and responsibility.

WILLINGNESS. Any member of any organization can declare himself willing to tackle problems or perform tasks that are clearly beyond the expectations held by others for the position that she or he holds. However, willingness alone is not enough. Is the willingness due to ambition or desire for more money, or is it based on awareness of competence? Almost every organization has someone who is trying to curry favor by eagerly volunteering for whatever is needed. But if he or she compounds or exacerbates the problem or the tasks are sloppily done or left incomplete, one does one's cause more harm than good. The would-be leader must be able as well as willing.

[1] C. E. Blocker, et al. *Two year college: A social synthesis.* Englewood Cliffs, N.J.: Prentice-Hall, 1965.

ABILITY. Having voluntarily taken on a problem or task, a person is under a far greater onus to produce satisfactory results than if the problem or task had been assigned to him or her. Yet one who does only what is assigned often does not attract sufficient attention to earn consideration for a position as leader or a promotion if he or she already is a leader. Thus, a volunteer must be certain that he or she has the ability necessary to do what is required, and must demonstrate what he or she has. That ability may be of at least three types: intellectual, demonstrable skills, or affective.

Intellectual abilities would include knowledgeability or recognizing and utilizing relationships. Skills might include ability to work with people, routine office management, organizing time, people, activities or resources, or locating or retrieving information. Affective ability might include loyalty to the organization and its people, personal performance standards, and values, beliefs, and feelings. How one may acquire new abilities is discussed later in this chapter. But willingness to do a job, even when one knows that one has the ability, is still not enough to qualify as a leader since responsibility also is involved.

RESPONSIBILITY. Without question, there are people in almost every school, college, training system, or other agency of education who would be willing to do necessary tasks and who have the ability to do them but who still do not volunteer. Many times this is because they are unwilling to be responsible for results. One needs to engage in soul-search to determine if one is willing to make oneself visible, to chance the risk that might be involved, and to bear the consequences if one's abilities *should* prove insufficient or one's solutions inadequate. Those who are willing to be responsible for whatever happens become the leaders; those who are unwilling remain followers.

The Effects of Crisis
An often-remarked phenomenon is that a crisis produces a leader. Innumerable examples could be cited from politics and government, in this and other countries. Under other circumstances, Churchill was unacceptable to the British people as premier, but he was welcomed as the savior of the empire during World War II. Lincoln probably would not have become President had this country not been facing the crisis of emancipation and the attendant threat of secession of the southern states. Some cities have chosen police commissioners, who, the citizens believed, could deal with crises involving crime.

As Maria wrote to Malvolio in *Twelfth Night,* "Some are born great, some achieve greatness, and some have greatness thrust upon 'em." In education, some, such as Plato, Aristotle, and Comenius, are born great. Some, perhaps, have greatness thrust upon 'em by crisis, although few such have been recognized in history. Most leaders in education, great and small, have to achieve any recognition they get. Occasionally, a purely local crisis thrusts into office a dean, a college president, a union or association president, a principal, a director of training and management development, a coordinator of some special program, or a superintendent of schools who thereby attains a local greatness but they are the exceptions.

Growing to Fit

Some employers operate on the premise that if there is a job to be filled they can name a person of intelligence and demonstrated competence, even if the shoes to be filled are obviously too big, and he or she will grow to fit. Government, at both the federal and state levels, has had some notable successes—and some colossal failures—with this practice.

In education, many a person has been named to a position on a supposedly temporary basis while a search was made for a qualified person outside, only to find that the incumbent had grown to the point where she or he looked better than other candidates. Several such instances which resulted in temporary appointees taking over in permanent assignments are personally known to the authors. Positions include those of university president, vice-president, dean, department head, superintendent of schools, assistant superintendent, director of curriculum, and building principal.

A temporary appointment may be a route to a permanent one. The individual may be able to prove to himself that he has ability and to others that he can grow to fit. Thus, one should not necessarily turn down an appointment because it is deemed to be temporary. However, there also have been many cases of "always a bridesmaid, but never a bride." Some individuals have been called on to fill a succession of leader posts on a temporary basis without ever being named to fill one of them permanently. One wonders if this may have been due to "creative incompetence" (Peter and Hull, 1969)—deliberate concealment of ability because of an unwillingness to permanently assume responsibility of the office—to lack of ability, to inability to grow, or to having done nothing other than keep the shop open—perhaps because it was thought that greater effort would be unrewarded. Perhaps it was because no course had been charted.

CHARTING A COURSE

"Will you please tell me, sir, which way I ought to go from
    here?" asked Alice.
"Well now that depends a good deal on where you want
    to get to," said the cat.
"I don't much care where," said Alice.
"Then it doesn't much matter which way you go," said the cat.

*"Just so long as I get somewhere," Alice added as
an afterthought.*[2]

If, like Alice, one does not much care where one goes, then perhaps it does not matter much what direction he or she takes. However, for anyone who wishes to get somewhere, charting a course becomes very important, and several steps are required. The first is to decide on and to state goals.

Statement of Goals

While "it is a long road that knows no turning," and it is recognized that many, if not most, persons change career direction one or more times, nevertheless progress is not made by wandering in one direction and then another. The individual needs to determine, as best he or she can, two things: his or her long-range goal and the nature of the first position that might be a step toward that goal.

THE LONG-RANGE GOAL. It seems that few people in education conform to the ages, periods, and stages of occupational-choice theory. Furthermore, many of us, if we were honest, would admit that we are in our present positions because of some particular juncture of circumstance, significant others, and time; still, few of us are in positions totally remote from those to which we aspired. The many persons who annually seek graduate degrees "so I will be qualified for whatever comes along" probably should yield their places in the universities (as they almost certainly will in the job market) to those with more sense of direction. It is unrealistic to believe that any degree will get one into "whatever comes along." Though there may be exceptions, most educators have to choose a direction—public schools, private schools, parochial schools, community colleges, private colleges, technological institutes, government training, industrial training, alternative schools, youth organizations, universities, or whatever—and take step after plodding step to move in that direction. At least the direction and the starting road must be clear.

THE NEXT POSITION. It is unrealistic for one to expect that he be the next president of the community college where he is now an instructor. A logical next step would be to the position of department chairman. The only way to get to position B, other than by chance, is to *know* position A, one's starting point. The aspirant should concentrate on what it takes to be chairman (position B) and compare his or her qualifications (position A) with the requirements. Only then

[2] L. Carroll, *Through the looking glass.*

does charting a course become possible. Chapter 15 will help the reader to establish where she or he now is (position A).

Anyone looking toward a next position should ask oneself: (1) what must an individual in that position *have* (what degree? what experience? what certification? what else?), (2) what must the position holder be able to *do* (what competencies are desirable? which of them are absolute minimums?), (3) what are the political facts of life that may affect *my* getting the job? Anyone charting a course in an unknown sea needs to be aware of reefs that may be encountered. Among such reefs in a job search are certain political realities.

Political Realities

Some realities that need to be considered concern whether the job aspirant is on a real or imagined plateau insofar as promotion is concerned, whether he (or she, particularly) is a member of a minority group that may be discriminate aganst, and whether he or she may be overqualified for the job.

PLATEAUS. If an individual has "reached his or her level of incompetence"—and there is more truth to the Peter Principle (Peter and Hull, 1969)—than most of us like to admit—he or she is unlikely to promoted. However, Reeves (1962) described six other reasons for an individual finding oneself on a job plateau, namely: (1) lack of encouragement, due to poor leadership on the part of one's superordinate, (2) health factors that keep one below peak efficiency, (3) fear of the effects of aging, because of the emphasis that this is a "young person's world," (4) higher positions are not opening up, for whatever reason, (5) loss of initiative or drive, and (6) the competition and internal politics, which increase geometrically with each successive level, have become distasteful to one. Of course, members of minority groups have particular reasons for finding competition and internal politics distasteful.

DISCRIMINATION. Despite years of educating the public, copious propaganda, affirmative action plans, and laws intended to prevent it, discrimination still exists. Employers should consider only who is the best-qualified applicant for a particular job, but the truth is that race, sex, religion, country of origin, age, and even appearance may be used as bases on which to disqualify someone, whether the announced reasons include those or not.

Milner (1973) compared data from the 1970 census to data from 1960 and concluded that nonwhites (black *men*, actually) with college training are "overrepresented" among the professions, but that the same group is still significantly underrepresented in the managerial category. He speculated as to causes, as shown in Figure 14-2.

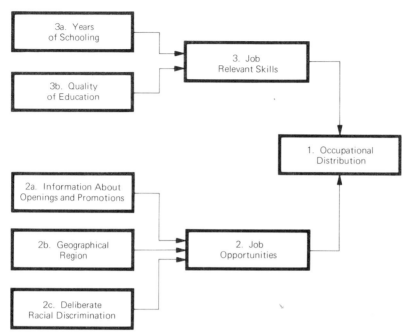

Figure 14-2 *Simplified Causal Model of Factors Producing White-Nonwhite Occupational Dissimilarity*
Source: Milner (1973), p. 292.

While Milner's study did not relate to educational administration and supervision, personal observations by the present authors indicate that his findings would also apply there. Milner hypothesized that the principal difference lies in access to job information through informal channels of communication; since fewer blacks have high-status jobs and most of their family and friends are black, blacks are less likely to hear about the better job opportunities through their network of personal relationships. The same reasoning may be applied to Chicanos, Indians, women, or any other minority group. To the extent that employers rely on informal channels to find and select candidates, as most of them do, they necessarily—even if unknowingly—discriminate against any group that does not presently have proportional representation among educational leaders.

Milner's study was limited not only to blacks, but to black males, because as he said, the data available for women are not adequate for this type of analysis. While many women have become militant over discrimination against them in recent years, the problems facing those who want to work at the executive level have been around a long time. In 1935 Tead had a chapter in his classic work on leadership relating to the problems of women leaders. In 1972, Hackamack and Solid listed as obstacles standing in the paths of women executives these things:

1. Stereotyped notions, such as that women are highly emotional and easily disturbed, transiency, "woman's place," women have higher rates of absenteeism and illness, women do not understand statistics.
2. Counselors do not encourage girls to train for important career jobs.
3. Women have to work harder and be better to "prove themselves" than do men.
4. Few male spouses are understanding.
5. Men do not like the idea of working for a woman.

The editors summarized the Hackamack and Solid 1972 article with this overly optimistic conclusion:

Women achieved their footing in the business world during World War II. From 1950 to 1960, the number of women executives nearly tripled. However, men continue to dominate the executive market and to earn larger salaries. Although women are credited with a number of characteristics desirable in business, traditional obstacles block their progress. As training becomes more accessible, however, and as managerial manpower resources dwindle, the day may soon come when men and women will be considered for the same job on the basis of their ability alone [p. 89].

Heaven speed the day! It seems further off than "soon," at least in education.

Most of the antidiscrimination laws that have been passed have specified that employers cannot discriminate on the basis of age, among other things. However, the person who decides to try for a first principalship, supervisor's job, training directorship, superintendency, or similar job after the age of 45 is deluding herself or himself. A person already in such a job may, perhaps, get a promotion after that age, but an individual over 45 must be unusual indeed to merit consideration when qualified younger candidates are available. Maturity is viewed with more tolerance in higher education, but even there a cut-off age is often established, whether announced or not.

Quota systems may work to the detriment of those whom they were established to help. If a person is employed because she is a woman, because he is a black, because she is Chicano, or because he is an Indian, rather than on the basis of ability alone, that person has more visibility than others who were employed on the basis of ability, and thus must work doubly hard to prove that she or he can do the job.

OVERQUALIFICATION. More than one young person has gone on to attain an advanced degree when employment opportunities were scarce—or while he or she was single and thus financially able to do so—only to find himself or herself overqualified. An inexperienced teacher with a Master's degree, for example, would be so high on the salary schedule of many school districts that employers would hesitate to give one with unproven capability a chance. The same is true of the person with no administrative experience who obtains a Specialist's or Doctor's degree. Despite protestations from the neophyte that he or she is willing to take less than a schedule calls for, most employers would be reluctant, in these days of professional negotiation, to contract employment with an individual at a lower salary than the schedule specifies.

Finding the Right Job
Supposedly, the job aspired to has been analyzed in terms of the degree, experience, and certification requirements, along with the skills needed to perform the job successfully. The individual needs to compare what the job requires with what he has to offer in order to ascertain what he must still do to prepare himself for that next job.

PREPARATION
In qualifying for leadership, one needs to examine how experience may be used, how authority may be gained, how skills may be acquired, the relative parts played by preservice and in-service education, and the modes of learning available.

Using Experience
Anyone can take advantage of many opportunities to both administer and lead, whether in formal or informal settings. As a matter of fact, any mature person aspiring to a position of leadership who has not already demonstrated some capacity to lead and interest in leading should be considered suspect. From a very early age, some persons find and enjoy opportunities to lead child, youth, and church groups; be officers of clubs, political or civic organizations; conduct discussions, or serve as elected officials.

A "good" teacher or instructor both administers and leads in the classroom. There are leadership opportunities in department or other types of faculty meetings. Local, state, regional, and national organizations all seek and use leaders, and some of those have full-time positions that aspiring leaders need to know of and consider. A PTA office can be a dreaded duty or an opportunity for significant leader experience. A person who has been responsible for the performance of others in business, industry, or the armed forces has performed many of the same actions and used many of the same techniques used in education.

One who is qualifying for educational leadership should seek and utilize opportunities to lead in other endeavors, and when preparing a resume for job-seeking purposes, he or she should list all leadership experience.

Gaining Authority

If the definition "authority is the legitimized right of one individual to make decisions or take actions that affect others" is accepted, then it is obvious that one must earn authority, that one cannot be given it except in a very limited sense. We have already pointed out that one way to earn authority is to take on tasks that go beyond the call of duty *if* able to do the job and willing to be responsible for results. The individual who knows more about what is to be done, who can proficiently perform on group-relevant tasks, or can help others to achieve their goals can always gain authority. Being liked or respected can help, although one does not have to be liked to gain authority. To repeat what was said earlier about the basis for authority, the basis always lies in what the authority figure *is* or *can do*, or in what others *feel* about her or him.

Acquiring Skills

How can a leader on the way up determine his or her future position aims well enough to acquire those skills which he or she ultimately will need? How can one get to that ultimate position without burdening oneself with skills which one needs now in the lower echelons but which will become dysfunctional as one climbs?

Katz (1955) has given some assistance by suggesting that an effective administrator should somehow acquire the following:

1. *Technical skill,* defined as ". . . an understanding of, and proficiency in, a specific kind of activity, particularly one involving methods, processes, procedures, or techniques [p. 34]."
2. *Human skill,* defined as "the executive's ability to work effectively as a group member and to build cooperative effort within the team he leads [p. 34–35]."
3. *Conceptual skill,* defined as ". . . the ability to see the enterprise as a whole; it includes recognizing how the various functions of the organization depend on one another, and how changes in any one part affect all the others [p. 35–36]."

It should be apparent that the top person in any organization needs conceptual and human skill in far greater degree than he or she needs technical skill, while a middle-level leader may need a wealth of human skill and only a modicum of conceptual and technical skills, as shown in Figure 14-3.

The leader is apt to get his or her first administrative position

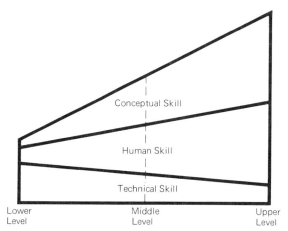

Figure 14-3 *Mix of Skills Needed by Leaders at Various Levels*

on the basis of some rather narrow technical skill, and of course the specific skills that one needs at a given time are determined by the job immediately ahead.

Education
Anyone interested in qualifying for leadership must, of course, be concerned about getting whatever education is required for the job in which he or she is interested. Much of that education may be preservice, before he or she starts on an administrative or supervisory job, and some can be in-service.

PRESERVICE. The potential educational leader must be identified early, either by self or by others, must be encouraged and guided in his development, and must set his sights and course at an early date. It should be recognized, however, that graduate° school is not a place for making up deficiencies in an undergraduate background, and if an individual has such deficiencies, they should be remedied before she or he starts on a professional leadership program, *not as a part of it.*

The characteristics of a model program for school administrators described by the AASA (1960) seem germane to programs for all educational leaders, namely:

1. A strong undergraduate background that includes work from the social sciences, the natural and physical sciences, the communications arts, and the humanities.
2. Two or more years of graduate study in a professional program.
3. Careful selection of students and program components.

4. Necessary resources, both human and material, including a strong faculty with demonstrated competencies in teaching, scholarly pursuits, and the practice of leadership.

In addition to being concerned about having the breadth of undergraduate background indicated, the student should select an institution for graduate study where certification requirements (if any) for the desired job may be met and where the degree that she or he needs may be earned. One also should be concerned about what accreditation the institution holds, since that is likely to be the most important factor affecting the regard in which its degrees will be held. Also vital to the future leader are the quality of libraries, laboratories, materials centers, study spaces, and learning modes available.

At its 1973 meeting, the NCPEA for the first time had "continuing interest" group meetings regarding competency-based educational programs for school administrators. It remains to be seen what comes of this movement.

IN-SERVICE. Once in a position as leader, the individual cannot stop learning. The leader must involve himself or herself in continued study and analysis, either formal or informal, of society and its cultural values, problems, and issues; must systematically keep abreast of professional literature; must utilize research findings relating to learning and to leading; and must seek ever-more-effective ways of meeting the expectations held for one in one's leader role.

Numerous learning modes are available to an individual for both preservice and in-service education.

LEARNING MODES. Whether alone, with a companion or mentor, or in a group, a person may learn through reading, listening, speaking, viewing, or writing. One also may learn by reacting to, interacting with, or emulating another person.

Simulation has come into vogue in recent years and, despite its limitations, it seems to have more potential than activities which are more abstract in nature. Simulation forms include case studies, experimentation, in-basket exercises, internships, role-playing, and skits. Aside from internships, simulated experiences seem to have the following deficiencies: there are no traditions to affect leader behavior, rewards often are too small to motivate anyone to the extra effort required for real leading, outside pressures do not affect one as they do in real life, and the size of group or complexity of task often is not at all in keeping with what is found in "real" life. However, some simulations are extraordinarily effective, especially when used in combination with tools such as videotape.

On-the-job learning modes include emulation, experimentation, observation, and actual participation. Indeed, there are those who say that no one becomes a leader unless he has a model to emulate. Even on the job, the unavoidable deficiencies of contrived experimental settings should be noted.

Another thing the would-be leader needs to qualify for leadership is to become familiar with those characteristics that may serve as predictors of success. These were discussed in Chapter 13.

SUMMARY

Theories of occupational choice neatly outline the ages, periods, and stages of life at which the young supposedly make career choices. Desirable as such processes may seem, innumerable case histories do not conform and the changing times probably presage even less conformity to theory. This in no way decreases the importance of career choice.

The idea of stepping stones to educational positions, too, is negated by the career patterns of many practicing educators. For positions as principals and superintendents of schools, there are some rarely disregarded stepping stones. A fixed path to any other position probably is not nearly as definite as has been believed, and almost any educational position today can be reached without utilizing traditional stepping stones.

To qualify for leader positions, one needs to be willing, able, and responsible for tasks beyond those presently expected of one. Crisis often "makes" leaders in some fields, but few national leaders in education have resulted from crises. Some leaders result when individuals grow to fit shoes initially thought to be too large for them, though.

To chart a course to an education career, one needs a long-range goal and a definite idea of the next position to which one aspires. One also needs to face political realities such as plateaus, discrimination, and overqualification, and must carefully check personal qualifications against the requirements of the job sought to assure finding the "right" job.

In preparing for a career as an educational leader, the individual must know how to use both formal and informal experience and how to gain authority. Skills needed must be analyzed and acquired, either preservice or on the job. The institution in which one gains needed education should be carefully selected in terms of resources provided and learning modes utilized.

A reader of this book who has followed the steps suggested previously has before her or him a long-range goal and she or he knows which is the most logical type of position to be sought. If he will undertake careful self-examination, as outlined in Chapter 15, he may determine what he "does do"—his performance on his present job—and the kinds of work patterns that he finds most rewarding. He may learn something of what he "will do"—his predictability, since that is directly related to past and present performance.

Through self-testing he may ascertain what he "can do"—his potential. He will find indicators—not measures—of his personality, his needs, drives, and wants; the kind of position, and the life-style that are likely to provide him with the most satisfaction.

SOME SUGGESTED RESOURCES

C. T. Dale, Women are still missing persons in administrative and supervisory jobs. *Educational leadership,* 1973, **31**(2), 123–127.

J. J. Fendrock, Ch. 3, A wasteland of unused manpower, pp. 41–60, and Ch. 4, Women on executive row, pp. 61–78. In *Managing in times of radical change.* New York: American Management Association, Inc., 1971.

L. C. Hackamack, and A. B. Solid, The woman executive. *Business Horizons,* 1972 (April), 89–93.

W. R. Lane, R. G. Corwin, and W. G. Monahan, Scope and character of administrative leadership. Ch. 12 in *Foundations of educational administration: A behavioral analysis.* New York: Macmillan, 1967. Pp. 301–342.

H. J. Leavitt, Developing managers: Applied ideas about influence, learning and groups. In *Managerial psychology* (2nd ed.). Chicago: University of Chicago Press, 1964.

V. Miller, G. R. Madden, and J. B. Kinchloe, In-service professional development. *The public administration of American school systems* (2nd ed.). New York: Macmillan, 1972. Pp. 418–420.

J. W. Taylor, Develop what, how? Ch. 7 in *How to select and develop leaders.* New York: McGraw-Hill, 1962. Pp. 103–157.

O. Tead, How do people become leaders? Ch. 3, pp. 22–32, and Ch. 13, Problems of women leaders, pp. 237–256 in *The art of leadership.* New York: McGraw-Hill, 1935.

V. Voeks, *On becoming an educated person* (2nd ed.). Philadelphia: Saunders, 1964.

CHAPTER 15

SELF-EXAMINATION

And there were three men
Went down the road as down the road went he:
The man they saw, the man he was, the man he wanted to be.
                                                                    —Masefield

It behooves every leader or would-be leader to learn how much or how little similarity there is between the individual he or she wants to be, the individual he or she is, and the individual whom others see. One way to learn this is through examination of the self, largely by the self, and this chapter explores what should be examined, how and by whom examination can be done, and what should result.

> *The function of self-examination is to lay the groundwork for insight, without which no growth can occur. Insight is the "oh, I see now" feeling which must, consciously or unconsciously, precede change in behavior. Insights—real, genuine glimpses of ourselves as we really are—are reached only with difficulty and sometimes with real psychic pain. But they are the building blocks of growth. Thus self-examination is a preparation for insight, a groundbreaking for the seeds of self-understanding which gradually bloom into changed behavior [Brouwer, 1964, p. 170].*

In anyone's attempt to determine whether or not she or he is suited to the rigors of a leader role, an account must be made of the perceptions that are held by others of that individual. Clearly these perceptions do have an influence on whether or not an individual will have opportunities in which the functions of leading could be carried out. This would be true even when an individual utilizes his or her own perceptions of oneself and believes that he or she possesses an adequate preparational background and many, if not all, of those other characteristics which are necessary and desirable aspects of leader makeup. The perceptions of others about an individual often are not consistent with the perceptions of an individual about himself or herself; it probably is a truism to state that no tyrant views his or her decisions and behaviors as anything but right and just. It probably also is true that the benevolent, though autocratic, leader has difficulty in understanding why some subordinates resist what he or she believes to be perfectly legitimate means for achieving his or her desired ends.

Some account also must be made of what a particular leader is like—of the "self" that one would have to be to hold a position to which he or she aspires. For example, if one aspires to be a director of a proprietary school, what does one believe such a director is like?

Figure 15-1 depicts not three but five "selves" that are of concern to everyone who must function in a social system. The degree of congruence between selves 1 and 2 determines self-adequacy; that between selves 2 and 3 determines integrity; congruence among selves 1, 2, and 3 determines self-perceived effectiveness; that found among selves 1, 2, 3, and 4 determines authenticity. Congruence between selves 3 and 4 determines conformity, while that between selves 4 and 5 determines acceptance, and congruence among 3, 4, and 5 establishes effectiveness as perceived by others.

Some description of self 4 must be developed in terms of expectations held for persons in the position to which the reader is aspiring. The purpose of self-examination is to reveal information about selves 1, 2, and 5. Insights or understandings about potential, predictability, and performance can result in changes of self-perception, self-expectations, or both, with resultant change in behavior, or self 3.

Since there is an almost infinite number of factors that one might explore in self-examination, it is necessary to limit the "groundbreaking for the seeds" and thus it is proposed that the reader first determine the expectations held for persons in positions such as that to which she or he aspires. Second, the individual should establish some criteria for determining those expectations. Third, it is important to consider which factors of one's own potential, predictability, or performance might need to be examined. Fourth, it will be necessary to ascertain what instruments, techniques, or other means may be available for examination of the self, by the self or by others. Fifth, the reader can examine his or her own need-dispositions to see if they are similar to those that leaders are believed to exhibit. Finally, painful as it may be, the data collected must be used for comparison of the five possible selves.

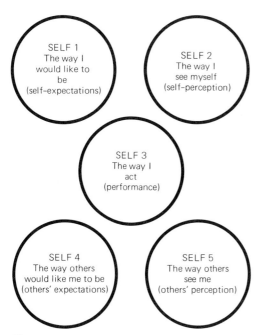

Figure 15-1   *The Five "Selves" of an Individual*

DETERMINING EXPECTATIONS

How far the reader may be able to go in determining the expectations that people hold for individuals in a position such as he or she aspires to may depend in large measure on the nature of that position. Certainly for any position, the expectations held by one's superordinates, by one's peers, and by one's subordinates are important, along with one's own expectations.

Superordinates' Expectations

It should be a fairly simple matter to check with a limited number of superordinates as to what expectations they hold for those in positions below theirs in an organization. For example, if one wishes to be a community college dean, what do presidents and vice-presidents expect of deans? An instrument such as could be made by utilizing items from Table 12-1 might be used to elicit responses from a few administrators in the reader's immediate geographic area.

Peers' Expectations

Sticking to the same example, the instrument used to solicit responses from presidents and vice-presidents of community colleges might be used also to determine what expectations deans believe to be held for them. Asking that respondents, both superordinate and peer, indicate the importance of various expectations by use of a scale, such as from zero to five, might be valuable to the individual who wishes to examine himself or herself in regard to measuring up to the expectations considered by respondents to be most important.

Subordinates' Expectations

Again using the same example, it would seem important that a would-be dean learn what chairpersons and faculty members in departments such as those with which he or she would be working expect of their dean. The same instrument and response scale could be used with a sample of such persons as was used with deans, presidents, and vice-presidents.

Self Expectations

Before any results are in from other respondents, the job aspirant should use the same instrument and response scale to indicate the expectations that he or she believes are held for persons in a position such as he or she aspires to.

Once returns are in, the individual can then compare responses for similarity of items and means (averages on the scale) of importance. The next step would then be to check perceived expectations against some criteria which he or she believes to be important.

CRITERIA

It is likely that the lists of expectations assembled will be quite diverse, with individual items far too numerous for any meaningful self-examination. Thus, the lists need to be combined and delimited by checking each stated expectation against the criteria of validity, reality, modernity, comprehensibility, and specificity.

Validity

Validity of an expectation boils down to the question, "Does this seem definitely related to success or failure in the position to which I aspire?" If the answer is "yes," then the item should be left in the list and consideration should be given to how information can be obtained that is relevant to one determining whether he or she is likely to be able to meet the expectation. If the answer is "no," then the item should be given no further consideration. A number of respondents placing high importance on an item indicates probable validity, but a lone respondent indicating high importance may indicate either validity or idiosyncrasy.

Reality

Reality of an expectation is determined by the question, "Is it practical?" If the job seems, in the eyes of those who indicated that the expectation is held, to demand a physical stamina that no one can exhibit, a prescience not to be found among mortals, or a record of accomplishments and an age range that are incompatible, then the expectation is unreal and may be ignored. No self-examination is necessary in regard to an unreal expectation.

Modernity

Is the expectation up-to-date and appropriate for modern conditions? Does it anticipate probable future conditions? For example, some superintendents of schools who have been in their present jobs for many years advise teachers who aspire to be superintendents that they should secure Masters' degrees in administration—even though all except a few rural school districts now expect their superintendents to have formal education beyond the M.A. level, and many have done so for two decades or more! As another example, professors of educational administration of long experience may advise that one is expected to have worked for a number of years as a public school administrator before seeking a professorship, but that no longer is true in a number of universities.

Comprehensibility

The criterion of comprehensibility requires an answer to the question, "Is the expectation understandable to me and to those persons with whom I may be working?" For example, corporation vice-presidents may indicate that they expect a training director to "have the right attitude," but that is meaningless unless "right attitude" is explained.

Specificity

An expectation against which one examines his or her characteristics should be sufficiently well defined to permit measurement or reasonable estimation. It does no good to examine for "responsibility," for example, unless expected responsibility is delimited as to nature and extent. Self-examination in regard to the type of life-style exhibited is pointless unless one knows what life-style a desired position may impose.

After the above-described five gauges have been applied to lessen the number of listed expectations, it is possible to examine the areas of one's own potential, predictability, and performance with a view to ascertaining what indicators may be found that he or she can or cannot meet those expectations.

POTENTIAL

To self-examine for potential, one needs to see which factors of overall potential, specific potential, acquired potential, and demonstrated potential could provide indicators of what one "can do."

Overall Potential

Overall potential involves aptitudes and capacity for work. By referring to Table 12-1, it may be seen that aptitudes thought to be desirable for leaders in general include enduring stress; tolerating ambiguity; working with people, things, or ideas; intelligence; and scholarship. It would seem that self-examination could yield information about all of these.

Capacity for work includes alertness; energy, vigor, or drive; physical condition; and industry. Again, it seems that self-examination might extend into each of these areas.

Specific Potential
Specific potential involves physical condition, mental health, and attitudes, and some self-examination could be done in each of these areas. Examination of attitudes should look into how one gets along with others; loyalty to and identification with a group; self-reliance, or whether one makes one's own decisions and stands on one's own feet; spirit of cooperation, willingness to take risks, and willingness to work.

Acquired Potential
Acquired potential factors include knowledges and judgment. Knowledges that should be examined for include those of learning theory, dynamics of leading, and dynamics of administering, plus technological knowledges that are job-specific. For example, job-specific knowledges necessary for a secondary school principal would include how to schedule classes, how to handle internal accounts, how to organize student records, how to organize and schedule activities, and basic school law.

The best source for discovering what knowledges are necessary in a given job probably is those persons now holding jobs of the sort desired. The knowledges that a college president is expected to have, for example, might be determined by asking a number of college presidents.

Some self-examination seems possible in the area of judgment, also, by comparing one's own judgment to the judgment of others.

Demonstrated Potential
Demonstrated potential can be examined in terms of the skills exhibited to date. Among the skills that should have been demonstrated in varying degrees according to position sought are accuracy, conversational ability, general vocabulary, grammar, pronunciation, spelling, persuasiveness, writing fluency, coherence, management, and organization.

PREDICTABILITY
Among the factors of predictability are work interests and aspirations, personality, wants, attitudes, values, mental health, preferences, and access to educational and job opportunities. Of these,

work interests and aspirations probably cannot be examined in and of themselves, but all of the others probably can be examined and can provide indicators of what a person "will do."

Personality
Examination of one's personality can yield information in regard to work habits such as stability, industry, and perseverance. It may also provide data about characteristics such as loyalty, compatibility, dedication, and commitment, and a great deal of information about attitudes.

Wants
There probably is no way for one to do meaningful self-examination in regard to one's goals and one's goal-orientation, or motivation, valuable as the information to be gained might be. Deficiencies in the perceived means of satisfying needs could be examined, but the degree of objectivity that is possible in self-examination is debatable. Whether one sees authority, competition, excellence, money, perfection, power, security, service to others, status, or some combination of these as necessary to satisfy one's needs might provide some indication of potential for a particular position.

Values
One's values and value-orientations undoubtedly are elements of predictability, but measurement of them is a bit tricky. To really understand one's values and value-orientations, it would be necessary to examine both the nature and the applicability of one's values. Nature, it was suggested in Chapter 12, is determined by intent, content, and modality of values. Applicability concerns extent, generality, intensity, and explicitness of values. Perhaps the best that can be done at this time is to examine in terms of content classification of one's values. *If* one can determine whether most of one's actions result from choices made and cherished because of principles, because of messages from significant others, or because of detailed, conforming behavior (see Figure 12-2) one will know far more about one's values than most people do about theirs. If an individual takes one of numerous available tests, he or she will know more yet.

Mental Health
In Chapter 14, mental health was indicated among those attributes that it takes to lead, and it is thus one of the "will do" factors to be considered. Many years ago, Overstreet (1949) listed some "Criteria of Maturity" that could be used for a rough self-examination as to whether one is mature, as immaturity is almost certain to be reflected in the state of one's mental health. Frank acknowledgement of strengths and weaknesses probably is possible only in the mentally healthy.

Preferences

At least two types of preferences can be indicators of predictability. The first type relates, of course, to the work setting, and the second to life-style.

WORK. Through introspection, an individual may be able to answer some questions relating to preferences which could help in determining *what kind* of work he or she enjoys. Honest answers to the following questions may indicate that some readers do not prefer the kinds of things most status leaders are called on to do, and may help those persons to decide that leader positions are not for them.

Do I prefer:

Risk, or stability?
Problems to solve, or serenity?
Structuring my own time, or having fixed hours?
Routine tasks, or variety?
To work alone, in competition, or cooperatively?
Dependence, or independence?
Environment that is rigid, or adaptable?
Status, money, or challenge?

LIFE-STYLE. Again, there are questions to be asked. Preferences as to life-style probably indicate little about job predictability, but may help to predict *where* one may perform better, given a choice of positions.

Do I prefer:

Roots and family ties, or mobility?
Visibility, or privacy?
Access to nature (rural), or a variety of cultural affairs (urban)?
Living conveniences, or being self-sufficient?

Access to Desired Position

One of the chief indicators of predictability would seem to be whether the reader has access to the type of position desired. Milner's model, Figure 14-2 (p. 297), helps to raise some pertinent questions in this regard, since it suggests that both job-relevant skills and job opportunities are important in determining occupational distribution. Although the model is theoretical and was developed in regard to black males, it seems valuable in explaining any occupational distribution.

JOB-RELEVANT SKILLS. Questions related to job-relevant skills seem to lie in two areas, namely:

1. Have I had or can I get the required years of formal education? Do I have or can I get the necessary degree or
   certificate?
2. Has the quality of my education been such that I now have
   the necessary skills and knowledges, or know how to get them
   on the job?

JOB OPPORTUNITIES. Imperative questions in regard to job opportunities are at least three in number:

1. Do I have access to those formal and informal channels of
   communication through which I am likely to learn about positions I might want?
2. Are there positions of the type I want in the geographic area
   where I now am located or wish to settle? Does location make
   an important difference to me?
3. Am I a member of a group against whom there may be deliberate discrimination? For any individual who is either female
   or nonwhite and is seeking an educational leadership position,
   the answer, at this writing, is almost certain to be "yes."

Probably the best overall indicator of a person's predictability
is his present performance.

PERFORMANCE

Among the indicators of performance are temperament, emotional
stability, personal development record, and productivity. Along with
these matters, one must examine his or her present or past work
assignments and conditions of work to see whether a change in those
might have made "does do" indicators different than they now are.

Temperament

Although psychologists are not agreed on a definition of temperament, most seem to believe that temperament is an individual's tendency to act in certain characteristic ways, not at any specific moment, but over extended periods of time. Thus, it is closely related
to "style" as leader style was defined and described in Chapter 11.
An individual whose behavioral tendencies are extreme or in severe
conflict is said to be maladjusted. While individuals with whom one
works or has worked often can reveal much significant information
about one's tendencies, they are unlikely to make such revelations
to anyone whose temperament is perceived as negative. Several in-
ventories have been developed to indicate tendencies on a single
component, such as Allport's Ascendance-Submission Test. Others
are multiphasic and intended to give indicators of several components of temperament, including emotional stability.

Emotional Stability

No one expects that an individual who is capable of functioning normally will be devoid of emotions. Emotions often are satisfying, adding to the color and variety of life and breaking the monotony of routine. If there were no hope, fear, indignation, love, hate, excitement, or anger life would be dull indeed. One needs to do self-examination to determine, not whether he or she has emotions, but whether he or she is guilty of emotional excess or instability to the point where it does or might affect interaction with other persons. Excess may be either in being too frequently moved by a single emotion or in being more extreme in showing an emotion than most people in similar situations. The unstable person may shift instantaneously from affection to anger, from self-confidence to depression. The extreme example of instability is the classic manic-depressive person.

Personal Development

The reader could do meaningful self-examination in terms of what she or he has done and is doing to develop competence in these four basic goal areas:

Meeting needs of others
  Identifying others' goals
  Assisting performance
Innovating
  Identifying organization goals
  Revising organization goals
  Decision-making
  Persuading others to change
Providing learning opportunities
  Programing
  Problem-solving
    Locating problems
    Specifying (delimiting) problems
    Finding alternatives
    Considering possible consequences of alternatives
    Deciding "best" course to pursue
    Getting feedback
Maintaining the organization
  Coordinating the work of others
  Utilizing conflicts

Productivity

"The purpose of work is to bring about some planned alteration of the physical, intellectual, or cultural environment, so that human living can be made more secure, more comfortable, or in other ways more desirable," according to Neff (1968, p. 154). He indicated these psychological attributes of the productive role:

— It is the outcome of a prolonged period of personal development.
— People vary greatly in the ease and efficiency with which they can assume it, and some cannot assume it at all.
— It is related to prevailing cultural values.
— One must be able to cope with a wide array of specialized social conditions, in addition to being motivated.
— It is a function not only of the kind of person one is, but the kind of work he or she is required to perform.

A person can examine how effective he is in his present position, or was in his previous position, by ascertaining how well his performance measured up to the expectations held for him. This can be done through formal "evaluations" by superordinates, by peer opinion, or by self-opinion, remembering always that both expectations and perceptions of performance vary with the point of view.

Work Assignments
A person doing self-examination needs to be scrupulously honest with himself as to whether his work assignment has been such that his performance in one setting has been better or worse than it might have been in a different setting, as the work assignment is used by some persons as an excuse for shoddy performance. However, there can be little doubt that an instructor who must develop two or three new courses each semester must work harder to achieve the same level of performance as an equally capable colleague who teaches the same courses over and over. Neither can there be any doubt that a cushy assignment can make even a mediocre performer look good.

Conditions of Work
Again, the self-examiner is urged to scrupulous honesty, as conditions of work also are used as an excuse by the inept. It is easy for a school principal to explain a poor showing by saying, "But I didn't have adequate supplies . . . or staff . . . or money . . . or space . . . or whatever." But what evidence has he or she that adequate supplies would have made performance any better? Conversely, would his or her performance look as good as it now does had the work situation not provided the supplies (or staff, money, space) that have been available?

SOME TESTS
There probably is no way of learning whether one can lead except to try it, but tests can indicate (not measure) ability to do the work

required of leaders, interest in doing the work, and, to some extent, ability to get along with self and others in the work. Any instrument or procedure that elicits systematic information about a person, for the purpose of appraising his or her potential, predictability, or performance, is a test.

It must be remembered that tests are only small samplings which can indicate something of a person's tendencies, potential, and possible disabilities, and that tests, whenever possible, should be objective rather than subjective. Also whenever possible, any test indication, objective or subjective, should be verified by other means.

As Taylor (1962) said so well:

If we employ the most comprehensive test battery consistent with a reasonably liberal specification as to economy, accuracy, and completeness, we must expect that our methods will yield some significant information—but they will also leave some indeterminate amount of significant information entirely unrevealed [p. 250].

With the above admonitions in mind, the following are suggested as some of the tests that an individual could initiate in order to accumulate information about his or her various selves, if the expectations that are held for persons in positions such as he or she aspires to seem to warrant such tests.

Published Tests

By turning to a textbook such as Lawshe and Balma's (1966) or the Buros (1970) standard reference, the reader may discover one or more published tests that he or she might take in each of the areas indicated below. Since such an extensive testing program would be beyond the financial capabilities of most individuals, some secondary means of testing are suggested in certain areas.

Characteristic	Secondary Test
Attitudes	Subjective opinions of superordinates and/or peers, using a structured list and a five-point response scale
Aptitudes	Introspective analysis, using the list provided under Overall Potential earlier in this chapter
Accuracy	Subjective opinions of superordinates, peers, or professors
Language skills	Subjective opinions of superordinates, peers, or professors; verbal section of the Graduate Record Examination

Characteristic (*Continued*)	**Secondary Test** (*Continued*)
Leader skills	Subjective opinions of peers
Mental ability	Grade-point average
Emotional stability	Subjective opinions of peers
Personality	Subjective opinions of peers or family members
Supervision skills	None suggested
Temperament	None suggested
Values	"Value Clarification" exercises; introspective analysis as to nature and applicability

Goldman and Saunders (1974) have instituted an annual compendium of test instruments utilized in education, psychology, and sociology, which are available but not commercially published.

Clinical Examinations
For at least two characteristics, clinical examination is required to find any meaningful indicators:

Physical condition, as determined by a physician.

Mental health, as determined by thorough clinical checkup. A secondary test in this area might be subjective opinion of peers or family members, given anonymously, or self-opinion as to Overstreet's "Criteria of Maturity."

Opinions of Others
The primary tests in certain areas almost have to be the opinion of other persons, with the secondary test being the self-examiner's own opinion.

Characteristic	**Primary Test**	**Secondary Test**
Alertness, vigor	Superordinates' opinions	Self-opinion
Judgment	Opinions of superordinates, peers, or family members	Self-opinion
Organization skills	Opinions of superordinates, peers, or family members	Self-opinion

Characteristic *(Continued)*	**Primary Test** *(Continued)*	**Secondary Test** *(Continued)*
Persuasiveness	Opinions of peers, or family members	None suggested
Productivity	Superordinates' evaluations	Peer opinion; self-opinion

Introspective Analysis

There are a number of characteristics, thought to be desirable for leaders in general, for which no better test can be suggested than the self-examiner trying to be analytical about himself or herself, with whatever degree of objectivity is possible.

Characteristic	**Test**
Administrative skills (said by others to be job-relevant)	Opinion as to capability on each listed skill, using a five-point response scale
Conditions of work	Questioning and answering whether one's performance has been affected to the extent that it might have been different under other conditions
Innovation skill	Creativity checklist (see Bellows et al., 1962, pp. 326–328); questioning and answering whether one has the ability to get others to accept change
Job knowledge (said by others to be relevant to the position sought)	Opinion as to extent of knowledge on each listed item, using five-point response scale
Job opportunities	Answering questions raised in regard to opportunities earlier in this chapter
Learning theory knowledge	Opinion
Personal development	Comparison of present capability in each of the areas listed earlier in

Characteristic *(Continued)*	Test *(Continued)*
	this chapter with capability one year (or two years) ago
Preferences	Honest answers to each of the questions raised in regard to this characteristic earlier in this chapter
Wants	Rank-ordering of the wants listed earlier in this chapter
Work assignment	Questioning and answering whether one's performance has been affected to the extent that it might have been different under other conditions

SUMMARY

There are five "selves" with which a leader or aspiring leader must be concerned: the ideal self, the perceived self, the real self as revealed by performance, the self that others expect in terms of the work role, and the others-perceived performing self. The degrees of congruence among the various selves determine self-adequacy, integrity, self-perceived effectiveness, authenticity, conformity, acceptance, and effectiveness as perceived by others.

The self that others expect in terms of one's work role can be established with some clarity by determining what expectations are held by superordinates, peers, subordinates, and self. The other four selves can be defined, with varying degrees of clarity, by self-examination in regard to the elements of potential, predictability, and performance.

Self-examination can be done by using instruments or procedures to test for indications of a person's tendencies, potential, and possible disabilities. Tests should be objective in preference to subjective, but that is not always possible, and any test indication should be verified by other means. Among the forms of tests that an individual can initiate for purposes of examining his various selves are published tests, clinical examinations, opinions of others, and introspective analysis.

The next section of this book is devoted to consideration of educational leadership as an occupation. Chapter 16 challenges the would-be leader to think about the difference that he or she wants to make in the course of events through being in that occupation, of the people he or she will have to lead in order to make that difference, why he or she wishes to lead them, the direction in which they are to be led, and how he or she will get them to follow.

SOME SUGGESTED RESOURCES

A. W. Combs, The human aspect of administration. *Educational Leadership,* 1970, **28**(2), 197–205.

A. W. Combs and D. Snygg, The adequate personality. Ch. 12 in *Individual behavior: A perceptual approach to behavior* (Rev. ed.). New York: Harper & Row, 1959. Pp. 237–264.

D. A. Goslin, What ability tests measure. Cy. 6 in *The search for ability.* New York: Russell Sage, 1963. Pp. 123–152.

E. E. Jennings, The problem: Who am I? In *An anatomy of leadership.* New York: Harper & Row, 1960. Pp. 220–222.

A. T. Jersild, *In search of self.* New York: Bureau of Publications, Teachers College, 1952.

K. McIntyre, Guides for screening applicants to administrative preparatory programs. In R. E. Wilson (Ed.), *Educational administration.* Columbus, Ohio: Merrill, 1966, 830–833.

A. Wheelis, *The quest for identity.* New York: Norton, 1958.

SECTION FOUR
THE
OCCUPATION

*The crux of leadership is the acceptance of responsibility—
the idea or fantasy that one can make a difference in
the course of events. This sense of personal involvement
in life is not simply a passive experience. It is an impelling urge
to make a difference and use oneself in effecting outcomes.*
                                                        —Zaleznik

This final section of this book is essentially a series of challenges. The would-be leader is challenged to think about the difference that one wants to make in the course of events and the people that one would have to lead in order to do it. He or she is challenged to think of the individual learner and the part that schooling plays in the learner's total education.

Education in the future is considered; challenges to the schools and to school administration in dealing with pressing social issues are laid down. The part to be played by school administrators in the overall pattern of educational leadership is critically questioned.

Finally, the rewards and the constraints of positions of educational leadership are examined, and the types and numbers of such positions in terms of society's manpower needs are cataloged. The section ends on a note of optimism.

CHAPTER 16

SOME CHALLENGES TO LEADERS AND WOULD-BE LEADERS

And the pilot—that is to say, the true pilot—is he a captain of sailors or a mere sailor?

A captain of sailors.

The circumstance that he sails in the ship is not to be taken into account; neither is he to be called a sailor; the name pilot by which he is distinguished has nothing to do with sailing, but is significant of his skill and of his authority over the sailors.

—*Plato,* The Republic

Paraphrasing Plato, one might say, "the name [title] by which the leader is distinguished may have little to do with the work that others do in an organization, but is significant of his skill and of his authority over the workers." In this chapter, the reader is urged to try to discover or to identify: (1) the type of educational agency in which he or she wishes to lead, (2) the title by which he or she wishes to be known, (3) the types of activities in which the workers of the agency will be engaged, (4) the manner in which organizational direction will be determined, (5) the bases on which he or she can demonstrate "skill and . . . authority over the sailors," and (6) his or her reasons for wanting to lead. To aid in the discovery or identification, a number of questions are put directly to the reader, and those questions should be considered as challenges, each requiring a specific and individual answer.

WHOM DO YOU WISH TO LEAD?

If you have not yet decided who you wish to lead, it may be helpful to consider the type of agency to which you feel most strongly drawn, the level of organization at which you wish to be employed, the philosophic level which accords with your values, the age level of learners whom you wish to serve, the position specialization in which you most wish to and can most readily demonstrate "skill and authority over the sailors."

Type of Agency

Informal agencies of education, as described in Chapter 4, are not permanent or semipermanent social systems in which there are *designated positions* whose incumbents are expected to lead. Thus, an individual who aspires to be a leader on a career basis, doing work for which one is paid, is limited to making a choice from among the many formal and nonformal agencies of education where there are such positions.

FORMAL. Of course, the formal agency familiar to most people is the public school. In the public school, one may lead other workers as a department chairperson, association or union representative, principal or assistant, administrative assistant, supervisor, coordinator, director, business manager, or superintendent or assistant. Alternative and free schools offer many of the same types of positions, sometimes with a headmaster designated, and with perhaps more freedom of action, or autonomy, for the agency and for individual staff members. Parochial and private schools, too, afford many of the same kinds of opportunities for leading, with perhaps less freedom of action or autonomy, for the agency and for individuals, than would be found in the public school. Vocational and technical institutes usually utilize chairpersons, coordinators, and directors and assistants. Community and junior colleges often designate chairpersons or department heads, deans, registrars, business managers, directors, coordinators, vice-presidents, presidents, and numerous specialists having esoteric titles. Four-year colleges usually have department heads or chairpersons, deans, registrars, business managers, directors, coordinators, vice-presidents, and presidents. Graduate schools and universities usually afford the same array of possible jobs, and sometimes have chancellors, provosts, and bursars. Many also have professors who are expected to lead in the professional preparation of other leaders. Professional associations and unions often have directors or executive secretaries. The U.S. Office of Education (USOE) employs specialists in all areas of subject matter and other specialties relating to the public school and to higher education.

NONFORMAL. Some structured, systematic, nonschool agencies provide learning activities and usually do not transfer credit to other agencies. They are nonformal, and abound in present society. Even though most traditionally oriented educationists do not look on them with favor, generally, they are with us and likely to remain. Many of them offer positions in which individuals can lead. In the mass media, there are authors, lecturers, script writers, and reporters. Many larger churches are designating ministers of education, superintendents of church schools, or directors of religious education. Some of the hundreds of youth-serving groups have full-time paid directors and assistants, particularly the YMCA-YWCAs. The armed forces academies, overseas dependents' schools, and other schools of the military have superintendents or directors and assistants. A number of special government programs and government schools employ directors and other administrators who are expected to lead. Civic and cultural centers, as well as other types of social organizations, usually have directors aided by assistants and other persons having a variety of titles. Company schools, or training and development programs, both at home and abroad, typically employ directors and a variety of assistants with staff specialties. Special-needs schools, proprietary schools, and correspondence schools often are structured in similar fashion.

Levels
You are challenged to ascertain the organizational level at which you wish to be employed, to define the learners with whom and the programs with which you wish to work, and to consider the philosophic level that accords with your values.

ORGANIZATION LEVEL. A few organizations—among them UNESCO, scouting, several youth-service organizations, and the World Health Organization—are international in scope and employ directors and assistants with varying titles.

Professional associations, unions, and the USOE have national headquarters that must be staffed in some instances in addition to regional, state, and local offices. At the national level also may be found certain of the mass media, some church school headquarters, many of the youth-service groups, and armed forces educational programs, various government programs and schools, some company schools, a few special-needs schools, numerous proprietary school headquarters, and several correspondence schools. Among the formal agencies of education having a national level of organization are the USOE, some parochial school groups, and an organization of independent schools. Some accrediting associations, such as NCATE, also have national headquarters, although most of them are only regional, or multistate, in scope.

There may be found at the regional level also some mass media, church school groups, a few of the government schools and programs, some company schools, special-needs schools, correspondence schools, and offices of the USOE.

Size, organizational plan, and jurisdiction of the state departments of education vary considerably from one state to another, but every state has a department employing from a few dozen to several hundreds of professional staff personnel. Parochial schools, too, usually have state headquarters, and many universities are organized at the state level, even though they draw students from far outside the state or even the nation. Professional associations or unions frequently have state offices, and many professional journals are published at the state level.

Some of the youth-serving agencies have state organizations, and numerous civic and cultural organizations having educational purposes are organized at the state level.

In several states, there are vocational and/or technical schools or institutes that are area-wide in organizational plan: that is, larger than county but smaller than state. Also at the area level may be found journals, civic and cultural agencies, parochial school agencies, and most of the community and junior colleges.

A few of the states still have county units of the public schools as intermediate or service units serving constituent local school districts. At this level also are some libraries and other cultural agencies.

The local level of organization encompasses all of the public school districts, the parochial schools, the private schools, the alternative or free schools, and the four-year colleges, although many of the latter draw their students from a far larger than local base. Numerous proprietary and company schools, civic and cultural centers, youth-service agencies, and mass media function as local units.

LEARNER LEVEL. There is the challenge of defining those learners with whom one wishes to work in terms of age, ability, and type of learning. A decision must be made as to whether one would rather work with preschool, early elementary, middle school, high school, college age, post-college adult, or senior citizen levels. Also, whether there is a wish to help the typical, the atypical, or both; if atypical, whether the faster-than-average learner or the slower-than-average. Further, there is a need to be certain as to whether one wishes to work with programs that: (1) provide basic skills, (2) provide the general learning needed by all citizens of this country, (3) equip the learner to make better use of leisure time, (4) provide occupational learning or recycling, or some combination of these.

PHILOSOPHIC LEVEL. There is a challenge to decide whether one prefers to work in an agency that announces, "Here are the kinds of learning opportunities that we believe we can best provide, and we welcome those learners who think they can find what they want here," or in an agency that announces, "We welcome all learners, will try to help them find what they, as individuals, need to learn, and will try to help them find learning opportunities."

In addition to selecting the type of agency and the level of organization at which to work, there is the challenge of deciding on the type of position to seek.

Position Sought

Is there a wish that personal "skill and authority over the sailors" be related most closely to learners, to teachers or instructors, to support staff, to the learning process and opportunities provided, to facilities, to finance and business matters, to maintaining the organization, or to communicating between the agency and its supporting constituents? In other words, is there a wish to be expert in pupil personnel services, teaching personnel, support personnel, curriculum and learning, facilities, business, administration, public relations, or some combination of these? If one's wish is to be a staff specialist, is the desire to help people to develop their potentials, to supervise what they do, to evaluate their efforts, or to do some combination of these? If the aspiration is to be an authority on learning, does one's skill lie in curriculum development, instructional techniques, research on learning, evaluation of what has been learned, or evaluation of learning programs? If interests are in facilities, are personal skills to be gained in developing sites and structures that accommodate learning, in providing equipment, furnishings, resources, and tools that aid learners, or in using technological devices that can take some of the burden off teachers or instructors?

If one has decided on the type of agency in which one prefers to lead, the level at which leading is both appealing and possible, and the nature of the position from which one expects to lead, there is a challenge to consider the types of activities in which one prefers to lead.

IN WHAT ACTIVITIES DO YOU WISH TO LEAD?

The actions of leading, as opposed to administering, consist of the broad actions of meeting the needs of individuals and innovating, or changing what is.

Meeting Individual's Needs

Those readers familiar with the research work of Herzberg (1959) and of Myers (1964), who think their findings generalizable to education, must be aware that individuals have task-centered motivation needs that relate to the goals of achievement, growth, responsibility, and recognition. Those needs may be met through satisfiers such as merit increases, discretionary awards, utilized aptitudes, work itself, inventions, and publications. Such needs demand of the leader day-to-day behavior that allows delegation; involvement of others in goal-setting, problem-solving, work simplification, and performance appraisal; giving access to information, allowing freedom to act, and providing an atmosphere of approval, as indicated in Figure 16-1. Not everyone is capable of such behavior.

Individuals also have a series of needs that Myers termed "maintenance" needs. Physical needs may be satisfied by such things as providing supplies necessary for the job, equipment, desired location, aesthetics, lunch facilities, rest rooms, desired temperature, and other conditions. Economic needs may be satisfied by salary, automatic increases, and fringe benefits. Security needs may be satisfied by fairness, consistency, reassurance, seniority rights, and grievance procedures. Orientation needs may be met by handbooks, instruction, group meetings, bulletins, memos, or the grapevine. Social needs may be met by work groups, coffee groups, lunch groups, recreation groups, social events, professional groups, or interest groups. Status needs may require satisfiers such as room or office furnishings, privileges, classification, or title.

You are challenged to avow whether you are able and willing to meet your own needs and help others to meet theirs. Also, are you able and willing to innovate?

Innovating

Bringing about change is not a sideline for a leader, it is one of the basic activities in which he or she must engage. To describe a person who strives to maintain the status quo as a leader would be a contradiction in terms. An educational leader may change the concept of learning to which a nation subscribes, the pattern of staffing in a college, or the devices used in a company training program, but changing things is central to leading. The forms of innovation will be discussed in the next section of this chapter, How would you determine direction?, but some kinds of change are described briefly here and one is challenged to decide in which types to lead.

CHANGING SOCIETY. In the earlier discussion of accountability, it was pointed out that some persons expect education programs to serve as the agents of social change and that, indeed, schools have been and are being used for that purpose. Many nonschool agencies of education have as their basic purpose the changing of some aspect of society. A list of social issues current in 1974 was presented, but a similar and probably much longer list probably could be assembled with minimal effort at any given time. Do you want to lead in using some agency of education to bring about social change? If so, do you want to take sides on social issues by influencing others, with whatever means you control, to take your side? Do you want to use your agency as a forum for having both sides of social issues presented, with the will of the people prevailing? Should you,

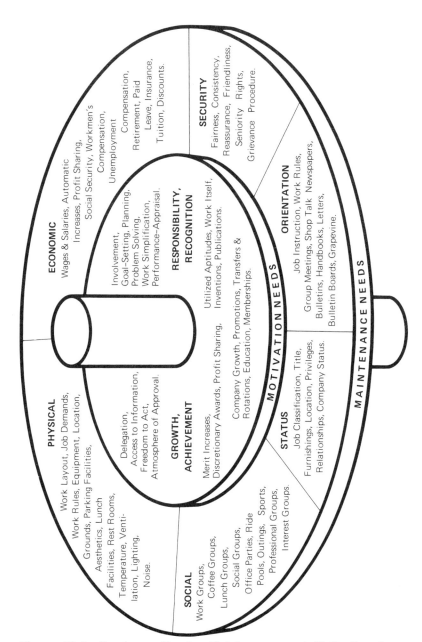

Figure 16-1 *Employee Needs—Maintenance and Motivational*
Source: Myers (1964), p. 86.

in your role as leader, be a partisan on social imperatives, such as those of Justice Douglas listed in Chapter 5?

CHANGING STRUCTURE. There are islands of theory about the effective structuring of human relationships in organizations, but there are no bridges between or among the islands. There is an island of theory about hierarchy and status; there is another about nondirective relationships; still another about the flexible organization as described by Berkley (1971) and others. Theory about hierarchy is, of course, most familiar and has been around for a very long time. Rogers (1952) and others have been developing their nondirective theory over a quarter century or more. The flexible structure theory is relatively new, and not yet clearly described by many. Perhaps it is best conceived by considering it analogous to Jay's (1967) description of a theatrical production:

> *I remember once talking to a successful theatrical director about producing a play. I assumed that he studied it extremely carefully and thought about it until he had a complete picture in his mind of how it ought to appear to the audience, then cast it and rehearsed it until the actors finally came as close as he could get them to the ideal production which was taking place in his mind. Not at all, he said. Certainly he read about it and thought about it, but he only formed a broad general idea of what the play should be like. It was in rehearsal that it really started to grow, as the actors and he together discovered more and more meanings and nuances and possibilities. My method would restrain the play within the limits of the director's imagination; his liberated all the creative abilities of the cast [p. 75].*

Does one feel impelled to maintain the hierarchical structure that now characterizes virtually every agency of education, except for a few alternative, free, or independent schools? Could one try to develop a nondirective structure? Would one call upon each individual to interpret his or her role to the utmost capability of his or her imagination and skills?

CHANGING PEOPLE. Changing people is serious business that raises some grave moral questions. Leaders in educational agencies have two groups of people whom they may try to change: staff personnel and learners. We know that opinions can be changed, but what means should one use to change them? As has been mentioned before, Watson (1966) has proved that attitudes, too, can be changed, but how does one determine whose attitudes should be changed, what attitudes should be changed, and which attitudes would be "better"? Rokeach (1971) presented some experimental evidence that values can be changed, but questioned the morality of some of the possible methods. Do you believe that some people should be changed? If so, on what basis? To whose standards?

CHANGING GOALS. Is the search for a leader position based firmly in a belief that the goals of an established agency are to be perpetuated? And what of the place of one's own long-range preferred outcomes, and the need to seek an agency which can be used instrumentally, along with its people, to achieve those outcomes? Would "good ideas" simply be diffused from other leaders or would they be created? In order to alter social system outputs, should one seek feedback aimed at changing the input, the process, or both? Would one welcome, fuse, and utilize ideas as they emerge from people with whom one works in an agency? If the latter, would credit be given to the idea sources or claimed as personal? In short, how would *you* determine the direction that *your* agency should take?

HOW WILL YOU DETERMINE DIRECTION?

The privilege—and penalty—of your education is that over the coming decades you will be the pace setters for political and social thought in your communities. You may not accept this responsibility, but that makes no difference. It is inescapable. For if you decide to set no pace, to forward no new ideas, to dream no new dreams, you will still be pace setters. You will already have decided that there is to be no pace [Adlai E. Stevenson].[1]

Should one determine direction and set the pace for an educational enterprise through imitation, adaptation of others' ideas, creativity, or considering demand?

Imitation

Many leaders apparently feel compelled to make change but are unwilling to change in a way that has not already been tested by someone else. Thus, they are faddists. They imitate through diffusion of ideas or through adaptation of ideas.

DIFFUSION. Someone in a school somewhere had the guts to be the first to try a kindergarten, a bookkeeping course, a language laboratory, the "new math," Head Start, performance contracting, the open classroom, computer-assisted instruction, the voucher system, and accountability. Sooner or later hundreds rushed to get on the bandwagon. Not too many years ago, there was one proprietary, for profit, school for heavy equipment operators; now there are several, some of them with specializations. One company tried a training program with success, others followed suit. One psychology de-

---

[1] Quoted in O. Tead, Responsibility and personal potential. *Educational Forum, 1963,* **28**(1), p. 9.

partment went all out for behavior modification and others emulated it. One management development program tried an encounter approach for improving human relations; soon there was a rash of encounter sessions. The taking of an idea from one setting and trying it in another is imitation by diffusion of an idea. It is also possible, and sometimes more effective, to imitate through adapting ideas to new uses or settings.

Adaptation

That diffusion of an idea, willy-nilly, does not always result in permanent improvement is exemplified by the dozens, if not hundreds, of portable science units and language laboratories, bought with federal monies, that are now standing idle in schools throughout the United States. Yet the first language laboratory seems to have been an adaptation, based on the needs of individuals in a specific situation, of a technological system used successfully by the armed services during World War II to teach Morse code efficiently. If one is to imitate, then one should make sure that: (1) the idea or practice has worked successfully where it has been tried, (2) it can be adapted to one's situation, and (3) it is understood, desired, and will be used by the persons for whom it is planned.

Often, it may be better to create than to imitate, and most people *are* capable of creativity.

Creativity

One may determine organizational direction and pace by being creative. Change must become the dominant concern of the top leaders in all educational enterprises. The days are over when school people could expect learners to flock to them because attendance was required and because they had a monopoly on the learning-services market. The days are also over when an individual could start his or her own educational enterprise and expect an automatic following. Growth plans for any present or proposed educational agency must be geared to acceptance of the idea of a shared market and to projected changes in wealth, demand patterns, birth rate, available resources, population distribution, technology, use of time, habit, and taste. Educational leaders must be able to invent, synthesize emerging ideas, and analyze needs.

INVENTION. Creativity is not a rare human quality like ESP or the ability to wiggle one's ears; it is a normal and common quality like intelligence or manual dexterity, as any kindergarten teacher can attest. If aspiring educational leaders in graduate classes do not demonstrate creativity in the same degree as do five-year-olds, then that is a reflection on their schooling, not on them. In their "Creativity Checklist," Bellows et al. (1962) suggested the use of the old who, what, why, when, where, and how questions applied to the more specific questions of: What other uses? Adaptation? Modification? Substitution? Addition? Multiplication? Subtraction? Division? Rearrangements? Reversal? Combination?

It appears that an imaginative person applying this checklist to education could develop new ideas for application in a specific agency. Whether these ideas would be inventions is debatable, as some writers maintain that it is impossible to invent anything, idea or tangible product, today. They maintain that anything "new" is, in reality, just a new application or a new synthesis of existing ideas. We believe that when anyone does something in a way that is new to him he is being creative. If that action results from ideas that he does not *know* that anyone else has used, he has invented. If he cheerfully admits that all he has done was to put together two or more ideas obtained from other people, he has synthesized, but still created.

SYNTHESIS. People synthesize ideas all the time. This book is acknowledged to contain more synthesis than invention, and most synthesis is extension or enlargement of component ideas. However, when two unconnected facts or ideas are put together in bisociation, resulting in a single new idea, creation has taken place, as Koestler[2] explained. One of the examples of creation to be found in this book is in Chapter 12, where the ideas of values and experiences with social agencies were combined to create a testable hypothesis concerning one's acceptance of societal values.

Ideas are never in short supply where there are educated people, but sometimes individuals who can select the significant from among the ever-emerging ideas, or are willing to synthesize them, are missing.

Considering Demand
There are two ways of looking at demands: inward or outward, at what services an agency can supply or at what learners want, at supply or demand. The best learning opportunities, like the best of any other products, have to spring from what consumers (learners) want and not from what the agency presently is best equipped to provide; in these days, surely no one would start up a new educational enterprise without being convinced that learners would buy the opportunities to be produced. However, it is not the new educational agencies that have a supply syndrome, it is the old ones. "Here is what we offer, come and get it" has been the prevailing thought of public schools and those agencies that have been spun off from the public schools. There has been no provision for feedback and gratuitous feedback has been resented if not rejected.

---

[2] A. Koestler, *The act of creation.* London: Hutchinson, 1964.

Schools and other agencies of education need to look outward, to their markets. What is it that learners want to learn, and how do agencies get information that is significant regarding the directions that they should take and how fast they should go?

The challenge to you, the reader, is, "How will you determine the direction that your agency will take? How will you determine the pace?" Whether you choose to use imitation or creativity, whether you invent, synthesize, or consider demand, the determination must be made. You must also determine by what means you propose to lead.

HOW DO YOU PROPOSE TO LEAD?

In order to lead, there is a need for power or authority, or both. However, Jay (1967) noted, "it seems to be characteristic of the creative leader that his personal loyalties are downward and not upward [p. 174]." Then if one expects to be creative, one must get authority from below; but the more one gets from below, the less likely that it will come from above. Conversely, if authority is positional, coming from above, the less of it one is likely to get from below *unless* one can demonstrate "skill and authority over the sailors." This is the crunch. Again quoting Jay (1967):

> *It is now becoming accepted that leadership is not necessarily hindered by a deep knowledge and lifelong experience of the area in which it [sic] is leading, even if the battle to establish imagination as a prerequisite of leadership is not yet won. But we are now in danger of over-compensation, of accepting the rival heresy that success . . . can be achieved not by leadership at all, but by management science, without a man [or woman?] of courage and vision and experience at the head of the enterprise to tell the management scientists what to study and for what purpose [p. 26].*

Recognition and acceptance of a leader by others has considerable impact on his or her performance in a leader role. Unless a person is viewed by others as either a controller or provider of need-satisfactions, there would seem to be little chance for a particular individual to function efficiently and effectively in such a role. Although in many ways the relationship between leader and followers is a symbiotic one, a leader cannot attract a following unless he or she is viewed by potential followers as being able, in some measure, to gratify their needs. This particular relationship was described by Knickerbocker (1948) as a "mutual means" concept of the dependencies existing between leader and followers, and it relies on authority or power. Influence is not enough when one occupies a status position.

Authority

In an authority relationship, the leader so structures environmental situations that his or her objectives, the objective of the educational agency, and the objectives of the subordinates have something in common with one another. When this is the case, subordinates' activities become "mutual means" for the achievement of the leader's and the organization's objectives and theirs as well. The activities of the people in achieving their objectives are the activities the leader desires from them so he or she can achieve his or her objectives. People grant such authority only when they are involved in the critical decisions of the organization.

The pivotal function of the educational leader has changed from knowing more than anyone else does about how learners learn to interpersonal, innovative, and administrative competence. The challenge to the reader is to determine on what basis, if any, authority can be developed. Is there a need for interpersonal competence? Innovative competence? Competence in producing improved learning opportunities? Competence in maintaining the organization? Is one basically interested in being a leader or an administrator? What plans are there for continually updating personal knowledge, skills, and behavior? Of course, if one has power—enough power—competence doesn't really matter; one can get people to go in the directions and at the pace one desires, regardless.

Power

Power—the capability of imposing sanctions—nearly always comes from above in the organization, almost never from below, except in revolutions. The reason should be obvious. Even though many people willingly make themselves dependent on others, few willingly cede to others the capability to reward or punish. Jay (1967) warned:

> *Worry and responsibility are part of the price of power. Real power does not lie in documents and memos outlining your terms of reference and area of jurisdiction: it lies in what you can achieve in practice. The boss's secretary can wield great power, like the king's mistress, without any authority at all—or at least not the sort you can show anybody. Equally, the head of a big division or company can be powerless, just as [King] Lear was powerless, despite any number of theoretical powers. Power lies in the acceptance of your authority by others, their knowledge that if they try to resist you they will fail and you will succeed* [p. 142].

If one expects to be in a position in which power is inherent or can be acquired, the challenge becomes, "On what basis, if any, will power be distributed? Will it be retained by one person, or will it be shared with a team whose skills and competencies fit and work together?'' If the latter, how will the team members be chosen, the power distributed?

Consideration of how one will lead raises the question of why lead. What satisfactions are to be gained?

WHY LEAD?

Perhaps the greatest challenge of all lies in the question, "Why lead?" It must by now be apparent that there are many reasons why not everyone should consider positions in which leading is expected. If you believe that you are one who should, you should be able to give your rationale, and that rationale should explain what you have to offer, what you stand to gain, and why those gains are important to you.

What Can Be Offered

The product of an educational agency is a service, the provision of learning opportunities. The improvement of that product depends largely on leaders who have superior imagination, stress tolerance, risk capability, knowledge, and skill. Can one honestly say that he has those qualities in such measure that he should be one of the leaders?

IMAGINATION. Perhaps the most valuable of all qualities in the educational leader is the ability to locate hidden demands, to think of something learners are not getting but need. Can a person be creative and help others to be creative? It is essential to find a cause and to enlist others in that cause.

STRESS TOLERANCE. We have spoken before of the need for any individual to be able to tolerate stress in order to maintain one's mental health, and the tolerance level must be particularly high for a leader. Jay (1967) described the "raw nerve" of the leader which must always be kept alive and sensitive, however painful, since it receives even very faint signals when all is not going well. It is one of the paradoxes of leading that the leader cannot succeed without confidence or without doubt; in the worst of times one's certainty keeps others going, in the best of times one must be alert for even the vaguest danger signals. The constant tension produces stress, and to speak of comfortable leaders is a contradiction in terms. Some persons have much higher stress thresholds than others do.

RISK CAPABILITY. The toughest decisions are the leader's, and they cannot be made without some degree of risk. He or she gives subordinates direction, and in return they pay with a part of their freedom and autonomy, through an "authority tax," to use Jay's term. Like any taxpayers, they are apt to be upset if they think they are paying too much for the services they are receiving. Byrd (1971) provided a formula by which one may gauge the amount of risk that he can afford to take, but take risk he must if he is to lead.

Knowledge and skill required have been discussed in earlier sections of this chapter. Of those qualities necessary for product improvement, what does the reader have to offer?

What Can Be Gained

The Daws Occupational Satisfactions Scheme described by Midler (1970) suggests that the satisfactions for which people work may be classified as material, status, skill, dominant value, associational, or perceptual. The reader is challenged to analyze which of these make him or her tick.

MATERIAL SATISFACTION. The material job satisfaction that comes most readily to mind is salary. During the several decades that teachers' and instructors' salaries were far too low, before the advent of negotiations, many individuals saw administrative positions as the only route to substantially increased salary. There is still considerable difference between the salaries of those who work directly with learners and those who have positions higher in the hierarchy. Since fringe benefits generally are closely tied to salary, those, too, are higher for administrators.

STATUS. With added responsibility comes added status; in the work organization, in the community, and in the profession. Often one's self-esteem is increased by attaining a personally valued position, or by gaining the attention of significant others whose opinions matter.

SKILL USE. The reader who has done careful self-examination should know rather well what skills he or she possesses or hopes to develop. Some individuals look to new positions in order to be able to exhibit mastery or to exercise skills for which present positions provide few or no opportunities. Some skills may be exhibited only when one has autonomy and the right to self-determination. Some may demand more responsibility for their exercise. Skill in the use of authority and/or power may be used to get others to do what one wants or to achieve established goals of the enterprise. Skill in providing learning opportunities may impel one to seek wider fields in which to use that skill. Some individuals are wise enough to recognize that they do not have the skills necessary to teach and, rather than lose face and schooling investment by leaving education, they seek to learn if they have skills in administering.

DOMINANT VALUE SATISFACTION. It is quite conceivable that the satisfaction one most seeks relates to a dominant value as indicated by cathexis, or concentration of desire on a particular value. For example, if the reader believes so strongly in a principle, such as learning by doing or having corrective programs in penal institutions, that he or she seeks a leader position in order to make the principle operative, he or she is seeking dominant value satisfaction.

ASSOCIATIONAL SATISFACTION. Some people seek the satisfaction of associating with certain individuals or groups whom they perceive as significant others. If one wishes above all else to associate with community college presidents, or with directors of training and management development, then the obvious way to obtain satisfaction is to become a community college president or a director of training and management development. If one gets one's satisfactions from association with adolescents, then one might try to become a middle school or junior high school principal. The association from which one derives satisfaction may be with either a work group or a target-learner group.

PERCEPTUAL SATISFACTION. Perceptual satisfactions, according to the Daws classification, are of three types: variety, outdoors, and travel. Educational leaders can almost be guaranteed variety, but there are few positions in which one would be outdoors for a significant part of the work day. However, the authors personally know a professor of educational administration who turned down an offer of a distinguished chair at the midwestern university where he was employed because he had a young family with whom he wished to share hiking, camping, and hunting experiences. Thus, he took a lower-salaried position in a western state and, at last report, had no regrets for having done so.

The reader is challenged to ask himself or herself, "What can I offer as an educational leader that others can't? What can I gain by being or becoming an educational leader that I cannot gain, or cannot gain as readily, by being a follower? Why is the potential gain important to me? Is it sufficiently important for me to make the very real effort necessary for leading?" Anyone who does not get completely satisfactory answers to these questions from himself or herself should take another route.

SUMMARY

Being designated as a leader is significant of some skill and authority over other people, and any leader or would-be leader needs to determine what skill and what basis of authority he or she has. To do this, several determinations must be made. This causes many questions to be raised that only the reader can answer.

Does one wish to lead in a formal or a nonformal agency of education? At the international, national, regional, state, area, or local level? With infants, children, youth, young adults, mature adults, or senior citizens? With typical or atypical learners? If atypical, in what way atypical? In programs in basic skills, general learnings, leisure-time use, career education, or some combination of these? In an agency that seeks learners for its programs or programs for its learners? With learners, staff, the learning process, facilities, finance and business, organization, or public relations?

The would-be leader also needs to assess whether one is able and willing to meet one's own motivation and maintenance needs and to help others meet theirs; whether he or she expects to change society, organizational structure, people, or organizational goals.

Will one determine direction and pace for one's organization through imitation, adaptation of others' ideas, or creativity? Can one be creative through invention, or only through synthesis of existing ideas? To what extent should learner demands be considered?

Since influence is insufficient to the demands of leading on a sustained basis, should one seek and use authority or power or both? If power, should the power be shared with others or jealously kept to oneself?

Only the individual knows whether he seeks to be a leader because of what he can offer, because of what he can gain, or because of what potential gains mean to him. Each reader is challenged to consider these matters.

In the next chapter, the questions of beliefs regarding who should determine how much an individual should learn, the agencies from which one should learn, when one's learning should end, the state's responsibility, and the desirability of compulsory schooling are raised and answered, at least to the authors' satisfaction.

SOME SUGGESTED RESOURCES

C. **Argyris,** Organizational effectiveness under stress. *Harvard Business Review,* 1960, **38**(3), 137–146.

R. C. **Doll,** *Leadership to improve schools.* Worthington, Ohio: Charles A. Jones, 1972.

H. D. **Drummond,** *Leadership for human change. Educational Leadership,* 1964, **22**(3), 147–148, 202.

C. L. **Hughes,** *Goal setting.* New York: American Management Association, Inc., 1965.

P. H. **Irwin and F. W. Langham, Jr.,** The change seekers. *Harvard Business Review,* 1966.

T. R. **McKague,** LPC—A new perspective in leadership. *Educational Administration Quarterly,* 1970, **6**(3), 1–14.

L. J. **Rubin,** Epilogue. In *Frontiers in school leadership.* Skokie, Ill.: Rand McNally, 1970. Pp. 140–150.

N. V. **Sullivan, T. D. Wogaman, and R. Barshay,** *Walk, run, or retreat: The modern school administrator.* Bloomington, Ind.: Indiana University Press, 1971.

R. **Tannenbaum,** The nature of authority. In M. D. Richards and W. A. Nielander (Eds.), *Readings in management.* New Rochelle, N.Y.: South Western, 1960. Pp. 708–714.

K. **Wiles,** Supervision is leadership. Ch. 3 in *Supervision for better schools* (3rd ed.) Englewood Cliffs, N.J.: Prentice-Hall, 1967. Pp. 31–50.

CHAPTER 17

LEARNERS AND LEARNING

> . . . is it not possible to teach by giving the student an
> opportunity to learn in a natural way?
>
> Unfortunately, a student does not learn simply when he is
> shown or told. Something essential to his natural curiosity is
> missing from the classroom. What is missing, technically
> speaking, is "positive reinforcement." In daily life. the student
> looks, listens, and remembers because certain consequences
> then follow.
>
> —Skinner

The educational leader who can see beyond the school may have
difficulty determining who is a learner and what is learning since
all existing educational-philosophy systems arc really school-philos-
ophy systems whose adherents apparently are incapable of recognizing learners other than children or agencies of education other
than schools.

The educational leader may be unique in that he serves four
classes of people, namely: (1) the learners who utilize the learning
opportunities "produced" by the agency that he or she heads, (2)
those who work in the organization to produce the opportunities,
(3) the extraorganizational clients who provide jobs for the learners,
and (4) the patrons who pay the bills. To lead, one must keep all
four groups satisfied to a reasonable degree, remembering that all
of them have a basic concern for learners and learning.

This chapter is the nub of what educational leadership is about. The chapter will differentiate among the terms schooling, educating, and learning; will examine what one must have for life and for the developmental tasks of learning one's way through life; and will consider how learners learn and may be helped.

LEARNING > EDUCATING > SCHOOLING

Learning is greater than educating and educating is greater than schooling. This belief must permeate the actions of anyone who is to be an educational leader rather than "just" a school administrator. Distinctions among the terms need to be internalized, avowed, cherished, and acted upon, so that a value becomes established.

Schooling

Schooling has, in our society, traditionally been a process of learning, in a particular place, for children and youth from about age 5 to about age 18—or age 21 for those who went to college. Some activities for adults take place in school buildings, but they generally take place in special programs, rather than as part of the schooling process.

Some kinds of learning, or learning for certain individuals, may be accomplished most efficiently in a special place, with necessary facilities conveniently at hand. That place is called a school, and the fact that a special place is involved distinguishes schooling from other kinds of learning. Much of one's learning can occur wherever one happens to be, but schooling cannot. Historically, societies have developed schools as places where certain kinds of learning are supposed to be effected for certain learners. However, with the advent of industrialization and resultant urbanization it should have become apparent that the best place for certain learning outcomes desired by the society often is not the school.

Some schools become so entangled in rules and regulations that it becomes difficult, if not impossible, for learners to go where they can best learn. And of course not all of the places where one could learn are available to learners on a nondiscriminate basis. Yet Skinner and others maintain that the place—the environment—is in fact the shaper of the individual learner.

Cremin (1965) has been among those able to see beyond the school to achieve an awareness that there are many agencies that educate, and he pointed out that the school's job should be to: (1) make children aware of the constant bombardment of facts, opinions, and values to which they are subjected, (2) give them the intellectual resources with which to make good judgments and deal with this bombardment, and (3) enable them to assess and to clarify which values are significant in their own lives. These things are not what schooling concentrates on currently, but they would constitute educating in the finest sense of that word.

Educating

Learning for predetermined purposes constitutes educating, regard-less of who determines the purposes or where it takes place. From the time of the first recorded societies of the human race, the elders of the tribe have required all of their young to learn certain things in common, for purposes that the elders deemed essential. Those purposes constitute institutionalized expectations. Adjustment con-sists of compromise between the individual's own purposes and the purposes of the social system, as those purposes are represented by expectations.

In the socialization process, a child often gives up more than he gets. He exchanges autonomy for conformity, aggressiveness for control, and privileges for responsibilities or, if he does not, he is called delinquent. The exchange must be reasonably equal if delin-quency is to be avoided.

The purposes for which the young have been required to learn have varied from society to society. The schools of ancient China prepared selected persons for government positions, and ancient Athens had citizens-to-be learn emphasis on character, moral train-ing, and aesthetic appreciation. Judeo-Christian societies teach the worth of the individual, thus perpetuating an ethic. The founding fathers of the United States held it important that each person be able to read the Bible and the catechism in order that his church might make him a better person. As the country developed, needs for public records brought demands for writing and computation ability, and thus the purposes imposed by society changed.

However, educating knows no age limits. A person of any age can learn for certain purposes, one's own or others', regardless of where one learns, and that is not true of schooling. An individual who learns for his own purposes is self-educated, and indeed there are some well-educated persons who have had little schooling. Many persons engage in learning with no specific purposes in mind, or learn incidentally.

Learning

Learning is a process in which an individual acquires facts, habits, or skills. It may be purposeful, but it does not have to be. It can take many forms and involve many people, but it doesn't have to. However, it *must* involve the learner and his or her action, reaction, or interaction. One can learn through independent action, but learn-ing of a social nature involves reaction to or interaction with an en-vironment, which may, but does not have to, include people. The actions of the learner may be conscious, as may be reactions or interactions, but any of them also may be unconscious.

It now is accepted fact that a sizable chunk of what one learns—and most of one's "intelligence"—is acquired by the age of seven or eight. However, educators in general seem to proceed from the premise that learning stops at a relatively early age. There is much discussion in regard to theory of teaching or instruction, but little in regard to theory of learning. Much of the "research" on learning is done in bits and pieces, with hypotheses that are unrelated, and with no unifying theory. Most of the findings are trivia.

Career educational leaders are needed who can perceive education as clearly as Adiseshiah (1971) did and who will develop philosophy and theory that can accommodate this concept:

> *learning,*
> *learning how to learn,*
> *a combination of different sets of learning skills to meet different needs.*
> *learning through the systematic use of all modern management techniques and all the technologies available from computer-assisted programmed instruction to educational television, terrestrial, satellite-based or hybrid; and using all the methodologies we have learned in business and adult education, learning in school, factory, farm, home, church, club, theatre, cultural centre, evening classes, correspondence courses, a learning experience is to be had, . . . [p. 5.]*

The philosophy and the theory of career educational leaders must consider whether learning can be forced, as present compulsory attendance laws seem to imply. They must also specify what learning is necessary for life.

LEARNING FOR LIFE[1]

Years ago, Linton (1936) cataloged ten elements that anthropologists found to be common among all of the cultures they had investigated up to that time. Chase (1948), reviewing the work of Linton, stated that:

> *The list shows the elements of every child's real education, what he must have for life, in contrast with the formal education* taught in the schools [*emphasis added*] *of Western civilization. When we get the two curricula a little closer together, perhaps so many child years will not be wasted in school [p. 78].*

The following discussion attempts to show how the two curricula may be brought a little closer together, and asterisks indicate the elements identified by Linton. Some of the comments have been adapted from Overstreet's (1949) criteria of maturity, and the list represents what the present writers believe one must learn to be functional in present society.

---

[1] Much of the material in this section is adapted from H. W. Boles, Careers and the educated person. *Illinois Career Education Journal*, 1974, **32**(1), 33–36.

Basic Skills
Certain skills are necessary if further learning is to be possible, and these skills may be divided into those relating to the use of muscles per se, those involved in communication, those having to do with learning itself, and those necessary for computation.

MUSCLE USE. Most children first learn the use of the large muscles by means of which they stand, walk, run, jump, throw, etc., and later develop proficiency in controlling small muscles such as those used in marking, cutting, fastening, and similar activities.

*LANGUAGE. Every person who functions in society must learn to speak (or to transmit signals in some other fashion), to listen (or to receive signals in nonaural form), to read, to write, and to interpret the signals that he or she receives. One must become increasingly articulate, throwing off communications restrictions imposed by early associations, by early rebuffs, or by lack of self-perception.

LEARNING. The individual must recognize that, at any instant of life, one's present knowledge is insufficient for the future. One must develop function habits—become orderly and organized. One must learn how to learn—to use facilities for learning and to seek sources of information. One must determine when and how to unlearn and to relearn, painful though those actions may be.

COMPUTATION. Ability to count, to add, subtract, multiply, and divide is essential in any developed society. Ability to compute ratios and percentage is necessary for everyone in the present-day society of the United States, and some persons in some occupations need much more sophisticated computation skills.

Social Learnings
There are a number of things that all individuals need to learn in common, including the following:

*FAMILY RELATIONSHIPS. All societies have found it necessary to help the individual convert his or her innate egocentricity to sociocentricity, through the agency of the family. A universal quality seems to involve a group of some permanency, which protects its young; is kind to its childbearers; includes both sexes, even though they need not necessarily be the biological parents; divides the labors; cares for its aged; is basically monogamous; frowns on cross-cultural liaisons, because it knows they are exceptionally difficult; holds incest taboo; and provides siblings.

*STATUS IN THE SOCIETAL GROUP. The individual must learn to accept his human role. Perhaps one did not ask to be born into this world—but who did? This larger need may be broken into smaller needs for: (a) eliciting response from the group of which one is a part, (b) knowing where one stands, whether one's status be ascribed

or achieved, in the group, (c) opportunities to lead or be led, (d) friends, (e) ways to relieve frustrations, (f) means of recognizing that one is, by nature, illogical, and (g) a society built on and led by average individuals.

RULES FOR PROPERTY AND TRADE. Most cultures seem to recognize that they cannot long remain at stark survival level, and have thus sanctioned the acquisition and transfer of property by individuals and by nations; the rules that apply in a particular culture must be learned by all of its members.

GOVERNMENT AND LAW. That punishment follows violation of group rules seems to be a further universal quality of the human race and must be learned if society is to survive.

ETHNIC DIFFERENCES. In a culture where all members are native-born, of the same skin color, and of a single religious belief, the teaching of ethnic differences might be unnecessary. In cultures where one or more variations occur, ethnic differences can be perceived, and thus taught, either as a source of pride and something to be cherished or as a source of conflict.

ETHICS. Apparently people in all societies feel a need to have each succeeding generation learn some guides for personal behavior that extend beyond laws.

SEXUALITY. The mature individual learns to develop a specific and creative sexual relationship. Society might help by reassessing values and distinguishing sexuality from eroticism, and both from hedonism.

STRATEGIES FOR CONFLICT RESOLUTION. Deplorable though it is, the fact remains that all of the cultures reported by Linton formalized ways of engaging in conflicts with rival tribes or societies. Of those cultures reported since 1936, the Tasaday tribe of the Philippines seems to be the lone exception. Perhaps the present need is for nations to learn a substitute for war, and certainly every individual needs to learn strategies for conflict resolution at various levels.

SYSTEMS FOR EXPLAINING NATURAL PHENOMENA. Depending on the culture, natural phenomena have been explained through myths, magic, religion, or science. Factions in our own society have lined up with both the latter two systems of explanation since the days of the Scopes trial, each faction insisting on its own explanation of how man relates to his environment. Some system for explaining phenomena is essential to the educated person, who must develop a philosophical linkage with all the world about him; must see wholes rather than isolated parts; must see his own relationship to such wholes. One must be able to see applications of what one has learned to what one is doing.

Understanding of Leisure Time

A third area in which an educated person must learn is that of understanding the uses to which leisure time can be put, uses which are at least three in number. Leisure time may be viewed either as a rejuvenator for career tasks, as a time in which pleasure may be sought, or as a time when one may be of service to others. That society does a poor job of preparing people for the use of leisure time is attested by the large number of persons who find that they do not know what to do with themselves when forced into early requirement.

There are at least four kinds of activities that an educated person should learn about as possibilities for using leisure time whenever one has such time.

ART FORMS. As indicated earlier, one may consider oneself creative whenever he is doing something in a way that is new to him, and anyone can be creative so long as he maintains a curiosity and an open mind. Many people express their creativity through the arts, another of the universals that Linton reported anthropologists had found among all of the cultures they had studied. While the forms and levels of sophistication vary, all known cultures have developed numerous forms, in both the fine and the performing arts, that give expression to the creative urge for no apparent purpose other than pure enjoyment.

RECREATION. Any activity that exposes an individual to sensory stimuli not usually experienced by him or her can refresh after toil or anxiety. A Robert Kennedy may shoot the rapids of the Colorado River or climb a mountain, a Walter Mitty may plant a shrub or rake the lawn, or a Lillian Roth may write a book.

ENTERTAINMENT. There are times in the lives of most people when they wish to make no physical or mental effort and only want something on which to focus attention. That focus may be a television program, a movie, a personally attended athletic event, a cocktail party, or any of the hundreds of other intellectual opiates available to most of us. One needs, however, to learn the dangers of developing anomie when one too frequently indulges in a particular form of entertainment; one may become personally disorganized, resulting in unsocial behavior.

SERVICE. Some psychologists state that every human being has an innate desire to be needed, and this desire can be turned to advantage by individuals with time on their hands. Some such start new or secondary careers that allow them to do things for other people, such as the retired banker who does home maintenance chores only for the elderly, at nominal cost. Others respond to some of the many calls for volunteers in a variety of service activities. There now is a national organization of retired people who serve as unpaid consultants to others who are having problems with small businesses.

Many otherwise educated persons have not learned to use leisure time well, with the result that recreation and entertainment have become big industries, providing new career opportunities for many individuals.

Career Education

The fourth element of every educated person's "*real* education, what he must have for life . . ." is career education. This is *not* a euphemism for vocational education introduced at an earlier age. In order to understand the present writers' admitted bias in regard to career education, it is necessary to look at six underlying assumptions. If one agrees with the assumptions, no proof is necessary; if one disagrees, no proof is possible. The six assumptions are:

1. Career education is a never-ending process that should start when the basic skills have been acquired. Woodring (1964) said: ". . . many students now in school will spend their adult lives in types of work that do not yet exist, cannot be predicted, and consequently cannot yet be specifically prepared for [p. 47]." These people may change careers as many as five times, and they need career education each time a change is imminent.

2. Our system of plural subcultures should be maintained and taught as a source of pride, but the schools have an obligation to teach common elements of acculturation, and the 13 years generally spent in the schools is a minimum time in which to do this job. Career education thus must be a part of liberal education, not a substitute for it.

3. The purpose of career education is to allow each individual to learn: (1) about a variety of careers and the requirements for people who pursue them, and (2) whether one prefers to work with things, with people, with ideas, or with some combination of these. Some elaboration of this point of view follows the list of assumptions.

4. The period from age 17 or 18 to the age of 22 or 23 may as well be spent by each individual in some kind of intensive career preparation since persons in this age group have little place in the labor market. In order to maintain a reasonable level of employment in the face of increasing technology, it has been necessary to advance the age at which individuals begin work and to retire them at ever-earlier ages. Increasing numbers of women in the labor force also work against the admission of the young.

5. The most fruitful activity for persons in the age span from 17 or 18 to 22 or 23 is further education, even though college may not be the best place for large numbers of them.

6. High schools cannot afford the equipment necessary to provide skill development for very many of the 22,000 or more jobs currently cataloged by occupational titles. Thus, the best places for

learning such skills are *regional* vocational-technical centers; business, industry, armed forces, and other government schools; proprietary schools; and on-the-job.

It should be obvious from the above assumptions and the brief rationale given that the present writers do not believe that the public schools have any business trying to teach specific vocational skills. What is not obvious is what they believe the schools *should* teach by way of career education. That description follows.

*THE NATURE OF WORK. Everyone can learn the nature of work; that it is done to get food, clothing, and shelter; that in a complex society, labor must be divided in order that tasks may be done by skilled persons; that people thus become interdependent, so that one exchanges one's services for another's services or goods that one needs or wants, and that work gives status, according to what people do.

WHAT PEOPLE DO. Everyone can learn that the status which work gives a person depends on: (1) the contribution that one's efforts make to society and (2) the competency and proficiency with which one does one's work. Everyone needs to learn about the need for and contributions made by architects, bakers, carpenters, die makers, engineers, farmers, garbage collectors, haberdashers, investigators, jockeys, knitters, lawyers, machinists, nurses, oculists, physicians, quarterbacks, receptionists, secretaries, truckers, undertakers, veterinarians, wholesalers, X-ray technicians, yardmasters, zookeepers, and a host of others. All need to learn that each occupation has its own skill requirements.

SKILL REQUIREMENTS. An individual must discover whether he or she prefers to work with things, with people, with ideas, or with some combination of these. Each person can learn the skill requirements of specific occupations that make use of the preferences one exhibits and can develop the kinds of skills required in those occupations to which one is most strongly inclined.

OPPORTUNITIES. Individuals can learn about the opportunities that certain careers may afford for satisfying work, advancement, responsibility, salary, travel, or whatever other opportunities they are interested in.

CONSTRAINTS. Individuals also can learn the constraints imposed by certain careers, such as the visibility of a politician, the lack of promotion for a professional, the lack of autonomy for an assembly-line worker, or the lack of time control experienced by a fireman. Fixed salary constraints can be compared to benefits, and geographic constraints of certain careers can be understood.

CONSUMERISM. Career education programs can help learners to become intelligent consumers of the services and products provided by other people and other nations. The effects of both domestic and international trade on various careers can be stressed.

For life, a person must learn basic skills, experience some social learnings that are common to all members of the society, understand how to use leisure time wisely and well, and be thoroughly grounded and continuously immersed, lifelong, in career education. The concept of developmental tasks can provide for an orderly sequence of the necessary learnings.

DEVELOPMENTAL TASKS

A developmental task is a task which arises at or about a certain period in the life of the individual, successful achievement of which leads to his happiness and to success with later tasks, while failure leads to unhappiness in the individual, disapproval by the society, and difficulty with later tasks [Havighurst, 1972, p. 2].

Developmental tasks may also be viewed as cultural expectations which are rewarded when achieved by individuals. When one fails on such tasks or is delayed in their achievement, one usually may expect punitive consequences from society.

Havighurst invented the seminal concept of developmental tasks in 1948, and catalogued the tasks that are necessary for one to "learn his way through life," from infancy through old age. The tasks give a pattern to "learning for life." The Havighurst booklet has been published in three editions, innumerable printings, and at least eight languages, and it has served as the basis for many of the child development courses taught in recent years, as well as for other types of courses in education and psychology. But the question arises as to why so many people have seen the concept as important to the learning of children and youth, yet seem not to have questioned its nonapplication to learners of other ages.

In discussing the characteristics of developmental tasks, Havighurst stressed that there is no developmental task of children or adolescents that the *school* can ignore, that developmental tasks are dependent on the culture in which they are to be accomplished, and that some tasks (such as participating responsibly as citizens) are recurrent, while others (such as learning to walk) usually are not. He did suggest that selection of a career was a nonrecurrent task, but that idea has changed. Can society afford to ignore the developmental tasks and their significance for learners of all ages? If some individuals are to have careers in educational leadership, must they not be concerned about all of the tasks at all age levels and must not certain of them prepare themselves to function in all of the agencies that can help learners?

Infancy and Early Childhood

The eight tasks listed by Havighurst as essential to the period of infancy and early childhood generally are accomplished through the agency of the family, before the child is ever introduced to school. They are: (1) learning to walk, (2) learning to take solid foods, (3) learning to talk, (4) learning to control bodily elimination, (5) learning sex differences, (6) forming concepts of social and physical reality, (7) getting ready to read, and (8) learning to distinguish right and wrong. The child who was no biological family usually has a surrogate family to help her or him cope with these fundamental tasks, but society must assure that some agency of education does the job. The family or surrogate family may be assisted by nursery school, church, or "regular" school—public, parochial, or private.

Middle Childhood

It seems that the family should be the agency of education having primary responsibility for nine tasks listed at the middle childhood level, also, with secondary responsibility being shared by the school and the church. For nonchurchgoing families or those families that abdicate primary responsibility, however, the full burden seems to fall on the school. The tasks are: (1) learning physical skills, (2) building wholesome attitudes toward self, (3) learning to get along with age-mates, (4) learning the appropriate sex role, (5) developing basic skills [it may be noted that the list of such skills provided earlier in this chapter is more extensive than that advocated by Havighurst], (6) developing abstract conceptualizing ability, (7) developing morality and a set of values, (8) achieving independence, and (9) developing attitudes toward social groups and institutions.

Peers and many neighborhood agencies assist with these tasks.

Adolescence

In learning to cope with the developmental tasks of adolescence, the self seems to be the agency of education having primary responsibility, with the family having secondary responsibility and the school—and perhaps the church—serving a more or less remedial function.

The eight tasks of this age level are: (1) achieving more mature relations with age-mates, (2) achieving a sex-related social role, (3) accepting and using one's body effectively, (4) achieving emotional independence, (5) preparing for marriage and family life, (6) preparing for a career, (7) acquiring a set of values and an ethical system as behavior guides, and (8) desiring and achieving socially responsible behavior.

Many youth-serving organizations function as supplemental or remedial agencies of education in helping adolescent learners.

Early Adulthood

The self is the obvious education agency for learning to cope with these eight tasks that Havighurst listed as developmental for the early adulthood stage of life: (1) selecting a mate, (2) learning to live with a partner, (3) starting a family, (4) rearing children, (5) managing a home, (6) getting started in an occupation, (7) taking on civic responsibility, and (8) finding a congenial social group.

Some may reasonably argue that only tasks 5 through 8 apply to those individuals who do not wish to marry.

While the self is the primary agency for learning to cope with these tasks, there are no agencies having specific secondary responsibility. This may be one reason why so many young adults do poorly at coping with the tasks, and why some of them sometimes cast about frantically to find agencies that can help them learn what they must learn. Most nonformal education agencies are intended to serve young adults, but patrons may have difficulty locating those they need. The church has increasingly taken responsibility for helping young adults in recent years, and some hospitals and other social welfare agencies have been making conscious efforts to help learners. Some school-based adult education and recreation programs also cater to the young.

Here and there scattered developments of other types in recent years indicate awareness of the needs that learners of this age group have. For example, in 1973 the Junior League of Flint, Michigan, sponsored a project designated as "Leadership Flint" to help promising young people prepare for civic and cultural responsibilities in their city.

Middle Age
A number of nonformal agencies of education are structured to help those persons of middle years cope with the varied roles that each person plays simultaneously, regardless of sex, through aiding with the seven developmental tasks that Havighurst listed for this age group.

The tasks are: (1) assisting children in becoming responsible and happy adults, (2) achieving civic and social responsibility, (3) reaching and maintaining satisfactory career performance, (4) developing leisure time activities, (5) relating to one's spouse as a person, (6) adjusting to physiological changes, and (7) adjusting to aging parents.

Most of the agencies to which adults of middle age can turn for help with these tasks are proprietary in nature, but the numbers of such agencies that have been developed and continue to exist attest to the need. Some school systems and some colleges make special attempts to provide programs for middle-aged people, some for credit and some without.

Old Age
The euphemism "later maturity" was applied to this group by Havighurst, but the tasks that he listed have to do with aging. They are: (1) adjusting to decreasing strength and health, (2) adjusting to retirement and reduced income, (3) adjusting to death of spouse, (4) establishing an explicit affiliation with one's age group, (5) meeting

social and civic obligations, and (6) establishing physical living arrangements.

As numbers of older persons and interest in geriatrics have increased, the agencies that can assist with the tasks of this age group have multiplied. Many churches and some schools and hospitals have provided special learning programs for older people. Nevertheless, many of them are ill-prepared to cope with the tasks that face them.

Havighurst raised highly significant questions, under the heading Educational Implications, regarding each of his age groupings except "later maturity." We believe there are educational implications for that group, as well, and educational leaders and would-be leaders are urged to read the implications in detail and to ponder well what the implications augur for their own careers. They also should analyze their beliefs about how learners learn.

HOW LEARNERS LEARN

Learning is a very complex matter, and there is no theory of learning per se to which educators and psychologists in general subscribe. It is apparent that many skills are learned subtly and informally, through interaction of the learner and a person who is more experienced, as in the case of the infant learning language skills through interaction with parents or older siblings. Most primitive skills probably are learned in similar fashion, but that leaves much learning unexplained. An educational leader who hopes to understand how learners learn must address the questions of what psychology we can trust, whether there are "rules" of learning, the importance of learners' own purposes, how other persons can help learners, and what is community education.

What Psychology Can We Trust?

What psychology can we trust? was the title of an intriguing pamphlet written by Watson (1961) which came close to presenting a theory of learning. Nothing newer is known to the present authors that improves on Watson's formulation. He listed 50 propositions under the headings of (1) Learning Process, (2) Motivation, (3) Teaching Methods, (4) Subject Matter, (5) Evaluation, (6) Growth, (7) Individual Differences, (8) Group Relations, and (9) Stratification. The propositions touched on essentials of how learners learn ranging from positive reinforcement through involvement, developmental stages, and effects of socioeconomic class. Educational leaders might do well to rely on Watson's formulation until it is improved upon. Morris (1967), the British zoologist, listed some "rules of play" that can be observed among animal young that also merit consideration.

Rules of Learning?

According to Morris, the pattern of exploration exhibited by the young of many animal species consists of the same order of actions, here paraphrased:

— The unfamiliar is investigated until it becomes familiar.
— Rhythmic repetition is imposed on the famlar.
— Repetition is varied in as many ways as can be thought of.
— The most satisfying of the variations discovered are selected and developed to the exclusion of other variations.
— Variations are combined and recombined one with another.
— All this is done for its own sake, as an end in itself.

This sounds suspiciously like Dewey's "learning by doing," especially when no external controls or extrinsic rewards are imposed on the learner. It may be that the animal play rules are "learning rules," at least for the learner who is trying to satisfy his curiosity— reduce his uncertainty—about something with which he is unfamiliar. As Skinner pointed out (see p. 340), "something essential to his natural curiosity is missing from the classroom." But does it have to be missing, or can efforts to help the learner direct attention to his or her natural curiosity, utilizing his or her own purposes for learning? This is one of the foremost challenges for persons who are going to make careers of leading educational enterprises.

Learner's Purposes

Society and the community establish minimum goals for the learning that they expect of all learners, but beyond these minimums individuals continually aspire to their own levels of accomplishment in their own selected areas. Some learn muscular development and coordination in order to become proficient bowlers, hockey players, swimmers, acrobats, draftsmen, potters, truck drivers, and so on ad infinitum.

Other persons learn in order to become, either for employment or enjoyment purposes, writers, carvers, photographers, ballet dancers, musicians, data processors, police officers, or bakers. Some learn in order to manage or manipulate others, to enact laws, to heal, to teach, to make speeches, to prosecute or defend litigants, or to interpret the laws.

It seems indisputable that a learner's own purposes are important to what one learns and how one learns, but little attention is given to the learner's own purposes in most of the agencies of education.

How Others Can Help

That no one ever learns from another person has been stated flatly by Postman and Weingartner (1969), and many other persons would agree with them. Yet there are hundreds of thousands of teachers, instructors, directors, coordinators, and others who are devoting their lives to trying to help individuals learn. Virtually all of the emphasis to date has been on what teachers should do to "motivate" learners in school rather than on what learners should do wherever they can best learn and on how teachers or others could help them do it. The absurdity of the past and present emphasis has been highlighted by Bruner (1968):

*The result of "teaching the culture" can, at its worst, lead to
the ritual, rote nonsense that has led a generation of critics to
despair. For in the detached school, what is imparted often has
little to do with life as lived in the society except insofar as the
demands of the school are of a kind that reflect indirectly the
demands of life in a technical society. But these indirectly imposed demands may be the most important feature of the detached school. For school is a sharp departure from indigenous
practice [p. 71].*

But are there not ways in which people can help learners? Ways
that do not sharply depart from "indigenous practice"? Ways in
which positive reinforcement for the learner, now missing from the
classroom according to Skinner, can be present in the classroom.
and can be related to the learner's own purposes for learning?

Such ways of helping learners to learn depend on teachers being
able to lead, not push; help, not goad; demonstrate the personal
authority of competence rather than the authority of position. To
demonstrate the authority of competence and to make use of learner-
valued positive reinforcement the teacher must prove that he or she
can help learners to reduce their uncertainties. Anyone who seeks
to help a learner must *help him or her to answer these questions
for himself or herself,* not supply ready-made answers to the
individual:

1. What uncertainties do I have?
2. How and where can I, through my own *action, reaction,* or
   interaction, get information that will help to reduce my
   uncertainties?
3. How can I handle the ever-present conflict between the crav-
   ing for novelty and the fear of leaving the familiar?
4. How can we know if I am ready to deal with those unfamiliar
   things about which I am uncertain?
5. How can I learn what I want to or must learn with the least
   waste of effort and other resources?
6. What tools are available to me for this task?
7. What example can you provide that will be meaningful for
   me to emulate?
8. What actions and what tools will be most effective for *me* to
   learn?[2]
9. How can we establish a climate in which I can learn, through
   following the learning rules, what society says I must learn
   plus what I wish to learn?

How learners learn and how others can help them to learn are
the essence of educational leadership. Anyone contemplating a

[2] The first 8 questions are from H. Boles, *The 3 Rs and the new religion.*
Midland, Mich.: Pendell, 1973, p. 55.

career as an educational leader must be sure of his or her convictions about these matters, and of his or her values. What alternatives are to be chosen, cherished, avowed as "right," and acted upon repeatedly, until they have become a part of one's life-style?

Community Education

There is as great diversity of view regarding where and how learners *should* learn as regarding how they do learn. "De-schoolers" such as Illich and Reimer hold that learners in this society would be better off without schools, learning through other agencies and individuals who can be of more help than can the schools. At the opposite extreme are some radical educationists who avow that the schools can give all the help necessary to learners of all ages for them to achieve their developmental tasks and learn their way through life. Some community school programs almost attempt to do this. Advocates of free and alternative schools seem to be saying that "the right kind of schools" can do the job.

The burgeoning Community Education movement, as described by Seay (1974), documents a belief that schools can be used in better fashion and for more purposes than they have been in the past, and a belief also that *all of the educative agencies of a community should be used to help all of the people learn to solve problems, individual and collective.* This may be the epitome of the philosophy of learning that is needed by educational leaders of the future.

SUMMARY

The educational leader needs a philosophy of learning rather than a philosophy of schooling such as most persons now working in education seem to have. The leader serves four classes of people: learners, educational workers, employers, and bill-paying constituents, but all are concerned with learners and learning.

Learning involves people of all ages, and some learning is purposeful while some is not. Educating consists of learning for predetermined purposes, some of which are imposed on the learner by society and some by the agency through which he or she is learning. Some purposes may be self-determined if the individual is lucky or sufficiently persistent. One may be self-educated even though one has little or no schooling. Schooling, in our society, has been an activity of children and youth, conducted in a particular place.

The educational leader must be concerned with change—human change. Unfortunately, some people never seem to develop the aspirations, the drives, or the skills necessary to achieve at a level near their potential. Trying to assure that everyone gets the learnings essential to living may help to reduce waste of human resources, and those learnings include basic skills, some social learnings common to all, leisure time use, and career education.

What an individual learns and the order in which it is learned are patterned to a great extent by developmental tasks that characterize various age levels from birth to death. Successful achievement of developmental tasks at a given level is fundamental to further development, and learning connected with the tasks comes in spurts of intense effort, interspersed with plateaus where learning levels off. There are educational implications of developmental tasks with which leaders must be familiar, and there are many agencies through which learners and leaders must work.

While there is no learning theory that unifies the bits and pieces of what is known and hypothesized about learning, there is a psychology that can be trusted and that could unify efforts to help learners learn. There are also some rules of play that the young of various animal species conform to when exploring, and they may constitute the rules for learning by doing. Certainly, the purposes that learners themselves have for wanting to or needing to learn are important, to them and to people who try to help them learn. Those who wish to help learners must lead, not push, and leading depends on competence in helping learners answer questions that are significant to them and that relate to reducing their many and ever-present uncertainties.

The philosophy of learning needed by educational leaders of the future may be embodied in the creed of the burgeoning Community Education movement: all of the agencies of education should be used to help all of the people learn to solve problems, individually and collectively.

In Chapter 18, questions will be raised about whether society needs experts, generalists, or both; who is to be educated, in what manner, and by which agencies of education; what, indeed, will constitute the education of the future; and for how much of that education, if any, should schools be responsible.

SOME SUGGESTED RESOURCES

H. **Boles,** *The 3 Rs and the New Religion.* Midland, Mich.: Pendell, 1973.

J. **Calam and J. Patenaude,** The schools ain't what they used to be—and probably never were. *Saturday Review Education,* 1972, **55**(18), 52–53.

B. R. **Clark,** The study of educational systems. In D. L. Sills (Ed.), *International encyclopedia of the social sciences.* New York: Macmillan, 1968. Vol. 4, pp. 509–516.

J. D. **Grambs,** Society as educator. Ch. 3 in *Schools, scholars, and society.* Englewood Cliffs, N.J.: Prentice-Hall, 1965. Pp. 14–24.

N. **Postman and C. Weingartner,** *The school book.* New York: Delacorte, 1973.

M. **Rossman,** How we learn today in America. *Saturday Review of Education,* 1972, **55**(34), 27–33.

R. L. **Saunders, R. C. Phillips, and H. T. Johnson,** How learning takes place. Ch. 7 in *A theory of educational leadership.* Columbus, Ohio: Merrill, 1966. Pp. 56–73.

CHAPTER 18

EDUCATION IN THE FUTURE

Imaginative planning and vigorous action are necessary to maintain a viable educational system. The educational system of the future will be shaped by men in purposive fashion, or it will, by default, be shaped by accident, tradition, and the senseless forces of environment.

—Irvine

There is much talk and discussion about futurism or futureness and about the implications of the future for education in this and other countries. This chapter will attempt to explain the concept of futurism and discuss the import of that concept for learners, for teachers or other persons who expect to help future learners, for the learning process, for the places in which learning takes place, for educational organization, for educational leadership, for educational finance, and for relations between those engaged in education and those who are not. That is an immodest undertaking, as the reader no doubt recognizes.

FUTURISM
Although he was using the term "innovation," and using it in a very special sense, Drucker (1965) seems to have been talking about *futurism,* as that term was being used in 1974, when he wrote:

> . . . we increasingly believe that there is a conscious disci-
> pline—already learnable though perhaps not yet teachable—for
> the imaginative leap into the unknown. We are developing rigor-

ous method for creative perception. Unlike the science of yester-
day, it is not based on organizing our knowledge. It is based
on organizing our ignorance [p. 28].

It was suggested by Toffler (1970, p. 373) that a leader is expected, with each successive promotion, to concern himself with events further in the future. If Toffler is correct in this intimation, then the top leaders of education should be expected to concern themselves with the furthermost fringes of education in the future. Some of the matters that should be encompassed in such concern may be discovered by considering some criteria for and risks inherent in the education of the future.

Criteria

The dimensions of "futureness," or futurism, include the questions of how much, how far, and what control, according to Toffler.

HOW MUCH. Anyone concerning oneself with the future must decide how much of one's time one can devote to the future as compared with the present, and how much of one's resources of imagination, energy, and finance can be committed without so impoverishing the present that one is unlikely to get beyond it. One's decisions as to "how much" depend on the factors of age and cultural conditioning, among others.

It has long been recognized that the very young are incapable of seeing beyond the immediate situation, and one of the marks of maturity is supposed to be the ability to defer immediate gratifications to longer-term potential benefits. Thus, there is an implication that those persons who have the capacity to shape the future will be found among the mature.

HOW FAR. Individuals who try to look into the future seem to experience unusual difficulty in putting their visions into words, and often the characters, events, and scenes they describe have an unreal and stilted quality not found in writings about the present or the past. Examples may be found in Bellamy's (1887) *Looking Backward,* Pediwell's (1939) *The Saber-Tooth Curriculum,* Halle's (1963) *Sedge,* or any of the host of science fiction works. Distortion may be directly proportional to how far one tries to peer into the future.

Still, as the tempo of life increases, as the future explodes into the present, the necessity for extending one's horizon further and further ahead becomes more and more imperative. Toffler (1970) likened the situation to that of the automobile driver on a freeway: at low speed the driver has plenty of time in which to make his move even if a sign is close to the exit, but as his speed increases he is compelled to lengthen his time horizon or risk being overtaken and unable to turn where he should have turned.

Then it seems that if one aspires only to a low-level leader position, one's ability to project forward, to examine and evaluate alternative courses of action that are open, needs to be able to reach only a relatively short distance into the future. However, for the person who aspires to lead a university the forward reach must be greater, and for the individual who would lead a nation's educational endeavors, concerns must extend far, far into the future.

WHAT CONTROL. Toffler indicated that a dimension of futurism must relate the questions of "how much" and "how far" to that of what control can be exercised in regard to technology. He pointed out that we must ask about the future accelerative implications of each major technological innovation, must assure ourselves of what or whether control can be exercised. Does the innovation help control and direct any further innovation that it is likely to breed, or does it tend to set in motion or accelerate forces or processes over which there will be no control? An example would be computer-assisted learning, with a console in every living room. Would that help to control and direct further learning innovations or might it set in motion a Big Brother governmental takeover? Implications for the schools of control, or lack of control, of technology are considered in Chapter 19.

Risk

The bold course of deliberately taking risk and creating risk by innovating for the future was advocated by Drucker (1965) as the only feasible alternative to the blind chance of premodern times and the modern belief in "inevitable progress, both chanceless and risk-less." He pointed out that the risk involved in deliberate futurism is threefold: the risk of exposure, or being overtaken by innovation; the risk of failure of a deliberate attempt; and the risk of an attempt succeeding. While Drucker was referring specifically to geopolitical matters, it would seem that the same three types of risk inhere in attempts to innovate educational systems for the future.

EXPOSURE. Indeed, Drucker warned that "each technology, each industry, each business lives under the risk of being destroyed or damaged by innovation, technological or social [p. 47]." There is always the possibility that a landslide of events may overtake educators even though they have anticipated it and are running to keep out of the way. It may be that the landslide is already upon us, in the guise of television. Any attempt to prevent or ignore the pervasive effects of this or other forces on education can only increase rather than obviate this particular risk.

FAILURE. To date, there has been no convincing proof that any human being can predict the future. However, as the staid *Business Week* (1974) reported, there has been increasing interest in and support of psychic research by responsible people, corporations, and even the federal government. One of the facets of ESP in which there is intense interest is the matter of precognition, or predicting the future. If research can establish that certain individuals actually are prescient, their services will no doubt be in great demand. Mihalasky and Dean (1974) argue that successful executives have a sixth sense, an inexplicable ability to predict the future. In addition to reports from laboratory experiments, their data include startling empirical findings regarding the high correlation of the track records of 25 selected individuals, in terms of their profit-making prowess, with their scores on a precognition test.

If precognition is possible, it could decrease the high rate of failure of innovation experienced previously and generally attributed to faulty vision, insufficient design, or injudicious timing. Drucker paradoxically concluded that more and speeded-up innovation alone can protect against the avalanche of innovation by others, but this necessitates the commitment of more and more resources to a gamble in which the odds of success are ever decreasing. Precognition could help to change these odds.

SUCCESS. Risk attaches even to the success of innovation because of unanticipated changes that it may produce, because of possible obsolescence by the time it is achieved, or because of possible inappropriateness if achieved.

A minor example may be seen in performance contracting. Some school districts in which patrons and officials were unhappy with the results being achieved by the schools contracted with for-profit corporations to provide learning opportunities for schoolchildren with the understanding that the corporations would be paid in terms of their performance in increasing the achievement levels of the children. Results in most of the experiments have been judged unsatisfactory because the standards by which the children's accomplishments were measured were deemed, ex post facto, inappropriate. Yet the innovation, having a nonschool educational agency paid in terms of demonstrated results, was achieved, and was successful.

Futurism in education must focus on learners, those persons who help them learn, and the learning process.

LEARNERS
Planning for learners of the future must relate to who the learners will be, their characteristics, their involvement in decisions regarding their own learning, and their career recycling.

Who They Will Be
The learners of the future will consist of the entire population, regardless of age. Learning will be—now it is for some persons—a cradle-to-crypt, womb-to-tomb, conception-to-resurrection activity of everyone. Even those people responsible for helping others to learn continue to be learners themselves.

Their Description
Learners of the future will be physically larger than past generations, with more variation in their sizes. Each generation will be more

sophisticated than any previous generation. The people of each new generation will know more about the world into which they are born than will anyone older than they. They will feel that there must be a better way to conduct human affairs than any discovered so far, and will be dedicated to lifelong learning in a search for that way. Virtually everyone will be engaged in trying to help learners who are younger than himself or herself. Some will learn in ways of which we cannot now conceive. More of them will be considered "normal," because ways of helping those now considered atypical will have been discovered and put to use. All will be starting formal learning activities at earlier ages than have been considered proper according to past "readiness" concepts.

Their Involvement
Future learners will be involved in making decisions about their own learning. Irvine (1972) provided a cogent rationale in his specifications for an educational system of the future:

> The system should progressively involve the learner in making decisions about his educational program so that ultimately the learner controls his own learning. *As learning becomes a life-long process, the learner must have, in addition to learning skills, the ability to plan and decide on his own learning needs. An educational system which provides for decisions to be made for the learner without involving him in the decision-making process is likely to produce docile, indecisve individuals. The system of the future must help the individual learn to make decisions; the most obvious starting point is in his educational program* [p. 363].

Recycling
In the decade of the 1970s it became apparent that people must recognize the limits of the resources available to humankind, must learn to conserve them, and must learn to live in symbiosis with other living creatures. Recycling changed from a "do-gooder" vogue to necessity. Attention was directed to conscious career recycling of human beings. Changes of occupation have occurred since the beginning of recorded history, but changes made in an earlier day usually were made because of preference. Now changes of occupation often are made because of necessity. Just as the automobile industry put most of the blacksmiths, carriage makers, and buggy-whip manufacturers out of business and the linotype and computer put many typesetters out of business, each new machine or process puts an end to or drastically reduces the number of persons employed in certain occupations. However, with each new machine or process, new occupations are developed and it becomes necessary to recycle human resources. Most of the workers of the future will

engage in occupations not yet known. As an individual's occupation is phased out, he or she must be prepared for another, and this will become a major purpose of the educational system (*not* just the school) of the future.

Many learners of the future will be engaged in helping others to learn.

LEARNER'S HELPERS

Substitution of the term "learners' helpers" for the terms teachers, instructors, and professors is deliberate and is made for several reasons. First, one person does not teach another, one only helps the other to learn. Second, the terms in current use at least imply that the positions they describe all exist in formal agencies of education, as if those were the only places in which learners learn, and that is untrue. Third, the terms in current use do not recognize parents, siblings, peers, and others from whom one learns much of whatever one learns. Fourth, no one knows what professional learners' helpers of the future may be called, even though the nature of what they will *do* is known, in general. Any planning for education in the future must include determining the numbers and types of helpers required, organizing their efforts, and assisting them in acquiring the skills they will need.

Numbers

The numbers of learners' helpers required by the educational system of the future will be greater than ever before. Those who work directly with groups of learners will work with many groups smaller than the 30 or so pupils per teacher that was standard in schools of the past. There will be many more situations in which the helper works with one or a few learners. There will be many more individuals in roles supporting those of the principal helpers who will be in direct contact with learners. Individuals in most of the thousands of occupations that will exist will be expected to help learners learn about their occupations.

Types

The central professional figure among the learners' helpers of the future will have a role comparable to that of the producer-director of a drama; he or she will get agreement on the play, be responsible for designating necessary props and arranging the setting, do the casting, help individuals to interpret their roles, coordinate, suggest actions, and, in general, make the production possible. A support team, to use Loughary's (1966) term, will consist of: "(1) content research specialists, (2) media specialists, (3) systems specialists, and (4) engineers [p. 216]." These individuals would be comparable to the electricians, prop people, wardrobe, and make-up people required for a dramatic production. At present, they would be considered paraprofessionals in education; in the system of the future they may be among the professionals. Secretaries, clerks, and technicians will be needed and they would be comparable to the stagehands who are necessary to production of a play.

Organization

The *producer-director* of learning will: (1) get agreement on common goals, (2) help each learner determine individual objectives that he expects will get him to those goals, (3) determine the props needed, (4) coordinate and direct activities of all concerned, and (5) help each individual ascertain how well he is performing in terms of his individualized objectives.

The *content research specialist* will identify and synthesize subject matter relevant to the learners' objectives, helping them utilize a computerized information-retrieval system so sophisticated and so sensitive that it would be breathtakingly awesome to us if it were suddenly available now. He or she will analyze staggering amounts of materials in terms of content and suitability to specified learning criteria.

The *media specialist* will determine the most effective modes of presentation and then assemble learning materials, given the learners' goals and objectives, using a media laboratory and production shop. Staff specialists will include artists, photographers, audio programers, material programers, and draftspeople.

The *systems specialist* will put various resources together and design control procedures to enable the producer-director to exercise and maintain maximum surveillance and control over the learners' activities, approximating individualized learning as closely as possible. As Loughary (1966) noted, with man-machine systems for education the potential for chaos—the failure of anyone to learn anything—increases sharply, and it is the systems specialist who must prevent this from happening. She or he must anticipate problems and possible consequences of actions.

The *engineer* will understand learning, the machines that can be used to help learners, and the ways in which those machines can be used. He or she will determine which of essential information-retrieval systems is best for each of the types of information to be stored.

Skills Needed

Most writers about education in the future speak little, if at all, about the skills needed by the people who will be responsible for helping learners to learn. Loughary (1966) did say that as more machines are used to help learners the emphasis of the professionals will turn to decision-making and planning. Toffler (1970) provided a brief discussion of three crucial areas in which learners themselves will need new skills, namely: learning, relating, and choosing. The present writers described, in Chapter 17, some rules of learning and listed some questions to which learners' helpers should be able to help learners find answers, implying some skills. It would seem that helpers should themselves possess the skills that they expect to help others acquire; thus, we will try to subsume what the helper of the future needs to be able to do under the areas of learning, relating, and valuing.

LEARNING. "Facts" will grow increasingly perishable, and the individual must know ways to manipulate data and to cope with what Michael (1968) and others have called "information overload." In behavioral terms, the individual demonstrates learning skill when she or he:

— ascertains areas of uncertainty that are of interest to him or her.
— follows the "rules of play" to reduce uncertainty.
— classifies and reclassifies information.
— evaluates the veracity of information.
— determines readiness for new explorations.
— changes categories for classifying information as necessary.
— moves from the concrete to the abstract and back again.
— looks at problems from various directions.
— locates sources of useful information.
— locates tools that aid in learning.
— uses learning tools.

RELATING. Transience of individuals from job to job, from home to home, from group to group, from neighborhood to neighborhood, or from community to community poses real problems in making and maintaining rewarding human relationships. The difficulty was highlighted by Toffler (1970), but he made no suggestions as to what behaviors are involved or what skills can overcome the problems. Relating skills are demonstrated when an individual:

— seeks or arranges situations in which he or she meets new people.
— actively solicits information from others regarding their interests.
— listens to the concerns of others.
— puts oneself in the shoes of others.
— puts trust in others.
— shows compassion for others.
— exhibits growth.
— tolerates ambiguity.
— acknowledges errors.
— shows patience.

VALUING. As stated earlier, a value is the result of choosing among alternatives, cherishing that choice above others that might have been made, openly affirming the choice, and acting on it, repeatedly, until it becomes part of one's life style. Skill in valuing may be evidenced by the following behaviors:

— choosing among alternatives.
— affirming reasons for choices.
— exhibiting the effects of standards in one's behavior.

Simon, Howe, and Kirschenbaum (1972) listed 79 strategies that an instructor could use to help others clarify their values. Learners' helpers of the future will need to be adept at using all strategies available.

THE LEARNING PROCESS
In 1965 Hutchins tried to answer the questions of how to educate for an undecipherable future and how to prepare individuals for a world in which work has lost the significance that it once had. Educational leaders must grapple with those problems, and to do so they need to do imaginative thinking about the future purposes of learning, information overload and what can be done about it, biological effects on learning, the content to be learned, and the modes and means of learning that will be used.

Purposes
That the purpose of learning, for children and youth, is to develop the desire for lifelong learning and the capability to do that learning was affirmed by Hutchins (1965). Clark and Sloan (1962) expressed their conviction that learning, especially that which takes place outside the formal agencies, is an essential force for national well being, and perhaps for national survival. Irvine (1972, pp. 362–364) listed 15 specifications for an educational system of the future, and among those were five having to do directly with the purposes for learning, as follows:

BREADTH OF VIEW. "The system must develop broadly educated specialists" because the size of population and the complexity of the world, the speed of communication, and intricate organizational patterns demand such specialists, according to Irvine. Hutchins was espousing that view in 1965. In 1962 Clark was asking:

> *Can the educational enterprise develop the capability to educate broadly as the curriculum turns toward technical thought and men train for specialized occupations? . . . The efforts to bring liberal education to the expert constitute a social response to*

the strain, an attempt to avoid a barbarism of men acute in techni-
cal judgment but myopic in social affairs, politics, and cultural
understanding. The future of the expert society challenges edu-
cation to close a gap that in the natural course of affairs will
ever widen [pp. 290–291].

In 1959 Snow was voicing a world need for:

trained scientists and engineers adaptable enough to devote
themselves to a foreign country's industrialization for at least
ten years out of their lives. . . . These men, whom we don't yet
possess, need to be trained not only in scientific but in human
terms. They could not do their job if they did not shrug off every
trace of paternalism [p. 45].

HUMAN RELATIONS. According to Irvine, *"The system must empha-*
size human relations," because of population mobility, transportation advances, and communications developments making all of the
peoples of a nation and all of the nations of the world neighbors
in a very literal sense. It is notable that the arguments of Hutchins,
Clark, and Snow on behalf of a broad education all contained strong
emphasis on the need for improved human relations.

LIFE'S MEANING. Irvine's specification was, *"The system must pro-*
vide the means by which individuals can determine overriding pur-
poses in their lives." The very stimuli that one admits to one's consciousness are filtered through a perceptual screen comprised of
one's values, and thus whatever one does depends indirectly or
directly on those values. Toffler very properly and very sharply criticized educators for having gone through a period in which they
backed off from indoctrinating the young with the values of their
elders and taught only facts, "letting the student make up his own
mind." The present writers agree with Toffler that new conditions
demand new values, and that does not mean that society can tolerate
citizens having *no* values. Any society must, for survival, have some
standards that give meaning to the lives of its citizens. What is
needed is a means of helping individuals find, define, and explicate
their values, with each person testing his or her values against those
of other persons in the society and each society testing its values
against those of other societies.

REDEFINING WORK AND PLAY. Irvine (1972) said it all:

The system must help individuals break down the dichotomy between work and play. *In order to accomplish his life purposes,*
the educated person of the future will have to look at work and
play as part of a total plan: Work will be play in the sense that
it is enjoyable and challenging; play will be work in the sense
that it is meaningful rather than merely time consuming [p. 363].

RELEASING POTENTIAL. Even human resources are not unlimited, and it is essential to conserve those as well as material resources. Irvine pointed out that society as well as the individual loses whenever there is discrimination, and that getting rid of discrimination is one of the major ways of assuring that human resources are conserved and used to best advantage. His specification was, *"The system must help each individual, regardless of characteristics and previous condition, to release the potential he possesses* [p. 364]."

HANDLING INFORMATION OVERLOAD. The proliferation of literature in every field and the continuing addition of new fields of knowledge make it imperative that the learning process give each learner some capability for handling information overload. Michael (1968) said, "We must educate so people can cope efficiently, imaginatively, and perceptively with information overload [p. 108]." There are basically two ways of doing this. Learners can learn *principles,* the essence of concepts, if those who help them learn recognize that, as Halle (1963) said, "new knowledge generally takes the place of old, rather than adding to the sum [p. 107]." As the same author explained," . . . knowledge tends to shake down and become compact, taking up no more room than it had before [p. 107]." Second, learners can learn that they need not store huge quantities of data in their memory "banks" because electronic data-storage-and-retrieval systems are becoming ever-more sophisticated. The learner needs to understand the nature of those systems, their locations, and how he or she can go about retrieving stored information. One needs thorough acquaintance with the many indexes of those systems and how they may be used.

Biological Effects
Since the 1962 award of the Nobel prize to Drs. Watson and Crick for their description of the DNA molecule, genetic advances have, in Toffler's words, "come tripping over one another at a rapid pace." Scientific discoveries seem to be at hand that will allow at least three types of developments that have great significance for the learning process, namely: (1) alleviation of learning handicaps, (2) increase of intelligence, and (3) genetic manipulation.

ALLEVIATION OF HANDICAPS. The field of medicine probably will develop means for alleviating many forms of what is now known as mental retardation. Almost certainly there will be developments in the delay of the aging process and in offsetting the handicaps of senility.

INCREASING INTELLIGENCE. Scientists are learning how the various organs of the human body develop and sooner or later they no doubt will experiment with ways of modifying those organs; thus, it is not too farfetched to believe that it may be possible to increase the size of the brain. For almost a decade scientists have been devising ways of making so-called "normal" individuals smarter, and the time when one does or does not take one's "smart pill" each morning is almost here, making a tired old joke a sharp reality. As Drury (1966) noted, "If we have the chemistry to make topflight brains, we'll need a topflight educational system to train them."

GENETIC MANIPULATION. The "Brave New World" is almost upon us. Toffler said "new genetic knowledge will permit us to tinker with human heredity and manipulate the genes to create altogether new versions of man [p. 176]." The ethical, moral, political, and educational questions raised by this biological possibility are staggering. Toffler suggested that a new birth technology, using implanted embryos, is possible that may shatter traditional notions of sexuality, motherhood, love, child-rearing, and learning. Who will decide what should be done, what will be done, and who will do it? Choice will be critical, and this adds an argument for the necessity of having learners and learners' helpers who are capable of making choices.

Content
The earlier section of this chapter on Purposes implied, to some extent, the content of what is to be learned. Toffler suggested the skills that learners of the future should have, and the present writers proposed that learners' helpers should have those same skills. Toffler also proposed that educational bets should be hedged by having a range of subject matter that would deal not only with the known but also with the unknown, the unexpected, the possible.

Three of Irvine's (1972) specifications dealt with content, to wit:

RESOURCE USE. "The system must accommodate itself to changes in the natural resources available to man." The learner needs to learn how to adapt, to find new sources of energy and raw materials, to utilize resources in new ways.

KNOWLEDGE ORGANIZATION. "The system must be capable of coping with increased amounts of information." The possibility of information overload and some ways of avoiding it were discussed earlier. Part of the content of the futurist's learning must involve how to organize his or her own knowledge rather than to follow a rigid organization which was useful, perhaps, to an earlier generation but which made no allowance for creative thinking.

LEARNING SKILLS. "The system must emphasize the development of learning skills." This matter was discussed earlier, under the heading of skills needed by learners' helpers.

Modes of Learning
An individual learns through his or her own action, through interaction with other persons or machines, or through reaction to some other person's ideas or actions.

ACTION. It seems possible that an individual could, through his or her own actions of discovery, learn what others have learned in almost every field. For example, a person with interest in chemistry could be placed in a laboratory with necessary apparatus and supplies and it is conceivable that, over a sufficient period of time, she or he might learn much of what others have learned about chemistry. Desirable as this mode might be, the means of learning would be so inefficient that it could not be tolerated in educational systems of the present, and certainly not in those of the future. Thus, the mode of most learning in the future probably will be a combination of interaction and reaction.

INTERACTION. There can be little question that a machine can store and retrieve information more efficiently than can the human brain. A memory that was fed and retained everything, with no automatic "forgetter" to dispose of the irrelevant, could soon become so cluttered that it would lose its capacity to separate the germane from the useless.

In the splendid *Saturday Review* (1966) special issue on "The New Computerized Age," such writers as Bushnell, Sarnoff, and Suppes made eloquent cases for computer-assisted instruction at three levels of interaction between learner and computer program: drill-and-practice systems, tutorial systems, and dialogue systems. Most of the writers in this issue, as well as many who have since written on the subject, stressed the limitations of what computers can do, and the fact that they cannot totally replace human beings with whom learners interact. Ideally, computer systems will be tailored to the individual needs of learners, but human beings are needed both to do the tailoring and to provide those interactions that no machines can provide.

Interaction with other learners also is essential to the interaction learning mode, and it may range from a general bull or rap session through directed discussion and role play to esoteric and exotic planned interactions such as computer-mediated seminars and the games, instructional games, and instructional simulation games described by Thiagarajan (1974).

REACTION. The learner of the future will learn also through reaction to the ideas of other persons, presented either in person, in various programed or nonprogramed forms, in one medium or in multimedia, by teaching machines, or through the proliferating electronic media. Reactions may range from informal to a formal critique and may or may not involve instructional material (which may or may not be programed), instructional simulation, and simulation games. The latter three also were defined, described, and differentiated by Thiagarajan (1974).

Means of Learning
Within the three modes of learning, attention in the education of the future will be focused on the means by which learners learn. Irvine

(1972) specified that *"The system must be concerned with economy of learning."* Greater resourcefulness will be needed to integrate human and technological resources in the "man-machine systems" described by Loughary (1966), utilizing human resources for those things they do best and those things machines cannot do.

Many of the means of learning were, necessarily, mentioned under Modes. Both mode and means should be adapted to the learner and to the rate at which his abilities indicate as appropriate for him. This customizing can only be done by human helpers who can empathize, appraise, synthesize, assert, and reinforce.

PLACES FOR LEARNING

In the education of the future, the industrial model of a central "plant" (school) in which raw materials are processed by workers will be passé. All of the informal and nonformal agencies of education will be recognized as having important parts to play, and the formal agencies' roles in providing places for learning will be greatly diminished, while the role of the home will be greater.

As noted by Taylor (1971), some of the experimental colleges have for years assumed that the world is their campus and that a particular college is only a central learning place with which the learner can identify and where she or he can make her or his temporary intellectual home. Even formal classes will move more and more into the community and the larger world where learners can participate in the "real" world while they learn from it.

Taylor also called attention to the fact that:

A good many students are staying out of college for a year or two, working at a job, living in a commune, travelling and studying on their own, going to concerts, the theater, art galleries, museums, tutoring children, working in VISTA, and are finding that a rangier attitude to their own education is a first step toward improving its quality [p. 93].

It is to be expected that more and more learners will make that discovery, and may seek to learn from various persons in the community in addition to faculty members of formal agencies. Toffler said that the proposal of Harold Howe II—for bringing stores, beauty parlors, and printing shops into the schools, giving them free space in return for free lessons by the adults who run them—could be given more "bite" by including also architects, computer services, broadcasting stations, advertising agencies, and perhaps even medical laboratories.

The need for extending the places of learning was encapsulated by Irvine (1972) in these specifications:

The system must capitalize on the many other educational forces which exist in society [p. 362].

> *The system must be able to bring learners in contact with a wide variety of realistic learning experiences [p. 363].*

The present already calls for less reliance on the formal places of learning called schools and colleges; the future will demand it.

ORGANIZATION FOR LEARNING

The ways in which geographical boundaries, populations, learners, time, learning experiences and materials, and staff are organized all affect learning, and all will undergo radical changes for education in the future. The organization of staff and learning experiences have been discussed in earlier sections of this chapter.

Geography and Population

Sociologists have for years been calling attention to sharp decreases in the population of rural areas. More recently, there have been shifts from inner-city areas to fringe and suburban areas. "Strip cities," some of them extending for hundreds of miles, are clearly identifiable, as anyone who has done extensive night flying across this country in recent years is aware.

Irvine called attention to a trend toward metropolitan governmental systems, and said that educational systems will need to reflect this trend. He also noted that even state boundaries are being all but erased in strip city and other metropolitan areas. He specified that, for education in the future, *"The system must accomodate itself to new and different population patterns [p. 362]."*

Boundaries of educational districts of the future almost inevitably must be more flexible, more readily changed, than are boundaries of present school or community college districts.

Learners

Age groupings of learners, such as are now prevalent in schools and colleges, will all but disappear; the mature and the young who have similar interests will learn together and from each other. Numbers of learners in various groups will range from two to several hundreds. There will be much more individualized learning, even though learners may, in some instances, be in close physical proximity. Learners will have more to say about the organizational patterns in which they organize for learning activities.

Time

Learning activities of the future will be less rigidly structured than most now are. They will not be confined to the present "school hours" of 9:00 A.M. to 3:00 P.M., nor to Monday through Friday, nor to September to June. The portion of a learner's day that is devoted to purposeful learning will increase, along with the portion of his or her lifetime so devoted.

In 1966 McGill, the unheralded and late lamented prophet and friend of education, was saying that education should serve the entire community—"not just the younger half of it. This will mean a six-day, 18-hour-a-day school, with at least two teaching staffs that include a necessary variety of full-time and part time specialists."

Taylor (1971) expressed the view that higher education, the most reactionary of the many agencies of formal education, may even change the time organization on which credits are based. The number of hours to be spent in learning activities may be decided by the learners and their helpers, and the amount of credit may be related to the amount of work the learner does and the time it takes her or him to do it!

Time organization for computer-assisted instruction might be the most flexible of all. Suppes (1966) suggested that a young child might spend as little as 15 minutes per day at a console, a secondary school student might have one 30-minute session in the morning and another in the afternoon each day; an adult might take an entire course in this fashion, perhaps choosing his or her own time blocks for doing so.

EDUCATIONAL LEADERSHIP

In the education of the future, the schools will be integrated with all of the other educational agencies of the community, and all will be tied together in an organizational structure which is *not* bureaucratic in nature. The structure will be the ad hoc or fluid type described by Bennis and Slater, Berkley, Toffler, and others. The chief educational leader of a community will have a power base in the total community, rather than in the schools, and will be responsible for coordinating the efforts of the various directors, supervisors, presidents, superintendents, and other heads of the individual agencies of education. She or he may be called the director of education and, along with the director of transportation, the director of streets and Roads, the chief of police, and others of like title, will report to and be directed by a council of the future.

Toffler conceived and described councils of the future as comprised of men and women "devoted to probing the future in the interests of the present." He warned that specialists are vitally needed in the councils, but that the councils will not succeed if they are captured by *any* unrepresentative elite, including educators.

It was Macy (1966), speaking of computer use in government, who reminded that much of what has, in the present, been dignified as "decision-making" actually is clerical in nature, requiring the identification of facts and the selection of one of possible alternative and predetermined actions based on those facts; this computers are able to do better than humans. Using computers for such purposes can free educational leaders, at all levels, for the risk-taking of forward-looking innovation, for being *shapers* of the future.

McGill (1966) opined that a major national task is that of discovering and developing leaders for the job of reconstructing the educational system to fulfill new purposes. Irvine said that "shaping the future . . . may be the most important role for leaders of the *educational* enterprise during the balance of this century [p. 364]." Bennis (1970) described the task as "inventing relevant futures."

FINANCE

As this book was being written, there was widespread discussion and debate throughout the nation about the best means of financing the schools. A number of court cases related to the matter were pending. Bills were before the legislatures of a number of states proposing to change tax laws to make the financing of schools more equitable. Abert (1974) had just called attention to the fact that the United States spends a larger proportion of its GNP on educational services than does any other industrialized nation, and that those expenditures have grown faster than the GNP for 20 years—*and he was talking only about expenditures for schools!* Seven other educators responded to Abert's suggested strategies for reversing the trend, and not one of the eight mentioned the vast array of educational agencies now functioning outside the schools, and the portion of the GNP that goes to these!

If *school* financing is a problem at present, *educational* financing in the future will surely demand the best thinking of the best minds in the country. Questions to be answered include: (1) Shall schools continue to be the only educational agencies which have universal public financial support? (2) Shall we continue to have a patchwork system of finance in which each agency competes with others for scarce support dollars? (3) Does the conservation of human resources require making funds for education available to those persons who cannot supply their own (as now is done on a *very* limited basis with some college and graduate students)? (4) Should each tax-paying individual have a right to deduct educational expenses for himself and family (and if so, for what type of education) before paying taxes for other purposes? (5) Should all legitimate (and how is legitimacy determined) agencies of education be federated and their present sources of income pooled? (6) Should all revenues for educational purposes be collected nationally and vouchers issued to those citizens who wish to learn something of their choice? (7) Should the total tax structure be rebuilt? (8) Should all formal and nonformal learning be on a straight tuition basis, with no dependence on tax monies? If so, where would indigent but worthy "human resources" get the tuition they lack?

As with any conflict, the conflict of agencies seeking educational financing must be settled by one of three means: (1) domination (perpetual competition to see which can muster the most political clout), (2) compromise (perpetual competition in which each party gives up something now in order to get something now, but vows to get at a later time what it gave up today), or (3) integration (cooperation in finding a cooperative and superordinate goal that all parties recognize as "better" than any one of them now has). Which will it be?

SUMMARY

Educational leaders need to "organize their ignorance" and make deliberate innovations for the future, using as criteria the questions of how much innovation, how far in the future, and what control can be exercised over the innovations. The young need to be included so they can ask the questions that would never occur to their elders, and all concerned need to recognize that they face triple risk: the risk of being overtaken by the innovations of others, the risk of failure, and the risk of success.

Learners of the future can be identified and described, and they must be involved in controlling their own learning. It is a foregone conclusion that most, if not all, will have to be "recycled" one or more times in terms of learning a new occupation. Teams of people will help learners, and more persons will be involved in helping others to learn than has ever been the case anywhere in recorded history. Team members will be organized to take advantage of their specialties, and all will need some new skills in addition to those now possessed by effective teachers. Particular skills will be needed in the areas of learning, relating, and valuing.

The purposes of the learning process will be changed and explicated, emphasizing a broad view, human relations, life's meaning, redefining work and play, releasing individual potential, and handling information overload. Biological effects will be used to alleviate learning handicaps, to increase intelligence, and for genetic manipulation. Content of the learning program will emphasize resource use, knowledge organization, and learning how to learn. Modes of learning will include the learners' own actions, their interaction with both machines and human beings, and their reactions to the ideas of others presented in many forms and in multimedia. The means of learning will include computer-assisted drill-and-practice, tutorial systems, and dialogue systems; person-assisted lectures, discussions, and seminars; computer-mediated seminars; games, instructional games, instructional simulation games, programed and nonprogramed instructional material, instructional simulation, and simulation games; and perhaps means not yet conceived will also be used.

The place for learning in the future will be any place in the world; all existing and many new agencies will be involved. Boundaries of future educational districts will be far more flexible than present school district boundaries and will conform to population distribution and social interests rather than geographic lines per se.

Age-level groupings of learners will be much less common than now, the patterns of time organization will be more flexible, and the time for learning will not be certain hours, certain days, certain weeks, or certain years.

Two major national tasks are: (1) finding and preparing educational leaders to structure the educational system that can adequately meet the challenges of the future and (2) determining the financial structure of an educational system that will conserve and make the best possible use of human resources.

Schools are facing unprecedented challenges, and some critics are saying "school is dead." In the opinion of the present writers, schools are not dead, but they *are* moribund. If they are to recover and regain their health, they must respond to the challenges facing them. Some of the more serious are detailed in Chapter 19.

SOME SUGGESTED RESOURCES

C. A. Anderson, Education in the national interest. In D. Gibson (Ed.), *Social foundations of education.* New York: Free Press, 1967. Pp. 129–161.

T. Brameld, Imperatives for a future-centered education. In *The climactic decades– Mandate to education.* New York: Praeger, 1970.

C. S. Brembeck, and T. Thompson, *New strategies for educational development: The cross-cultural search for non-formal alternatives.* Lexington, Mass.: Lexington Books, 1973.

J. Holt, Beyond schooling. In *Freedom and beyond.* New York: Dutton, 1972.

J. Lear, Where is society going: The search for landmarks. *Saturday Review Science,* 1972, **55**(16), 34–39.

G. B. Leonard, No school? Pp. 101–117. Also, The future how? Pp. 213–228 In *Education and ecstasy.* New York: Dell, 1968.

W. A. McClelland, *The process of effecting change.* Alexandria, Va.: Human Resources Research Office, George Washington University, 1968. Done under contract to the Department of the Army (DA 44-188-ARO-2).

E. Reimer, *School is dead.* Garden City, N.Y.: Doubleday, 1971.

K. A. Ringbakk, Why planning fails. Reprint from *European Business,* date unknown.

L. J. Rubin (Ed.), Leadership and educational reform: Potence and impotence. In *Frontiers in school leadership.* Skokie, Ill.: Rand McNally, 1970. Pp. 103–116.

H. G. Shane, *The educational significance of the future.* Bloomington, Ind.: Phi Delta Kappan, 1973.

H. Taylor, *How to change colleges: Notes on radical reform.* New York: Holt, Rinehart & Winston, 1971.

H. A. Thelen, Plan: Predicament and promise, pp. 4–15, and Suppositions: Four models for education, pp. 74–87. In *Education and the human quest.* New York: Harper & Row, 1960.

A. Toffler, Education in the future tense. Ch. 18 in *Future Shock.* New York: Random House, 1970. Pp. 353–378.

CHAPTER 19

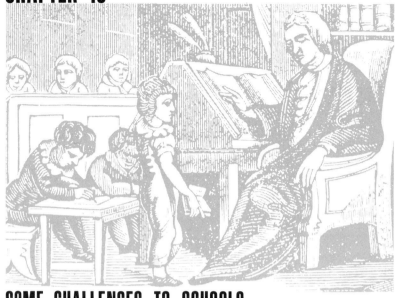

SOME CHALLENGES TO SCHOOLS

Everyone learns to live outside school. We learn to speak,
to think, to love, to feel, to play, to curse, to politick, and to work
without interference from a teacher. Even children who
are under a teacher's care day and night are no exception
to the rule. Orphans, idiots, and schoolteachers' sons learn
most of what they learn outside the "educational" process
planned for them.

—Illich

Increasing numbers of persons are asking whether schools are necessary to purposeful learning. Every educational leader, whether he or she proposes to work in schools or not, must consider the challenges being presented to the schools and decide for himself or herself whether the schools should continue to exist. This chapter will delineate a number of the current challenges to schools, some of them related to delimiting that portion of educating, if any, that schools can best do; some related to schools and society; a number related to schools and learners; and some related to schools' use or abuse of technology. The term "schools," as used in this chapter, refers to publicly financed schools, nursery through professional. However, some of the challenges apply as well to private or parochial schools as to public schools.

SCHOOLING AND EDUCATING
Among the challenges relating to schooling and educating are questions of what the schools can do about: (1) those who are indifferent

or incapable of learning, (2) the unending uncertainty experienced by every human being capable of thought, (3) arguments of the "deschoolers," (4) justifying the continued existence of schools, (5) improving the learning process, and (6) the deleterious effects of compulsory school attendance.

Indifference and Disability
As long as attendance is mandatory for certain age groups of learners, schools will have to cope with a variety of learner difficulties. Among these are: (1) learner indifference, (2) culturally induced handicaps, and (3) learner brain damage due to protein malnutrition during the first few years of life.

As Ebel (1972) pointed out, schools must develop the means to accommodate and to resolve problems related to unwilling learners. The present authors recognize that the sources of learner indifference are quite varied, with some being based in the nonschool life of the learner, some having their origins in nonrelevant instructional content, and some associated with a learner's continuing interactions with uninspired, disinterested teachers. Unless the problem is to be lifelong, the schools are challenged to overcome the indifference of some learners, regardless of how it was induced.

It is obvious that when a child is reared in a cultural setting which provides little positive evidence of the value of schooling, there will be few chances for the child to view schooling as desirable. The literature fairly abounds with research evidence which confirms the negative impact of cultural paucity on the school performance of learners.

As for nutritionally induced brain damage, both the U.S. Department of Agriculture and the United Nations' World Health Organization in recent years have been inquiring into the effects of early protein malnutrition on the intellectual development of young children. The findings have uniformly revealed that apparent irreversible brain damage results when there is severe protein deficiency in a child's diet during the first few years of life, and that by age six the intellectual performances of the nutritionally deprived children were significantly lower than for those children who started life with appropriate diets.

Thus, the schools are faced with the challenge of overcoming indifference to learning and learning disability which divert attention, time, and ever-diminishing economic and material resources from the majority of learners who manifest unending uncertainty.

Unending Uncertainty
The concept that information consists of reducing uncertainty for a message receiver has been mentioned several times in this book. It is our belief that every human being capable of thought has an insatiable curiosity, numerous continuua of uncertainty, that impel

him or her to try to determine relationships and causes for everything that he or she can observe or experience. Pfeiffer (1962) said, "We are, above all, learners. We cannot help learning, and certain studies of our unique capacity for neurosis indicate that we may suffer from not learning [p. 197]."

Exploration results from uncertainty. Is there something better "out there"? What lies just beyond the known? The "rules of play" followed by the young of various animal species and observed and reported by Morris (1967) indicate that humans are not alone in their proclivity for exploration. The present writers have defined education as "learning for a purpose," and the learner's own purpose often is nothing more than trying to reduce his or her immanent uncertainty. For most persons, as one uncertainty is reduced—as uncertainty becomes certainty, or fact—another is introduced. When one finds a new sensation, one wonders what others one has not yet experienced. When Roger Bannister ran the first four-minute mile, he and others immediately wondered how much faster a human being would be capable of running. When we reached the moon, we immediately wondered to what other planets we might go.

Schools have, traditionally, chosen certain purposes for which they have said that all of the children sent to them must learn, thus implying that society knows, better than the individual himself, which of his uncertainties he should explore. Over a period of years, the individual often is conditioned to subordinate or forget his or her own interests. Illich (1971) said, "By making men abdicate the responsibility for their own growth, school leads many to a kind of spiritual suicide [p. 60]."

One of the greatest challenges to the schools is to determine how the not-unwilling learner's own unending uncertainty may be used to motivate him to learn both what he wants to know and what society says that he must know. Otherwise, de-schooling arguments will, increasingly, be seen as valid.

De-schooling Arguments
Arguments that school is dead and that society should be de-schooled have been provided by Reimer (1971) and Illich (1971), with milder arguments being offered by Holt (1972), Farson (1974), and others. It does no good for educational leaders to ignore them, denigrate them, or turn away in embarrassment. The arguments must be faced and either accepted or refuted. Among those arguments are the following, all of which present challenges to schools.

FUNCTIONS. The functions of custodial care, indoctrination, and selection of social roles need to be separated from the proper function of education, namely learning for the purposes that the individual finds important to him or her and to society.

DISCRIMINATION. Schools discriminate in at least three significant ways: they appropriate resources available for education which might be better utilized by other educational agencies, at least in part; they use resources for providing learning opportunities over which learners have no control; and they use the resources available to them in educating children, adolescents, and youth to the almost total exclusion of infants, adults, and the old.

INEQUITY. Schools polarize a society, separating the advantaged from the disadvantaged. Instead of equalizing learning opportunities, schools monopolize their distribution. Even compensatory education programs do little or nothing to give the poor child learning opportunities which the middleclass takes for granted, such as books and conversation in the home, vacation travel, and feelings of self-worth. Equal schooling not only is unfeasible but is economically impossible and to attempt it is, according to Illich (1971), "intellectually emasculating, socially polarizing, and destructive of the credibility of the political system which promotes it [p. 10]."

FALSE CLAIMS. Schools claim, or their existence at least allows an observer to infer, that most learning is the result of teaching. But most learning happens casually, most of the agencies through which one learns are not schools, and most of the uncertainty reducing that most people have experienced has occurred outside of schools. Children learn to speak, to think, to respond, to feel, to stand-walk-run, to play, to wash-dress-groom, to politic, to work, and to do a host of other things with no specific teacher. Those adults who continue to learn often do so without benefit of teachers.

FUND MONOPOLY. Schools preempt most educational funds. Even though there are more effective ways of learning some skills and certain subject matter than by going to school, such as by means of programed materials or computer-assisted dialogue, those means are now a privilege of the relatively few learners who are: (1) financially able to bypass the schools, (2) sent to military service or other government schools, or (3) given on-the-job training in some of the big industries.

INCONSIDERATENESS. Schools tend to ignore the interests and problems of learners. Creative, exploratory learning should make it possible for peers—peers in terms of common puzzlement, regardless of age or status—to interact in solving problems chosen and defined by their own uncertainties. Such learning is rarely possible in most schools, never in some.

INSUFFICIENT RESOURCES. Even with their preemption and monopolization of funds available for education, schools do not provide access for everyone to the four types of "networks" or "webs" of resources needed for real learning, namely: things, models, peers, and elders. Reimer (1971) said that the things of special educational value are of two kinds: "those which embody symbols and those which translate, transmit, or receive information coded in symbols [p. 115]."

The greatest challenge posed by the de-schoolers lies in making a choice between using the technology now available to develop independence and learning and using it to further bureaucracy and teaching. Reimer (1971) demanded that the traditional model of the school be used in reverse order:

> First attention must be given to the availability of information in the form of records, the instruments that produce and interpret these records, and other objects in which information is stored. Second priority must be given to the availability of skill models, people who can demonstrate the skill to be acquired. Third priority must go to the availability of real peers, fellow learners with whom learning can be actually shared. Fourth and last priority must go to the provision of educators who by virtue of experience can facilitate the use of the more essential learning resources [p. 129].

Those educational leaders who believe that schools should remain a part of society are challenged to justify their continued existence.

Justifying Schools

Some persons who have not argued that society should be de-schooled have nonetheless offered evidence that schools are ineffective, thus putting schools and school employees on the defensive. One of the principal arguments of school defenders has been that schools are the only integrative institution in our society that, theoretically at least, has contact with all of the young. It has been argued that the schools are the agency through which the individual exercises his or her right to equal opportunity. Yet the massive Coleman Report (1966b) said that the schools and their resources appeared to have little influence on a child's academic or economic achievemen, but that his social-class background was very closely related to his performance in the classroom.

Cass (1974), soberly reflecting on whether schools make a difference, reported that the International Association for the Evaluation of Educational Achievement (IEA) study, undertaken to identify those *factors that determine students' success in the schools* of 22 countries, drew some conclusions that are bound to be disturbing to school personnel. The factors found to be most closely related to student achievement were all home-related: the father's occupation, the father's and mother's levels of education, and the number of books in the home. Even "the basis for future verbal ability, the most vital capacity for academic success in contemporary schools" was conceded to have been developed before the child ever entered school.

The more sanguine findings of the IEA study reported by Cass included that the principal variables accounting for differences in student achievement among national systems of schooling were: (1) the degree of student exposure to given areas of a subject, (2) teacher competence, and (3) the time devoted to a subject. Hardly startling conclusions, and those modest findings relate only to one national school system as compared to another, not to schools as compared with possible alternative means for learning!

Clearly, the people who are interested in preserving and perpetuating the schools had better get their heads out of the sand and, before it is too late, set about discovering what, if anything, it is that schools can do better or more efficiently than can any other agency of education.

One of the educators willing to state clearly how he thinks the continued existence of schools can be justified is Ebel (1972), who said:

> *Schools ought to be held accountable. One way or another, they surely will be held accountable. If they persist in trying to do too many things, things they were not designed and are not equipped to do well, things that in some cases can not be done at all, they will show up badly when called to account. But there is one very important thing they were designed and are equipped to do well, and that many schools have done very well in the past. That is to cultivate cognitive competence, to foster the learning of useful knowledge. If they keep this as their primary aim, and do not allow unwilling learners to sabotage the learning process, they are likely to get an excellent accounting of their effectiveness and worth [p. 7].*

If one accepts Ebel's thesis, then the continued existence of the schools perhaps can be justified. Whether compulsory attendance can be justified is another matter.

Compulsory Attendance

At the time of this writing, every state of the United States except Mississippi has a statute on the books requiring children of certain ages to attend school. Many of the other countries of the world have followed suit. The implication is that not only can the child be compelled to attend school, but she or he can be compelled to learn, and some of the accountability programs now in vogue seem to be based on that premise. One of the challenges to schools is to either determine a rational and defensible position on the matter of compulsory attendance or to get the laws repealed. The origins of the attendance movement and the present-day effect of the practice need to be examined.

ORIGINS. Compulsory school attendance appears to have been rooted in four separate and distinct ideas and developments. One was the invention of childhood, as a special phase of life, in Europe some 400 years ago (see Aries, 1962). The second was the Protestant work ethic, developed in this country, which contended that the devil would find work for idle hands. A third was the court ruling that public monies could be used for secondary schooling, and the fourth was the industrial revolution.

Until Europeans invented childhood, the child was treated no differently than other family members except in a few privileged families. She or he, along with others, worked either on the farm, at crafts in the home, or in the shop. Everything that the child learned was learned in the home or at work. There were no special activities for the young, no special toys, no period of coddling. What schooling there was might be taken advantage of by those who wished and could afford it, regardless of age, and often schools were peopled by adults as well as children from wealthy families. The idea of schools as places reserved to children could not exist until the concept of childhood was accepted.

The notion that the devil finds work for idle hands was recognized in the act of 1642 that required parents and masters to teach children and apprentices to read. It was believed that if one read the Bible, the catechism, and "the capital laws of the country," one's family and church could then make one a moral being. The act of 1647 ordered towns of 50 householders to provide for teaching children to read and write, and referred to "that old deluder Satan."

In 1832, the right to use tax monies for public schools was established in Massachusetts. However, it was not until 1872 that the question of whether that right applied to secondary schooling became a legal issue. In 1874, in the celebrated Kalamazoo case, the Michigan Supreme Court established the right of school districts to levy taxes for the support of secondary schools.

The introduction of power-driven machinery in the textile industries of England and Scotland took place between 1750 and 1800 and marked the beginning of the modern factory. With factories came the growth of cities, and soon in most industrialized countries children were being exploited as cheap labor. Of course, there were some persons with humanitarian concerns who objected to this, but there were also adults who aspired to the jobs held by children, and together they managed gradually to get child labor outlawed. The Knights of Labor union, which had its origins as a secret society in the garment industry where child-labor exploitation was prevalent, had gained between 600,000 and 700,000 members by 1886. Publicly, it and other labor organizations were taking the stance that children

should be in school in order to achieve the American dream of upward mobility through education. It can hardly be doubted that privately some members coveted the jobs held by the low-paid
children.

In any event, child labor laws were enacted, and rather than have
gangs of children with idle hands, particularly in the quantities found
in cities, it seemed desirable to have them in schools where they
would be "doing something constructive." The best way to get them
there was to require, by law, that they attend. The first compulsory
attendance law had been enacted in Massachusetts in 1852, and
by 1918 most states had similar laws. Until school attendance became compulsory, those children not suited by the schools had other
educational options.

EFFECT. The effect of compulsory school attendance was stated
harshly but accurately by Reimer (1971):

> *The school itself, as custodian of ever-larger numbers of people,*
> *for increasing proportions of their life span, for an ever-growing*
> *number of hours and interests, is well on the way to joining*
> *armies, prisons, and insane asylums as one of society's total in-*
> *stitutions [p. 37].*

A CHALLENGE. Do the people who work in schools want them to
become a total institution in the sense in which Reimer used the
term? What are the alternatives?

SCHOOLS AND LEARNERS
Some further challenges to schools of the future lie in the areas
of what is to be learned, how it is to be learned, who is to learn,
and where learning resources are to be found.

What is to be Learned
Possible content material to be learned in the future is certain to
be more extensive and more complex than ever before. People will
have more interests, and the personnel of schools must decide
whether to cater to all of those interests or whether to determine
what learners can learn better in schools than elsewhere and stick
with that. For example, it seems likely that learning to read can
best be done or can be improved in schools, but reading specialists
seem agreed that 10 to 14 percent of children have difficulty in mas-
tering the skill of reading. Needs for special help are greatest among
children of the lowest-income families, according to a study cited
by Quie (1973), and such help is needed by 68 percent of students
by the time they get to fourth grade. Obviously, disparities widen
with each year in school unless special help is given.

Mathematics, too, is an area in which the schools may be the best place for learning, but in this field the need for special help among those from low-income families is as high as 59.5 percent of fourth grade students.

Schools must get out of the box of trying to teach everything. Their staff people must determine what useful knowledge they can provide more readily than can any other agency of education. They must decide how they can utilize what is known about how children learn.

How Children Learn

Challenges in regard to how children learn are at least fivefold. First, teachers must be aware of and believe in the "self-fulfilling prophecy," the Pygmalion effect evidenced by the Rosenthal (1973) research. Second, ways must be found to avoid restrictive categories for students and to "desort" children who have already been harshly—and "finally"—categorized. Third, means of providing individualized learning opportunities for far more students in far more phases of their learning must be identified and put to use, assisting each to utilize his or her capabilities. Fourth, acceptance into a learning program that presupposes certain skills must be based on ability to demonstrate those skills rather than on some rigid process through which the skills are presumed to have been acquired. Fifth, the tryanny of testing must be brought to an end.

The slowness of educators in accepting research findings is understandable if one considers the shoddiness and shallowness of much of what is passed off in the literature as research. However, the research regarding learners performing according to the expectations held for them seems to be clear-cut, and the schools must find some way to get teachers to accept it.

The term "special education" should mean special in that it is tailored to the needs of individuals, and what is known about learning must be put to use to help every child learn. It must be recognized that no two children are identical in mental characteristics, in sensory abilities, in neuromuscular characteristics, in social and emotional manifestations, in ability to communicate, or in the presence or absence of "handicaps." No one should be sorted into a stigmatized "box" and left to wither there.

So-called "individualized" learning programs are presently of three types: learning paced to individuals, learning in which resources are varied for individuals, and learning in which the purposes are the learners' own. Most programs are of the first type, and they are better than the traditional lock-step, but not much better. All learners are expected to assimilate the same content, but at different paces. In the second type of program, one learner may use the printed page only, another may have audiovisual supplementary resources, and a third may interact with a computer, but in most programs of this type the content is similar if not identical for all learners, and the learners' own purposes are seldom if ever considered. The third type of program allows each child to be the architect of his or her own learning experiences, and is the only one that can properly be called individualized learning. We are *not* advocating that the learning experiences have no structure, because we agree with Skinner (1965) that "A Summerhill is therapeutic [but] not educational." Individualized learning can be accomplished, if at all, by having teachers who are willing to help the learner find his own answers to the questions listed under How Others Can Help in Chapter 17.

Acceptance into programs that presuppose certain skills should not be based upon years in school or presumed prerequisites, but upon demonstration of the skills. In other words, the graded system and prerequisites should give way to performance criteria. The learner should read or do mathematics or foreign language at the level at which he can perform, and there should be no artificial barriers to his learning as much as he is capable of during the time he is in school. Some may master reading in two years, some in four, and others may require eight or nine years.

Testing undoubtedly will continue to have a place in schools of the future, but it is to be hoped that the place will not be nearly as prominent as it now is. Any test that requires the use of language is to some degree "culture bound," and any such test puts some learners at a disadvantage. Far too many tests are given, and far too many of them purport to measure "achievement" while bearing little or no relationship to assessment of human performance in terms of the objectives of learning. Testing must be a part of the *means* of learning, not the end.

Who is to Learn

In *Brown vs. Board of Education,* a unanimous Supreme Court held that:

> *In these days it is doubtful that any child may reasonably be expected to succeed in life if he is denied the opportunity of an education. Such an opportunity, where the state has undertaken to provide it, is a right which must be made available to all on equal terms. . . .*

Apparently the schools face the challenge of providing "compensatory" education as early as possible in order to minimize differences which, in the normal course of schooling as it presently is practiced, can only become wider with each year in school. Reimer (1971) and others emphasized that something must be done to give all children the advantage that some now get through having such things as literate parents, books in the home, and opportunities to travel. As Riles said:

*Where better to begin than at the beginning? About 50 percent
of a child's learning potential is developed by age 5, 80 percent
of it by age 8. By age 8, the end of the third grade, every child
should be reading, computing, communicating and—above all
things—excited about learning.*[1]

Such dreams require attention to resources for learners if they are
to become more than dreams.

Resources for Learners

Schools are challenged to put themselves in competition with other
agencies of learning. Schools should stand or fall on their appeal
to learners. One method of competing is by means of a voucher
system in which resource credit is accumulated by each individual
and expended as he or she wishes. As advocated by Reimer (1971),
the parents would administer the resource account in very early
childhood with the learner taking over the administration at an early
age. Admittedly, there might be some abuses, but it is questionable
whether abuses would be worse, more flagrant, or more pervasive
than if the schools continue to monopolize the bulk of the funds
available for education.

As long as compulsory attendance is maintained, schools are
among the institutions that Illich (1971) classed as *manipulative,* and
most learners will be in them due to duress. Can the schools become convivial, existing to be used as a privilege and providing opportunities within defined limits while the learner remains a free
agent?

SOCIETY AND SCHOOLS

Once more it is stressed that the schools, kindergarten through university, constitute only one of the agencies of the education institution which has been imbued with value by society. Society must decide whether the schools are to educate for conformity or for freedom; they cannot do both. Also, they can advocate equality, but
advocacy will not achieve it, and furthermore it is justice that is
needed. They could perpetuate, at least for a while, what Illich has
called the "myth of unending consumption," or they can educate
for conservation of resources, but they cannot do both. They can
attempt to perpetuate the melting-pot idea which is a myth, too, or
they can have as a goal the understanding of cultural pluralism as
a source of pride; they cannot do both and do either well. If society
recognizes that more and more of its people have more and more
discretionary time which they should learn to use to advantage, the
schools can educate for use of that time. In general, educators who

[1] W. Riles, quoted in S. Alexander, 4 million lucky kids. *Newsweek*, 1974,
83(15), 40.

work in schools are challenged to decide whether schools should reflect society or lead society.

Conformity or Freedom?
There are some kinds of knowledge that have met the tests of time and of validation through having been discovered as necessary in various cultures throughout the world. The elements of such knowledge were briefly described in Chapter 17, and no serious educator would question the wisdom of having all citizens learn those things. Since the learnings described are needed early in life, it seems proper that the schools, if they are to continue, help learners to learn basic skills, those things designated by the present writers as "social learnings," career information, and "worthy" use of leisure time.

But as children grow toward adulthood they increasingly face unending uncertainty and discover that they and others have differences of values that are irreconcilable. Each person must develop the discipline of mind essential to live with tentative conclusions or downright ambiguity. Unless one is in a closed society, dealing with questions, particularly those relating to social issues, to which there are no immediate or conclusive answers becomes an indispensible experience. In the matter of issues, schools are challenged to expose, not impose—to help learners explore, not indoctrinate. Each person must learn to abide by majority opinion, even as she or he works to change that opinion.

Equality or Justice?
To advocate absolute equality of human beings is to advocate mediocrity. Since not everyone can be raised to the level of excellence, it follows that some must be forced to substitute mediocrity for excellence if all are to be equal. Human beings are *not* all born equal, nor is any amount of schooling likely to make them so. All *should* be able to find justice, however.

The political system of the United States is making some headway in forbidding unjust discrimination in hiring or voting, less in forbidding discrimination against learners. The Braginskys (1974) documented their distressing charge that a large segment of the total population, "the surplus population of the unneeded and unwanted," is unjustly discriminated against in daily living, and that the children of those people are subject to ever more brutal discrimination:

"Surplus" adults, who have no hope of participating in mainstream society, have a fixed reward-cost ratio before a child ever enters their life. For large segments of this population, the costs of life are so high and the rewards so low that they are predisposed to reject and often eject their children. The social conditions that lead to such despair and futility guarantee that new

*children will inherit membership in the surplus population of the
unneeded and unwanted. The child may also contribute to the
reward-cost ratio himself. Children born with noticeable defects
or who get into trouble with the community, for example, are
likely to increase the costs to the parents [p. 29].*

What is needed is a system of justice that will assure that no
child will be denied a right to learning opportunities regardless of
what his or her parents were or were not. Such a system must come
from society, not from the schools, although the schools are challenged to help provide those opportunities.

Unending Consumption: A Myth

The myth that "progress" involves unending consumption had been
called to the attention of the American public by Illich (1971) and
others before the crises and shortages of the early 1970s impressed
it indelibly upon the consciousness of all. The writers pointed out
that social reformers of the 1940s had held forth hope that the problem of justly distributing the world's goods could be licked by creating an abundance of them, but that we as a people are just coming
to the sad realization that there are not enough resources to make
available to every person in the world all of the goods, services,
and want satisfiers now available to the poor of the "more developed" (or more resource-exploited) countries.

Again, society must decide what it wants its schools to do. Shall
they continue to dangle before each learner the hope that he or
she will be among the privileged few who *can* enjoy whatever they
wish by way of goods, services, and want satisfiers? Can school
personnel be honest and point out what an individual's ever-decreas-
ing odds are? The schools are challenged to determine what less
materialistic and more realistic hope can be offered instead.

Cultural Pluralism

The concept of society as a melting pot, too, is a myth. While a
degree of cultural homogeneity is necessary to the continuing existence of a society, and the learning of some common elements thus
a goal of the society's educational agencies, still a look about provides firsthand evidence that subcultures based in ethnic differences
abound. Schools can be expected to pretend that such differences
do not exist or they can be expected to offer opportunities for each
individual to learn about other cultures and to appreciate them.
Knowledge of a number of cultures can be seen as one mark of
the truly educated person and the "culturally deprived" can be defined as one who knows only one language and little or nothing
about how others live. One can be taught to view ethnic differences
with pride or with shame; society must decide which view it expects
its schools to perpetuate.

For those school personnel who believe in cultural pluralism, Stent (1973) and the contributors to her volume have provided pragmatic suggestions. The means are available but the social mandate is not.

Discretionary Time
In his de-schooling arguments, Illich (1971) stressed the fact that technology has increased the ability of human beings to relinquish to machines the "making" of things, thus leaving them with discretionary time which they can decide how to use. Time that does not now have to be devoted to earning a living can be used in deliberately chosen ways, but the schools have not done well in helping individuals learn to make those choices. Illich said, "Man must choose whether to be rich in things or in the freedom to use them [p. 62]."

The same author pointed out that providing added durability in a limited range of the products made by human beings would allow even more discretionary time that could be spent in institutions that might increase the opportunity for and desirability of human interaction, provided the necessary institutions were accessible. As "making" things requires less and less time, more and more time can be devoted to "doing." Instead of the Weber notion that leisure is necessary for human beings to be able to work, Illich advocated the Aristotelean concept that work is necessary for people to have leisure. The challenge to the schools is to help young learners learn to "do"—to act, to participate, to reduce uncertainty—rather than to "make."

SCHOOLS AND TECHNOLOGY
"Technology has quietly and unobtrusively evolved into a megamachine of gargantuan power and influence," according to Sine (1974, p. 471). He made the somber prediction that *if* international corporate structures continue extending their influence in response to the single value of unrestricted "progress," humanity will increasingly have to be altered to fit the needs of technocracy. The challenge to schools is to find ways to: (1) use technology to the benefit of learners and (2) resist the megamachine without being crushed by it.

Technology and Learners
Technology needs to be used to develop independence and learning. Testing, programed text material, computers, and other teaching machines can be utilized for that purpose, along with many other types of hardware and software now available or soon to be available. All must be used according to values which enhance the dignity of the individual, not according to values which make him or her subservient to the technocracy. Already thousands of students

have experienced frustration at not being able to change their regis-
tration, or at getting grades only after long delay, because of computer convenience.

COMPUTERS. Sarnoff (1966) described how computers will leave
"No life untouched," since they will be used to analyze a student's
learning experience at intervals, will be the base of teaching machines that instruct one at one's individual rate, will team with a
teacher in tutorial service, will simulate dangerous or remote systems, and will provide continuing self-instruction and career mobility. He also stressed the tremendous capability of computers for processing information storage and retrieval. As mentioned before,
Bushnell (1966) saw computers as providing a teacher for each
student. Pfeiffer (1968) emphasized the versatility of computers for
planning, simulating, and individual life-planning. Simon (1965) described computer simulation of human thought. All of these uses
could be to the advantage of learners.

TEACHING MACHINES. As long ago as 1962, Clark and Sloan were
describing teaching machines of great variety and differing degrees
of complexity. Many types have been manufactured, while others
exist in prototype, and most educators are familiar with at least some
of them. They range from simple, manually operated devices to elec-
trically controlled machines that coordinate presentations of materials in various media. Many use programed content, but with all
of them learning is essentially accomplished through a do-it-yourself
tutorial process. Some machines are supplemented or comple-
mented by group instruction that may use lecture, films, film strips,
videotapes, or other aids. Video cameras and monitors also are used
as teaching machines when tapes are made and the learner is confronted with a playback of performance followed by discussion or
critique.

  Not all technological developments are as benign as those described above, however, and the personnel who work in schools
must be concerned about how to oppose some of the more insidious
aspects of the megamachine without being ground to bits by it.

The Megamachine
Planetary technocracy is a megamachine capable of overrunning
all of the social institutions and ruining the globe, insofar as human
living is concerned. The late President Eisenhower warned the American public of the growing power and danger of the military-indus-
trial complex, but he was little heeded. Heilbroner's (1960) *The
Future as History* focused on the same theme. That there is credibility to the claim of individual and even national interests being sacrificed to international industrial complexes is attested by such events
as the defeat in late 1973, in the U.S. Congress, of an energy bill

that would have prevented oil companies from making windfall profits during the then-new energy crisis.

Electrical and chemical intervention and genetic manipulation to control human beings, altering their beliefs and values and thus their personalities, are now possible or soon will be. Whether such means are to be used to get individuals to conform or to give them freedom will depend to a great extent on what learners learn in schools at an early age. How far freedom may be allowed to extend is a very real question. Sine (1974) couched the challenge thus:

> Among the questions confronting the sanctuaries of schooling
> are not only whether they are willing to consider other views
> of the cosmos, but whether they will be able to tolerate the possi-
> bility of using other truth systems that approach reality through
> the subjective, intuitive, and mystical [p. 472].

Neither the "scientific method," behavior modification, nor any other single line of thought can be allowed to seduce school personnel into excluding competing thought. Yet *already there is a single line of thought in regard to the necessity for unlimited industrial and military growth,* but the calendar does not yet read 1984!

ADMINISTRATORS AND SCHOOLS

In Chapter 18, the opinion was expressed that in the education of the future the chief educational leader of a community is likely to be based in the community at large rather than in the school system. If schools continue to exist, as the present writers believe they will, there will be administrators in them, and those administrators will be faced with problems of coordinating the work of schools with the work of other educational agencies, finding more effective forms of organization, getting all who work in schools to utilize research findings about learning, providing ever-better learning opportunities for individuals, and responding to the de-schooling critics.

Schools and Other Agencies

The demand for educational leaders will continue to increase, and school administrators will find places among them. They will be among the architects of resource networks, and will administer units catering to distinct target populations. Those units will be more closely allied with other types of agencies in helping all of the people of a community to use all of the community institutional forces to solve problems, individual and collective.

As early as 1938, Seay was stating that two principles of education were: (1) Education is a continuous process, and it cannot be confined within fixed administrative divisions; it demands coordination of all its services, and (2) educational activities should be based upon the problems, needs, and interests of those for whom they are planned (pp. 43–55). In 1945, the same author was stating that there were two distinct emphases for what he was then calling the "community school": service to the entire community, not merely to the children of school age; and discovery, development, and use of the resources of the community as part of the educational facilities of the school. The schools are still faced with the challenge of implementing these principles. Administrators must consider them to be serious goals.

School Organization

The need, as Boyer (1973) so aptly put it, is for administrators "to come to terms with change, not fight it, not surrender to it [p. 169]." There must be a "tomorrow climate," with staff personnel, students, and administrators all looking forward—not at the past, not at the ground where they are now standing, but at where they are going. The bureaucratic hierarchy with hard and fast lines of authority and decision-making must go, to be replaced by a flexible structure such as described by Berkley (see Chapter 4). People must be relatively free to pursue their own means of achieving agreed-on objectives. They must find ways of acting together in personally chosen ways, not ways forced upon them by superior power. Administrators must exist, and they must be expected to lead, but those whose efforts administrators direct must have some choice as to who is to lead them. Administrators must be accountable to persons whom they supervise as well as to those to whom they report, and subordinates must have the right of periodically reviewing administrators for accountability purposes. There must be more policies and fewer rules, and policies must emanate from those who will be affected by them. Organization must be in terms of doing a job for learners and their purposes, and administrative facility or computer convenience must never be allowed to take priority over those purposes.

These matters pose staggering challenges for schools.

Using Learning Research

Administrators must be sophisticated consumers of research, and must influence others to use research findings. However, a person must be able to distinguish research that relates to learning from research that relates to teacher performance or methodology and from the spate of publications that purport to report research but do not. Any "study" in which the reader cannot easily identify these steps should be immediately suspect: (1) the investigator started with a hypothesis about learning that is related to what is already known about the phenomenon, (2) a means of collecting data that could either support or refute the hypothesis was selected or devised, (3) varying conditions were taken into account, (4) data were collected and analyzed, (5) a clear statement was made as to whether the hypothesis was supported or refuted, and (6) implications of the findings were clearly stated.

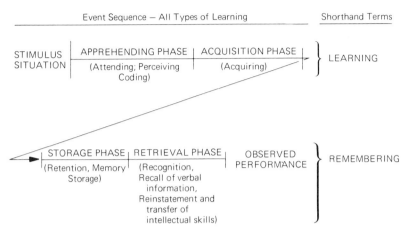

Figure 19-1 *The Sequence of Events in Learning*
Source: Gagne (1970), p. 71.

The above steps should be obvious in any research study, regardless of the area in which the research is done. However, a further test is necessary to determine whether a study relates to learning. If it does, one of the following three questions should have an affirmative answer:

Will the results help the learner in answering the nine questions found in the How Others Can Help section of Chapter 17?

Do results relate to "the elements of the learning event" (Gagné, 1970, pp. 4–5), namely the learner, the stimulus situation, or the response?

Do results relate to one or more of the four phases of the learning sequence shown in Figure 19-1?

Research studies in which at least the six steps are evident are worth giving attention to if they relate to learning. The challenge to schools is to utilize the true research after distinguishing it from academic tinkering.

What Schools Must Do[2]
School administrators must bear the burden of getting school personnel to decide what schools must do to justify their continued existence. The major tasks are at least six in number. First, schools must extend cultural boundaries and constraints, becoming multicultural and teaching that cultural differences are to be respected, rather than continuing to be oriented to the white middle-class culture. Second, schools must place their emphasis on individual worth and the learner's own needs to a far greater extent than has been

[2] The first four of these points are from a presentation by Leon Cohen to the Field Seminar of Western Michigan University in Battle Creek on March 16, 1974.

the common pattern of the past. Learners must not be asked to mindlessly perform school-determined tasks. Third, the schools must be organized for continuous monitoring of learning, for purposes of fact-finding and improvement, not for putting blame on learner or teacher. The monitoring must include annual testing of each learner—physical, achievement, and adjustment. Fourth, schools must emphasize the future and prepare learners to tolerate ambiguity. Fifth, schools must foster, not repress, differences of opinion. Sixth, people who work in schools must be mindful of learners, rather than be mindlessly performing tasks. These are no mean challenges.

Deschooling? No!

One of many responses to the de-schoolers was an article by Jackson (1972) under the title of "Deschooling? No!" In it, he pointed out that school people might take the course of ignoring the critics and getting on with their work, they might counterattack by exposing weaknesses of the critics' arguments, or they might learn from the critics. Jackson advocated the latter course, and suggested that two shortcomings brought to mind by the critics involve lessons to be learned. The first is that many school people are sure of what they are *against* but uncertain of what they are *for*. In his words:

> After all, it is easier to put oil on squeaky wheels than to ask about where the vehicle is headed in the first place and to ponder the necessity for a change in direction [p. 21].

The second shortcoming is lack of a conception of what education leads toward, and in implying a challenge to school people in this matter, Jackson quoted John Dewey, thus:

> There is a present tendency in so-called advanced schools of educational thought . . . to say, in effect, let us surround pupils with certain materials, tools, appliances, etc. and then let pupils respond to these things according to their own desires. Above all, let us not suggest any end or plan to the students; let us not suggest to them what they shall do, for that is an unwarranted trespass upon their sacred intellectual individuality since the essence of such individuality is to set up ends and aims.
> Now such a method is really stupid. For it attempts the impossible, which is always stupid; and it misconceives the conditions of independent thinking. There are a multitude of ways of reacting to surrounding conditions, and without some guidance from experience these reactions are almost sure to be casual, sporadic, and ultimately fatiguing, accompanied by nervous strain. Since the teacher has presumably a greater background of experience, there is the same presumption of the right of a teacher to make suggestions as to what to do as there is on the part

of a head carpenter to suggest to apprentices something of what they are to do.

Dewey's admonition still has not been heeded, although it was written about 50 years ago. Everyone connected with schools needs to take it seriously, since it presents one of the counterarguments to the de-schooling critics.

SUMMARY
The difference between schooling and educating is becoming increasingly clear to noneducators, and must become so to school-based educators if they are to be able to justify the continued existence of schools. A number of influential voices are demanding that schools be abolished and that better ways be found to provide education to the young. Education is unending, because an individual's uncertainty is unending, but the proper functions of the schools in dealing with learner indifference, culturally induced handicaps, learner brain damage, and learner uncertainty have not yet been determined. It is charged that schools discriminate unjustly, are inequitable, make false claims, monopolize the funds available for education, are mindless of learners and what they are about, and do not provide access to enough resources for those learners they hold captive.

Compulsory attendance must be abolished, and schools must stand or fall on the basis of functions that they can perform for learners in better fashion than can any other agency of the educational institution. Those functions include helping learners to learn the basic skills, introductory social understandings and skills, use of leisure time, and career information.

More attention must be given to helping more learners learn more in individualized patterns. Progression of learners in schools must be based on skill competency, but testing needs to be greatly reduced and what is allowed to remain must be related to human performance much more closely than some of it now is. Schools must compete with other agencies of learning and prove that they can exist when the learner is a free agent, choosing among agencies that are used as a privilege, not an obligation.

Society cannot hold the schools accountable until a clear mandate is given that they are to teach freedom and justice, that unending consumption is a myth, that cultural pluralism is desirable and a source of pride, and that discretionary time is to be used as the individual chooses so long as it is not inimical to society. Technology, particularly that using computers and other teaching machines, must be harnessed and used for the benefit of learners. Dangers of the international technocratic megamachine must be faced squarely, and no single line of though *on any matter* can be allowed to seduce school personnel into excluding competing thought.

School administrators face particularly difficult challenges. They and others must acknowledge that they are not the zenith among educational leaders, but that all of the educational agencies of the community must be much more closely united in efforts to help all of the learners of all ages. Since the people working in schools are all educated persons, the demands for flexible-relationships structures in schools are even stronger than similar demands in other organizations. School personnel must learn to identify research regarding learning, come to trust it, and utilize it until such time as better research is done.

Schools must discard cultural constraints, cater to learners' needs, continuously monitor learning for fact-finding and improvement, prepare learners to handle ambiguity, foster differences of opinion, and be mindful of learners. People who work in schools must constantly ask questions about what schools are for and where they are going; they must be sure that they, through the authority of competence, are qualified to navigate the way.

The final chapter of this book explores the satisfactions being an educational leader, the constraints within which a leader must operate, and the opportunities one may find for leading. It examines numbers and types of educational positions whose holders are expected to lead and suggests some strategies for getting desired positions.

SOME SUGGESTED RESOURCES

R. E. Agger and M. N. Goldstein, *Who will rule the schools: A cultural class crisis.* Belmont, Calif.: Wadsworth, 1971.

B. M. Braginsky and D. D. Braginsky, Stimulus/response: The mentally retarded: Society's Hansels and Gretels. *Psychology Today,* 1974, **7**(10). 18, 20–21, 24, 26, 28–30.

R. C. Doll, *Leadership to improve schools.* Worthington, Ohio: Charles A. Jones, 1972.

R. C. Ebel, What are schools for? *Phi Delta Kappan,* **54**(1), 3–7.

R. Farson, The right to educate oneself. Ch. 7 in *Birthrights: A bill of rights for children.* New York: Macmillan, 1974. Pp. 96–112.

E. Fromm, Escape from freedom. *Intellectual Digest,* 1971, **2**(3), 45.

R. M. Holmes, *The adademic mystery house, thc man, the campus and their new search for meaning.* Nashville, Tenn.: Abingdon, 1970.

J. Holt, Schools against themselves. In *Freedom and beyond.* New York: Dutton, 1972. Pp. 236–265.

I. Illich, *De-Schooling society.* New York: Harper & Row, 1971.

J. A. Peddiwell, *The saber-tooth curriculum.* New York: McGraw-Hill, 1939.

E. Reimer, *School is dead.* Garden City, N.Y.: Doubleday, 1971.

L. J. Rubin (Ed.), *Frontiers in school leadership.* Skokie, Ill.: Rand McNally, 1970.

T. Sine, The megamachine and the schoolhouse. *Phi Delta Kappan,* 1974, **55**(7), 470–473.

H. Taylor, *How to change colleges: Notes on radical reform.* New York: Holt, Rinehart & Winston, 1971.

K. R. Toole, *The time has come.* New York: Morrow, 1971.

CHAPTER 20

THE OPPORTUNITIES AVAILABLE

> *Follow the Leader—A Modern Fable*
> *A parade was passing in the street, and from the crowded*
> *throng that watched, a voice was heard to cry: "Beware,*
> *you fools, you march the wrong way. That street leads*
> *nowhere—it is a dead-end!"*
>
> *The paraders paused . . . alarmed . . . "But, can*
> *this be?" they thought, and looked as one toward the front*
> *where, tall and proud, their handsome leader made his way.*
> *"He must be going the right way," they thought, "for look*
> *how well he marches, and look how tall he stands—oh yes,*
> *he is most certainly going the right way!" . . . and they*
> *marched on.*
>
> *The handsome leader paused . . . alarmed . . . "But*
> *can this be?" he thought, and stole a glance behind.*
> *"I must be going the right way," he thought, "for look how*
> *many follow me—oh yes, I am most certainly going the right*
> *way!" . . . and he marched on.*
>
> *Redifer*

Certainly the individual who believes that he or she is going the right way in education today can, with some effort, attract a following; having attracted a following, it is easy to convince oneself that followers assure that the chosen way is correct. Thus, it behooves anyone who would like to seize any of the many opportunities available to educational leaders today to determine in advance that she or he really does know the path to be followed, what it leads to, and the dangers likely to be encountered.

This chapter will discuss satisfactions that a leader may find in seizing or seeking opportunities, some of the constraints under which one will have to operate in taking advantage of those opportunities, finding opportunities in present job situations, positions that might afford opportunities, and what is necessary for getting a desired position.

SATISFACTIONS

The satisfactions that one may expect from finding and seizing opportunities to lead probably depend on the values that are dominant in one's life. If an individual's dominant values relate to *motivation* needs, one may experience quite different satisfactions than if one's values relate to *maintenance* needs or to *perceptual* needs.

Motivation Needs

Motivation, as used in this book, refers to a person's orientation to goals. This meaning is not inharmonious with the meaning of motivation in the "motivation needs" idea expressed by Myers (1964) and as shown in Figure 16-1, p. 329. Myers said that motivation needs consist of growth, achievement, responsibility, and recognition. Certainly most educational leaders can find or make opportunities for all of these.

GROWTH. Growth involves such satisfactions as being the recipient of delegated authority, having access to information having freedom to act, and working in an atmosphere of approval. Peter and Hull (1969), with tongue in cheek, described the "lateral arabesque," in which a person is moved sideways to another position because his superordinates know that he has reached his "level of incompetence," or a level above which he cannot perform satisfactorily. While the reason for such moves was not established, Boles (1952), in a study of the prior-year moves made by chief school executives in Ohio, concluded that a high percentage of those moves had been made to situations that involved no added responsibility, no more freedom to act, no greater salary. It might be hypothesized that some moves were made because individuals were on the verge of being, or had been, forced out of incumbencies. Regardless of reason, lateral moves rarely provide growth opportunities or satisfactions.

ACHIEVEMENT. Feelings of achievement result from satisfactions such as knowing that one's aptitudes, skills, and knowledge are being utilized, getting the necessary tasks done, helping others, achieving publication, and invention. Educational leaders generally have ample opportunities to experience some or all of these satisfactions.

RESPONSIBILITY. If one needs and enjoys responsibility, she or he may find satisfaction in being involved in decision-making, goal-setting, planning, solving problems, helping others to get the resources they need and simplifying their work, and performance appraisal. Performance appraisal is basic to continued improvement of any organization and is the essence of accountability, but it probably is the facet of responsibility that is least enjoyed by anyone and relished by few. To many, it is downright painful.

RECOGNITION. Recognition comes through satisfiers such as being respected, esteemed, or loved; receiving testimonials or plaudits, merit increases, discretionary awards, or bonuses. Most educational leaders must settle for being respected or esteemed; one who feels that he or she must be loved by everyone will likely wind up being either disappointed or a poor administrator. There simply are times when actions that must be taken for the good of the organization will be displeasing to certain factions or to numbers of individuals. Testimonials and plaudits for educators generally are reserved for retirement parties and funerals, unfortunately. Merit increases, discretionary awards, and bonuses are almost unknown in most educational agencies, largely because the value systems of superordinates are such that they are unwilling to make the judgments on which these satisfiers must be based.

Maintenance Needs

Maintenance needs relate to matters such as status, security, economic considerations, social contacts, physical arrangements, and orientation. While satisfiers of many of these needs may be found in educational leader positions, the present writers are of the opinion that few successful leaders have dominant values that tie them directly to such needs.

STATUS. Having and being able to use power is one of the seldom acknowledged satisfactions of status, but in this book there has been repeated stress on the uninvestigated hypothesis that leaders have certain need-dispositions in common, among them enjoyment of the use of authority and power. Some individuals appear to gain satisfaction from capricous power display, some from rational use of power to benefit individuals or the organization, and some from use for oligarchic purposes. Positional status, of course, has concomitant authority which some persons find satisfying, while others are satisfied by the status that comes with personal authority. The satisfactions that come from either power or authority tie directly to one's relationships with other people, both inside the organization and outside. Some individuals also find satisfaction in such perquisites of status as title, office location, furnishings, and rights such as being able to arrange one's own schedule, having a private parking place, or having a private toilet.

SECURITY. Security needs often are manifest by one who seeks satisfactions such as reassurance, friendliness, consistency, fairness, seniority rights, and use of grievance procedures. Those who aspire to positions as union or association representatives may hold security as a dominant value. It seems doubtful that the top executives of many educational agencies have that dominant value or, indeed, that they are likely to experience reassurance and friendliness in great measure. If driven by security needs, executives may have to seek their satisfactions in social systems other than those in which they work.

ECONOMIC. The satisfiers of economic needs include salaries, automatic pay increases, retirement benefits, paid sick leave, compensation for job-related injury or uemployment, insurance, tuition for self or family members, and, perhaps, purchase discounts. In the past, it seems that numerous persons sought positions in educational administration primarily for economic satisfiers, but as salaries of teachers, instructors, trainers, and professors have become more equitable probably fewer administrators have had these satisfiers as their impetus. The present writers would hypothesize that persons who seek administrative positions basically for economic-needs satisfiers will be unsuccessful, or, at best, mediocre in their performance as leaders.

SOCIAL. Social needs are related to associational satisfactions as the latter are expressed in the Daws Occupational Satisfactions Scheme (see Midler, 1970). Social needs may be satisfied by associating with others in professional groups, interest groups, recreational groups, or hobby groups. Some individuals may satisfy all of their social needs by association with individual friends. However, it should be noted that the top executive in most educational agencies is a lonely person. Such a person often has no professional colleagues within the same organization with whom to share confidences or problems, and thus must look outside for associational satisfactions if they are important to him or her.

PHYSICAL. Certain needs may be satisfied by such physical matters as office arrangement, equipment, aesthetics, lunch arrangements, temperature and humidity control, lighting, and noise reduction. When wants include couches, easy chairs, and private sauna baths, there may be a question as to whether the needs are physical or status in nature, but such accoutrements as those named are rarely found in the offices of educational leaders at the present time.

ORIENTATION. Orientation needs may be met by satisfiers such as job instruction, group meetings, regulations, rules, handbooks, house publications, bulletins, memos, and grapevine reports. While educational leaders should have little need for most of those satisfiers, they should not overlook the grapevine, or unofficial communications, which can help them become oriented to reality, whether or not the messages received satisfy.

Perceptual Needs

The work of Herzberg and of his disciples Myers and Sergiovanni makes no mention of the satisfiers that Daws listed as perceptual. The latter indicated that perceptual satisfactions are of three types, and the three seem to the present writers to be relevant to the opportunities for satisfaction that educational leaders may experience. They are variety, outdoor stimuli, and travel.

VARIETY. While a school principal who allows himself to get so enmeshed in maintaining the organization that he has no time for anything else may come to believe that he deals with the same problems over and over, his life does not have to be that way. Any educational leader can periodically change his or her focus among the four basic goals of the enterprise, can work with different individuals and groups, can concentrate on different aspects of learning opportunities, can use alternate approaches to problems, or can seek new inputs from staff personnel. For an imaginative and resourceful person, there should be no dearth of satisfactions resulting from perceptual variety.

OUTDOOR STIMULI. Although few educational leaders have jobs that can be done wholly or even in large part outdoors, some perhaps can be. For example, a director of park rangers should be able to spend a fair amount of his work time outdoors. Many persons in other more prosaic leader positions may find that there are aspects of their jobs that can take them outdoors frequently if they do not allow themselves to become slaves to paperwork, and those who learn to manage time often can arrange their schedules to include regular rounds of golf, fishing trips, or other rejuvenating outdoor activities.

TRAVEL. One of the perquisites of the educator's job most envied by persons in other occupations is the amount of "break," holiday, and vacation time allowed. The leader who becomes so desk-bound that she or he "can't take a vacation" doesn't hold recreation-through-travel as a dominant value. Furthermore, professional responsibilities often make attendance at conferences or visitation to other agencies of education desirable. As more and more efforts are made to coordinate the total range of educational agencies of a given community, possible travel satisfactions are likely to become more numerous.

The list of possible satisfiers seems quite extensive, and indeed it is. However, not all satisfiers are equally appealing to all leaders, and no one is likely to experience all of them on any job. Besides, each leader has constraints within which he or she must operate and often the constraints outweigh the potential satisfactions of a particular position.

CONSTRAINTS

Constraints within which every educational leader must operate include those imposed by the expectations of various individuals and groups, by inordinate visibility, by pressures of time and from groups, by risk, and by the possibility of heading into dead-end avenues.

Expectations

An educational leader is always constrained in what he can do by the expectations held for his performance by individuals and groups both inside and outside the organization and unit within which he works. One must be ever vigilant to learn what people's expectations are, and having learned them one must strive to get as much congruence as possible among them. If some reasonable degree of congruence cannot be attained, the leader can either try to use power (if he has it) to force his expectations on others, function in a constant state of ambiguity, or seek another position in which there may be more congruence of expectations. The rational means of trying to obtain congruence is through persuasion, but emotional means are often used also.

INSIDE. The leader must be concerned abut the expectations held by all of the individuals and groups within the organization or unit in which she or he is the designated leader. Each leader has his own expectations, of course, but he must compare them to those expectations that seem to be held in common by his superordinates, those shared among peers, and those subscribed to by subordinates as a group.

OUTSIDE. The expectations of certain individuals and groups outside the unit or organization are also of importance to the leader. Individuals who are either community influentials in general or power figures in regard to educational issues must be given special attention, and ignoring those political constraints can lead to professional suicide. In every community there are a number of noneducation social systems that can and frequently do bring to bear great pressures on education agencies, as any practicing administrator can attest. For example, at the time of this writing the ministerial association in one Michigan community was creating a community uproar, requiring several special public meetings, because of some jokes and skits that students in the high school had been allowed to use in a publicly performed musical revue. In another community, an affirmative action group was generating a lot of heat on community college administrators and trustees because the college had no women on its administrative staff.

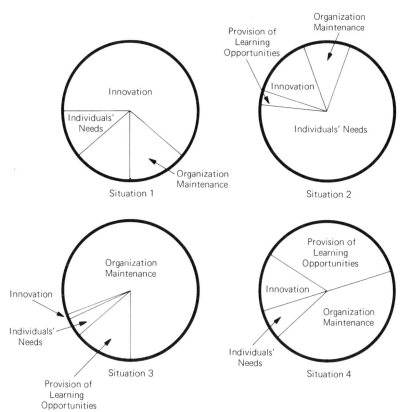

Figure 20-1 *Hypothetical Illustrations of Expectations Regarding Distribution of a Leader's Time Among the Four Basic Goals of an Educational Agency*

EFFECT. The effect of expectations is at least two fold: Expectations always set boundaries within which educational leaders must perform and they sometimes exclude certain individuals from consideration for certain positions. The four hypothetical situations shown in Figure 20-1 illustrate the latter circumstance. In situation 1, assumed common expectations are that the educational leader will spend a major portion of his or her time in innovation, and obviously not everyone can do that because some will lack the abilities or the convictions necessary. In situation 2, the leader would be expected to devote the major portion of his or her time to meeting the needs of individuals, and again not everyone would be prepared to do that. In situation 3, a leader focused on maintenance of the organization almost to the exclusion of other goals would be needed. Situation 4 would require that the leader devote most of his or her time and energies to the provision of learning opportunities and maintenance of the organization, with a fair amount of innovation being expected, but it seems likely that the needs of individuals would suffer. Perhaps the four situations depicted are illustrative of the constraints imposed on a leader's performance by followers' expectations. Further constraints are imposed by visibility.

Visibility

One must achieve a certain visibility if one is to become a leader. Having achieved a position as leader, many an individual finds that he has more visibility than. he desires or can live with comfortably. Even his actions in private life, as well as the actions of members of his family, may be held up for public scrutiny. The friends he has and the social activities in which he and family members engage may be subject to comment by individuals and by media reporters. For those leaders who work in public schools, particularly, there is still, in many communities, an expectation that they will serve as models of propriety for the children and youth of the community. Parents may expect that the school principal or superintendent not smoke or drink, even though they themselves may do so.

Probably school personnel in small communities face constraints that are more limiting than do their counterparts in large cities, but the large-city educator is visible to far more persons and such of his or her actions as are criticized are likely to become points of contention more readily. Factions are likely to develop in communities of any size, and the educational leader who aligns himself or herself with one faction on an issue can expect nothing but continuing harassment from those in opposing factions. Either personal or professional actions of the leader can become issues. Antagonizing reporters for any of the mass media often heighten visibility and the concomitant pressure that attends any controversy. Every year, some promising educational leaders leave their positions, thereby demonstrating that they have heeded Harry Truman's admonition: "If you can't take the heat, get out of the kitchen!"

Visibility of personnel in private or parochial schools often is as great as for their counterparts in public schools, but usually the viewing audience is more limited. Visibility of college and university personnel may be as great or greater than for public school personnel, but tolerance of idiosyncrasy probably is greater also. Visibility of leaders in nonformal agencies of education usually is less than for those in formal agencies, and tolerance of idiosyncrasy usually is higher. Tolerance of school constituents for leader idiosyncrasy may be inversely proportional to the compulsion for learners to attend or to forced financial support, or to both. Visibility certainly provides one of the pressures under which educational leaders must work.

Pressures

Pressures on an individual who has positional authority not only serve as constraints to what she or he can do but are the source

of stress which can, in some instances, become so severe as to inca-
pacitate the person. Pressures include those of time and of vested-
interest groups, and anyone seeking opportunities to lead should
be aware that he or she will encounter both, but that they can be
handled if one is prepared for them.

TIME. Everyone has exactly the same amount of time, as Mackenzie
(1972) pointed out, but some manage it to their advantage and to
the advantage of the organization in which they work, while others
fall into "the time trap" and find their lives being managed and their
energies vitiated by time. In his succinct description of "how to
spring the time trap," Mackenzie provided a list of the "time wasters" that he has most frequently encountered in consulting with
executives in a dozen countries, along with possible causes and
some suggested solutions. The time wasters, which many educational leaders doubtless are guilty of allowing, include lack of planning, lack of priorities, overcommitment, management by crisis,
haste, paperwork and reading [the tyranny of paper], routine and
trivia, visitors, telephone, meetings, indecision, and lack of delegation. Mackenzie provided realistic suggestions for solutions, thus
giving hope that the leader who is knowledgeable can avoid many
of the pressures of time. Drucker (1967) also developed this theme.

VESTED INTERESTS. Every person having positional authority in an
educational agency is beset almost daily by representatives of various groups having interests that they would like to further by using
the agency to propagandize. Undoubtedly, the pressures are more
numerous in public agencies than in private agencies, stronger in
those close to the general public than in those that are remote, more
nearly irresistible in agencies having public support than in those
that rely on private support. Internally, learner groups pressure for
everything from curriculum and personnel changes to special privileges, while staff groups pressure for even more diverse and far-
ranging interests. Externally, there are pro and con factions for every
one of the social issues listed in Chapter 10, plus a host of others.
Each group tries to get anyone having leader status to be the advocate of its interests. Each time a group is refused, personal risk for
the leader becomes greater.

Risk

Some sources of risk, for the leader and for the organization, have
been considered previously. Thus, the discussion here is limited to
risk arising from perception or from lack of unity.

PERCEPTION. One of the constraints under which a leader must
operate involves the degree to which a course of action that he or
she is proposing is perceived as creating risk for the organization

and for individuals in it. Most of the individuals could not care less about whether the action poses risk for the leader himself or herself. If the action is seen as creating a high degree of risk for the organization, the number of willing followers is likely to be small. High risk, few followers; low risk, many followers, other things being equal. A leader's action which a follower perceives as involving high risk to himself or herself, as an individual, is going to be strongly resisted. High personal risk, high resistance; low personal risk, low resistance. The leader proposing innovation must think in terms of individuals, and must either be prepared to show each that the advantages to him or her will outweigh the disadvantages or be prepared for the resistance of those for whom the disadvantages, which they perceive as personal risk, weigh more heavily than perceived advantages.

LACK OF UNITY. Unity is hard to achieve in any organization, and the greater the lack of unity the greater the risk to the organization and to the leader. Having as many employees as possible unified in their efforts is essential if a creditable job is to be done in achieving the four basic goals of an educational agency. Probably few if any leaders can expect to be loved by everyone, and most must settle for being respected. Respect begets loyalty and loyalty begets unity. Competence, sincerity, and understanding must be combined to beget respect.

Dead Ends
The leader seeking further opportunities must be aware of and do his or her best to avoid dead-end positions. It is possible to get oneself into a situation from which there is little hope of further promotion. The matters of poor stepping stones, the Peter Principle, and the top job must be considered as possible constraints.

POOR STEPPING STONES. It was indicated in an earlier chapter that the present writers believe that clearly defined patterns of career stepping stones: (1) probably never were as important as many persons thought them to be, (2) probably have never existed for certain educational leader positions, and (3) are not as important for *any* educational position as they may have been at one time. We did not intend to totally negate the concept, however, as there can be little doubt that, at the present time, certain positions are very poor launching pads to further success. For example, few directors of military schools or superintendents of public schools become college or university presidents. Few directors of training and management development ever move into positions of greater responsibility in the formal agencies of education. Few principals of parochial or private schools or directors and coordinators in public schools ever are appointed superintendents of public schools. Few

business managers move to different *types* of jobs, few staff personnel move to line positions, few intermediate school superintendents
ever become anything else. When considering whether to take a particular position, one must look ahead to what one might wish to do
in the future and assess, honestly of course, whether even successful
experience in the position might help in further aspirations. The individual must also assess whether the Peter Principle has already become operative in his or her case or whether it might do so in the
next position.

THE PETER PRINCIPLE. One may need to recognize that he has
already reached his level of incompetence. One *does* tend to be
promoted so long as others see in him potential for greater performance and to have his upward progress arrested if performance
is perceived by others as mediocre or worse. It is the wise college
dean—or director of training and management development, or
school principal—who recognizes that he presently is doing a job
in a fashion that others applaud but might not do as well in the
next-more-responsible position. Many a person continues year after
year in a job that he and others know that he does more than passing
well, enduring the uncomprehending head-shakes of colleagues, because of such recognition within himself.

THE TOP JOB. One further constraint is imposed on the individual
who already is in the top job in his or her educational agency—top
in terms of responsibility and opportunity. Where does one look for
advancement if one is already a college president, a corporation
vice-president for management development, or a superintendent of
schools? Often, changing to a position in the same type but larger
agency only means doing the same job on a larger scale without
commensurate achievement, growth, responsibility, or recognition,
so those who are responsive to motivation needs may be reluctant
to move. Longer hours, more problems, and more risk may be sought
by persons motivated by the maintenace needs of status, security,
economic gain, or social association, however.

A STARTING POINT
A would-be leader cannot always, as advised in the trite old story,
"go somewhere else to start." An individual may have to begin where
she or he is. Some ways of doing this are through increasing
one's influence or authority, through achieving increased visibility,
through shrewd timing of action, or through being alert to fortuitous
circumstance.

Increasing Influence and Authority
Table 20-1 lists some of the factors that the present writers believe
to be of major importance in giving one influence or authority over
others, along with some judgments as to how much one might delib-

TABLE 20-1
FACTORS THAT GIVE ONE INFLUENCE OR AUTHORITY OVER OTHERS

FACTOR	AMOUNT OF EFFECT THE INDIVIDUAL CAN DELIBERATELY HAVE ON THIS FACTOR		
	LITTLE OR NONE	SOME	MUCH
HAVING:			
—an engaging personality		X	
—attractive physical appearance		X	
—certain blood lines	X		
—commanding voice (tone or quality)		X	
—greater than average height	X		
—organizational status		X	
—persuasive ability			X
—societal status		X	
—superior strength		X	
—the "proper" skin color	X		
—the "right" family name	X		
—wealth		X	
BEING:			
—able to manipulate others		X	
—admired			X
—identified with a cause		X	
—identified with a familiar figure		X	
—identified with the organization			X
—liked			X
—loved		X	
—respected			X
—visible in group-approved fashion			X
DEMONSTRATING:			
—ability or knowledge			X
—accomplishment			X
—commitment to a cause		X	
—commitment to the organization			X
—ethical standards			X
—group-sanctioned rituals			X
—physical skill or dexterity		X	
—responsibility			X
—sexuality		X	
—use of group-sanctioned language			X

erately do, either in one's present position or in a new one, to increase one's personal influence and authority. Each reader must determine for himself or herself those factors that may be important to his or her present situation.

Being Visible
The elements of visibility are at least four in number, namely: what one does, who one knows, by whom one is known, and alertness to organizational needs.

WHAT ONE DOES. How well or how poorly a person is perceived as doing his or her job is certainly a major facet of visibility. One may have to "go someplace else to start" because of having less competition elsewhere, because one's talents or accomplishments are unrecognized ("a prophet is not without honor save in his own country"), or because the present pond is too big for a small frog to make a splash. In the latter instance, one must either find ways to become bigger or seek a smaller pond. The particular position that one holds and how well one can discharge its responsibilities are, of course, important to visibility. While actions of private life may in no way reflect capability for doing one's job, they do increase or decrease visibility and thus cannot be ignored. The person looking for opportunities can gain visibility through positively sanctioned community activities as well as organizational activities.

WHO ONE KNOWS. Many a career has been founded on "getting to know the right people," and many a promotion has resulted from a person having deliberately made himself or herself known to those who were in positions where they could either recommend or select candidates. When one is seeking a position, it is just good political sense to ascertain who the individuals are who will be able either to recommend or to decide the appointment and then to do whatever one can to draw the attention of those persons to oneself. One of the best means of doing that is to demonstrate outstanding performance on one's present job.

WHO KNOWS ONE. An often-overlooked fact is that an individual may be known, through reputation, by persons with whom one is not acquainted. Perhaps the persons who knows one are at least as important as those whom one consciously sets about knowing. It was speculated previously that Milner's model (Figure 14-2, p. 297) may have more general applicability than he attributed to it, and the persons by whom an individual is known seem to affect information that he receives about job openings, whether he learns of job opportunities in one or several geographical regions, and whether he may or may not be discriminated against in position appointments.

ALERTNESS TO NEEDS. Many an individual has found himself or herself suddenly in the organizational limelight because he or she sensed and articulated needs of which other organizational members were conscious, but about which little or nothing was being done. Being alert to needs, being able to articulate them, and having reasonable courses of action to propose are excellent ways of making oneself visible. Individuals who can do these things become emergent leaders insofar as the immediate situations are concerned, and every incident of emergent leadership in which positive results are achieved adds to the likelihood that the emergee will become a positional leader, or advance to a higher position if he or she already has positional authority. Alertness to organizational needs is closely related to timing, another of the major constraints under which all positional leaders must operate.

Timing
A person seeking opportunities as an educational leader must be almost as attuned to timing of actions as the already practicing leader. He must recognize that premature action may be every bit as harmful to his cause as waiting too long to make a move. He must not move to grab a position for which there has not as yet been an announcement of vacancy; such an action will be viewed by others as gauche at best and unethical at worst. Perhaps one of the worst mistakes of timing is made by the individuals who rush to secure administrative credentials only as an alternative when teaching-staff jobs are scarce. One who is going into the demanding work of leading other educators should do so by choice, not as a desperation move. Credentials should be secured when the individual is convinced in his own mind that it is time, in his planned professional development, to make that move. This admonition does not negate the possibility of a person recognizing a fortuitous circumstance and taking advantage of it.

Fortuitous Circumstance
Many educational leaders, if they were honest, would admit that they are where they are because of fortuitous circumstance. The senior author of this book became an administrator because of a circumstance in which a board of education, in order to meet a competitive salary offer, named him high school principal without his knowledge and without paper credentials when he had applied for a teaching post! As a matter of fact, every significant development in his professional career seems to have resulted from a juncture of fortuitous circumstance and the presence of one or more significant others!

The would-be leader must recognize situations in which one has ego-involvement that impels one to action, knowledge that can help the group, skill that can bring about action, or commitment that can provide others a cause around which to rally. However, it is hoped that he or she will distinguish the finding of opportunities through fortuitous circumstance from the opportunism that sometimes motivates, in which there is little regard for principles or ultimate consequences. We have seen few educational leaders who tried to make a ladder to success from the bloody bodies of colleagues who ever enjoyed or were very successful in the positions they achieved in such fashion.

POSITION POSSIBILITIES
Too many persons consider the opportunities for educational leaders as being restricted to positions as school principals and supintendents. In order to extend the horizons of those who read this book,

a list is provided in Table 20-2. Neither the agencies nor the position titles shown are exhaustive listings and both are meant only to be indicative.

Because data regarding numbers of persons employed, salary ranges, degree requirements, and organization addresses are so transient, such data have not been included. A reader who thinks he or she may have a serious interest in a particular type of agency or position should experience little difficulty in securing current data regarding position titles, numbers employed, salaries paid, and degree requirements if he or she is industrious and has access to a good library.

If the reader has followed the advice given in this book, he or she should now know a great deal about his or her own performance, potential, and predictability. Having assured oneself, through some investigation of the data suggested in Table 20-2, that there *are* opportunities for educational leaders one should now have a real soul-searching session in which to ascertain honestly why he wishes to leave his present position and why certain of the possibly available positions are of interest. These matters should be openly discussed with members of one's immediate family, if any are involved, and together they should weigh all of the personal, family, and professional factors that they can think of. If the conviction remains that the anticipated move would be to the overall benefit of the family (or the individual if he or she is alone), then the steps necessary for getting from here to there should be taken.

GETTING FROM HERE TO THERE

There are five steps in getting from a present position to a desired one, namely: getting the necessary paper qualifications, securing a quality education, sorting out germane and demonstrable competencies, locating job opportunities, and developing strategies for getting oneself considered in preference to other applicants.

Paper Qualifications

The applicant needs to ascertain the paper qualifications required of candidates for the position to which one aspires and then make sure that one can present those qualifications or their equivalents. Such qualifications may include a specific type of degree, a specific type of certificate, and specific courses taken, considered singly or in combination. It is the applicant's responsibility to determine the qualifications that are being called for and to check one's own against those listed. If one applies for a position knowing that his or her credentials are at considerable variance with those specified for the position, one should accompany the application with a strong rationale for applying despite the discrepancy.

Quality of Education

Three elements of the quality of one's education are the university attended, the types of learning experiences encountered, and the

TABLE 20-2

POSITION POSSIBILITIES FOR EDUCATIONAL LEADERS

TYPE OF AGENCY	TYPICAL POSITION TITLE[1]	POSSIBLE SOURCE OF INFORMATION
FORMAL[2]		
International Cooperative Administration		I.C.A.
National Institute of Education		The Institute
National Foundation of the Arts and Humanities		The Foundation
National Science Foundation		The Foundation
U.S. Office of Education		USOE
Regional Laboratories	Director	USOE
Research and Development Centers	Director	USOE
U.S. Academies		
Air Force Academy	Superintendent	The Academy
Army Academy	Superintendent	The Academy
Coast Guard Academy	Superintendent	The Academy
Merchant Marine Academy	Superintendent	The Academy
Naval Academy	Superintendent	The Academy
Other U.S. Government Schools		
American Overseas Dependents' Schools	Principal	A.A.S.A.
Indian schools	Principal	Burea of Indian Affairs
Schools in national parks	Principal	U.S. Park Service
Schools in trust territories	Principal	Dept. of Interior
Professional associations and unions	Executive Director	The association
	State Director	The association
Special-interest associations[3]	Executive Secretary	The association
Special-position associations[4]	Executive Secretary	The association
Regional accrediting associations	Executive Secretary	The association
Education Commission of the States	Executive Director	The commission
State Departments of Education	Superintendent	The department
	Assoc. or Asst. Supt.	The department
	Consultant[5]	The department
Universities and Graduate Schools	President	The specific institution
	Vice-president	The specific institution
	Chancellor	The specific institution
	Provost	The specific institution
	Dean	The specific institution
	Dept. head or chairperson	The specific institution
	Director	The specific institution
	Professor of Admin.	U.C.E.A.
College, two- or four-year	President	The specific college
	Vice-president	The specific college
	Dean	The specific college
	Dept. head or chairperson	The specific college
	Director	The specific college
Vocational and Technical Institutes	Director	The specific institute
	President	The specific institute
	Vice-president	The specific institute
Schools, public	Superintendent	The specific school system
	Asst. Supt.	The specific school system
	Director[6]	The specific school system
	Coordinator[7]	The specific school system
	Principal	The specific school system
Schools, private	Superintendent	The specific school system
	Director	The specific school system
	Headmaster	The specific school system
	Principal	The specific school system
Schools, parochial	Superintendent	The specific school system
	Principal	The specific school system
Schools, independent or free	Principal	The specific school system
Schools, American Overseas Dependents[8]	Principal	The controlling corporation
Schools, correspondence	Director	National Home Study Council
NONFORMAL[9]		
Mass media		
Magazines, general	Education Editor	The magazine
Newspapers	Education Editor	The newspaper
Book publishers	Education Editor	The publisher
Professional journals	Editor	The journal

TABLE 20-2 (Continued)

TYPE OF AGENCY	TYPICAL POSITION TITLE[1]	POSSIBLE SOURCE OF INFORMATION
Child, youth, and adult groups		
Agricultural Extension	Agent	U.S.D.A.
Boy and Girl Scouts		Nat'l Hdqtrs.
Brownies		Nat'l Hdqtrs.
Campfire Girls		Nat'l Hdqtrs.
Fraternal groups[10]		Nat'l Hdqtrs.
Home Extension	Agent	Nat'l Hdqtrs.
Service clubs[11]		Nat'l Hdqtrs.
Armed services base	Education Director	Service Hdqtrs.
Armed services research and		
development programs	Director of Evaluation	Service Hdqtrs.
U.S. Government-sponsored programs		
Head Start		USOE
National Institutes of Mental Health		The Institute
National Monuments		
National Museums		
National Parks		U.S. Nat'l Park Service
Training programs within agencies	Training Director	A.S.T.D.
VISTA		National Hdqtrs.
Washington Intern Program		USOE
Work-study		
U.S. Government-agency schools		
F.B.I. Academy		F.B.I.
Law Enforcement schools		F.B.I.
Meteorology school		Dept. of Commerce
Philanthropic foundations	Education Director	Council on Foundations, Inc.
	Evaluation Director	Council on Foundations, Inc.
Civic and cultural centers		
Citizenship schools	Director	The specific school
Art centers	Director	The specific center
Concert halls	Manager	The specific hall
Libraries	Director	The specific library
Museums	Director	The specific museum
Theater	Manager	The specific theater
Social organizations		
Ameliorative associations[12]	Director	The specific association
Guidance clinics	Director	The specific clinic
Employment offices (nonprofit)	Manager	The specific office
Penal institutions	Education Director	The specific institution
Welfare agencies	Director	The specific agency
Research corporations	Director	The specific corporation
Company schools	Director of training and Management Development	A.S.T.D.
Special-needs schools[13]	Director	The sponsoring ass'n.
Proprietary schools	Director	The specific school
	Manager	The specific school
	President	The specific school
Correspondence schools		The National Home Study Council

[1] Full-time, *paid* positions only, for persons who are expected to *lead*.

[2] Providing structured, systematic activities for distinct target populations; either direct learning experiences for individuals or services to those schools that do; are part of the hierarchical school system.

[3] Such as audiovisual higher education, NCATE, PTA, and subject-matter associations.

[4] Such as chief state school officers, classroom teachers, school administrators, elementary school principals, secondary school principals, etc.

[5] In any of many subject areas and other specialities.

[6] Of adult education, career education, community education, pupil personnel services, etc.

[7] Of art, music, elementary education, for example.

[8] Financed and controlled by private corporation.

[9] Providing structured, systematic, nonschool activities aimed at a different target population; activities do not advance one to a higher level of the hierarchical school system.

[10] For example, Eagles, Elks, Knights of Columbus, Knights of Pythias, Masons, Moose, Odd Fellows, or Redmen.

[11] For example, Kiwanis, Lions, Rotary, or Sertoma.

[12] Any association conducting educational, nonschool activities aimed at a distinct target population for the purpose of ameliorating a specific social ill; for example, Goodwill Industries (help for the handicapped), Salvation Army (help for indigents), American Cancer Society, Multiple Sclerosis.

[13] Such as those operated by poultry raisers, milk producers, etc.

types of on-the-job experience that may be pertinent to the desired position. If one graduated from an unrecognized or poorly accredited college, it may be necessary to get advanced work or a further degree from a more reputable institution. Whether it is justified or not, there is bias in the minds of some employers against an applicant who has two or more degrees from the same institution. That condition is not an insurmountable obstacle, and may have no connection with the quality of one's education, but there is a suspicion of provincialism when an individual has experienced only one institution of higher education. Furthermore, there are certain institutions whose graduates get more than a proportionate share of certain positions. For example, according to Campbell and Newell (1973), 50 percent of the professors of educational administration received their doctoral degrees from the 20 universities identified by Sims (1970) as having the highest-quality departments of educational administration.

The university attended no doubt holds some key to the kinds of experiences one has had. However, the applicant needs to consider whether his or her education has been strictly academic, providing only or largely cognitive learning (perhaps conceptual skill), or whether experiences such as simulations, games, and internships have been included that may have contributed to the acquisition of human and technical skills.

Regardless of the quality of institution and the quality of academic learning, there are some skills and knowledges that are only acquired on the job. The applicant who has conscientiously learned the requirements of the position that he seeks should rigorously examine whether his experience has given him those qualifications that his education has not. He must ascertain what competencies he has that are demonstrable.

Demonstrable Competencies

Throughout this book, the authors have attempted to highlight the variable dimensions of leadership roles in educational institutions. Implicit in the discussions has been the view that where opportunities to lead are concerned there are primary bases, or criteria, which potential leaders must satisfy. We believe that the bases are embedded in at least four demonstrable competencies, these being: (1) knowledgeability, (2) technical skills, (3) organizational responsiveness, and (4) the ability to work with and to be sensitive to human needs.

KNOWLEDGEABILITY. Knowledgeability, as used here, is related to the Katz (1955) version of "conceptual skill" in that a potential leader must possess not only an ability to see the organization as a whole but must have as well a deep insight into the inner workings of the organization of which she or he wishes to become an integral part.

TECHNICAL SKILLS. The technical skills necessary for the would-be leader obviously will vary with the hierarchical level at which a position is sought. In the upper echelons of organizational life, it is of far greater importance to be able to direct the activities of others, to be capable of leading meetings and discussions, and to achieve agreements about organizational needs and objectives than it is to demonstrate skill in typing, filing, and the making of minor assignments for subordinates.

ORGANIZATIONAL RESPONSIVENESS. Organizational responsiveness is an entirely different dimension, in that the requirement is placed on an aspirant to recognize and to attend to an organization's needs, accept its goals as legitimate, give more of himself or herself than the actual contract would require, and make every effort necessary to achieve its objectives.

HUMAN SKILLS. A fourth, but no less important, demonstrable competence resides in the area of human relationships. The ability to work with people in such a way as to provide them with satisfying experiences while at the same time making use of their individual and collective talents to enhance organizational viability is clearly a high-priority competence. Awareness and sensitivity to human needs is also of considerable importance, as Graves (1966) pointed out. In this regard, it seems imperative to utilize leader styles which are compatible with the developmental level of subordinates in order to increase productive activity as well as to provide for individual satisfactions.

The present writers believe that, unless these competencies can be demonstrated, no matter where leadership opportunities lie individuals who fall short will be thwarted in their efforts to lead. Each individual should keep in mind the competencies that he can demonstrate when he goes job hunting.

Job Hunting
The literature in regard to job hunting in education seems almost nonexistent. Good guides for persons seeking positions in any field are scarce, but the best that the present authors have seen is Jameson's (1972) for industrial executives. Most of its pointers can be adapted by persons seeking positions as educational leaders, and the pointers relate to the areas of planning a campaign and learning of vacancies.

PLANNING A CAMPAIGN. In planning a campaign, a plan-of-action checklist should be developed, an immediate position goal should be set, an outstanding resume *must* be developed, a series of three or four short standard (but *never* dittoed or mimeographed!) letters should be developed, and strategies should be planned. The reference cited gives detailed suggestions on all of these matters, along with examples of resumes and letters. Throughout the campaign the objective should be to present honest information that nevertheless gives the impression that the applicant is above the average. A short version of the resume in letter form is particularly essential for an individual considering a variety of types of positions.

LEARNING OF VACANCIES. Most job opportunities probably come from developing and using personal contacts. A good memory for names and position titles is invaluable and can be cultivated by most individuals. Contacts may include present or former employers, professional colleagues, professors, publishers' representatives, social and community acquaintances, friends, relatives, congressmen, senators, fellow alumni, fraternity or sorority friends, and others. The importance of personal contacts cannot be overemphasized.

Answering advertisments may provide some leads. While public school positions are seldom advertised in newspapers except in a few states, some, particularly for administrators, are. *The Chronicle of Higher Education* regularly carries advertisements of position vacancies, as does the *AAUP Bulletin* and the *Training and Development Journal. Saturday Review* regularly has such a column in its classified advertisements. Professional journals in one's specialty field should be examined to see whether they carry advertisements.

Placing "Situation Wanted" advertisements may develop some leads also, although the practice is looked at askance by many educators. Almost any newspaper, along with periodicals such as those mentioned above, will accept such advertisements.

Direct letters may be effective if they are individually typed and sent to carefully selected individuals. Unless it is known that a vacancy exists, a direct letter should only inquire about the possibility of a vacancy or indicate the writer's interest in working in that particular agency should a vacancy develop. If possible, a direct letter should indicate some familiarity with the agency addressed and with its strengths. Obviously duplicated letters not only may do the writer no good but may be an actual detriment, as each recipient immediately knows that he is only one of many and that there is no personal element, for him or his institution, in the message. There is a widespread feeling that persons who send letters or resumes on a broadcast basis are either exceedingly naive or extremely desperate.

Some placement agencies are operated by colleges or universities on behalf of their graduates, some by professional associations, and some are operated as profit-making businesses. While we have no data to support it, our belief is that few persons with advanced degrees in education are placed by placement agencies. Nevertheless, a job applicant should register with his university placement office, and perhaps with any agency operated in conjunction with professional associations of which he is a member. One should not expect too much by way of results unless one makes unusual efforts to acquaint those persons who make recommendations with one's unique qualifications and needs. Otherwise, the individual may be viewed as one of dozens or hundreds having similar qualifications. Proprietary placement agencies which charge a fee to the person placed often can be worth the fee charged, but seldom have to be resorted to by individuals of superior ability. Some management-consultant or executive-search firms operate in filling high-level educational positions for businesses, industries, government agencies, or foundations, and their fees usually are paid by the employing organizations.

The conventions or conferences of professional associations often serve as valuable sources of job information. Such events often are used by universities as opportunities to maintain headquarters suites where selected job seekers may meet prospective employers and where notices of vacancies can be received. Employers frequently make the rounds of the headquarters of their favorite universities making their needs known. A job seeker who happens to be present has a distinct advantage over others who will learn of vacancies only after they are announced in the placement bulletin.

Some Strategies

Four strategies that should prove helpful, if they are carefully developed and executed, are: (1) know *how* the application procedure *should* work, (2) show how your qualifications fit those required for the job, or (3) make yourself an expert in an area where an expert is needed, or (4) make your own job.

KNOW HOW. Most people not only do not know how to seek and apply for a job, but neither do they know what to expect of employers or how procedures should dovetail to make the employment process easier for both employer and job seeker. Hence the following performance objectives.

   A. "Ideal" performance objectives of the employer include:
      1. Determining staff needs
      2. Establishing qualification to be sought, both minimum and desired
      3. Developing a job description that includes:
         a. job title, building assignment
         b. reason for the opening
         c. reasons why the agency should be considered a good place to work
         d. compensation: salary, extras possible, fringe benefits

         e. other conditions of work
            (1) contract provisions
            (2) physical environment
            (3) social environment (including administrative climate)
            (4) stability of employment
4. Locating qualified applicants
5. Receiving applications
6. Screening applications against listed qualifications
7. Selecting "best qualified" candidates for interview
8. Interviewing candidates
9. Recording information relating to "Can Do" factors (from both application *and* interview)
10. Checking with previous employers and peers regarding "Does Do" factors
11. Recording information relating to "Will Do" factors (from application, interview, and employer-peer checks)
12. Providing testing (if any is required) for likely candidates
13. Analyzing all available information for each candidate in terms of matching desired qualifications
14. Selecting the "best" candidate
15. Making an (acceptable) offer
16. Appointing the person
17. Notifying all unsuccessful candidates
18. Assigning job responsibilities
19. Inducting the individual into the system
20. Orienting the individual to the job
21. Working out performance objectives with the individual
22. Evaluating the individual in terms of his/her objectives

B. "Ideal" performance objectives of the job seeker include:
1. Determining job requirements, both minimum and desired (including community characteristics)
2. Developing a resume that includes (but perhaps is not limited to):
    a. Name, address, phone number, age, marital status
    b. Educational record
    c. "Can Do" factors, such as
        (1) aptitudes
        (2) knowledges
        (3) skills
        (4) intelligence
3. Notifying present employers and peers of decision to seek new employment
4. Discussing reasons (for desiring change) with present employer and peers
5. Locating job openings

6. Submitting applications and resumes
7. Receiving information about possible jobs and communities in which they exist
8. Screening information received against job requirements
9. Interviewing likely employers in terms of asking questions and seeking information regarding how job and community match up to expectations
10. Recording information from the interview
11. Taking tests required by any employers being considered
12. Receiving job offer
13. Visiting the community and agency of the prospective employer
14. Analyzing all information received
15. Accepting job offer
16. Working out performance objectives with new employer

SHOW HOW. There has been repeated emphasis in this book on the applicant fixing his mind on the immediate position to which he aspires. Having done this, and having followed up by planning a campaign that has located one or more position vacancies, the next vital step becomes one of showing potential employers how one is qualified by education and experience to do the job. No one else can do this for the candidate—it is strictly a do-it-yourself job that requires imagination, resourcefulness, persuasiveness, and sales ability. However, if a rigorous campaign has failed to locate a single position vacancy, the candidate should not despair as there are still at least two viable strategies available. They are making oneself expert and making one's own job.

BECOMING EXPERT. In these times, there are always positions to be filled in educational institutions for which there are few or no candidates, or for which candidates are, at best, only marginally qualified. At the time of this writing, one student of the authors' acquaintance seemed to be first in line for a job because, through an internship experience, she had discovered that a community college in which she wanted to work had a need for and wished to employ a director of institutional research. Recognizing that qualified candidates would be few indeed, she set about devoting all of her further formal learning experiences to becoming the best-informed, most-skilled person with a community-college background who would be likely to apply! This is opportunism of a sort, but not the sort that is oblivious of consequences.

MAKING ONE'S OWN JOB. One further strategy available to the resourceful person is to literally carve out a job for himself or herself where none has existed peviously, including finding and developing a source of funding. Again, an example known to the authors is that

of a student who was vitally interested in the matter of program evaluation but could not find a position vacancy commensurate with his
abilities and aspirations. He launched a sophisticated sales campaign to convince the administrators in a state department of education that they should have an evaluation unit. Having developed more
than passing interest on the part of decision-makers, he then wrote,
advocated, and presented a proposal for a federal grant to fund such
a unit on an experimental basis. There should be little doubt that,
if the proposal is funded, he will be employed as director of evaluation. His skills are such that he doubtless can, within the experimental period, demonstrate the worth of the unit. If he does, the state
department will no doubt take over the unit, supporting it with "hard"
money. More than one individual has literally made his or her own
job in similar fashion.

SUMMARY

It is easy—and soothing to the spirit—for a person who can command some sort of following to delude himself that he or she indeed
knows the only path to the Holy Grail. The individual who wishes
to be a career educational leader would do well, though, to ascertain
the satisfactions that he seeks, the constraints under which he will
perforce operate, the point from which he is starting, the position
possibilities that may be open to him, and how he can get from where
he is to where he wishes to go.

Odds of success appear to be better for individuals seeking satisfactions of motivation needs, or a combination of motivation and perceptual needs, than for those driven by maintenance needs alone.
One could almost predict mediocre performance, if not failure, for
the would-be leader seeking satisfactions of maintenance needs
alone.

Constraints under which every educational leader must operate
include expectations of individuals and groups both inside and outside the employing social system, fishbowl visibility, pressures of
time and vested-interest groups, risk, and possible dead ends. The
leader is also constrained by having to start from where she or he
is, but ways of doing this include increasing influence and power
in one's present position, achieving more visibility, judicious timing,
and taking advantage of fortuitous circumstance.

Position possibilities are far more numerous and of infinitely
greater variety then generally conceived by most educators, and
ways of achieving a desired position include getting the necessary
paper qualifications, making sure that one has a quality education,
having demonstrable competencies, planning a campaign, and using
a variety of means for learning of vacancies. The cultivation of personal contacts and the wise use of them unquestionably is the most
fruitful of the means for learning about vacancies.

Helpful tactics that the job seeker may employ to his advantage include knowing how the employment process *should* operate, showing how his education and experience make him uniquely qualified for the job, becoming expert in a specialty that he knows is needed by an agency in which he would like to work, and making his own job.

SOME SUGGESTED RESOURCES

E. M. Bridges, R. F. Campbell, J. E. Corbally, Jr., R. O. Nystrand, and J. A. Ramseyer, *Introduction to educational administration* (4th ed.). Boston: Allyn & Bacon, 1971. Ch. 12, Choosing educational administration as a career, pp. 362–393, and Ch. 14, Challenge of administration, pp. 421–449.

R. F. Campbell and L. J. Newell, *A study of professors of Educational Administration.* Columbus, Ohio: UCEA, 1973.

K. Goldhammer, J. E. Suttle, W. D. Aldridge, and G. L. Becker, Superintendents' perceptions of their problems. Ch. 2 in *Issues and problems in contemporary educational administration.* Eugene, Ore.: Center for the Advanced Study of Educational Administration, University of Oregon, 1967. Pp. 9–53.

M. S. Gordon (Ed.), *Higher education and the labor market.* New York: McGraw-Hill, 1974.

A. W. Halpin, A foggy view from Olympus. In W. G. Walker, A. R. Crane, and A. R. Thomas (Eds.), *Explorations in Educational Administration,* St. Lucia, Australia: University of Queensland Press, 1973. Pp. 377–390.

R. Jameson, *The professional job hunting system.* Verona, N.J.: Performance Dynamics, Inc., 1972.

V. Miller, G. R. Madden, and J. B. Kinchloe, Careers and opportunities in educational administration. Ch. 16 in *The public administration of American school systems* (2nd ed.). New York: Macmillan, 1972. Pp. 397–420.

R. H. Ostrander and R. C. Dethy, Educational administration—a panorama. Ch. 15 in *A values approach to educational administration.* New York: American Book, 1968. Pp. 381–402.

B. M. Sachs, Educational administration as a profession. Ch. 15 in *Educational administration: A behavioral approach.* Boston: Houghton Mifflin, 1966. Pp. 217–233.

B. Sandler, Women: The last minority. *Journal of College Placement,* 1971, **32**(2), 49–50.

R. E. Wilson (Ed.), To point the direction for educational administrators. Ch. 16 in *Educational administration.* Columbus, Ohio: Merrill, 1966.

P. Woodring, On the origins and nature of educational leadership. In R. J. Havighurst (Ed.), *Leaders in American education,* 70th yearbook of NSSE, Part II. Chicago: Unversity of Chicago Press, 1971. Pp. 495–499.

GLOSSARY

Action: An action is a function of the human body or one of its parts.

Administrator: An administrator is a person who puts into effect policies and rules of an organized social system. The term is typically used in regard to persons in governmental or public agencies.

Agency: An agency is a person or an organization that carries on certain activities on behalf of individuals or of social systems.

Appearance: Appearance is the sense impression of reality received by a particular individual.

Authenticity: Authenticity is the degree of congruence between the way a person sees oneself and the way one acts.

Authority: Authority is that relationship which exists when (1) one person rationally legitimizes another individual or a group to make decisions or take actions that affect him or her, or (2) recognizes in another a skill or knowledge that he or she does not possess.

Behavior: Behavior is a pattern of actions.

Charisma: Charisma is a personal quality which results from unusual persuasive ability, power to arouse deep emotions in others, and espousal of one or more causes.

Communication: Communication is a process through which an individual receives a sense impression of another.

Conceptual Skill: Conceptual skill is proficiency in developing and using ideas; the ability to see the whole of an enterprise as well as its parts, to grasp the interrelationships among the elements in a complex situation, and to establish and maintain the delicate balance that fosters both unity and diversity.

Conformity: Conformity is the degree of congruence between the way others would like one to be and the way one acts.

Coordinator: A coordinator is a person responsible for integrating the work of two or more individuals, each of whom is performing a task related to tasks being performed by other members of the social system.

Counselor: A counselor is a person responsible for helping individuals or groups to understand, and sometimes helping them to rechannel, their own need-dispositions.

Cultural System: A cultural system is a collectivity of people adhering to a common value held in such high esteem that its transmission to younger members or other systems is deemed desirable.

Decision-making: Decision-making is a process of carefully discovering and evaluating alternatives in light of clear objectives, aimed at taking action.

Delinquent Behavior: Delinquent behavior is that behavior of an individual or a group that falls outside the general limits of tolerance of the larger society.

Deviant Behavior: Deviant behavior is a series of actions, by an individual or a group, which fall outside the expectation limits accorded to the specific individual or group by a social system of which he/she or it is a part.

Discipline: A discipline is a body of subject matter made up of concepts, facts, and theories, so ordered that it can be deliberately and systematically taught.

Director: A director is a person responsible for getting a given function performed within an organization.

Drives: Drives are action tendencies which appear to the actor to be necessary to achieve some state which seems to him or her to be desirable. They should not be confused with the physiological energy called drive.

Dynamics: Dynamics is the action of forces in producing or changing motion.

Education: Education is a process by means of which one or more individuals set about helping one or more others to learn for a recognized purpose.

Educational Agency (Formal): A formal educational agency is an organization that helps individuals to learn for a purpose through structuring content, and it is a part of a system in which there is unity of purpose and an interaction of units.

Educational Agency (Informal): An informal educational agency is a person or a group through which an individual achieves purposeful learning without structure of content.

Educational Agency (Nonformal): A nonformal agency of education is an organization that helps individuals in a distinct target population to learn for a purpose through providing structured, systematic, nonschool activities that are unrelated to those of similar agencies.

Effectiveness: Effectiveness is the ratio of expectations to performance.

Effectiveness (Self-perceived): Self-perceived effectiveness is a ratio of the way one perceives one's own action to the way one would like to be.

Efficiency: Efficiency is the ratio of benefits to costs.

Ethos: Ethos is a cluster of characteristics, consisting of values, practices, and individual behaviors, that distinguishes one cultural system from another.

Executive: An executive is any person who, by virtue of his or her position or knowledge, is responsible for a contribution that materially affects the capacity of the organization in which he or she works to perform and to obtain results.

Expectation: An expectation is a belief held by an Individual in regard to how he/she or another should perform in a particular role.

Fact: A fact is an aspect of a situation selected by an individual from reality as being relevant to a specific problem.

Facility: A facility is a physical object that aids task performance.

Goal: A goal is an aim or purpose which defines the field of desire and the direction of effort of an individual or a group.

Group: A group is a collectivity of individuals having a common purpose or goal and having communication with each other.

Human Skill: Human skill is proficiency in working with people; the ability to understand people and how they work and get along together, and the use of that ability in getting the best out of people, individually and in groups.

Influence: Influence is a relationship in which one individual affects the thoughts or attitudes of another. The effect often is manifest in actions.

Information: Information is a communication that reduces uncertainty for the receiver.

Inner-directed Person: An inner-directed person is an individual whose dominant values are principles, and whose motivation is self-approval.

Institution: An institution is an established practice, law, custom, or belief to which sufficient value is attached that efforts are made to insure its perpetuation.

Integrity: Integrity is the degree of congruence between the self a person would like to be and the self one exhibits through one's acts.

Kinesics: Kinesics is a science of body behavioral communication; it is in the early-development stage.

Learning: Learning is a process of acquiring information or finding meaning in information. It always requires action, interaction, or reaction of the learner.

Leader: A leader is a person who helps an individual or a group to move toward goals that group members find acceptable.

Leader Style: Leader style is a consistent manner in which an individual performs actions in helping a group move toward goals acceptable to its members.

Leadership: Leadership is a process in which an individual or a group of individuals take initiative to assist a group to move toward production goals that are acceptable, to maintain the group, to dispose of those needs of individuals within the group that impelled them to join it, and to innovate.

Legalism: Legalism is undue strictness in conforming to rules or procedures as a means of justifying behavior.

Manager: A manager is a person who gets work done by people or things. The term is typically used in regard to persons in business or industry, where it is further defined to mean one who makes decisions about utilization of machines, manpower, materials, and time.

Model: A model is a visual representation of an idea that is believed to be more effective than words alone.

Motivation: A motivation is an orientation toward certain goals sufficient to bring about action.

Need: A need is a relationship of an individual to his or her environment.

Need-disposition: A need-disposition is a tendency of an individual to act with respect to objects or persons in certain manners and to expect certain consequences.

Neurotic Behavior: Neurotic behavior is a series of actions of an individual which are concentrated within a very narrow sector of the expectation limits accorded her or him by a social system of which she or he is a member.

Norm: A norm is an expectation limit held generally by social system members for each member.

Objective: An objective is a measurable action which is expected to help an individual or a group to reach a goal.

Observation: Observation is the conscious noting of reception of sensory impression.

Operant Behavior: Operant behavior is a group of actions patterned according to the interactions of the members of a specific social system.

Organization: An organization is a structure intended to perpetuate a more or less fixed relationship within a social system.

Other-directed Person: An other-directed person is an individual whose dominant values are messages from significant others and whose motivation is group approval.

Perception: Perception is the interpretation given to reality by an individual.

Personality: Personality is the means by which a person is recognizable from day to day other than by appearance.

Policy: A policy is a general guide to individuals' limits of discretion adopted by a formal group.

Position: A position is a status in an organization as defined by the task or tasks allocated to the holder and by the predispositions of organization members.

Power: Power is that relationship in which one individual has the capability to apply sanctions to another.

Principle: A principle is a statement of order or relationship that is so generally accepted that it seldom is stated or challenged.

Problem: A problem is a deviation from some pre-set standard of performance; an imbalance between *what should be* and *what is.*

Problem Specification: Problem specification is a process in which a deviation from the standard is precisely identified, located, and described.

Problem Analysis: Problem analysis is a process of observation and comparison, aimed at finding cause.

Procedure: A procedure is an established manner of performing a task.

Process: A process is a series of actions or operations definitely conducing to an end.

Reality: Reality is the world of things as they are.

Respondent Behavior: Respondent behavior is a group of actions patterned according to the *expectations* of certain members of a specific social system.

Regulation: A regulation is a statement of expectation held by an individual or a group for all subgroups under his/her or its jurisdiction.

Risk: Risk is a situation which poses some possible threat for an individual, a group, or an organization.

Role: A role is the total of expectations held by the members of a social system for an individual within that system.

Rule: A rule is a statement of the way in which an individual is expected to perform in a specific situation.

Sanctions: Sanctions are reactions of one individual to another's actions, and consist of rewards and punishments.

Schooling: Schooling is that part of the education process in which structure of content is provided to help individuals to learn in a particular place.

Science: A science is a body of knowledge of systematized facts resulting in laws or principles.

Self-adequacy: Self-adequacy is the degree of congruence between the way a person sees oneself and the way one would like to be.

Significant Other: A significant other is a person whose approval is meaningful to an individual.

Social System: A social system is a group of persons in which the action of one affects the actions of others.

Status: Status is the state of condition of an individual compared to other members of a social system.

Structure: A structure is a pattern of relationships of interdependent parts.

Style: A style is a consistent manner of behaving.

Superordinate: A superordinate is a person whose position in an organizational hierarchy is above one's own.

Supervisor: A supervisor is a person responsible for helping others to improve their work.

Teacher (Instructor, Professor): A teacher is a person responsible for helping others to learn.

Technical Skill: Technical skill is proficiency in dealing with things; the ability to use the facilities and tools that can aid in task accomplishment.

Teaching: Teaching is that part of the process of education through which one individual directly helps another to learn.

Theory: A theory is a framework for raising intelligent questions about a phenomenon and about data which might be relevant to answering those questions, and for relating those questions to what is already known or generally assumed.

Tool: A tool is any thing or process which serves as a means to an end.

Tradition-directed Person: A tradition-directed person is an individual whose dominant values are detailed, conforming behavior and whose motivation is society's approval.

Training: Training is a process by means of which an individual learns (1) to utilize or coordinate certain muscles in an increasingly skillful manner, (2) to recall certain learning on demand, or (3) a conditioned response.

Value: A value is a choice of an individual or a social system as to what is worthy of effort, devotion, and allegiance.

Variant Behavior: Variant behavior is a series of actions by an individual which is not conforming in all its aspects but which occurs within tolerable limits prescribed by a social system of which one is a member.

Want: A want is a perceived deficiency of the means for gaining a desired reward or avoiding a punishment.

REFERENCES

Abbott, M. G. Intervening variables in organizational behavior. *Educational Administration Quarterly*, 1965, **1**(Winter), 1–13.

Abel, A. *The great American hoax*. New York: Trident, 1966.

Abert, J. G. Wanted: Experiments in reducing the cost of education. *Phi Delta Kappan*, 1974, **55**(7), 444–445.

Adair, J. *Training for leadership*. London: McDonald, 1968.

Adiseshiah, M. S. Life–long education. *Indian Journal of Adult Education*, 1971, **32**(4), 3–6, 19.

Allport, G. W. *The person in psychology*. Boston: Beacon, 1968.

American Association of School Administrators. *Inservice education for school administration*. Washington, D.C.: The Association, 1963.

American Association of School Administrators. Professional administrators. *Professional administrators for America's schools*. Washington, D.C.: The Association, 1960.

American Association of School Administrators. *The education of a school superintendent*. Washington, D.C.: The Association, 1963.

Anderson, C. M. The self-image: A theory of the dynamics of behavior. In L. D. Crow and A. Crow (Eds.), *Readings in child and adolescent psychology*. New York: Longmans & Green, 1961. Pp. 406–419.

Anderson, D. F. Leadership effectiveness in education as related to human behavior and leadership style. Unpublished doctoral dissertation, Western Michigan University, 1973.

Anderson, J. G. Bureaucratic rules: Bearers of organizational authority. *Educational Administration Quarterly*, 1966, **2**(Winter), 7–34.

Argyris, C. *Personality and organization*. New York: Harper & Row, 1957.

Argyris, C. The CEO's behavior: Key to organizational development. *Harvard Business Review*, 1973, **51**(2), 5–14.

Aries, Philippe. *Centuries of childhood*. New York: Random House, Vintage, 1962.

Association for Supervision and Curriculum Development. *Leadership for improving instruction*. Washington, D.C.: The Association, 1960.

Atkinson, J. W., and Feather, N. T. *A theory of achievement motivation.* New York: Wiley, 1966.

Barnard, C. I. *The functions of the executive.* Cambridge, Mass.: Harvard University Press, 1938.

Barnard, C. I. The nature of leadership. In S. D. Hoslett (Ed.), *Human factors in management.* New York: Harper & Row, 1946.

Bartky, A. J. The moral aspect of leadership. In *Supervision as human relations.* Lexington, Mass.: Heath, 1953.

Bass, B. M. *Leadership, psychology and organizational behavior.* New York: Harper & Row, 1960.

Bell, E. H. *Social foundations of human behavior.* New York: Harper & Row, 1961.

Bellamy, D. *Looking backward.* Boston: Houghton Mifflin, 1887.

Bellows, R., Gilson, T., and Odiorne, G. *Executive skills: Their dynamics and development.* Englewood Cliffs, N.J.: Prentice-Hall, 1962.

Bennis, W. G. A funny thing happened on the way to the future. *American Psychologist,* 1970 (July), 595–608.

Bennis, W. G. Chairman Mac in perspective. *Harvard Business Review,* 1972, **50**(5), 139–143.

Bennis, W. G., and Slater, P. T. *The temporary society.* New York: Harper & Row, 1968.

Berelson, B., and Steiner, G. A. *Human behavior.* New York: Harcourt Brace Jovanovich, 1964.

Berelson, B., and Steiner, G. A. *Human behavior.* (Shorter Ed.) New York: Harcourt Brace Jovanovich, 1967.

Berkley, G. E. *The administrative revolution.* Englewood Cliffs, N.J.: Prentice-Hall, 1971.

Berlo, D. K. *The process of communication.* New York: Holt, Rinehart & Winston, 1960.

Betz, R. L. A proposed typology for group processes. *Michigan Personnel and Guidance Journal,* 1973, **4**(2), 18–23.

Birdwhistell, R. L. Kinesics. In D. L. Sills (Ed.), *International encyclopedia of the social sciences.* Vol. 8. New York: Macmillan, 1968.

Blake, R. R., and Mouton, J. S. *The managerial grid.* Houston, Tex.: Gulf, 1964.

Boles, H. W. Changes in local school executive positions in Ohio during 1951. *Educational Research Bulletin,* 1952, **31**, 118–128.

Boles, H. W. The real issue. *Contemporary Education,* 1970, **41**, 263–268.

Boyer, E. L. Managing tomorrow's education. Ch. 5 in *Challenge to leadership.* New York: Free Press, 1973.

Braginsky, B. M., and Braginsky, D. D. Stimulus/response: the mentality retarded: society's Hansels and Gretels. *Psychology Today,* 1974, **7**(10), 18, 20–21, 24, 26, 28–30.

Branden, N. *The psychology of self-esteem.* Los Angeles: Nash, 1959.

Brouwer, P. J. The power to see ourselves. *Harvard Business Review,* 1964, **42**, 166–182.

Brown, A. F. Reactions to leadership. *Educational Administration Quarterly,* 1967, **3**(1), 62–73.

Brown, C. T., and Keller, P. W. *Monologue to dialogue.* Englewood Cliffs, N.J.: Prentice-Hall, 1973.

Brown, D. S. *Understanding the management function* (monograph). Washington, D.C.: Leadership Resources, Inc., 1966.

Brown, R. E. *Judgment in administration.* New York: McGraw-Hill, 1966.

Bruner, J. Culture, politics and pedagogy. *Saturday Review,* 1968, **51**, 69–72.

Bugenthal, J. F. T. *The search for authenticity.* New York: Holt, Rinehart & Winston, 1965.

Buros, O. K. *Personality tests and reviews: Including an index to the mental measurements yearbooks.* New York: Gryphon, 1970.

Bushnell, D. D. For each student a teacher. *Saturday Review,* 1966, **49**(30), 31.

Business Week. Why scientists take psychic research seriously. 1974 (Jan. 26), 76–78.

Byrd, R. E. How much risk can you afford to take? *Management Review,* 1971, **60**(5), 4–9.

Campbell, R. F., Bridges, E. M., Corbally, J. E., Jr., Nystrand, R. O., and Ramseyer, J. A. *Introduction to educational administration.* (4th ed.) Boston: Allyn & Bacon, 1971.

Campbell, R. F., and Newell, R. J. *A study of professors of educational administration.* Columbus, Ohio: UCEA, 1973.

Carkhuff, R. R. *The development of human resources.* New York: Holt, Rinehart & Winston, 1971.

Cartwright, D., and Zander, A. *Group dynamics.* New York: Harper & Row, 1953.

Carver, F. D. and Sergiovanni, T. J. Complexity, adaptability, and job satisfaction: an axiomatic theory applied. *Journal of Educational Administration,* 1971, **9**(1), 10–31.

Cass, J. Do schools make a difference? *Saturday Review/World,* 1974, **1**(9), 59.

Cattell, R. B. Personality pinned down. *Psychology Today,* 1973, **7**(2), 40–46.

Chase, S. *The proper study of mankind.* New York: Harper & Row, 1948.

Clark, B. R. *Educating the expert society.* San Francisco: Chandler, 1962.

Clark, B. R. The sociology of educational administration. In *Perspectives on educational administration and the behavioral sciences.* Eugene, Ore.: CASEA, 1965.

Clark, H. F., and Sloan, H. S. *Classrooms in the factories.* Rutherford, N.J.: Institute of Research, Fairleigh Dickinson University, 1958.

Clark, H. F., and Sloan, H. S. *Classrooms in the stores.* Sweet Springs, Mo.: Roxbury Press, 1962.

Clark, H. F., and Sloan, H. S. *Classrooms in the military.* New York: Bureau of Publications, Teachers College, 1964.

Clark, H. F., and Sloan, H. S. *Classrooms on Main street.* New York: Teachers College, 1966.

Clear, D. K., and Seager, R. C. The legitimacy of administrative influence as perceived by selected groups. *Educational Administration Quarterly,* 1971, **7**(1), 46–64.

Coch, L., and French, J. R. P. Overcoming resistance to change. *Human Relations,* 1948, **1**, 512–532.

Cohen, W. J. Education and learning. In *Annals of the American Academy of Political and Social Science,* 1967, **373**, 79–101.

Coleman, J. S. Community disorganization. In R. K. Merton and R. A. Nisbet (Eds.), *Contemporary social problems.* (2nd ed.) New York: Harcourt, Brace Jovanovich, 1966a.

Coleman, J. S. *Equality of educational opportunity.* Washington, D.C.: USOE 38001, 1966b.

Combs, A. W., and Snygg, D. *Individual behavior* (rev. ed.). New York: Harper & Row, 1959.

Conant, J. C. The performance appraisal. *Business Horizons,* 1973 (June), 73–8.

Cook, D. L. *Program evaluation and review technique applications in education.* Washington, D.C.: GPO, 1966.

Coopersmith, S. *Antecedents of self-esteem.* San Francisco: Freeman, 1967.

Coyne, J., and Hebert, T. *This way out.* New York: Dutton, 1972.

Cremin, L. *Genius of American education.* Pittsburgh, Pa.: University of Pittsburgh Press, 1965.

Davenport, J. A. Educational decision-making: Who makes the decisions? *The Michigan Elementary Principal,* 1964, **39**(2), 9.

Delbecq, A. L. and Van de Ven, A. H. A group process model for problem identification and program planning. *The Journal of Applied Behavioral Science,* 1971, **7**(4), 466–492.

Deutsch, M. Conflict and its resolution. Presidential address presented before Division 8 meeting of the American Psychological Association, Personality and Social Division, Chicago, September 1965.

Diggory, J. C. *Self-evaluation: Concepts and studies.* New York: Wiley, 1966.

Drucker, P. F. Managing the educated. In D. Fenn (Ed.), *Management's mission in a new society.* New York: McGraw-Hill, 1959.

Drucker, P. F. *Landmarks of tomorrow: A report on the new "post-modern" world.* New York: Harper Colophon, 1965.

Drucker, P. F. *The effective executive.* New York: Harper & Row, 1967.

Drucker, P. F. Beyond stick and carrot: Hysteria over the work ethic. *Psychology Today,* 1973, **7**(6), 87–92.

Drury, T. Science is finding ways to make you smarter. *Nation's Business,* 1966 (June), 102–104ff.

Ebel, R. L. What are schools for? *Phi Delta Kappan,* 1972, **54**(1), 3–7.

Eisenstadt, S. N. Social institutions: The concept. In D. L. Sills (Ed.), *International encyclopedia of the social sciences.* Vol. 14. New York: Macmillan, 1968.

Emery, D. A. *The compleat manager.* New York: McGraw-Hill, 1970.

Fabun, D. *Communications: The transfer of meaning.* Beverly Hills, Calif.: Glencoe Press, 1968.

Farson, R. *Birthrights: A bill of rights for children.* New York: Macmillan, 1974.

Fast, J. *Body language.* Philadelphia: Lippincott, 1970.

Fielder, F. E. *Theory of leadership effectiveness.* New York: McGraw-Hill, 1967.

Fiedler, F. E. Style or circumstance: The leadership enigma. *Psychology Today,* 1969, **2**(10), 38–43.

Fiedler, F. E. Stimulus/response: The trouble with leadership training is that it doesn't train leaders. *Psychology Today,* 1973, **6**(9), 23, 25, 26, 29, 30, 92.

Follett, M. P. In H. C. Metcalf (Ed.), *Scientific foundations of business administration.* Baltimore, Md.: Williams & Wilkins, 1926.

Frank, L. K. How to be a modern leader. New York: Association Press, 1954.

French, J. R. P., and Raven, B. The bases of social power. In D. Cartwright (Ed.), *Studies in social power.* Ann Arbor, Mich.: Institute for Social Research, 1959.

Gagné, R. M. *The conditions of learning.* (2nd ed.) New York: Holt, Rinehart & Winston, 1970.

Gardner, J. W. *Self-renewal: The individual and the innovative society.* New York: Harper & Row, 1963.

Gardner, J. W. The anti-leadership vaccine. In *Annual Report.* New York: Carnegie Corporation of New York, 1965.

Getzels, J. W., and Guba, E. G. Social behavior and the administrative process. *School Review,* 1957, **65**(4), 423–441.

Getzels, J. W., Lipham, J. M., and Campbell, R. F. *Educational administration as a social process.* New York: Harper & Row, 1968.

Gibb, C. A. The principles and traits of leadership. In C. G. Browne and T. S. Cohn (Eds.), *The study of leadership.* Danville, Ill.: Interstate, 1958.

Gibb, C. A. Leadership: Psychological aspects. In D. S. Sills (Ed.), *International encyclopedia of the social sciences.* Vol. 9. New York: Macmillan, 1968.

Ginzberg, E. *The development of human resources.* New York: McGraw-Hill, 1966.

Goldenson, R. M. *The encyclopedia of human behavior: Psychology, psychiatry, and mental health.* Garden City, N.Y.: Doubleday, 1970. 2 vols.

Goldman, B. A., and Saunders, J. L. *Directory of unpublished experimental mental measures.* Vol. 1. New York: Behavioral Publications, 1974.

Goldman, H. Educational leadership, fact or fiction? *Theory Into Practice,* 1969, **8**(1), 11–13.

Golembiewski, R. T. *Men, management, and morality.* New York: McGraw-Hill, 1965.

Good, C. V. (Ed.) *Dictionary of education.* New York: McGraw-Hill, 1973.

Gordon, T. *Parent effectiveness training: The no-lose program for raising responsible children.* New York: Peter H. Wyden, 1970.

Goslin, D. A. *The school in contemporary society.* Glenview, Ill.: Scott, Foresman, 1965.

Gouldner, A. W. Cosmopolitans and locals: Toward an analysis of latent social roles, I and II. *Administrative Science Quarterly,* 1957, **2**, 281–306; 1958, **3**, 444–480.

Gouldner, A. W. In J. Litterer (Ed.), *Organizations: Structure and behavior.* New York: Wiley, 1963.

Graubard, A. *Free the children.* New York: Pantheon, 1973.

Graves, C. W. Deterioration of work standards. *Harvard Business Review,* 1966, **44**(5), 117–128.

Gronlund, N. E. *Stating behavioral objectives for classroom instruction.* New York: Macmillan, 1970.

Gunther, M. How to succeed at corporate visibility. *Signature,* 1971, **6**(1), 36, 37, 48, 50.

Hackamack, L. C., and Solid, A. B. The woman executive: There is still ample room for progress. *Business Horizons,* 1972 (April), 89–93.

Hägerstrand, T. Diffusion: The diffusion of innovations. In D. L. Sills (Ed.), *International encyclopedia of the social sciences.* Vol. 4. New York: Macmillan, 1968.

Hall, E. T. *The silent language.* Garden City, N.Y.: Doubleday, 1959.

Halle, L. J. *Sedge.* New York: Praeger, 1963.

Halpin, A. W. *The leadership behavior of school superintendents.* (2nd ed.) Chicago: Midwest Administration Center, University of Chicago, 1959.

Halpin, A. W. *Theory and research in administration.* New York: Macmillan, 1966.

Havighurst, R. J. *Developmental tasks and education.* (3rd ed.) New York: McKay, 1972.

Headlee, R. The nature and nurture of charisma. *Transactions,* 1969 (Spring), 3–7.

Heilbroner, R. *The future as history.* New York: Harper & Row, 1960.

Hersey, P., and Blanchard, K. H. Life cycle theory of leadership. *Training and Development Journal,* 1969, **23**(5), 26–34.

Hersey, P., and Blanchard, K. H. *Management of organizational behavior.* (2nd ed.) Englewood Cliffs, N.J.: Prentice-Hall, 1972.

Herzberg, F. The new industrial psychology. *Industrial and Labor Relations Review,* 1965, **18**, 364–376.

Herzberg, F. *Work and the nature of man.* New York: World, 1966.

Herzberg, F. One more time: How do you motivate employees? *Harvard Business Review,* 1968, **46**(1), 53–62.

Herzberg, F., Mausner, B., and Snyderman, B. B. *The motivation to work.* (2nd ed.) New York: Wiley, 1959.

Hicks, H. G. *The management of organizations: A system and human resources approach.* (2nd ed.) New York: McGraw-Hill, 1972.

Hochberg, J. E. Perception: Introduction, In D. L. Sills (Ed.), *International encyclopedia of the social sciences.* Vol. 11. New York: Macmillan, 1968.

Hollander, E. P. Conformity, status, and idiosyncrasy credit. *Psychological Review,* 1958, 65(2), 117–127.

Hollander, E. P., and Hunt, R. G. *Current perspectives in social psychology.* New York: Oxford University Press, 1967.

Holt, J. *Freedom and beyond.* New York: Dutton, 1972.

Homans, G. C. *The human group.* New York: Harcourt Brace Jovanovich, 1950.

Homans, G. C. *Social behavior: Its elementary forms.* New York: Harcourt Brace Jovanovich, 1961.

Hovland, C. I., Janis, I. L., and Kelley, H. H. *Communication and persuasion.* New Haven, Conn.: Yale University Press, 1953.

Hughes, C. L. *Goal setting: Key to individual and organizational effectiveness.* New York: American Management Association, Inc., 1965.

Hughes, J. F., and Hughes, A. O. *Equal education.* Bloomington, Ind.: Indiana University Press, 1973.

Hutchins, R. M. Are we educating our children for the wrong future? *Saturday Review,* 1965 (Sept. 11), 66–68.

Illich, I. *De-schooling society.* New York: Harper & Row, 1971.

Irvine, D. J. Specifications for an educational system of the future. *Phi Delta Kappan,* 1972, **53**(6), 362–364.

Jackson, P. W. Deschooling? NO! *Today's Education,* 1972, **61**(8), 18–22.

Jameson, R. *The professional job hunting system.* Verona, N.J.: Performance Dynamics, Inc. 1972.

Janis, I. L. Groupthink. *Yale Alumni Magazine,* 1973, **36**(4), 16–19.

Jay, A. *Corporation man.* New York: Random House, 1971.

Jay, A. Fame and feedback. Ch. 16 in *Management and Machiavelli.* New York: Holt, Rinehart & Winston, 1968.

Jencks, C. et al. *Inequality: A reassessment of the effect of family and schooling in America.* New York: Basic Books, 1972.

Jersild, A. T. *In search of self.* New York: Bureau of Publications, Teachers College, 1952.

Kaplan, L. *Mental health and human relations in education.* New York: Harper & Row, 1959.

Kast, F. E., and Rosenzweig, J. E. *Organization and management: A systems approach.* New York: McGraw Hill, 1970.

Katz, R. L. Skills of an effective administrator. *Harvard Business Review,* 1955, **33**(2), 33–42.

Kepner, C. H., and Tregoe, B. B. *The rational manager.* New York: McGraw-Hill, 1965.

Killian, R. A. *Managers must lead.* New York: American Management Association, Inc., 1966.

Kimbrough, R. B. *Political power and educational decision-making.* Skokie, Ill.: Rand McNally, 1964.

Kimbrough, R. B. *Administering elementary schools: Concepts and practices.* New York: Macmillan, 1968.

Kindall, A. F., and Gatza, J. Positive program for performance appraisal. *Harvard Business Review,* 1963, **41**(6), 153–160.

Kluckhohn, C. Values and value-orientations in the theory of action: An exploration in definition and classification. Ch. 2 of Part 4 in T. Parsons and E. A. Shils (Eds.), *Toward a general theory of action.* New York: Harper & Row, 1951.

Knickerbocker, I. Leadership: A conception and some implications. *Journal of Social Issues,* 1948, **4**(3), 23–40.

Knight, B. M. A study of selected variables associated with idiosyncrasy credit. Unpublished doctoral dissertation, Western Michigan University, 1971.

Koontz, H. *Principles of management.* New York: McGraw-Hill, 1968.

Kraai, J. L. The perceived effects of physical distance, intervening obstacles, and race during interviews between administrators and teachers. Unpublished Ed. D. dissertation, Western Michigan University, 1973.

Lane, W. R., Corwin, R. G., and Monahan, W. G. *Foundations of educational administration: A behavioral analysis.* New York: Macmillan, 1967.

LaPiere, R. T. *Collective behavior.* New York: McGraw-Hill, 1938.

Lawshe, C. H., and Balma, M. J. *Principles of personnel testing.* (2nd ed.) New York: McGraw-Hill, 1966.

Leavitt, H. J. *Managerial psychology.* (2nd ed.) Chicago: University of Chicago Press, 1964.

Lerbinger, O., and Sullivan, A. J. (Eds.) *Information, influence, and communication.* New York: Basic Books, 1965.

Levinson, H. Asinine attitudes toward motivation. Harvard Business Review, **51**(1), 70–76.

Levinson, H. *Executive stress.* New York: Harper & Row, 1970.

Levinson, H. *The great jackass fallacy.* Boston: Division of Research, Graduate School of Business Administration, Harvard University, 1973.

Likert, R. *Resolving social conflict.* New York: Harper & Row, 1958.

Likert, R. *Human organization.* New York: McGraw-Hill, 1967.

Likert, R. New patterns of management. New York: McGraw-Hill, 1961.

Linton, R. Concepts of role and status. In R. Linton, *The cultural background of personality.* Englewood Cliffs, N.J.: Prentice-Hall, 1945. (Republished: In T. M. Newcomb and E. L. Hartley (Eds.), *Readings in social psychology.* New York, Holt, Rinehart & Winston, 1947.)

Linton, R. *The study of man: An introduction.* Englewood Cliffs, N.J.: Prentice-Hall, 1936.

Lipham, J. M. Leadership and administration. In NSSE, *Behavioral science and educational administration,* 63rd yearbook. Part II. Chicago: University of Chicago Press, 1964.

Lippitt, R., and White, R. An experimental study of leadership and group life. In T. M. Newcomb and E. L. Hartley (Eds.), *Readings in social psychology.* New York: Holt, Rinehart & Winston, 1947.

Litchfield, E. H. Notes on a general theory of administration. *Administrative Science Quarterly,* 1956, **1**(1), 3–29.

Livingston, J. S. Myth of the well-educated manager. *Harvard Business Review,* 1971, **49**(1), 79–89.

Lonsdale, R. C. Maintaining the organization in dynamic equilibrium. In NSSE, *Behavioral science and educational administration.* 63rd yearbook. Part II. Chicago: University of Chicago Press, 1964.

Loughary, J. W. (Ed.) *Man-machine systems in education.* New York: Harper & Row, 1966.

McCarty, D. J. How community power structures influence administrative tenure. *The American School Board Journal,* 1964, **148**(5), 11–13.

McDavid, J. W., and Harari, H. *Social psychology.* New York: Harper & Row, 1968.

McGill, R. Educational problems pose a need for new leadership. *Kalamazoo Gazette,* February 4, 1966. P. 6.

McGregor, D. An uneasy look at performance appraisal. *Harvard Business Review,* 1957, **35**(3), 89–94.

McGregor, D. *The human side of enterprise.* New York: McGraw-Hill, 1960.

McGregor, D. *Leadership and motivation.* Boston; M.I.T. Press, 1966.

McLuhan, M. *Understanding media: The extensions of man.* New York: Signet (paperback ed.), 1964.

McNally, H. J. Evaluation of what? for what? *Educational Administration and Supervision,* 1949, **35**(1), 36–48.

McNally, H. J. Teacher evaluation that makes a difference. *Educational Leadership,* 1972, **29**(4), 353–357.

Mackenzie, R. A. *The time trap.* New York: American Management Association, Inc., 1972.

Macy, J. W., Jr. Automated government. *Saturday Review,* 1966, **49**(30), 23–25, 70.

March, J. G., and Simon, H. A. *Organizations.* New York: Wiley, 1958.

Maslow, A. H. *Motivation and personality.* New York: Harper & Row, 1954.

Maslow, A. H. *Eupsychian management.* Homewood, Ill.: Irwin 1965.

Mayer, M. *The schools.* New York: Harper & Row, 1961.

Mead, M. *Culture and commitment: A study of the generation gap.* Garden City, N.Y.: Doubleday, 1970.

Merrill, F. E. *Society and culture: An introduction to sociology.* (4th ed.) Englewood Cliffs, N.J.: Prentice-Hall, 1969.

Merton, R. K. Types of influentials: The local and the cosmopolitan. In P. F. Lazarsfeld and F. N. Stanton (Eds.), *Communications research.* 1948. (Republished: As addition to *Social theory and social structure.* (2nd ed.) New York: Free Press, 1957.)

Metcalf, H. C. (Ed.) *Scientific foundations of business administration.* Baltimore, Md.: Williams & Wilkins, 1926.

Michael, D. N. *The unprepared society: Preparing for a precarious future.* New York: Harper Colophon, 1968.

Midler, P. (Ed.) *Psychological assessment of mental and physical handicaps.* London: Methuen, 1970.

Mihalasky, J., and Dean, E. D. *Executive ESP.* Englewood Cliffs, N.J.: Prentice-Hall, 1974.

Miles, M. B. *Learning to work in groups.* New York: Teachers College, 1959.

Milner, M., Jr. Race, education, and jobs: Trends, 1960–1970. *Sociology of Education,* 1973, **46**(3), 280–298.

Mockler, R. J. Situational theory of management. *Harvard Business Review,* 1971, **49**(3), 146–155.

Morris, D. *The naked ape.* New York: McGraw-Hill, 1967.

Mort, P. R., and Ross, D. H. *Principles of school administration.* New York: McGraw-Hill, 1957.

Moser, R. F. The leadership patterns of school superintendents and school principals. *Administrator's Notebook,* 1957, **6**, unpaginated.

Mosteller, F., and Moynihan, D. P. (Eds.) *On equality of educational opportunity.* New York: Vantage, 1972.

Murray, H. A. Toward a classification of interaction. Ch. 3 of Part 4 in T. Parsons and E. A. Shils (Eds.), *Toward a general theory of action, q.v.* New York: Harper & Row, 1951.

Murray, H. A. et al. *Explorations in personality.* New York: Oxford University Press, 1938.

Myers, M. S. Who are your motivated workers? *Harvard Business Review,* 1964, **42**(1), 72–88.

Neff, W. S. *Work and human behavior.* New York: Atherton, 1968.

Nelson, D. P. Similarities and differences among leaders and followers. In C. R. Gibb (Ed.), *Leadership.* Baltimore, Md.: Penguin, 1969.

Nelson, R. R. Innovation. In D. L. Sills (Ed.), *International encyclopedia of the social sciences.* Vol. 7. New York: Macmillan, 1968.

Odiorne, G. S. *How managers make things happen.* Englewood Cliffs, N.J.: Prentice-Hall, 1961.

Overstreet, H. A. Criteria of maturity. In *The mature mind.* New York: Norton, 1949.

Page, E. B. How we all failed at performance contracting. *Phi Delta Kappan,* 1972, **54**(2), 115–117.

Parsons, T., and Shils, E. (Eds.) *Toward a general theory of action.* New York: Harper & Row, 1951. Harper Torchbook (paperback ed.), 1962.

Paulston, R. G. (Ed.) *Non-formal education: An annotated international bibliography.* New York: Praeger, 1972.

Pediwell, J. A. *The saber-tooth curriculum.* New York: McGraw-Hill, 1939.

Peter, L. J., and Hull, R. *The peter principle.* New York: Bantam, 1969.

Pfeiffer, J. *The thinking machine.* Philadelphia: Lippincott, 1962.

Pfeiffer, J. *New look at education: Systems analysis in our schools and colleges.* New York: Odyssey, 1968.

Pfeiffer, J. W., and Sabers, D. *Attrition and achievement in correspondence study.* Washington: NHSC, 1970.

Plachy, R. Leader power requires the consent of followers. *Modern Hospital,* 1973, **120**(3), 153–156.

Plumb, J. H. The great change in children. *Intellectual Digest,* 1972, 2(8), 82–84.

Postman, N., and Weingartner, C. *Teaching as a subversive activity.* New York: Delacorte, 1969.

Postman, N., and Weingartner, C. A careful guide to the school squabble. *Psychology Today,* 1973a, **7**(5), 76–78, 80, 82, 84, 86.

Postman, N., and Weingartner, C. *The school book.* New York: Delacorte, 1973b.

Presthus, R. *The organizational society.* New York: Vintage, 1962.

Punch, K. F., and Ducharme, D. J. Life cycle leadership theory: Some empirical evidence. *The Journal of Educational Administration,* 1972, **10**(1), 66–77.

Quie, A. H. Drastic reform proposed for compensatory education. *Compact,* 1973 (May–June), 33–35.

Randall, L. K. Common questions and tentative answers regarding organization development. *California Management Review,* 1971, **13**(3), 45–52.

Reddin, W. J. *Managerial effectiveness.* New York: McGraw-Hill, 1970.

Reeves, E. T. Applied psychology in the training director's job. Reprint from *The Journal of the American Society of Training Directors,* 1961, 1962.

Reimer, E. *School is dead.* Garden City, N.Y.: Doubleday, 1971.

Reisman, D. *The lonely crowd: A study of the changing American character.* New Haven, Conn.: Yale University Press, 1950.

Roethlisberger, F. J. *Man-in-organization.* Cambridge: Harvard University Press, 1968.

Rogers, C. R., and Roethlisberger, F. J. Barriers and gateways to communication. *Harvard Business Review,* 1952, **30**(4), 46–52.

Rogers, E. M., and Svenning, L. *Managing change.* USOE Grant for Operation PEP: A statewide project to prepare educational planners for California, September, 1969.

Rokeach, M. Persuasion that persists. *Psychology Today,* 1971, **5**(4), 68–71, 92.

Rorty, M. C. AMA's ten commandments of good organization. In C. Heyel (Ed.), *The encyclopedia of management.* Vol. 2. New York: Reinhold, 1963.

Rosenthal, R. The pygmalion effect lives. *Psychology Today,* 1973, **7**(4), 56–63.

Sanday, P. R. An alternative interpretation of the relationship between heredity, race, environment, and IQ. *Phi Delta Kappan,* 1972, **54**(4), 250–254.

Sarnoff, D. No life untouched. *Saturday Review,* 1966, **49**(30), 21–22.

Saretsky, G. The strangely significant case of Peter Doe. *Phi Delta Kappan,* 1973, **54**(9), 589–592.

Sawrey, J. M., and Telford, C. W. *Educational psychology* (4th ed.). Boston: Allyn and Bacon, 1973.

Saxe, R. W. (Ed.) *Opening the schools: Alternative ways of learning.* Berkeley, Calif.: McCutchan, 1972.

Schein, E. H. *Organizational psychology.* Englewood Cliffs, N.J.: Prentice-Hall, 1965.

Schmidt, W. H. Styles of leadership. In *Looking into leadership executive library.* Washington, D.C.: Leadership Resources, Inc., 1966.

Schmidt, W. H., and Tannenbaum, R. Management of differences. *Harvard Business Review,* 1960, **38**, 112–114.

Schroeter, L. C. *Organizational élan.* New York: American Management Association, 1970.

Seay, M. F. (Ed.) *Community education: A developing concept.* Midland, Mich.: Pendell, 1974.

Seay, M. F. Some principles of an educational program. In M. F. Seay (Ed.), *Adult education: A part of a total educational program.* Lexington, Ky.: Bulletin of the Bureau of School Service, University of Kentucky, 1938, **10**(4).

Seay, M. F. The community-school emphases in postwar education. In NSSE 44th yearbook, Part I. *American education in the postwar period.* Chicago: University of Chicago Press, 1945.

Selznick, P. *Leadership in administration.* New York: Harper & Row, 1957.

Sergiovanni, T. J. Factors which affect satisfaction and dissatisfaction of teachers. *Journal of Educational Administration,* 1967, **5,** 66–82.

Sergiovanni, T. J., and Carver, F. D. *The new school executive: A theory of administration.* New York: Dodd, Mead, 1973.

Sexton, P. K. *Education and income.* New York: Viking, 1961.

Shannon, C. E., and Weaver, W. (Eds.) *The mathematical theory of communication.* Urbana, Ill.: University of Illinois Press, 1949.

Shartle, C. L. *Executive performance and leadership.* Englewood Cliffs, N.J.: Prentice-Hall, 1956.

Sherif, M. *Social interaction.* Chicago: Aldine, 1967.

Silberman, C. E. *Crisis in the classroom.* New York: Random House, 1970.

Sills, D. L. (Ed.) *International encyclopedia of the social sciences.* New York: Macmillan, 1968. 17 vols.

Simon, H. A. *Administrative behavior.* (2nd ed.) New York: Macmillan, 1968.

Simon, H. A. *The shape of automation for men and management.* New York: Harper & Row, 1965.

Simon, S. B., Howe, L. W., and Kirschenbaum, H. *Values clarification: A handbook of practical strategies for teachers and students.* New York: Hart, 1972.

Sims, P. D. Assessment of the quality of departments of education administration. Unpublished Ph.D. dissertation, University of Wisconsin, 1970.

Sine, T. The megamachine and the schoolhouse. *Phi Delta Kappan,* 1974, **55**(7), 470–473.

Skinner, B. F. Why teachers fail. *Saturday Review,* 1965, **48**(October 16, 1965), 80–81, 98–101.

Skinner, B. F. *Beyond freedom and dignity.* New York: Knopf, 1971.

Smith, C. G., and Tannenbaum, A. S. Organizational control structure: A comparative analysis. *Human Relations,* 1963, **16**(4), 299–316.

Smith, M. B. *Social psychology and human values.* Chicago: Aldine, 1969.

Snow, C. P. *The two cultures and the scientific revolution.* London: Cambridge University Press, 1959.

Sommerville, J. C. Leadership that "rocks the boat," a boat that needs rocking. *Educational Leadership,* 1971, **29**(1), 45–49.

Stent, M. D. (Ed.) with Hazard, W. R., and Rivlin, H. N. *Cultural pluralism in education: A mandate for change.* Englewood Cliffs, N.J.: Prentice-Hall, 1973.

Stogdill, R. M. Personal factors associated with leadership. *Journal of Psychology,* 1948, **25,** 35–71.

Stogdill, R. M., and Coons, A. E. (Eds.) *Leader behavior: Its description and measurement.* Columbus, Ohio: Ohio State University Press, Bureau of Business Research, 1957.

Stoops, E. Keys to leadership. *Phi Delta Kappan,* 1963, **45**(1), 42–43.

Stufflebeam, D. L. Evaluation: Its meaning in an administrative context. Unpublished paper presented at the Workshop for Ohio School Superintendents, Columbus, Ohio, July 10, 1973.

Stufflebeam, D. L., Foley, W. J., Gephart, W. J., Guba, E. G., Hammond, R. L., Merriman, H. O., and Provus, M. M. *Educational evaluation and decision making.* Itasca, Ill.: F. E. Peacock Publishers, 1971.

Sullivan, H. S. *The interpersonal theory of psychiatry.* New York: Norton, 1953.

Sumner, W. G. *Folkways,* Boston: Ginn, 1906.

Suppes, P. Plug-in instruction. *Saturday Review,* 1966, **49**(30), 25, 29–30.

Swerdloff, A. *Styles of leadership* (film). Beverly Hills, Calif.: Roundtable Productions, 1961.

Swerdloff, A., and Fowler, O. *Overcoming resistance to change* (film). Beverly Hills, Calif.: Roundtable Productions, 1961.

Tagiuri, R. Person perception. In D. L. Sills (Ed.), *International encyclopedia of the social sciences.* Vol. 11. New York: Macmillan, 1968.

Tannenbaum, R. The nature of authority. In Richards, M. D., and Nielander, W. A., *Readings in management.* New Rochelle, N.Y.: South-Western, 1963, 708–714.

Taylor, H. *How to change colleges: Notes on radical reform.* New York: Holt, Rinehart & Winston, 1971.

Taylor, J. W. *How to select and develop leaders.* New York: McGraw-Hill, 1962.

Tead, O. *The art of leadership.* New York: McGraw-Hill, 1935.

Tessin, M. J. An investigation of the relationship between emergent leadership and several predictor variables in an academic setting. Unpublished doctoral dissertation, Western Michigan University, 1972.

Thelen, H. A. *Education and the human quest.* New York: Harper & Row, 1960.

Thiagarajan, S. Gamegame II. *Phi Delta Kappan,* 1974, **55**(7), 474–477.

Toffler, A. *Future shock.* New York: Random House, 1970.

Tracy, W. Goodbye IQ, hello EI (Ertl Index). *Phi Delta Kappan,* 1972, **54**(2), 89–94.

Trusty, F. M., and Sergiovanni, T. J. Perceived need deficiencies of teachers and administrators: A proposal for restructuring teacher roles. *Educational Administration Quarterly,* 1966, **2,** 168–180.

Urwick, L. F. Notes on the theory of organization. In C. Heyel (Ed.), *The encyclopedia of management.* Vol. 2. New York: Reinhold, 1963.

Watson, G. B. *What psychology can we trust?* New York: Bureau of Publications, Teachers College, 1961.

Watson, G. B., and Johnson, D. *Social psychology: Issues and insights.* (2nd ed.) New York: Lippincott, 1972.

Weber, M. The three types of legitimate rule. In *Preussiche Jahrbucker,* 1922. (Republished: In A. Etzioni (Ed.), *Complex organizations: A sociological reader.* New York: Holt, Rinehart & Winston, 1961.)

Wheelis, A. *The quest for identity.* New York: Norton, 1958.

Wiles, K. *The changing curriculum of the American high school.* Englewood Cliffs, N.J.: Prentice-Hall, 1963.

Wiles, K. *Supervision for better schools.* (2nd ed.) Englewood Cliffs, N.J.: Prentice-Hall, 1967.

Worthen, B. R., and Sanders, J. R. (Eds.), *Educational evaluation: Theory and practice.* Worthington, Ohio: Charles A. Jones Publishing Co., 1973.

Wurman, R. S. (Ed.) *Yellow pages of learning resources.* Cambridge, Mass.: MIT Press, 1972.

Zaleznik, A. *The human dilemmas of leadership.* New York: Harper & Row, 1966.

Zubek, J. P. *Perceptual deprivation.* In D. L. Sills (Ed.), *International encyclopedia of the social sciences.* Vol. 11. New York: Macmillan, 1968.

INDEX

75 76 77 7 6 5 4 3 2 1